Civic Resources and the Future of the European Union

This book shines new light on the political system of the European Union (EU) by focusing on *civic resources* as a keystone of the EU's ability to sustain. Less tangible resources such as trust, solidarity, mutual recognition and citizens' social and political participation have been, until now, largely ignored in the research on European integration.

Due to the fundamental changes to the EU in recent years and the challenges ahead, European citizens have become increasingly critical of a long-lasting unification process in Europe. This volume theoretically and empirically examines how the European citizens themselves may contribute to the long-term effectiveness, legitimacy and endurance of the EU. This book aims to examine the issues associated with the utilization of civic resources by the EU, and the ability of European citizens to develop transnational civic resources. Expert contributors in the field develop a framework to understand and explore the potential of citizens in the uncertain future of the EU.

Civic Resources and the Future of the European Union will be of interest to students and scholars of European Politics and European Union Studies.

Ireneusz Pawel Karolewski is Associate Professor of Political Science in the Willy Brandt Centre for German and European Studies at the University of Wroclaw, Poland.

Viktoria Kaina is Professor of Political Science at the Friedrich-Schiller University, Jena, Germany.

Routledge Advances in European Politics

1. Russian Messianism
Third Rome, revolution, Communism and after
Peter J.S. Duncan

2. European Integration and the Postmodern Condition
Governance, democracy, identity
Peter van Ham

3. Nationalism in Italian Politics
The stories of the Northern League, 1980–2000
Damian Tambini

4. International Intervention in the Balkans since 1995
Edited by Peter Siani-Davies

5. Widening the European Union
The politics of institutional change and reform
Edited by Bernard Steunenberg

6. Institutional Challenges in the European Union
Edited by Madeleine Hosli, Adrian van Deemen and Mika Widgrén

7. Europe Unbound
Enlarging and reshaping the boundaries of the European Union
Edited by Jan Zielonka

8. Ethnic Cleansing in the Balkans
Nationalism and the destruction of tradition
Cathie Carmichael

9. Democracy and Enlargement in Post-Communist Europe
The democratisation of the general public in fifteen Central and Eastern European countries, 1991–1998
Christian W. Haerpfer

10. Private Sector Involvement in the Euro
The power of ideas
Stefan Collignon and Daniela Schwarzer

11. Europe
A Nietzschean perspective
Stefan Elbe

12. European Union and E-Voting
Addressing the European Parliament's internet voting challenge
Edited by Alexander H. Trechsel and Fernando Mendez

13. European Union Council Presidencies
A comparative perspective
Edited by Ole Elgström

14. European Governance and Supranational Institutions
Making states comply
Jonas Tallberg

15. European Union, NATO and Russia
Martin Smith and Graham Timmins

16. Business, The State and Economic Policy
The case of Italy
G. Grant Amyot

17. Europeanization and Transnational States
Comparing Nordic central governments
Bengt Jacobsson, Per Lægreid and Ove K. Pedersen

18. European Union Enlargement
A comparative history
Edited by Wolfram Kaiser and Jürgen Elvert

19. Gibraltar
British or Spanish?
Peter Gold

20. Gendering Spanish Democracy
Monica Threlfall, Christine Cousins and Celia Valiente

21. European Union Negotiations
Processes, networks and negotiations
Edited by Ole Elgström and Christer Jönsson

22. Evaluating Euro-Mediterranean Relations
Stephen C. Calleya

23. The Changing Face of European Identity
A seven-nation study of (supra)national attachments
Edited by Richard Robyn

24. Governing Europe
Discourse, governmentality and European integration
William Walters and Jens Henrik Haahr

25. Territory and Terror
Conflicting nationalisms in the Basque country
Jan Mansvelt Beck

26. Multilateralism, German Foreign Policy and Central Europe
Claus Hofhansel

27. Popular Protest in East Germany
Gareth Dale

28. Germany's Foreign Policy Towards Poland and the Czech Republic
Ostpolitik revisited
Karl Cordell and Stefan Wolff

29. Kosovo
The politics of identity and space
Denisa Kostovicova

30. The Politics of European Union Enlargement
Theoretical approaches
Edited by Frank Schimmelfennig and Ulrich Sedelmeier

31. Europeanizing Social Democracy?
The rise of the party of European socialists
Simon Lightfoot

32. Conflict and Change in EU Budgetary Politics
Johannes Lindner

33. Gibraltar, Identity and Empire
E.G. Archer

34. Governance Stories
Mark Bevir and R.A.W Rhodes

35. Britain and the Balkans
1991 until the present
Carole Hodge

36. The Eastern Enlargement of the European Union
John O'Brennan

37. Values and Principles in European Union Foreign Policy
Edited by Sonia Lucarelli and Ian Manners

38. European Union and the Making of a Wider Northern Europe
Pami Aalto

39. Democracy in the European Union
Towards the emergence of a public sphere
Edited by Liana Giorgi, Ingmar Von Homeyer and Wayne Parsons

40. European Union Peacebuilding and Policing
Michael Merlingen with Rasa Ostrauskaite

41. The Conservative Party and European Integration since 1945
At the heart of Europe?
N.J. Crowson

42. E-Government in Europe
Re-booting the state
Edited by Paul G. Nixon and Vassiliki N. Koutrakou

43. EU Foreign and Interior Policies
Cross-pillar politics and the social construction of sovereignty
Stephan Stetter

44. Policy Transfer in European Union Governance
Regulating the utilities
Simon Bulmer, David Dolowitz, Peter Humphreys and Stephen Padgett

45. The Europeanization of National Political Parties
Power and organizational adaptation
Edited by Thomas Poguntke, Nicholas Aylott, Elisabeth Carter, Robert Ladrech and Kurt Richard Luther

46. Citizenship in Nordic Welfare States
Dynamics of choice, duties and participation in a changing Europe
Edited by Bjørn Hvinden and Håkan Johansson

47. National Parliaments within the Enlarged European Union
From victims of integration to competitive actors?
Edited by John O'Brennan and Tapio Raunio

48. Britain, Ireland and Northern Ireland since 1980
The totality of relationships
Eamonn O'Kane

49. The EU and the European Security Strategy
Forging a global Europe
Edited by Sven Biscop and Jan Joel Andersson

50. European Security and Defence Policy
An implementation perspective
Edited by Michael Merlingen and Rasa Ostrauskait

51. Women and British Party Politics
Descriptive, substantive and symbolic representation
Sarah Childs

52. The Selection of Ministers in Europe
Hiring and firing
Edited by Keith Dowding and Patrick Dumont

53. Energy Security
Europe's new foreign policy challenge
Richard Youngs

54. Institutional Challenges in Post-Constitutional Europe
Governing change
Edited by Catherine Moury and Luís de Sousa

55. The Struggle for the European Constitution
A past and future history
Michael O'Neill

56. Transnational Labour Solidarity
Mechanisms of commitment to cooperation within the European trade union movement
Katarzyna Gajewska

57. **The Illusion of Accountability in the European Union**
Edited by Sverker Gustavsson, Christer Karlsson, and Thomas Persson

58. **The European Union and Global Social Change**
A critical geopolitical-economic analysis
József Böröcz

59. **Citizenship and Collective Identity in Europe**
Ireneusz Pawel Karolewski

60. **EU Enlargement and Socialization**
Turkey and Cyprus
Stefan Engert

61. **The Politics of EU Accession**
Turkish challenges and Central European experiences
Edited by Lucie Tunkrová and Pavel Šaradín

62. **The Political History of European Integration**
The hypocrisy of democracy-through-market
Hagen Schulz-Forberg and Bo Stråth

63. **The Spatialities of Europeanization**
Power, governance and territory in Europe
Alun Jones and Julian Clark

64. **European Union Sanctions and Foreign Policy**
When and why do they work?
Clara Portela

65. **The EU's Role in World Politics**
A retreat from liberal internationalism
Richard Youngs

66. **Social Democracy and European Integration**
The politics of preference formation
Edited by Dionyssis Dimitrakopoulos

67. **The EU Presence in International Organizations**
Edited by Spyros Blavoukos & Dimitris Bourantonis

68. **Sustainability in European Environmental Policy**
Challenge of governance and knowledge
Edited by Rob Atkinson, Georgios Terizakis and Karsten Zimmermann

69. **Fifty Years of EU-Turkey Relations**
A Sisyphean story
Edited by Armagan Emre Çakir

70. **Europeanization and Foreign Policy**
State diversity in Finland and Britain
Juha Jokela

71. **EU Foreign Policy and Post-Soviet Conflicts**
Stealth intervention
Nicu Popescu

72. **Switzerland in Europe**
Continuity and change in the Swiss political economy
Edited by Christine Trampusch and André Mach

73. **The Political Economy of Noncompliance**
Adjusting to the single European market
Scott Nicholas Siegel

74. **National and European Foreign Policy**
Towards Europeanization
Edited by Reuben Wong and Christopher Hill

75. **The European Union Diplomatic Service**
Ideas, preferences and identities
Caterina Carta

76. **Poland within the European Union**
New awkward partner or new heart of Europe?
Aleks Szczerbiak

77. A Political Theory of Identity in European Integration
Memory and policies
Catherine Guisan

78. EU Foreign Policy and the Europeanization of Neutral States
Comparing Irish and Austrian foreign policy
Nicole Alecu de Flers

79. Party System Change in Western Europe
Gemma Loomes

80. The Second Tier of Local Government in Europe
Provinces, counties, départements and Landkreise in comparison
Hubert Heinelt and Xavier Bertrana Horta

81. Learning from the EU Constitutional Treaty
Democratic constitutionalism beyond the nation-state
Ben Crum

82. Human Rights and Democracy in EU Foreign Policy
The cases of Ukraine and Egypt
Rosa Balfour

83. Europeanization, Integration and Identity
A social constructivist fusion perspective on Norway
Gamze Tanil

84. The Impact of European Integration on Political Parties
Beyond the permissive Cconsensus
Dimitri Almeida

85. Civic Resources and the Future of the European Union
Edited by *Ireneusz Pawel Karolewski and Viktoria Kaina*

Civic Resources and the Future of the European Union

Edited by Ireneusz Pawel Karolewski
and Viktoria Kaina

LONDON AND NEW YORK

First published 2012 by Routledge
2 Park Square, Milton Park, Abingdon, Oxfordshire OX14 4RN

Simultaneously published in the USA and Canada
by Routledge
711 Third Avenue, New York, NY 10017

First issued in paperback 2014

Routledge is an imprint of the Taylor & Francis Group, an informa business.

© 2012 Ireneusz Pawel Karolewski and Viktoria Kaina for selection and editorial matter; individual contributors their contribution.

The right of the editors to be identified as the authors of the editorial material, and of the authors for their individual chapters, has been asserted in accordance with sections 77 and 78 of the Copyright, Designs and Patents Act 1988.

All rights reserved. No part of this book may be reprinted or reproduced or utilised in any form or by any electronic, mechanical, or other means, now known or hereafter invented, including photocopying and recording, or in any information storage or retrieval system, without permission in writing from the publishers.

Trademark notice: Product or corporate names may be trademarks or registered trademarks, and are used only for identification and explanation without intent to infringe.

British Library Cataloguing in Publication Data
A catalogue record for this book is available from the British Library

Library of Congress Cataloging in Publication Data
A catalog record for this book has been requested

ISBN 13: 978-0-415-68900-7 (hbk)
ISBN 13: 978-1-138-82223-8 (pbk)

Typeset in Times New Roman by RefineCatch Limited, Bungay, Suffolk

Contents

List of figures xi
List of tables xii
Notes on contributors xiv

Introduction: Europe's blues and Europe's future – civic resources for a European Union in trouble 1
VIKTORIA KAINA AND IRENEUSZ PAWEL KAROLEWSKI

**PART I
Trust, identity and support for the EU** 13

1 **Identification and trust – resources of support for the European Union?** 15
   BETTINA WESTLE

2 **What does the EU mean to you personally? Citizens' images of and support for the European Union** 37
   NICOLA BÜCKER

3 **Trust in co-Europeans and support for European unification: extending the identity approach** 59
   JAN DELHEY

4 **'In the Union we trust'? Institutional confidence and citizens' support for supranational decision-making** 80
   VIKTORIA KAINA

PART II
Civic resources, recognition and citizenship   103

5 Civic resources for European democracy in Central
   and Eastern Europe   105
   MATTHEW LOVELESS

6 Mobilizing civic resources through e-participation in the European
   public sphere: problem-solving, re-legitimizing or decoupling?   125
   SIMON SMITH

7 Conceptualizing (and tentatively mapping) the EU's
   social constituency   146
   JOHN ERIK FOSSUM AND MARIT ELDHOLM

8 Caesarean citizenship and its anti-civic potential in
   the European Union   196
   IRENEUSZ PAWEL KAROLEWSKI

PART III
Conceptual and theoretical considerations   219

9 From crisis to constitution? Europe's path from culture to politics   221
   ENNO RUDOLPH

10 Analysing European identity – the need for civic resources   229
   VIKTORIA KAINA

   Index   250

Figures

2.1	Ranking of the most important frames in the Eastern German sample	47
2.2	Ranking of the most important frames in the Polish sample	49
3.1	Support for European integration by level of trust	69
3.2	Impact of trust on support for European integration	72
4.1	Net trust in the European Parliament, 1999–2008	84
4.2	Net trust in the European Commission, 1999–2008	85
4.3	Net trust in the European Central Bank, 1999–2008	85
4.4	Net trust in the Council of the European Union, 1999–2008	85
4.5	Net trust in the European Court of Justice, 1999–2007	86
4.6	Trust in EU institutions, 2008	88
4.7	Preferred policy competence, 2008	90
5.1	Trust and support for the European Union	114
5.2	Collective thinking and support for the European Union	114
7.1	Illustration of the combined *catnet* strength of the nation-state	157
10.1	Configuring research foci in studying European collective identity	233
10.2	Systematizing EU citizens' orientations regarding a shared sense of belonging together	241

Tables

1.1	Representative samples of the voting population in 16 Western and Eastern European countries in 2007	19
1.2	Indicators of identity	19
1.3	Factorial structure of indicators of identification and trust	23
1.4	Correlations between indicators of identification and trust of national and European identification	23
1.5	Correlations between the different indicators of trust in people	24
1.6	Collective identification – distribution	25
1.7	Trust in people – distribution	27
1.8	Correlation between indicators of identification and indicators of trust	28
1.9	Correlations between indicators of collective identity and support for the authorities and the regime of the European Union	29
1.10	Multiple regression: support of identification and horizontal trust	30
1.11	Multiple regressions for subgroups	31
2.1	Easton's model of political support	39
2.2	A model of people's EU attitudes	41
2.3	EU frames in Eastern Germany and Poland	44
2.4	A typology of EU frames	52
2.5	Our country's main benefits from EU membership	54
2.6	Our country's main disadvantages from EU membership	55
3.1	Determinants of support for European integration – 'trust model'	70
3.2	Determinants of support for European integration – 'trust + identity model'	71
3.3	The salience of trust for support – geographical differences	74
4.1	Factor analysis: trust in European and national institutions, 2008	87
4.2	Factor analysis: preferred policy authority at the national and European level, 2008	89

4.3	Bivariate correlation between preferred level of policy competence and citizen assessment of the EU's democraticness	92
4.4	Bivariate correlation between preferred level of policy competence and citizens' trust in European institutions	93
4.5	Preferred level of policy competence for cross-border problems	95
4.6	Preferred level of policy competence for welfare and identity issues	96
5.1	Trust and collective thinking	113
5.2	Trust and collective thinking: VGAs, 'closed' networks, and psychological insecurity	116
5.3	Support for the European Union in CEE	117
6.1	Properties of a multi-tiered European public sphere	128
7.1	Ethnic minorities in 25 EU member states	166
7.2	Immigrant minorities in 25 EU member states	171
7.3	Religious minorities in 25 EU member states	175
7.4	Language minorities in 25 EU member states	181
10.1	An analytical framework for research on European collective identity	231

Contributors

Nicola Bücker received her PhD from the Jacobs University, Bremen (Germany), and currently works as a research associate at the Institute of Political Science at the University Marburg (Germany). Her research interests cover public EU attitudes and discourses, nationalism and right-wing populism in Europe, and the integration of migrants in European societies. Her recent publications include: 'Crossing the frontier: transnational social integration in the EU's border regions', *International Journal of Comparative Sociology* 51(1–2) (2010): 5–32. (with S. Rippl, A. Petrat and K. Boehnke); 'What does EU mean? Historical and current frames in Polish and German discourses on Europe', in: *The Nature of Society: Proceedings of the 33rd Congress of the German Sociological Association* in Kassel 2006, edited on their behalf by Karl-Siegbert Rehberg (Frankfurt/New York: Campus 2008).

Jan Delhey is Professor of Sociology at Jacobs University, Bremen. He holds a doctoral degree in sociology. His research interests include comparative research on social trust, subjective well-being and Europeanization. Selected publications include: 'How general is trust in "most people"? Solving the radius of trust problem', *American Sociological Review* 76(5) (2011): 786–807 (with Kenneth Newton and Christian Welzel); 'Do enlargements make the European Union less cohesive? An analysis of trust between EU nationalities', *Journal of Common Market Studies* 45 (2007): 253–79; *Life satisfaction in the enlarged Europe. European Foundation for the Improvement of Living and Working Conditions* (Office for Official Publications of the European Communities, Luxembourg 2004).

Marit Eldholm is Administrative Project Manager of the FP6-funded RECON project (Reconstituting Democracy in Europe) at ARENA – Centre for European Studies at the University of Oslo. She holds a master's degree in political science from the University of Oslo, with a thesis entitled *Towards a European constitution? A discourse-theoretical analysis of the European Convention* (2006) (in Norwegian).

John Erik Fossum is Professor of Political Science at ARENA – Centre for European Studies at the University of Oslo. His main fields of interest include political theory, democracy and constitutionalism in the EU and Canada, Europeanization and transformation of the nation state. Recent publications include *The European Union and the Public Sphere* (co-edited with Philip Schlesinger) (2008); 'Europe's American dream', *European Journal of Social Theory* (2009); *The constitution's gift: a constitutional theory for the European Union* (co-authored with Agustín J. Menéndez) (2011); 'Law and democracy', in D. Neil, *MacCormick's legal and political theory* (co-edited with Agustín José Menéndez) (2011); and *Rethinking democracy and the European Union* (co-editor Erik Oddvar Eriksen) (Routledge 2012).

Viktoria Kaina is Professor of Political Science and holds the Chair of Government at the Friedrich-Schiller University Jena (Germany). She received her PhD in political science from the University of Potsdam. Together with Ireneusz P. Karolewski, she is convenor of the ECPR Standing Group 'Identity'. Her main research interests focus on European identity and the EU's legitimacy problems, comparative politics and trust, elites and mass attitudes. Her recent publications include: 'Why do we trust strangers? Revising the institutional approach to generalized trust creation', *West European Politics* 34 (2011): 2: 282–95; '"We" and "the others" – European identity building as a construction of community and difference', *Zeitschrift für Politik* 57 (2010): 4: 413–33.

Ireneusz Pawel Karolewski is Professor of Political Science in the Willy Brandt Centre for German and European Studies at the University of Wroclaw (Poland) and holds a PhD and the professorial degree (Habilitation) in political science from the University of Potsdam (Germany). Research interests include European citizenship, collective identity in Europe, nation and nationalism in Europe and constitutionalism of the EU. Selected publications include: *Citizenship and collective Identity in Europe* (Routledge 2010); *Nation and nationalism in Europe* (with Andrzej Marcin Suszycki, Edinburgh University Press 2011); 'Pathologies of deliberation in the EU', *European Law Journal* (2011).

Matthew Loveless is a Lecturer in Comparative Politics at the University of Kent. He received his PhD in political science from Indiana University in 2005 and has taught quantitative methodology and courses in European politics at Georgetown University, George Washington University and the University of Mississippi. He is currently a member of European Consortium on Political Research Standing Group: 'Identity'. His recent publications include: 'Social inequality and social conflict: evidence from the new market democracies of Central and Eastern Europe', *Europe-Asia Studies* (forthcoming, with Stephen Whitefield); 'Being unequal and seeing inequality: explaining the political significance of social inequality in new market democracies', *European Journal of Political Research* 50 (2011): 239–66 (with Stephen Whitefield).

xvi *Contributors*

Enno Rudolph is Professor of Philosophy at the University of Lucerne (Switzerland) and a former director of the Institute for Cultural Sciences in Lucerne. His research fields include political philosophy and the philosophy of culture. His main areas of research cover the history of humanism and 'antihumanism' in Europe; concepts of power; and theory of metaphor. His recent publications include: *Brauchen die Europäer eine Identität? Politische und kulturelle Aspekte* (edited together with Furio Cerutti) (2010); 'Rousseau absconditus: Zur Kritik der Taylorschen Liberalismuskritik', in: Michael Kühnlein/Mathias Lutz-Bachmann, *Unerfüllte Moderne? Neue Perspektiven auf das Werk von Charles Taylor* (2011); *Machtwechsel der Bilder* (ed.) (2012).

Simon Smith is a Research Fellow at the Leeds Institute of Health Sciences and a visiting researcher at the Centre for Digital Citizenship, Institute of Communications Studies, University of Leeds. He obtained his PhD from the University of Bradford in 1998 for a thesis on spaces of independent cultural production in communist Czechoslovakia. Since then he has conducted research on a variety of topics, including interest representation in post-communist societies, community studies, partnership and public involvement in local and regional strategic planning, digital inclusion, e-participation and organisational knowledge creation. He is currently investigating issues connected with online cultural production, professional identities and collaborative research networks. His recent publications include: 'A three-layered framework for evaluating eParticipation', *International Journal of Electronic Governance* (2012, with Ann Macintosh and Jeremy Millard); 'eParticipation policies and initiatives in the European Union institutions', *Social Science Computer Review* (2011, with Efpraxia Dalakiouridou et al.); 'Contextualising public (e)Participation in the governance of the European Union', *European Journal of ePractice* 7 (March 2009, with Efpraxia Dalakiouridou).

Bettina Westle is Professor of Political Science (Research Methods in Political Science and Empirical Democracy Research) at the University of Marburg. She holds a PhD and a professorial degree (Habilitation) from the University of Mannheim. Research interests include political cognition, attitudes and participation in Western democracies, collective identities and European Union. Her recent publications include: 'Identity, social and political', in: Bertrand Badie *et al.* (eds) *International Encyclopedia of Political Science* 4 (Sage 2011): 1131–43; 'Politisches Wissen in Deutschland: Ein Vergleich von Bürgern mit türkischem Migrationshintergund und einheimischen Deutschen', *Zeitschrift für Parlamentsfragen* 42(4) (2011): 835–50; 'Orientierungen gegenüber Demokratie und Rechtsextremismus im Vergleich der Geschlechter', in: Ursula Birsl (ed.) *Rechtsextremismus und Gender* (Verlag Barbara Budrich 2011): 211–40.

Introduction: Europe's blues and Europe's future – civic resources for a European Union in trouble

Viktoria Kaina and Ireneusz Pawel Karolewski

Challenges for a 'polity in between'

The European Union expects heavy seas ahead. This prediction is based on a contradictory observation. Most Europeans show little interest in 'Europe'. At the same time, they do pay more and more attention to European decisions and their implementation at the national level. The origin of this puzzle is traced back not only to the way the European integration was pushed over the years, but also to the partly unexpected ramifications of the EU's unequalled success.

Intensified by the Maastricht Treaty of 1993, the European unification path has developed a power structure of supranational authority (Bach 1999, 2000). Scholars on European integration widely agree, therefore, that the European Union has taken root as a new type of governance (e.g. Marks *et al.* 1996; Stone Sweet and Sandholtz 1997; Kohler-Koch 1999; Jachtenfuchs 2000; Stone Sweet *et al.* 2001; Jachtenfuchs and Kohler-Koch 2004). For our purposes in this book, it does not matter if we describe the EU as a multi-level system of governance or as a political system. It is sufficient to say that today's European Union shows some features of a full-fledged national polity (Hix 2005: 2ff; Lepsius 2006: 112) while it lacks other characteristics of a modern polity. In particular, the EU is not a state (Böröcz and Sarkar 2005: 155). Moreover, the so-called input dimension of a political system is still underdeveloped at the European level (Kaina 2009). Thus, we may describe the current nature of the European Union as a 'polity in between' which governs citizens of a certain territory within 'a stable and clearly defined set of institutions for collective decision-making and a set of rules governing relations between and within these institutions' (Hix 2005: 2). As a result, the European Union can be analysed as a political collectivity inasmuch as a supranational authority, a Weberian *Herrschaftsverband*, has been established at the European level. Realizing a sort of (multi-level) governance, the EU is facing the challenge of justifying political rule since every sort of governance limits the self-determination and individual freedom of people. However, legitimizing European governance becomes harder the more the European integration process succeeds. This 'paradox of success' arises from three developments revealing the transforming character of the European Union as a 'polity in between'.

The *first* development describes the erosion of the so-called permissive consensus (Lindberg and Scheingold 1970). For a long time, this specific mélange of common citizen support for European integration and widespread indifference of the European publics (e.g. Hix 2005: 149; McLaren 2006: 8; Kaina 2009: 88f) has been conceded a generous room of manoeuvre to national and European elites to push the integration process on. By now, research on public opinion suggests the end of the permissive consensus.

Some people who regard themselves and their countries as winners of European unification see the integration process first and foremost in a positive light. A rising number of EU citizens, however, increasingly feel they cannot cope with the dynamics of that development. They are worried by the pace of European unification and increasingly unnerved by the demands of an expanding and ever more heterogeneous European Union. As a result, numerous EU projects have been rejected by popular vote: the Maastricht Treaty in Denmark (1992), the accession of Norway (1972, 1994), the Nice Treaty in Ireland (2001), the introduction of the euro in Sweden (2003), the European Constitutional Treaty in France and the Netherlands (2005) and, more recently, the Lisbon Treaty in Ireland (2008). In addition to such visible signs of disagreement between European citizens and their elites, a wealth of empirical examinations provide evidence that citizens' support for European integration has been decreasing since the early 1990s (of many: McLaren 2002, 2004, 2006, 2007; Deutsch 2006; Eichenberg and Dalton 2007; Hooghe 2007; Hooghe and Marks 2006, 2007, 2009; Hix 2008: 24–31; Taylor 2008: 24–31; Hix 2008: 51ff; Kaina 2009: 15–30; Thomassen and Bäck 2009; Weßels 2007, 2009). The very literature on the Euroscepticism phenomenon fortifies the fact that Europe suffers from the 'Post-Maastricht blues' (Eichenberg and Dalton 2007) and the permissive consensus has been displaced by a 'constraining dissensus' (Hooghe and Marks 2006: 248). The people's cognitive and emotional detachment from the EC/EU was hardly a severe problem as long as the permissive consensus allowed the national and European elites to push the European unification on. However, this matter of course obviously belongs to the past.

A *second* development refers to impending effectiveness shortfalls in the European multi-level system. In the wake of broadening the EU's scope of governance, Simon Hix (2008: 32) recently diagnosed a 'policy shift' at the European level. After the successful creation of the internal market, the EU policy agenda is now focused on the question of 'what economic and social policies should be pursued in the new European-scale polity' (Hix 2008: 89). The change of the European policy agenda is accompanied by an increasing conflict potential inasmuch as European decision-making involves redistributive consequences. As a result, coalition-building between the European Commission, Council and the European Parliament becomes more difficult and makes policy gridlock at the European level more likely (Hix 2008: 44ff).

The diagnosis of Hix is tightly related to a *third* development, namely growing distribution conflicts at the supranational level, which was particularly visible during the recent currency and debt crisis in the EU. The success of the European integration process has led to a stage where supranational decision-making increasingly affects the general living conditions of EU citizens (Bach *et al.* 2006: 7; Vobruba 2007: 10). The aforementioned 'policy change' and the resulting growth of redistributive European decision-making comes with the risk of increasing distribution conflicts at the European level which were formerly resolved within EU member states (Lepsius 1999: 210; Vobruba 2003: 41, 48; Bach 2006: 25). As a consequence of the European policy change and the increased heterogeneity of EU members, this 'Europe' in which most Europeans do not take an interest creates winners and losers and cannot always guarantee Pareto-rational results (Joerges 1999; Føllesdal and Hix 2006: 11; Hix 2008: 48). The more EU citizens become aware of this consequence, the more the success and legitimacy of the integration process depend on the EU's social cohesion and the union's capability for *societal* integration.

Referring to the 'paradox of success', the book is based on the following main thesis: as the European community has enlarged and the integration process has reached a deeper level, the process of European unification is increasingly susceptible to swings in public mood. Given the decreasing citizen support for European integration and the disquieting list of setbacks, the European Union is obviously in a squeeze: the more the European unification proceeds, the more its future success is going to be dependent on the active consent of the people. However, asking the people comes with the high risk of disagreement or even rejection (Vobruba 2007: 12). Thus, the question arises: how can the European Union get out of this plight in order to pave the road to the future?

Focus and aim of the book

Facing enormous challenges while lacking strong support among European citizens, the European Union is vulnerable to unpredictable stress. Against this background, the book opens up a new perspective on the political system of the European Union by focusing on *civic resources* as a crucial underpinning for the EU's ability to sustain. We seek to theoretically explore and empirically investigate potential civic resources that the European Union might need to become both effective and legitimate. To date, civic resources such as trust, solidarity, mutual recognition and citizens' social and political participation have been largely ignored in the research on European integration. In fact, a major part of research on the EU's legitimacy and effectiveness has explored three main factors: first, the role of *elites'* behaviour; second, the creation of efficient *institutions* for supranational governance; and third, the implementation of *policies* producing visible outputs in terms of perceivable benefits for EU citizens. These three factors mainly serve to realize Barroso's 'Europe of results' and thereby accentuate an output perspective for legitimizing the EU. Scholars who deal with the input side of legitimizing the EU mainly discuss various factors to reduce the EU's 'democratic deficit' by analysing the emergence of European parties, interest groups or a European public sphere.

4 *Viktoria Kaina and Ireneusz Pawel Karolewski*

This book extends both horizons by theoretically exploring and empirically scrutinizing whether and, if so, how European citizens *themselves* may contribute to the long-term endurance of the European Union. Due to the fundamental changes the EU has undergone as well as the challenges ahead, European citizens become increasingly critical regarding a long-lasting unification process in Europe. Accordingly, the book aims at three points:

- evolving a research agenda by theoretically exploring the significance of civic resources for a European Union in trouble;
- presenting first empirical analyses on this topic;
- identifying empirical desiderata and pointing to future research options.

In particular, the book takes a first step to explore the role of trust, identity, mutual recognition and citizens' social and political participation in the context of five main problems the European Union is facing:

- citizens' support for European integration and the EU's legitimacy;
- the problem-solving capacity of EU institutions;
- the societal integration capacity in the European Union;
- both the potential and problems of a European collective identity;
- democratic deficiencies in the wake of European integration.

Addressing these five main problems, the volume has *a double focus*: *on the one hand*, we want to deal with these issues pertaining to the 'utilisation' of civic resources by the EU, for instance in the context of the enhancement of its problem-solving capacity (institutional perspective). *On the other hand*, we are interested in the ability of European citizens to develop *transnational* civic resources of trust, solidarity, mutual recognition and engagement (societal perspective).

Civic resources and their relevance for EU studies

As the continuing series of crises in the recent years have shown, the EU has been subject to unpredictable stress, which has been dealt with mainly through institutional reforms, pushed through the ratifications of consecutive treaties. Shortly after the Lisbon Treaty came into effect, a new treaty reflecting 'the financial union' is supposed to be prepared and ratified. At the same time, the EU is keen on further enlargements, even though after the summit of the European Council in December 2011, a 'double-speed Europe' has been conjured. The EU elites learned apparently neither from the EU's democratic deficit (which remained part of the academic, rather than political discourse) nor did they take the 'too-much-too-soon problem' of the EU seriously (Eichenberg and Dalton 2007; see also Kaina's 'Analysing European identity – the need for civic resources' in this volume).

Against this background, the role of civic resources appears central for the further study of the EU. There are several aspects of EU studies in which civic resources promise an added value. *First*, future research might focus on the question of whether and to what extent civic resources are relevant for the legitimacy, stability and further existence of the EU. The book takes mainly the impact of civic resources on the support for the EU into account. However, there might be differences in impact of trust, solidarity and recognition. Moreover, these civic resources might also strengthen or neutralize each other depending on specific conditions of their operation. The book suggests, for instance, that the role of trust for the support of the EU is not straightforward. This might also hold true for other civic resources, which should be explored in more detail.

Second, the book argues that apart from the expected positive workings of civic resources concerning, for instance, the mass support and legitimacy of the EU, some EU policies or political practices might entail anti-civic consequences. This rather critical view of the EU implies that civic resources could be damaged or even depleted by the anti-civic impact of certain EU practices. For instance, under the conditions of exclusionary politics, generalized trust, solidarity and recognition might be turned into a generalized suspicion, panic and hysteria. This concept of anti-civic potential reflects also to some extent the question of how to measure civic resources: should they be measured binarily (presence/absence), gradually or even with a negative scale of anti-civic resources? In this context, there is a potential positive linkage between the research on civic resources and the Europeanization research, as in the latter the 'politics' level of analysis (as opposed to policy and polity levels) still shows empirical deficits. Thus, other research agendas can also profit from the exploration of civic resources.

Third, a conceptual clarification of different types of civic resources in the EU context, including trust, solidarity and recognition, seems to be necessary for further exploration of collective identity. In this book we argue, for instance, that identification and trust might be viewed as sub-dimensions of collective identity. It also refers to the relationship between various civic resources, which still remains largely unexplored. On the one hand, the book suggests that the relationship between civic resources and a 'we' feeling is a complex one. On the other hand, it is still uncertain whether, for instance, further integration of the EU is really contingent on institutional trust. Concerning the latter it appears to be still open whether institutional trust can be considered a civic resource and how it relates to European identity.

Fourth, EU studies would certainly benefit from exploration of the circumstances under which civic resources develop, are strengthened or weakened. Here, the issue of politico-cultural commonalities in the EU seem to play a central role. This is linked to the question of common supranational institutions embodying commonalities such as the European constitution. Some contributors argue in favour of cultural commonalities as a precondition for a smaller and more resilient community in the EU. This also touches upon the issue of how much heterogeneity the EU can bear. For instance, this book argues that civic resources can be distributed unequally across different EU societies. Because in some European societies there might be more social capital, trust and solidarity than in others, it can have consequences for EU legitimacy at large.

Fifth and final, civic resources relate to broader themes in European studies such as participation, citizenship, public space and democracy. They include the meanwhile classical research on democratic deficit, but also issues of democratic political culture or participative governance in the EU. In addition, civic resources are not only discussed in relation to mass support of the EU but also regarding ethnic minorities and dissatisfied groups in the context of the politics of recognition. Here, a more positive vision of the EU as a 'new recognition order' is put forward.

Brief overview of the book

The book consists of three main parts. In Part I, the contributions focus on the role of civic resources for citizens' mass support in the EU. Part II deals with broader themes concerning civic resources, recognition and citizenship. Part III offers conceptual and theoretical considerations, for instance, regarding civic resources in the context of cultural commonalities, constitution and collective identity.

Bettina Westle's chapter, 'Identification and trust – resources of support for the European Union?' opens up Part I of the book. She explores how far identification and trust as sub-dimensions of collective identity deliver a reservoir of diffuse support, working as a bulwark against system stress in the EU, which is caused by deficits in effectiveness and democracy in the EU. At the conceptual level the chapter examines the relationship between identification and trust. Empirically, it explores the potential of identification and trust as resources for an EU in times of crisis. It does so by linking identity and trust, on the one hand, and diverse aspects of support for the political regime of the EU, on the other hand. It focuses both on mass support and on dissatisfied subgroups.

Chapter 2 by Nicola Bücker, 'What does the EU mean to you personally? Citizens' images of and support for the European Union', departs from the position that citizens might hold different images of what the EU represents and also find different reasons for accepting the EU as a legitimate political order. The chapter explores the support model developed by David Easton and elaborates its application in European integration studies. In addition, the chapter discusses the concept of framing as a promising alternative for analysing people's stance towards the EU. In the empirical part of this chapter, Nicola Bücker presents the results of 46 qualitative interviews conducted by the author in Poland and Eastern Germany in 2005 and examines how these participants perceived and legitimized the European Union.

Chapter 3 by Jan Delhey, 'Trust in co-Europeans and support for European unification: extending the identity approach', offers a new line of argument concerning identity issues in the European Union. The chapter introduces the concept of 'transnational trust', based on the assumption that generalized interpersonal trust in people from other EU countries has an impact on mass support for European unification. Jan Delhey argues that the transnational trust approach is complementary to the existing identity approaches; in particular, it widens the spectrum of possible variants of 'sense of community'. The approach is operationalized and tested against data using the European Elections Study from 2004.

In Chapter 4, '"In the Union we trust"? Institutional confidence and citizens' support for supranational decision-making', Viktoria Kaina draws on the difference between the enlargement and deepening mode of European integration. The chapter is focused on the deepening mode of European unification and the scope of legitimate European governance. The author explores empirically the role of institutional trust for citizens' approval of competences' transfer from the national to the European level. The main hypothesis of the chapter is that European citizens are likely to support European decision-making in several policy areas if they tend to trust European institutions. Furthermore, the chapter presents some preliminary empirical findings regarding the hypothesis.

Part II starts with Chapter 5 by Matthew Loveless, 'Civic resources for European democracy in Central and Eastern Europe'. The chapter departs from the observation that EU studies have struggled with the perception that the EU suffers from a 'democratic deficit', in new and old member states alike. In contrast, the chapter seeks to deepen the insights on the nature and extent of national democratic culture as a resource for the EU, mainly with regard to Central and Eastern European countries. It focuses on trust and solidarity as both core elements of democratic political values and potential resources for EU support. The inquiry is underpinned by the notion that trust and inclusiveness can be regarded as the foundation for social cohesion and community. By formulating specific hypotheses, the chapter aims to identify national, civic resources of political cultures that can provide a safeguard to the ebb of support for EU membership in Central and Eastern Europe.

Chapter 6 by Simon Smith, 'Mobilizing civic resources through e-participation in the European public sphere: problem-solving, relegitimizing or decoupling?' explores the use of e-participation by the European Commission. It focuses empirically on an online consultation using the Interactive Policy-Making tool, combined with an online discussion forum, conducted to inform multilingualism policy in 2007–08. The chapter explores a case in which a public authority invites citizens to participate to relegitimize the dominant social contract in a polity. The citizens generate on their part loosely organized 'issue publics' – citizens' networks that coalesce around particular issues. The chapter discusses how a specific policy issue had been placed in the public domain and, by partially decoupling the discussion from the policymaking process, a process of problem redefinition had begun, enriching a multi-tiered European public sphere and empowering citizenship.

Chapter 7, by John Erik Fossum and Marit Eldholm, 'Conceptualizing (and tentatively mapping) the EU's social constituency', departs from the concept of the EU's social constituency, i.e. the structure of demands and expectations that citizens and groups place on the EU. The authors argue that an assessment of the EU's social constituency requires proper attention both to the recognition expectations that the EU establishes and to the structure of social demands that is oriented at it. It is of scholarly interest given the increased focus on recognition politics, not only within nation-states but also within the transnational realm. The chapter develops a conceptual–methodological framework with a set of structured tests to permit an analysis of the character of the EU's social constituency. It also provides some of the data that show the challenges of an exploration of the EU's social constituency. The conceptual–methodological framework of the chapter combines a philosophical approach to recognition with a sociological approach to contentious politics. Its central element is the notion of 'recognition order'. The chapter examines whether the EU might be said to make up a unique recognition order.

Chapter 8, by Ireneusz Pawel Karolewski, 'Caesarean citizenship and its anti-civic potential in the European Union', argues that there are certain traits of European citizenship that hold an anti-civic potential and are counterproductive concerning the development of civic resources in the EU. The concept of the anti-civic potential of citizenship draws on the literature highlighting the exclusionary nature of citizenship as an instrument of social closure. This perspective on citizenship (Caesarean citizenship) highlights the politics of insecurity carried out in the immigration policy of the EU. While more traditional conceptions of citizenship aim either for the common good or highlight the individual's rights, Caesarean citizenship is based on the idea of self-preservation of individuals who acknowledge the state authority for the sake of protection against (real or imagined) enemies. Ireneusz P. Karolewski applies the concept of Caesarean citizenship to the European Union by discussing the immigration policies of the EU and exploring the idea of the 'European corporate state' as the underpinning of European citizenship. He argues that even though exclusionary practices, institutions and policies have occurred mainly in the post-9/11 nation-state, the EU has also increasingly dealt with immigration as a danger to European societies and created institutions dealing with exclusion of immigrants.

Part III begins with Chapter 9, 'From crisis to constitution? Europe's path from culture to politics', by Enno Rudolph. He discusses the continuing currency and debt crisis in the EU against the background of a European constitution. The chapter refers to the recent essay by Jürgen Habermas. However, Enno Rudolph argues in favour of a smaller community in the EU, which is based on cultural commonalities, rather than a Habermasian postnational constellation. The chapter highlights that an applied recapitulation of European cultural history is essential for the answer to the question of what constitutes Europe's core. A collective appreciation of legal continuation of once-achieved unifications could prove to be indispensable for a new attempt at a constitution for a new, smaller EU.

Chapter 10 by Viktoria Kaina, 'Analysing European identity – the need for civic resources', wraps up the entire book by offering conceptualization of civic resources in the context of collective identity. The chapter argues that, notwithstanding a surge of publications on European identity, previous research on European collective-identity-building suffers from inconsistent evidence, contradictory conclusions and controversial diagnoses. This unsatisfying state of affairs is mainly caused by a severe theoretical deficit and ongoing problems to find an appropriate operationalization for empirical inquiry. Therefore, the author argues in favour of reconsidering the theoretical premises of European identity research as well as redesigning the common instruments to measure a sense of community among EU citizens. Viktoria Kaina discusses the relevance of civic resources such as trust, tolerance and solidarity for empirical studies on a mass European identity and brings together research on civic resources and collective identity.

References

Bach, Maurizio. 1999. *Die Bürokratisierung Europas. Verwaltungseliten, Experten und politische Legitimation in Europa*. Frankfurt/New York: Campus.

Bach, Maurizio. 2000. 'Die Europäisierung der nationalen Gesellschaft? Problemstellungen und Perspektiven einer Soziologie der europäischen Integration', in: Bach, Maurizio (ed.), *Die Europäisierung nationaler Gesellschaften*. Opladen: Westdeutscher Verlag, 11–35.

Bach, Maurizio. 2006. 'The enlargement crisis of the European Union: from political integration to social desintegration?', in: Bach, Maurizio, Lahusen, Christian and Vobruba, Georg (eds) *Europe in motion: social dynamics and political institutions in an enlarging Europe*. Berlin: edition sigma, 11–28.

Bach, Maurizo, Lahusen, Christian and Vobruba, Georg. 2006. 'The problem of the European Union: political integration leaving out society', in: Bach, Maurizo, Lahusen, Christian and Vobruba, Georg (eds) *Europe in motion: social dynamics and political institutions in an enlarging Europe*. Berlin: edition sigma, 7–10.

Böröcz, József and Sarkar, Mahua. 2005. 'What Is the EU?' *International Sociology* 20: 153–73.

Deutsch, Franziska. 2006. 'Legitimacy and identity in the European Union: empirical findings from the old member states', in: Karolewski, Ireneusz Pawel and Kaina, Viktoria (eds) *European identity: theoretical perspectives and empirical insights*. Münster: LIT Verlag, 149–78.

Eichenberg, Richard C. and Dalton, Russell J. 2007. 'Post-Maastricht blues: the transformation of citizen support for European integration, 1973–2004', *Acta Politica* 42(2–3): 128–52.

Føllesdal, Andreas and Hix, Simon. 2006. 'Why there is a democratic deficit in the EU: a response to Majone and Moravcsik', *Journal of Common Market Studies* 44: 1–30. (DOI 10.1111/j.1468-5965.2006.00650.x)

Hix, Simon. 2005. *The political system of the European Union*. 2nd ed. Houndmills: Palgrave Macmillan.

Hix, Simon. 2008. *What's wrong with the European Union and how to fix it*. Cambridge: Polity Press.
Hooghe, Liesbet. 2007. 'What drives Euroskepticism? Party-public cueing, ideology and strategic opportunity', *European Union Politics* 8(5): 5–12.
Hooghe, Liesbet and Marks, Gary. 2006. 'Europe's blues: theoretical soul-searching after the rejection of the European Constitution', *PS: Politics and Political Science* 39(April): 247–50.
Hooghe, Liesbet and Marks, Gary. 2007. 'Sources of Euroscepticism', *Acta Politica* 42(2–3): 119–27.
Hooghe, Liesbet and Marks, Gary. 2009. 'A postfunctionalist theory of European integration: from permissive consensus to constraining dissensus', *British Journal of Political Science* 39(1): 1–23.
Jachtenfuchs, Markus. 2000. 'Die Problemlösungsfähigkeit der EU: Begriffe, Befunde, Erklärungen', in: Grande, Edgar and Jachtenfuchs, Markus (eds) *Wie problemlösungsfähig ist die EU? Regieren im europäischen Mehrebenensystem*. Baden-Baden: Nomos, 345–56.
Jachtenfuchs, Markus and Kohler-Koch, Beate. 2004. 'Governance in der Europäischen Union', in: Benz, Arthur (ed.) *Governance – Regieren in komplexen Regelsystemen. Eine Einführung*. Wiesbaden: VS Verlag für Sozialwissenschaften, 77–101.
Joerges, Christian. 1999. '"Good Governance" through Comitology?', in: Joerges, Christian and Vos, Ellen (eds) *EU committees: social regulation, law and politics*. Oxford/Portland: Hart Publishing, 311–38.
Kaina, Viktoria. 2009. *Wir in Europa. Kollektive Identität und Demokratie in der Europäischen Union*. Wiesbaden: VS Verlag für Sozialwissenschaften.
Kohler-Koch, Beate. 1999. 'The evolution and transformation of European governance', in: Kohler-Koch, Beate and Eising, Rainer (eds) *The transformation of governance in the European Union*. London: Routledge, 14–35.
Lepsius, M. Rainer. 1999. 'Die Europäische Union. Ökonomisch-politische Integration und kulturelle Pluralität', in: Viehoff, Reinhold and Segers, Rien T. (eds) *Kultur. Identität. Europa. Über die Schwierigkeiten und Möglichkeiten einer Konstruktion*. Frankfurt: Suhrkamp, 201–22.
Lepsius, M. Rainer. 2006. 'Identitätsstiftung durch eine europäische Verfassung?', in: Hettlage, Robert and Müller, Hans-Peter (eds) *Die europäische Gesellschaft*. Konstanz: UVK, 109–27.
Lindberg, Leon N. and Scheingold, Stuart A. 1970. *Europe's would-be polity: patterns of change in the European Community*. Englewood Cliffs: Prentice-Hall.
Marks, Garry, Hooghe, Liesbet and Blank, Kermit. 1996. 'European integration from the 1980s: state-centric v. multi-level governance', *Journal of Common Market Studies* 34(3): 341–78.
McLaren, Lauren M. 2002. 'Public support for the European Union: cost/benefit analysis or perceived cultural threat?', *Journal of Politics* 64(2): 551–66.
McLaren, Lauren M. 2004. 'Opposition to European integration and fear of loss of national identity: debunking a basic assumption regarding hostility to the integration project', *European Journal of Political Research* 43(6): 895–911.
McLaren, Lauren M. 2006. *Identity, interests and attitudes to European integration*. Houndmills: Palgrave Macmillan.
McLaren, Lauren M. 2007. 'Explaining mass-level Euroscepticism: identity, interests, and institutional distrust', *Acta Politica* 42(2–3): 233–51.

Stone Sweet, Alec and Sandholtz, Wayne. 1997. 'European integration and supranational governance', *Journal of European Public Policy* 4(3): 297–317.
Stone Sweet, Alec, Sandholtz, Wayne and Fligstein, Neil (eds). 2001. *The institutionalization of Europe*. Oxford/New York: Oxford University Press.
Taylor, Paul. 2008. *The end of European integration: anti-Europeanism examined*. London/New York: Routledge.
Thomassen, Jacques and Bäck, Hanna. 2009. 'European citizenship and identity after enlargement', in: Thomassen, Jacques (ed.) *The legitimacy of the European Union after enlargement*. Oxford: Oxford University Press, 184–207.
Vobruba, Georg. 2003. 'The enlargement crisis of the European Union: limits of the dialectics of integration and expansion', *Journal of European Social Policy* 13(1): 35–62.
Vobruba, Georg. 2007. *Die Dynamik Europas*. 2nd ed. Wiesbaden: VS Verlag für Sozialwissenschaften.
Weßels, Bernhard. 2007. 'Discontent and European identity: three types of euroscepticism', *Acta Politica* 42(2–3): 287–306.
Weßels, Bernhard. 2009. 'Spielarten des Euroskeptizismus', in: Decker, Frank and Höreth, Marcus (eds) *Die Verfassung Europas. Perspektiven des Integrationsprojektes*. Wiesbaden: VS Verlag für Sozialwissenschaften, 50–68.

Part I
Trust, identity and support for the EU

1 Identification and trust – resources of support for the European Union?

Bettina Westle

Theoretical considerations

There is widespread consent among analysts that the development of the European Union (EU) towards a political system with increasing competences normatively and empirically needs the active consent of its citizens. Yet, unification steps taken in the last years show growing disagreement, as was seen in popular votes and as survey data show (e.g. McLaren 2004; Scheuer 2005; Deutsch 2006; Westle 2007a; Isernia *et al.* 2010). Against this background the editors of this book ask for certain civic resources as a possible basis for an ongoing European integration. This chapter explores how far identification and trust as sub-dimensions of collective identity deliver a reservoir of diffuse support, working as a bulwark against system stress in case of deficits in effectiveness and democracy. After defining the question, the available indicators are discussed and their distributions are presented. In the next steps, the relationship between identification and trust is examined. To estimate the potential of identification and trust as resources for an EU in trouble, the links between identity and trust, on the one hand, and diverse aspects of support for the political regime of the EU, on the other hand, in total as well as for dissatisfied subgroups, are analysed and finally conclusions are drawn.

Collective identity and trust are concepts which have experienced an enormous revival in the scientific debate of recent years in different disciplines reaching from philosophy, social-psychology and sociology to political science. Especially in the context of the social identification theory (SIT), the research about social capital (SC), and debates about the EU identity and trust play important roles. Yet, this popularity partly comes at the price of reinventing the wheel and partly of growing heterogeneity of the meanings of these concepts. Therefore, the first step shall be to clarify how both concepts will be used in this chapter.

Leaning on social-psychological concepts, *European identity* as like national identities can be defined as a social, collective identification of individuals with large-scale reference objects. Such identities consist of a self-image based on the perception of certain commonalities with others. As part of the personal identity, collective identities contribute to individuals' self-esteem and therefore can become relevant sources of behaviour, for example in order to defend or improve self-concept. According to SIT (Tajfel 1981; Turner et al. 1987), a social identity not only consists of cognitive and affective identification with an in-group, but also of distinction/discrimination against out-groups.

Different concepts of *social trust* have been developed within the SC approach. One concept, based on the rational choice frame, conceives of trust as a cognitive calculus, often arising in situations of common interests (e.g. Ripperger 1998; Hardin 2006). In contrast, another SC concept sees trust as a moral phenomenon, based on common cultural orientations, and often early socialization, so that trust forms a personality trait of the trusting, widely independent from the trusted objects (e.g. Fukuyama 1995; Uslaner 2002). In between these poles are a variety of different concepts of trust, referring to reciprocity, networks and information about trustworthiness as well as possibilities of sanctions or linked to friendship and feelings of closeness – but all presuppose some perceived knowledge about each other (e.g. Coleman 1988; Putnam 1994, 2000; Offe 1999; Gambetta 2001).

The social-psychological approach to collective identity and the latter concept of trust as a reciprocal relationship between a truster and trustworthiness/trusted are rather compatible with established, older concepts in political science, for example of Deutsch et al. (1957) or Easton (1975). Both describe collective identity as a sense of community, 'we' feeling, mutual trust, sympathy and loyalty, identification in terms of feelings of belonging, readiness to cooperate and, finally, as willingness to form or maintain a political community. In later research these broad concepts have often been reduced and systematized along two dimensions (e.g. Niedermayer and Westle 1995; Scheuer 2005): the vertical, which is the identification of the individual with the community, and the horizontal, which is the mutual trust that ties together people of a political community.

Within *Easton's concept of political support* and some closely related concepts, which will be used as a frame in the following, identification with a political community and trust between its members are two sub-dimensions of diffuse (value-based and/or affective, enduring) support of the political community. It is assumed that horizontal trust and identification are positively linked, albeit the causal direction between both is open.[1] The aim of this

---

1 At least four relationships are plausible: first, mutual trust within a political community as well as identification with it might arise separately from the same roots, for example from the perception of similarities or commonalities between the members, which additionally also generate the fundaments of the regime – as for example the values of Christianity within confessional communities or the values of democracy within political communities. Such a perception of commonalities makes trust feel less risky and fosters sympathy for a common frame of rules – thus, trust and identification are both dependent variables, which are shaped by the same independent variables and therefore might develop parallel in a similar direction. A second possibility is that trust comes first and identification is dependent on trust. This seems plausible in the situation where a community is built by the free will of its founders – the logic is, because we trust each other, we should work together. Yet, in regard to the founding situation of the EC, at least on the elite level the opposite argument played a role. Mistrust between nations was one of the motives for founding the EC and one of the hopes was that an intensified contact between the member nations in the long run might lead to its erosion. Also,

chapter is not to disentangle the determinants of and relationships between identification and trust. Rather, one can formulate the axiom that in an established community, there should be positive links between horizontal trust and identification, which in a process perspective well might reinforce (or erode) each other in both causal directions. Yet, the question whether identity or mutual trust can be a better resource for support of the EU only makes sense in the case that both are different concepts, but could substitute for each other in regard to their function.

Besides, a political community can also be supported in a specific mode, resting on considerations about costs and benefits of belonging to it. The same applies to the two other objects which Easton differentiates within a political system, namely the regime and the authorities. Both of them can be supported either because of their effectiveness (specific) or because of the values they ideally represent (diffuse) and, additionally, because of their performance in realizing these values (diffuse-specific support, see Westle 2007b).

Within Easton's concept, the three object-levels are distinguished but not thought of as totally independent from each other. Rather diverse spillover effects are discussed. The ones which are of interest in the following are spillovers between the political community on the one hand and the regime and authorities/outputs on the other hand. Such effects again are possible in both directions.[2] In regard to trust these effects were already theoretically discussed in the context of SC. Thus it is argued that face-to-face contacts as a basis of mutual trust are sparse in large-scale societies. Instead the durability of institutions, which are based on shared values of the members of the community, guarantees the trustworthiness of the fellow citizens (e.g. Offe 1999: 59; Hartmann 2002: 88). This argument has been transferred to the EU, stating that its democratic content gives reason for the trustworthiness of the fellow citizens (Kaina 2006: 123). This argument forms a plausible basis to implement more democracy in the EU before a widespread and resilient European identity exists. Yet, trust in the people of other member countries

---

it was hoped that economic benefits of the EC might foster the identification with this community in spillover effects. This assumes, thirdly, different determinants but similar outcomes with respect to growing mutual trust and identification. Fourthly, it is possible that identification works as a determinant of mutual trust. This assumption is based on the consideration that belonging to and supporting the same community is itself a reason for trustworthiness, because deviant and harming behaviour would affect all members negatively. In the long run deviance also would harm the deviators, insofar trust relies on reciprocity. Also, because the EC originally was conceptualized without the option of exit for the member states, it additionally fulfilled one condition of dense networks, which allow for sanctions in case of misuse of trust and thus reduces the risks of trust.

2 Some authors explicitly oppose the 'conclusion: if collective identity, then legitimacy' (e.g. Fuss and Grosser 2006; see also Karolewski and Kaina 2006). Yet, this conclusion is very farfetched and overtly based on a misinterpretation of the Easton model, which does not equate the different levels of political systems, but explicitly differentiates between collective identity as diffuse support of the political community on the one hand and support of the regime and of the authorities on the other hand. Yet, those levels are not totally immune to each other, but allow for links (overflows), especially in a process perspective.

does not necessarily arise out of face-to-face contacts or of European democratic institutions. Today, information about other countries is easily transported by mass media and thus can create certain feelings of similarity, familiarity and even commonalities with other countries. Thus, trust in the people of other countries can also rest on the knowledge that they support the same democratic values in their own countries as oneself does and have behaved in a peaceful way. Former empirical results about trust also hint to these factors. Thus, for example, Norway and Switzerland receive trust rates by the citizens of EU member countries as high or even higher than those ones of other EU peoples, whereas Eastern European countries in the transition period, countries with severe democratic defects such as Turkey and non-democratic countries such as China or Russia are much less trusted (Westle 2003b; Delhey 2004, 2007a, 2007b).

Thus, in the following the analysis will be restricted to the contrary causal arrow of possible spillover effects, namely the classical argument that collective identity delivers a reservoir of goodwill in cases of shortcomings of the political regime and the outputs of the authorities. If this is the case, one should find not only positive links between identification and horizontal trust but also evaluations of the political regime and outputs. Rather, identity should show its potential as a source of systems support, especially in cases of negative evaluation on the other levels.

Operationalization and structure of the indicators of collective identity

The survey data for the following analyses have been taken from representative samples of the voting population in 16 Western and Eastern European countries in 2007 (Table 1.1). These data deliver indicators of identification and trust as shown in Table 1.2.

The variable *'European belonging'* comes close to what SIT states as a presupposition for identification, namely the knowledge of belonging to a certain group and its relevance for their own life. Yet this indicator might carry the problem that it says nothing about whether felt consequences are positive or negative. According to SIT, perceived positive consequences should promote identification and negative consequences should injure identification. Thus this indicator seems to carry ambivalent meanings in regard to identity as a dimension of support.

'Feeling as European 1 and 2' should catch the self-identification as European. This question has first been asked early in the questionnaire and again some time later in an experimental setting with threat scenarios. The first indicator was designed to catch the usual day-to-day context, the second to catch a situation of gravity.

'Attachment to one's own country' and *'attachment to Europe'* have already been asked in the Eurobarometer in order to measure the extent of identification with different territorial and political units. Aims were to allow for independent

Table 1.1 Representative samples of the voting population in 16 Western and Eastern European countries in 2007

Country	Country-specific weight (n)	Total weight (n)	Year of EU accession
Belgium	1,004	404	1951
France	1,007	2,295	1951
Germany	1,000	3,315	1951
Italy	1,012	2,303	1951
Denmark	1,000	207	1973
United Kingdom	1,000	2,185	1973
Greece	1,000	434	1981
Spain	1,002	1,789	1986
Portugal	1,000	377	1986
Estonia	1,000	66	2004
Poland	999	1,488	2004
Slovakia	1,082	198	2004
Slovenia	1,018	81	2004
Bulgaria	1,006	311	2007
Macedonia	1,002	387	—
Serbia	1,005	297	—
Total	16,136	16,136	

Table 1.2 Indicators of identity

shortname	question, categories of answer and coding
	collective identification
European belonging	How far do you feel that what happens to Europe in general has important consequences for people like you? *a great deal (4), somewhat (3), not very much (2), not at all (1), (don't know), (refusal)*
feeling as European 1	How much does being a European have to do with how you feel about yourself in your day-to-day life? *a lot (4), some (3), a little (2), not at all (1), (don't know), (refusal)*
feeling as European 2	identical with q10, but asked in an experimental setting after three different scenarios of threat of the own country by globalization (split ballot) and a question whether, in order to deal with this threat, the power of the national government or the power of the EU should be increased.
attachment to nation and to Europe	People feel different degrees of attachment to their town or village, to their region, to their country or to Europe. What about you? How attached do you feel to the following? *very attached (4), fairly attached (3), not very attached (2), not at all attached (1), (don't know), (refusal)* (A – your town/village), (B – your region), C – our country, D – Europe
national or European	In the near future do you see yourself as . . . /nationality/ only (1), /nationality/ and European (2), European and /nationality/ (3), European only (4), (none of the above), (don't know), (refusal)

(Continued)

Table 1.2 (Continued)

shortname	question, categories of answer and coding
	horizontal trust
general social trust	Generally speaking, would you say that most people can be trusted or that you need to be very careful in dealing with people? *Please use a number between 0 and 10, where '0' means that 'you need to be very careful in dealing with people' and '10' means that 'most people can be trusted'. You can use any number from 0 to 10.* (don't know), (refusal).
trust in groups of people	Please tell me on a scale of 0 to 10, how much you personally trust each of the following groups of people. *'0' means that you 'do not trust the group at all' and '10' means you 'have complete trust'.* (don't know), (refusal). A – 'nationality', B – people in other European countries, C – people outside Europe

ratings of the objects of identification and for direct comparisons. Thus, these questions are meant to catch multiple identities.[3]

The question *'national or European'* also has often been asked in Eurobarometer, yet it is interpreted quite differently. Some see it as an indicator of dual identity, because it allows for the combination of the nation and Europe in two middle categories (e.g. Citrin and Sides 2004). Others interpret it as an indicator of European identity only, thus forgetting about its construction along a spectrum of the nation and Europe (e.g. Sanders *et al.* 2010). Here it is seen as a partly forced choice question because respondents have to decide which of the objects is more important. It is assumed that the indicator invokes a model of competition or conflict between the nation and the EU.[4]

All indicators referring to identification have 'Europe' as stimulus, not the 'EU'. Therefore they could be seen as catching primarily social instead of political identification. Yet, this is questionable, because the context established by the other survey questions is clearly political and thus it is reasonable that respondents associate Europe also with the EU.[5]

---

[3] This question originally was designed by the author in a German study of 1985 (Westle 1989) and then in 1991 integrated by K. Reif into the Eurobarometer. Earlier indicators forced the respondents either to choose between nation or EU, or to build a rank order, or they did not allow direct comparisons because of different stimuli (e.g. pride on the national level and feeling of belonging on the European level). For an analysis of multiple identity structures see Westle 2003a).

[4] It has been shown that the indicator indeed is especially sensible for real-life situations of conflict between the EU and its member countries (Westle 2003a; Duchesne and Frognier 2008).

[5] For a test of the Easton model, a clear political connotation of the indicators, EU instead of Europe, is preferable. Europe is a broader object of identification than the EU, probably involving more historical and cultural associations, whereas the EU should evoke more political evaluations. Yet, the empirical evidence is dubious. In Eurobarometer 36 (1991) the question was asked twice, one with the stimulus Europe and one with the stimulus EU – without significant differences in distribution. In Eurobarometer 65.2 (2006) both stimuli were asked in a split ballot, with Europe showing clearly stronger attachment than EU.

In regard to social trust, four indicators are available. *'General social trust'* has been used in a lot of studies before. Yet the indicator is rather vague because the stimulus 'most people' allows for diverse associations, ranging from 'most people in my closer surrounding' to 'most people in the world'. Yet it probably invokes the association of people as individuals.

In contrast the indicators *'trust in own nationality'* (asked as trust in Italians, Greeks, etc.), *'trust in people in other European countries'* and *'trust in people outside Europe'* have more clearly defined objects, which probably are understood less in the sense of single persons, but more in the sense of certain groups of people, the nation and other countries within and outside Europe. Thus, the type of possible risks linked to a misuse of trust, which respondents think of when answering these questions, might differ quite largely. In regard to single persons such risks are, for instance, to be cheated, robbed, exploited or misused. But inhumane and unsocial behaviours such as these seem rather strange when thinking of whole national populations and their international relations. Risks on these levels are of a different nature, as like becoming – as a nation – the victim of other nations engaging in international conflicts ranging from economic sanctions to armed conflicts. Because of these different types of risks the kind of trust might be different as well, more bound to the personal situation of respondents in the first case and more to the situation of the nation in the second case.

Compared with questions that ask for trust in single nations, these questions seem somewhat suggestive because they draw an explicit difference between European and non-European countries – which does not necessarily meet the citizens' perceptions, as mentioned above. Despite this, it can be assumed that respondents try to give an answer based on their own summary of perceptions of other countries' populations. Thus, this question format may also come as an advantage in the way that the comparison between European and other countries is not dependent on the coincidence of which single countries the researcher might have selected for evaluation. However, the questions about national trust and about trust outside Europe are useful to deliver realistic comparisons for trust in the people of European countries and to identify the line between in- and outsiders.

Trust in people has been asked with an 11-point scale, with the poles of 'no trust at all' and 'complete trust' and an additional category of 'don't know'. The first question arising here is, what does 'no trust at all' really mean? Is the absence of trust identical with the presence of mistrust? A second question concerns the meaning and handling of the category 'don't know'. Usually in analysing survey items this category can be defined as missing, based on the assumption that the few respondents choosing 'don't know' would distribute like the others, if they would have made up their mind. Yet, this assumption is always empirically troubled when frequencies of 'don't know' are high because then the question concerning causes and further prospects arises. In regard to trust the assumption of an identical distribution is moreover theoretically questionable. What does it mean to say 'I don't know whether I trust or not'? Since trust can be seen as a mechanism to reduce uncertainty about the behaviour of 'others' in a possibly precarious situation, the psychological status 'don't know' could easily be identical with 'I cannot trust' or 'I neither trust nor mistrust'. This vagueness of the concept(s) of trust and mistrust is a real problem for survey questions, which might lead to high frequencies of 'don't know' answers. If this is the case, they should be treated separately until their meaning becomes clearer.

The first step to prove the meanings of these indicators and their conceptual dimensionality on an empirical basis are factor analyses (Table 1.1 for the pooled data; because of limited space, single-country analyses are not shown in this chapter, but just reported.). They clearly reveal three different dimensions, namely on factor 1 all the indicators of trust, on factor 2 all the indicators of identification with Europe and the variable 'national or European' and on factor 3 the variables 'attachment to own nation' and 'national or European', together explaining 58 per cent of the variance. The double-loading of the variable 'national or European' on the European as well as on the national factor confirms the above classification of this indicator as a measure of a spectrum between national and European identification. The indicator 'belonging to Europe' shows an insufficient commonality and a rather low loading on the European factor, thus confirming the above doubts about this question as an indicator of a positive European identification. In regard to the dimension of trust, the general social trust shows a lower loading than the other indicators, followed by trust in their own countrymen. This supports the above considerations of different types of trust.[6]

This structure is nearly perfectly repeated in all countries. They all exhibit the three same factors with around 60 per cent of explained variance. Only in France, Italy and Greece does trust in the own nation show an additional, but still clearly lower, loading on the factor of national identity. Thus identity and trust can indeed be confirmed as separate constructs. The indicator 'national or European' shows double loadings, on the European and on the national factor, in eight Western as well as Eastern EU member countries. In the other eight cases this indicator shows only loadings on one factor, but these are in five countries on the national and only in three countries on the European dimension. Thus, this indicator again reveals a double nature. Finally, the indicator about consequences of belonging to Europe has low commonalities in seven countries and shows rather low loadings on the European dimension.

The correlations between the indicators of identification (Table 1.4) illustrate these main findings as well, insofar as they are strongest in between the two variables concerning the day-to-day EU feeling and attachment to Europe and somewhat lower with these and the variable about EU belonging. Additionally is to be seen that whereas attachment to the nation correlates only very low with the EU feeling, but rather modest and positive with attachment to Europe,

---

6 The assumption of a more individualistic connotation of the 'general social trust' is also supported by analyses of distributions and determinants, which cannot be reported here.

Table 1.3 Factorial structure of indicators of identification and trust

	F1 trust	F2 EU identification	F3 nat. identification
EU belonging	—	(0.46)	—
EU feeling day to day 1	—	0.75	—
EU feeling day to day 2	—	0.75	—
attachment Europe	—	0.69	—
national vs. European	—	0.55	–0.51
attachment nation	—	—	0.88
general social trust	0.62	—	—
trust: people of own country	0.72	—	—
trust: people of other EU countries	0.85	—	—
trust: people outside EU	0.82	—	—
Eigenvalue	2.85	1.73	1.18
cum % of variance		57.6	

only loadings above 0.39 shown;
( ) indicates commonality below 0.30

Table 1.4 Correlations between indicators of identification and trust of national and European identification

pearsons r	EU belonging	EU feeling day to day 1	EU feeling day to day 2	att. Europe	national vs. European
EU feeling day to day 1	0.21**	—	—	—	—
EU feeling day to day 2	0.25**	0.50**	—	—	—
attachment Europe	0.18**	0.39**	0.33**	—	—
national vs. European	0.15**	0.28**	0.24**	0.33**	—
attachment nation	0.06**	0.08**	0.09**	0.30**	–0.12**

n=14,840; 1-tailed significance: *–0.01, **–0.001.

the indicator contrasting the nation and Europe correlates positively with all variables concerning European identification, but negatively with attachment to the nation. This again shows its different status within the identity variables.[7]

[7] A closer inspection of the means of different indicators of identity according to each other also reveals this variable as an exception. The usual pattern between two indicators of European identification is a parallel increase of both. But in case the indicator 'national or European' is used as independent variable, the peculiarity exists that the group 'European only' systematically shows less intensive European answers than the group 'primarily European, but also national'.

Table 1.5 Correlations between the different indicators of trust in people

pearsons r	general social trust	trust in people of own country	trust in people of other EU countries
trust in people of own country	0.31**	—	—
trust in people of other EU countries	0.36**	0.53**	—
trust in people outside EU	0.37**	0.40**	0.68**

n=14,840; 1-tailed significance: *–0.01, **–0.001.

In order to compute a scale of European identification, four additional reliability analyses have been computed, with fairly similar outcomes. Using all five variables would result in an alpha of 0.67, leaving aside the 'EU belonging' in an alpha of 0.68, leaving aside the 'national or European' in an alpha of 0.64 and leaving aside both of these indicators in an alpha of 0.67.

Thus, the reported analyses do not tell only one unquestionable story about scale construction. But on their basis, the assumption that the indicator concerning EU belonging is probably more cognitively framed and also catches negative consequences on the high values leads to the decision not to use it anymore. The indicator about the future feeling as national or European will not be integrated into the scale of European identification, but used separately, mainly because it also catches national feelings. Thus, the index of EU identification is constructed with the two variables about the day-to-day feeling and attachment to Europe.

The correlations between the indicators of trust show for the pooled data (Table 1.5) and for every single country the strongest link between trust in people of other EU countries and trust in people outside the EU, followed by the link between trust in the own nation and trust in people of other EU countries, and on the third place trust in own nation and trust in people outside the EU. This hints to a main 'borderline' between the nation as in-group and others as out-groups, regardless of whether they are Europeans or not. Secondly, trust in Europeans is closer to trust in own countrymen than trust in non-Europeans, thus following a 'trust geography' of closeness. Besides, general social trust shows moderate correlations to all other trust variables. On the basis of these data the indicators depicting their collective object clearly will be used as single ones, leaving aside the general social trust.

Distributions of identity and trust

Similar to earlier years, affects are clearly more strongly developed in regard to the own country than to Europe (Table 1.6): more than the half of the respondents feel very strongly attached to their country, but only around 21 per cent feel very strongly attached to Europe and only around 12 per cent have a very strong feeling as Europeans in their day-to-day life. The most

Table 1.6 Collective identification – distribution

	not at all (1)	not very much (2)	somewhat (3)	a great deal (4)	mean	missing in % of total (n)
EU feeling day to day 1	24.9	26.2	36.2	12.7	2.37	2.0
EU feeling day to day 2	24.7	30.7	32.4	12.2	2.31	2.0
attachment to Europe	11.0	24.6	43.2	21.2	2.75	1.4
attachment to own country	2.9	8.8	33.8	54.6	3.40	0.2
index of EU identification	none (1) 4.9	6.2	10.0	13.1	14.6	15.4	17.7	10.1	5.0	strong (4) 3.1	2.48	4.5
	national only 37.3	national and European 49.7	European and national 8.2	European only 4.8	1.81	2.7
national or European						

frequent pattern here is to feel modestly European. Nearly one-quarter do not feel at all European in day-to-day life, but only 11 per cent deny any attachment to Europe. The indicator contrasting the feeling as national versus European again shows a much stronger position of the nation than of Europe, although the latter is accepted as a less central part of their identity by more than half of the respondents.

In most countries this pattern is repeated. The majority (ranging from half to three-quarters of the respondents) feels very attached to their own nation; exceptions are Belgium, Spain, the United Kingdom and Slovakia, where only around 40 per cent feel strongly attached to their nation, but most feel moderately attached. Attachment to Europe is clearly less intensive in each country. The most frequent category is the feeling of being somewhat attached (except for the UK with 'not very' and Macedonia with 'very' strong attachment). Whereas missing answers are below 2 per cent in regard to attachment to own nation, attachment to Europe arouses somewhat more insecurity: up to 12 per cent (in Bulgaria). Both questions about day-to-day life show a very similar pattern, with the category of feeling somewhat European as the most frequent, except for the UK, Bulgaria, Poland, Slovakia and Serbia with tendencies to lower Europeanness and Portugal to stronger Europeanness. Finally, the indicator about the future feeling as national or European again reveals in all countries the priority of the nation. This is the case either as an exclusive feeling as for majorities in the UK (69 per cent), Poland (53 per cent), Bulgaria (52 per cent), Estonia (49 per cent) and Serbia (46 per cent), in each country followed by the category 'nationality first and European second', or the other way round as in all other countries. Exclusive European identification varies between only 0 per cent and 9 per cent, and a priority of the feeling as European varies between 3 per cent and 13 per cent (both high values in Belgium). The index of European identification with a range from 1 to 4 shows in total of the countries a mean of 2.48, with Belgium and Portugal on top (but the latter with more missing values and more variance), Italy, Denmark, Macedonia, Spain, Poland, Germany and Slovenia in the middle and still above the scale mean of 2.5 and as such with a weak, but positive European identification, and the other countries below this mean with the UK at the bottom with 2.14. Just to reaffirm the above reported structures of the single indicators, the index also shows positive links to the future feeling as national or European (0.36) in all countries and to national attachment (0.21) in most of them (except for Poland, Bulgaria, Macedonia and Serbia).

The indicators of trust in groups of people reveal a pattern of geographical, cultural and political closeness as was observed in a similar way before (Inglehart 1991, 1999; Niedermayer 1995; Westle 2003b; Delhey 2004, 2007a, 2007b): trust in the people of their own country is strongest, followed by trust in people of other European countries and lowest is trust in people of countries outside Europe. Yet, the differences are very small, and between trust in own nation and other Europeans they are nearly the same (0.86) as the ones between trust in other Europeans and non-Europeans (0.83).

Table 1.7 Trust in people – distribution

percentages	careful									trusted		mean	missing in % of total
	1	2	3	4	5	6	7	8	9	10	11		
own country	2.6	0.8	2.2	4.0	6.5	23.1	13.2	18.8	16.5	3.3	9.0	7.21	1.1
other EU countries	5.1	1.1	3.2	6.5	9.0	29.6	15.7	15.9	9.4	1.7	2.7	6.35	5.5
outside EU	10.0	2.0	6.3	10.2	11.6	29.5	12.6	9.8	5.2	1.0	1.9	5.52	7.5

This ranking of trust is strongly grounded in answers surrounding the middle category (6) – either with a slight tendency towards the positive or the negative pole, but the more extreme categories are not frequent and, additionally, the middle category in each case shows by far the highest frequency. This nurtures the suspicion that the middle category is not only used to articulate a middle amount of trust, but also 'neither trust nor mistrust', 'trust and mistrust', 'insecurity about trust' and so on.

The same pattern of rising trust in people with their closeness is repeated in every country. Especially strong favouritism in trust towards own countrymen compared with trust in other countries is observed in Spain (regardless of Europe or not), Greece and Slovenia (with respect to outside Europe), and Serbia and the United Kingdom (with respect to Europe). In regard to all three questions, Denmark and Belgium show the highest trust rates, and trust is mostly somewhat stronger in Western than in Eastern European countries. But again the means hide somewhat unusual distributions, with extremely high frequencies on the middle category (up to 35 per cent), and in regard to trust in people outside Europe, with high frequencies of the lowest category 'no trust at all' (but not on the values in between) in some countries. Finally, the indicators of trust in people of other European countries and people outside Europe show remarkably high rates of 'don't know' in some countries (especially Portugal, Estonia, Poland, Slovakia, Bulgaria and Serbia, with between 10 per cent and 28 per cent of the total respondents), which again nurtures doubts about how the scale might be understood, or more generally, about the relationships between trust, absence of trust, mistrust and insecurity about trust.

Relationships between identification and trust

The empirical links between the indicators of identification and of trust (Table 1.8) show rather modest positive correlations. As is to be expected, they are highest when the similar object is referred to, as in the case of pearsons r=0.20 between attachment to own country and trust in own countrymen, and pearsons r=0.24 between the index of European identification and trust in

28   Bettina Westle

Table 1.8 Correlation between indicators of identification and indicators of trust

pearsons r	trust in people of own country	trust in people of other EU countries	trust in people outside EU
index of EU identity	0.12**	0.24**	0.16**
national or European	0.01	0.21**	0.15**
attachment to own country	0.20**	0.09**	0.04**

'don't know' coded as missing values; 1-tailed significance: *–0.01, **–0.001.

people of other EU countries.[8] All other correlations are somewhat lower and may be an effect of a general psychological tendency to trust or not to trust others, but they also reveal that identification with Europe is positively linked to trust towards the world outside Europe, whereas identification with the nation does not show a comparable positive link, thus probably hinting to a more parochial (thick) trust psychology. An inspection of the cross-tabulations (not shown) supports this assumption and reveals that respondents who tend to identify exclusively with their own nation articulate especially low trust in people as well outside Europe as in other European countries and high rates of 'don't know' answers, but they also show somewhat lower trust in their own countrymen than respondents who identify with their nation and with Europe.

Turning the perspective moreover shows that missing answers on trust in people of other European countries most often go along with rather low identification with Europe (mean of 2.30), which is between the low and moderate trusters. Yet, this pattern is not to be found in each country. In most Eastern European countries, which have the highest levels of 'don't know' on trust, respondents show the lowest identification with Europe. In most other countries, the identification of those respondents is only somewhat below the average. Thus, presumably missing values on trust can be interpreted as similar to low trust or mistrust in Eastern European countries, but not in Western ones.

Identity and trust as resources of European unification

If a political system exists for some time and at the moment does not experience a severe crisis, all levels of support – for outputs and authorities, the regime and the political community – should be positive and be linked positively because of mutual overflow processes in the past (the same, of course, applies

8 On first view it is irritating that the indicator 'national or European' correlates with trust in people of other EU countries with pearsons r=0.21, but not (negatively) with trust in people of the own country. This is due to respondents who feel exclusively as nationals because they articulate a bit less trust in their own countrymen (mean of 7.10) than those who feel primarily as nationals, but include Europe at second place (7.50). The ones who feel primarily or exclusively as Europeans articulate less trust in their own countrymen than the others (7.04 and 6.84). Yet, ethnocentrism (mean differences to trust in people of other European countries and in people outside Europe) decreases with stronger European feelings.

Table 1.9 Correlations between indicators of collective identity and support for the authorities and the regime of the European Union

pearsons r Coding 0 = none/negative to 1= very/positive	attachment to own country	national or European	index of European identification	trust in people of own country	trust in people of other European countries
responsiveness of EU authorities	0.06	0.14	0.29	0.13	0.24
satisfaction with democracy in Europe	0.11	0.16	0.31	0.16	0.25
EU benefit self and country	0.08	0.27	0.43	0.12	0.26
EU membership own country	0.08	0.26	0.36	0.09	0.24
transfer to EU in 4 policies	0.08	0.22	0.35	0.05	0.19
EU unification	0.05	0.21	0.32	0.13	0.25

all values significant at the level of −0.001.

to erosions of support). In the case of democratic national political systems, the ruling authorities can for some time also be evaluated negatively because the possibility to vote them out is the central blockade against an overall erosion of support as a consequence of output dissatisfaction. Yet in the case of the EU this possibility does not exist and therefore dissatisfaction with outputs and authorities may more directly injure the regime and the community.[9] Table 1.9 shows correlations between the indicators of identity and some variables of political support of the other levels of the EU. Because of the singular type of the EU these variables do not exactly represent Easton's different categories of support, but they come close to it. An index referring to the political authorities is 'responsiveness', whereas 'satisfaction with democracy in the EU' refers to the political regime and 'EU benefits' refer to specific support for outputs, though these are not assigned to concrete politicians or institutions. The question about the 'EU membership of own country' is also assigned to the EU as a whole and probably catches aspects of diffuse support. Finally, there are two indicators integrated which do not fit into the classical support model but aim at the uniqueness of the EU itself: the questions about 'transfer from the national to

---

9 Since the EU is linked with the national political systems in a complex way, support for these systems can also play a role for the evaluation of the EU. Research on the EU has over time and between countries found differing links to political support on the national level – thus, for example, in some countries satisfaction with democracy in the own nation and in the EU are linked positively, in others negatively and in some countries the EU is supported because the national economy benefits from EU membership, whereas in others the EU is accepted because and as long as things in the own nation go well (e.g. Martinotti and Steffanizzi 1995; Gabel 1998; Marks and Hooghe 1999; Kritzinger 2003).

Table 1.10 Multiple regression: support of identification and horizontal trust

dependent →	responsiveness		benefit		democracy satisfaction		membership		transfer		unification	
independent ↓	b	beta	b	beta	b	beta	b	beta	b	beta	b	beta
index of European identity	0.23	0.65	0.65	0.38	0.25	0.26	0.53	0.32	0.29	0.33	0.32	0.27
trust in people of other European countries	0.19	0.34	0.34	0.17	0.22	0.19	0.32	0.17	0.12	0.12	0.26	0.19
constant	0.23		0.08		0.29		0.39		0.44		0.27	
adj r²		0.12		0.21		0.13		0.16		0.14		0.14

all values significant at the level of –0.001.

EU responsibility' should catch support for a deepening of the integration in certain policy areas and the question about 'EU unification' should measure the most generalized attitude towards the future of the EU. All variables have been symmetrically recoded to a range from 0 to 1 for the coming analyses (for question wordings, see 'Appendix' at the end of this chapter).

Whereas attachment to own country and trust in its people show rather weak links to support of the different aspects of the EU, European identification and trust in people of other European countries reveal significant and somewhat stronger links to all aspects. The links between horizontal trust and other aspects of political support are in contrast to earlier observations, which could not find the hypothesized relationships between general social trust and political support (e.g. Kaase 1999; Gabriel et al. 2002), which is, by the way, here also the case (pearsons r between general social trust and political support range between 0.00 and 0.10). This again hints to a relevant difference in general social trust and trust in people of countries. In all cases the index of EU identification shows somewhat stronger links than trust in European people.

This bivariate observation also holds in the multivariate analysis (Table 1.10; because of possible problems of multi-co-linearity, the analysis is restricted to one indicator for each dimension).[10] Both aspects of European identity keep relevance in regard to other indicators of support, and identification as European again is somewhat more strongly linked with them than horizontal trust, which leads to the assumption that identification might be a somewhat better resource than horizontal trust.

Yet, until now it is still questionable whether identification and trust really are resources for an EU in trouble, since their links with the other support

---

10 Other analyses which also included national attachment and national trust reveal that these lose nearly any importance for the support of the EU (data not shown).

Table 1.11 Multiple regressions for subgroups

dependent →	unification					
	if responsiveness		*if benefits of country and self*		*if with democracy*	
subgroups	*negative*	*positive*	*none*	*one or both*	*not satisfied*	*satisfied*
n	11,128	3,714	4,189	10,220	5,826	9,339
independent ↓	b beta	b beta	b beta	b beta	b beta	b beta
index of European identity	0.29 0.25	0.34 0.30	0.31 0.24	0.21 0.19	0.35 0.27	0.23 0.21
trust in people of other EU countries	0.25 0.18	0.28 0.21	0.20 0.16	0.22 0.17	0.21 0.15	0.25 0.19
constant	0.28	0.28	0.20	0.39	0.24	0.28
adj r²	0.11	0.16	0.09	0.08	0.11	0.10

all values significant at the level of −0.001.

variables are rather strong. Therefore in the last step it will be tested whether these sub-dimensions of European identity are able to overcome the perception of diverse deficits as with low responsiveness, no benefits and unsatisfactory democracy when it comes to the question of whether unification should go on.[11] The idea is that if identity matters, support for an ongoing unification should be as strong (or weak) dependent on European identity regardless of whether deficits are criticized or not.

The empirical evidence (Table 1.11) supports this assumption: in the case of critique about authorities' responsiveness, the explained variance in the attitude towards unification is a only bit weaker than in the case of satisfaction with responsiveness and regardless of whether respondents see benefits or not and how satisfied they are with democracy in the EU; their European identity has nearly the same effect on their attitude towards unification.

Summary

The foregoing work has produced some results, but has also shown some problems of theory and of measurement. To start with the latter, there are primarily two problems: although the concept of trust has been considered in a lot of scientific work in recent years, this concept is neither theoretically nor

---

11 'Unification' probably taps the most principled question in regard to the future durability of the EU and its deepening. Another possibility for the dependent variable of this test would be 'membership of own country'. But since this question is directed towards the past and not the future, 'unification' is preferred here.

in terms of measurement instruments satisfactorily defined. It is an open question whether trust is something ranging from absence to strong existence or ranging from a negative pole as mistrust over absence to a positive pole. Respondents also seem to have these problems with the concept, which results in unclear, ambiguous handling of the measurement scales. A second open question for future research is how far citizens differentiate in their identity feelings between Europe as a geographical and cultural entity and the European Union as the political organization and what consequences this has for political support.

Substantially, to evaluate identity as a resource of the EU in stress affords to distinguish between the fulfilment of its function and its distribution. In sum, identity – as measured in terms of vertical identification and horizontal trust – individually does fulfil the function to work as a blockade against the withdrawal of support in case of dissatisfaction with outputs, authorities and democracy, although in a rather limited way (in terms of explained variance). But the distribution of an intense European identity until now has stayed rather weak, especially as compared with national identity. Because of the relative marginality of Europe in the minds of Europeans, it is questionable whether this part of identity really already can fulfil the functions which social-psychological approaches ascribe to collective identities as motives for behaviour – especially in case of a conflict with more central and stronger parts of collective identity, such as the national one.

Collective identity is not totally immune to other aspects of evaluation of the political system. Rather it develops out of long-enduring positive experiences on the other levels and it might also erode in the opposite case. Also against the background of nearly all Europeans' historical experience of the Janus-face of collective identities in nationalistic wars, it cannot be a promising option to construct a strong European identity from above by means of symbolic action. Instead, the development of a widespread, resilient and peaceful collective European identity might need a very long time of realistic positive experiences with outputs and with democracy in the European Union.

Appendix

Country	Country-specific weight (n)	Total weight (n)	Year of EU accession
Belgium	1,004	404	1951
France	1,007	2,295	1951
Germany	1,000	3,315	1951
Italy	1,012	2,303	1951
Denmark	1,000	207	1973
United Kingdom	1,000	2,185	1973
Greece	1,000	434	1981
Spain	1,002	1,789	1986
Portugal	1,000	377	1986

Country	Country-specific weight (n)	Total weight (n)	Year of EU accession
Estonia	1,000	66	2004
Poland	999	1,488	2004
Slovakia	1,082	198	2004
Slovenia	1,018	81	2004
Bulgaria	1,006	311	2007
Macedonia	1,002	387	—
Serbia	1,005	297	—
Total	16,136	16,136	

Variables of political support

responsiveness – meanindex: I am going to read a few statements on politics in /our country/ and in Europe. Could you please tell me whether you tend to agree or tend to disagree with each of them? (rotation of items). *strongly agree, agree, disagree, strongly disagree, (neither agree nor disagree), (don't know), (refusal)* • Those who make decisions at the European Union level do not care much what people like me think. • Those who make decisions at the European Union level are competent people who know what they are doing.

satisfaction with democracy: On the whole, how satisfied are you with the way democracy works in the European Union? *very satisfied, somewhat satisfied, somewhat dissatisfied, very dissatisfied, (don't know), (refusal).*

benefit country and self – countindex: Taking everything into consideration, would you say that /our country/ has on balance benefited or not from being a member of the European Union? *has benefited, has not benefited, (don't know), (refusal)* (in Serbia: . . .would benefit) And what about people like you? Have people like you on balance benefited or not from /our country's/ EU membership? *have benefited, have not benefited, (don't know), (refusal)* (in Serbia: . . .would benefit).

membership: Generally speaking, do you think that /our country's/ in the European Union is. . .? *a good thing, a bad thing, (neither good nor bad), (don't know), (refusal)* (in Serbia: . . .would the accession of).

transfer on European level – meanindex: Thinking about the European Union over the next few years or so, can you tell me whether you are in favour of or against the following. *strongly in favour, somewhat in favour, somewhat against, strongly against, (neither in favour nor against), (don't know), (refusal)* • a unified tax system for the EU, • a common system of social security in the EU, • a single EU foreign policy toward outside countries, • more help for EU regions in economic or social difficulties.

unification: Some say European integration has already gone too far. Others say it should be strengthened. What is your opinion? Please indicate your views using a 10-point-scale. On this scale, '0' means unification 'has already gone too far' and '10' means it 'should be strengthened'. What number on this scale best describes your position? (don't know), (refusal).

References

Citrin, J. and Sides, J. 2004. 'More than nationals: how identity choice matters in the new Europe', in: R. K. Herrmann, T. Risse and M. B. Brewer (eds) *Transnational identities: becoming European in the EU*. New York: Rowman & Littlefield Publishers, 161–85.

Coleman, J. 1988. 'Social capital in the creation of human capital', *American Journal of Sociology* 94(supplement): 95–120.

Delhey, J. 2004. 'Nationales und transnationales Vertrauen in der Europäischen Union', *Leviathan* 32(1): 15–45.

Delhey, J. 2007a. 'Grenzüberschreitender Austausch und Vertrauen. Ein Test der Transaktionsthese für Europa', in: A. Franzen and M. Freitag (eds) *Sozialkapital. Grundlagen und Anwendungen*. Wiesbaden: VS Verlag für Sozialwissenschaften, 141–62.

Delhey, J. 2007b. 'Do enlargements make the European Union less cohesive? An analysis of trust between EU nationalities', *Journal of Common Market Studies* 45(2): 253–79.

Deutsch, F. 2006. 'Legitimacy and identity in the European Union: empirical findings from the old member states', in: I. P. Karolewski and V. Kaina (eds) *European identity: theoretical perspectives and empirical insights*. Berlin: Lit Verlag, 149–78.

Deutsch, K. W., Burrell, S. A., Kahn, R. A., Lee, M., Lichtermann, M., Lindgren, R. E., Loewenheim, F. E. and van Wagenen, R. W. 1957. *Political community and the North Atlantic Area: international organization in the light of historical experience*. Princeton, NJ: Princeton University Press.

Duchesne, S. and Frognier, A. 2008. 'National and European identifications: a dual relationship', *Comparative European Politics* 6(2): 143–68.

Easton, D. 1975. *A systems analysis of political life*. Chicago and London: The University of Chicago Press.

Fukuyama, F. 1995. *Trust – the social virtues and the creation of prosperity*. New York: The Free Press.

Fuss, D. and Grosser, M. A. 2006. 'What makes young Europeans feel European? Results from a cross-cultural project', in: I. P. Karolewski and V. Kaina (eds) *European identity: theoretical perspectives and empirical insights*. Berlin: Lit Verlag, 209–42.

Gabel, M. J. 1998. *Interests and integration: market liberalization, public opinion, and European Union*. Ann Arbor: The University of Michigan Press.

Gabriel, O. W., Kunz, V., Roßteutscher, S. and Van Deth, J. W. 2002. *Sozialkapital und Demokratie*. Vienna: Wiener Universitätsverlag.

Gambetta, D. 2001. 'Kann man dem Vertrauen vertrauen?', in: M. Offe and C. Hartmann (eds) *Vertrauen. Die Grundlage des sozialen Zusammenhalts*. Frankfurt and New York: Campus, 204–37.

Hardin, R. 2006. *Trust*. Cambridge and Malden, MA: Polity Press.

Hartmann, M. 2002. 'Vertrauen als demokratische Erfahrung', in: R. Schmalz-Bruns and R. Zintl (eds) *Politisches Vertrauen. Soziale Grundlagen reflexiver Kooperation*. Baden-Baden: Nomos, 77–98.

Inglehart, R. 1991. 'Trust between nations: primordial ties, societal learning and economic development', in: K. Reif and R. Inglehart (eds) *Eurobarometer. The Dynamics of European Public Opinion.* Houndmills: Macmillan, 145–85.

Inglehart, R. 1999. 'Trust, well-being and democracy', in: M. E. Warren (ed.) *Democracy and trust.* Cambridge: Cambridge University Press, 88–120.

Isernia, P., Fiket, I., Serriccio, F. and Westle, B. 2010. 'European identity – a search in time and space', in: D. Sanders, P. Magalhaes, A. Freire and G. Tóka (eds) *Citizens and the European polity: mass attitudes towards the European and national polities.* Oxford: Oxford University Press.

Kaase, M. 1999. 'Interpersonal trust, political trust and non-institutionalized political participation in Western Europe', *West European Politics* 22(3): 1–21.

Kaina, V. 2006. 'European identity, legitimacy, and trust: conceptual considerations and perspectives on empirical research', in: I. P. Karolewski and V. Kaina (eds) *European identity: theoretical perspectives and empirical insights.* Berlin: Lit Verlag, 113–46.

Karolewski, I. P. and Kaina, V. 2006. 'European identity: preliminary conclusions and open questions', in: I. P. Karolewski and V. Kaina (eds) *European identity: theoretical perspectives and empirical insights.* Berlin: Lit Verlag, 295–314.

Kritzinger, S. 2003. 'The influence of the nation-state on individual support for the European Union', *European Union Politics* 4(2): 219–41.

Marks, G. and Hooghe, L. 1999. *National identity and support for European integration.* Berlin: Wissenschaftszentrum Berlin für Sozialforschung.

Martinotti, G. and Steffanizzi, S. 1995. 'Europeans and the nation state', in: O. Niedermayer and R. Sinnott (eds) *Public opinion and internationalized governance.* Oxford: Oxford University Press, 163–89.

McLaren, L. 2004. 'Opposition to European integration and fear of loss of national identity: debunking a basic assumption regarding hostility to the integration project', *European Journal of Political Research* 43(6): 895–911.

Niedermayer, O. 1995. 'Trust and sense of community', in: O. Niedermayer and R. Sinnott (eds) *Public opinion and internationalized governance.* Oxford: Oxford University Press, 227–45.

Niedermayer, O. and Westle, B. 1995. 'A typology of orientations', in: O. Niedermayer and R. Sinnott (eds) *Public opinion and internationalized governance.* Oxford: Oxford University Press, 33–50.

Offe, C. 1999. 'How can we trust our fellow citizens?', in: M. E. Warren (ed.) *Democracy and trust.* Cambridge: Cambridge University Press, 42–87.

Putnam, R. D. 1994. *Making democracy work: civic traditions in modern Italy.* Princeton: Princeton University Press.

Putnam, R. D. 2000. *Bowling alone: the collapse and revival of American community.* New York: Simon & Schuster.

Ripperger, T. 1998. *Ökonomik des Vertrauens. Analyse eines Organisationsprinzips.* Tübingen: Mohr Siebeck.

Sanders, D., Bellucci, P. and Torcal, M. 2010. 'The Europeanization of national politics? Citizenship and support in a post-enlargement Union', in: P. Belucci and D. Sanders (eds) *The Europeanization of national politics? Citizenship and support in a post-enlargement union.* Oxford: Oxford University Press.

Scheuer, A. 2005. *How Europeans see Europe.* Amsterdam: Vossiuspers.

Tajfel, H. 1981. *Human groups and social categories: studies in social psychology.* Cambridge: Cambridge University Press.

Turner, J. C., Hogg, M. A., Oakes, P. J., Reicher, S. D. and Wetherell, M. S. 1987. *Rediscovering the social group: a self-categorization theory.* Oxford: Blackwell.

Uslaner, E. M. 2002. *The moral foundations of trust.* Cambridge: Cambridge University Press.

Westle, B. 1989. *Politische Legitimität.* Baden-Baden: Nomos.

Westle, B. 2003a. 'Europäische Identifikation im Spannungsfeld regionaler und nationaler Identitäten. Theoretische Überlegungen und empirische Befunde', *Politische Vierteljahresschrift* 44(4): 453–82.

Westle, B. 2003b. 'Universalismus oder Abgrenzung als Komponente der Identifikation mit der Europäischen Union?', in: F. Brettschneider, J. W. van Deth and E. Roller (eds) *Europäische Integration in der öffentlichen Meinung,* Opladen: Leske & Budrich, 115–52.

Westle, B. 2007a. 'Europäische Identität und das EU-"Demokratiedilemma"', *Welt Trends. Zeitschrift für Internationale Politik und vergleichende Studien* 15(54): 69–83.

Westle, B. 2007b. 'Political beliefs and attitudes: legitimacy in public opinion research', in: A. Hurrelmann, S. Schneider and J. Steffek (eds) *Legitimacy in an age of global politics.* Houndmills: Palgrave Macmillan, 93–125.

2 What does the EU mean to you personally?

Citizens' images of and support for the European Union

Nicola Bücker

Introduction: What kind of EU for Europe's citizens?

Against all odds, the European integration process is moving forward. After the debacle of the failed European Constitution in 2005 and the rather fruitless 'period of reflection' of the following years, the Lisbon Treaty came into force in 2009 and basically reformed the European Union (EU) according to the constitution's original intentions (Kurpas 2007; Dougan 2008). This deepening of integration is paralleled by the EU's ongoing widening, which concerns five official candidate countries and four 'potential candidates' today.[1]

The integration process is moving forward, but apparently without the European Union's citizens. Far from being enthusiastic about the European project, the EU's citizenry has even denounced its former 'permissive consensus' and has developed a rather disapproving stance towards the EU, as demonstrated most visibly in three failed referendums since 2005.[2] This lack of public political support is highly problematic for the EU's future existence, because citizens have not only turned more critical, but have also gained more influence on the EU's political process over recent decades.[3] As a consequence, many observers argue that the deepened and widened EU will only hold together if its far-reaching economic and political integration is supplemented by a corresponding social integration of its population (e.g. Herrmann and Brewer 2004; Kaina and Karolewski 2006; Delhey 2007; Weßels 2007). According to this line of reasoning, only a sufficiently integrated European

---

1 The five official candidate countries are Croatia (which signed its Accession Treaty with the EU in December 2011), Iceland, Macedonia, Montenegro and Turkey. The 'potential candidates' are Albania, Bosnia and Herzegovina, Kosovo and Serbia (European Commission 2010).
2 But also the growing influence of Eurosceptic political parties, the declining expression of public EU support in social surveys and the ever smaller turnout at the European Parliament elections indicate that citizens have become more distanced and critical towards the EU (Fuchs *et al.* 2009; Kaina and Karolewski 2009: 15).
3 In addition to national referendums, citizens can directly impact the European political process via the European Parliament, which has gained considerably more power through the Lisbon Treaty. Moreover, several authors have highlighted an increasing politicization of the EU, meaning that voters can more and more directly influence their governments' EU policies, even though this development is still in a nascent stadium (see for example Ferrara and Weißhaupt 2004; Marks and Steenbergen 2004; Kriesi 2007).

people with an adequate sense of community and/or levels of mutual trust and solidarity will accept the EU's political decisions as rightful and appropriate, in other words as legitimate. This should hold true in particular in view of the EU's expanding activity areas and its stronger engagement in redistributive policies, which should increase political conflicts between its member states.

While many scholars agree on the necessity of a European society, this chapter examines whether EU citizens themselves share this rather 'federal' vision of the European Union. As previous research has demonstrated, people might perceive the EU and the European integration process in different ways and thus support it for different reasons (cf. Díez Medrano 2003). Accordingly, citizens might not view a European society as a necessary foundation of the European Union, because they might not conceptualize the latter as a supranational political system that potentially conflicts with their individual or national interests. Instead, they might find different reasons for supporting and accepting the EU as a legitimate political order.

In the following, I first elaborate on the theoretical concept of political support and discuss the model developed by David Easton and its application in European integration studies, as this model still provides a theoretical framework for many studies dealing with people's EU support today. Having presented some of the drawbacks of much of the 'established' empirical research in this field, I discuss the concept of framing as a promising alternative for analysing people's stance towards the EU. In the empirical part of this chapter, I present the results of altogether 46 qualitative interviews that I conducted in Poland and Eastern Germany in 2005 and examine how these participants perceived and legitimized the European Union. In order to put this qualitative data into a broader context, I also present some findings based on *Eurobarometer* concerning the EU advantages and drawbacks that people see for their country.

Examining political support in European integration studies: old and new approaches

According to David Easton, citizens' support is one of the decisive inputs of any political system (the second input being demands). Without a minimal level of support, no political system can survive in the long run. With regard to the political objects that people might support, Easton distinguishes between three fundamental elements of the political system (Easton 1965: 193, 212): the political regime (i.e. values, norms and institutional structure), the political authorities (i.e. the occupants of the authority roles) and the political community, which he defines as 'a group of persons bound together by a political division of labor' (ibid.: 177).[4] Moreover, Easton further elabo-

---

4 Easton further explains the last object as follows: 'The existence of a political system must include a plurality of political relationships through which the individual members are linked to each other and through which the political objectives of the system are pursued (. . .)' (ibid.).

Table 2.1 Easton's model of political support

Types of political support	Objects of political support		
	Political community	Political regime	Political authorities
Diffuse	'we' feeling; sense of community	sentiment of trust; sentiment of legitimacy	sentiment of trust; sentiment of legitimacy
Specific	—	—	instrumental output assessment (general performance; laws, etc.)

Source: Niedermayer and Westle (1995), own supplements according to Easton (1975).

rates on the different types of political support and puts forward his famous distinction between 'specific' and 'diffuse' support. Specific support results from people's satisfaction with a political system's outputs; in other words, it is a '*quid pro quo* for the fulfillment of demands' (ibid.: 268, original emphasis). This type of support is only directed at the political authorities. As this specific support strongly depends on political outputs, it is supposed to change if people perceive their valued outputs to increase or to diminish.

'Diffuse support', on the other hand, does not refer to any specific outputs, but to 'evaluations of what an object is or represents – to the general meaning it has for a person – not of what it does' (Easton 1975: 144).[5] This latter type of support supplies a 'reservoir of favourable attitudes or good will' that helps sustain sufficient levels of public support even when people's demands are temporarily disappointed (ibid.). Hence, diffuse support is supposed to be more stable than specific support, which makes it indispensable for any political system, because it will never be possible to satisfy all demands of all members immediately (Easton 1965: 269). At the same time, the former is more fundamental than the latter in a second way, because it is not only directed towards the political authorities, but also to the political regime and the political community. With regard to the authorities and the regime, diffuse support appears as two 'sentiments', that is, trust and legitimacy (Easton 1975: 453).[6] Table 2.1 displays the different combinations of types and objects of political support according to Easton.

Over recent decades, a number of authors have aimed at adjusting this general model of political support to the specific context of European integration

---

5 Still, Easton presumes that diffuse support might also result from long-term satisfaction with political outputs, that is, from specific support (Easton 1975: 445).
6 Easton defines trust in the regime as 'symbolic satisfaction with the processes by which the country is run' and trust in the authorities as belief that these will consider people's interests, even if they are not permanently controlled (Easton 1975: 447). On the other hand, legitimacy means the 'conviction that it is right and proper (...) to accept and obey the authorities and to abide by the requirements of the regime' (ibid.: 451).

(e.g. Lindberg and Scheingold 1970; Niedermayer and Westle 1995; Schmidberger 1997; Krouwel and Abts 2007; Kaina 2009).[7] While most authors adhere to the distinction between diffuse and specific support, many have suggested modifying Easton's three objects of political support. For example, some scholars have introduced specific EU policies as another object of support, as people might be more strongly aware of these and might not necessarily link them to the EU politicians (Niedermayer and Westle 1995; Schmidberger 1997: 67–8). Moreover, several scholars have argued that the components of Easton's 'political regime' rather capture distinct aspects of a political system and accordingly distinguish between a system's ideals and principles on the one hand and its institutional structure on the other hand (Niedermayer and Westle 1995; Fuchs *et al.* 2009). Finally, Easton's restriction of specific support to the political authorities has been questioned, as people might also support the other elements of a political regime because of their specific advantages (Schmidberger 1997: 58–9).

In this study, I adopt the distinction between the EU's institutional structure and its ideas and principles as two distinct elements of a political system that people might evaluate. I also agree that citizens are likely to judge EU policies without necessarily ascribing them to the responsible political authorities. Therefore, I conceptualize political authorities and policies as two distinct objects of people's EU support. Moreover, I extend citizens' specific support to all objects except for the EU's ideals and principles, as citizens might always rate the specific merits of these objects.[8]

In order to account for both people's positive and negative evaluations of the EU, the model put forward in this study also comprises citizens' diffuse and specific opposition to the EU's various political objects. Adopting some of the insights from research on people's Euroscepticism, I understand specific opposition as people's criticism on the EU's actual performance and its outputs, while diffuse opposition expresses their general disapproval of the EU's various political objects (e.g. Kopecky and Mudde 2002). Again, I assume that people do not oppose the EU's ideals out of specific output assessments. Table 2.2 displays the model of people's EU attitudes as employed in this study.

It is interesting to note that many empirical studies on citizens' EU support have not adopted any of the theoretical concepts mentioned in Table 2.2.[9] Put more technically, most scholars have not dealt with the different dimensions of their dependent variable, that is, EU support, but have put much more

---

7 Niedermayer and Westle deal with people's support for internationalized governance in general.
8 This even holds true for the object 'political community' because citizens might well reason about the specific advantages they get from being a member of this community, such as the right to vote in and run for election in local elections of their place of residence in any EU member state.
9 The situation looks different with regard to studies on public Euroscepticism. See for example Krouwel and Abts (2007) or Weßels (2007).

Table 2.2 A model of people's EU attitudes

Types of EU attitudes	Objects of EU attitudes				
	Political community	*Ideals and principles*	*Institutional structure*	*Political authorities*	*Policies*
Diffuse support	'we' feeling	sharing of ideals/ principles	trust legitimacy	trust legitimacy	legitimacy
Specific support	approval of political rights	—	positive output/ performance assessment	positive output/ performance assessment	positive output assessment
Specific opposition (criticism)	disapproval of political rights	—	negative output/ performance assessment	negative output/ performance assessment	negative output assessment
Diffuse opposition	rejection of 'we' feeling	rejection of ideals/ principles	distrust illegitimacy	distrust illegitimacy	illegitimacy

effort in finding out the independent factors that drive people's *overall* approval or disapproval of the EU.[10] But if one asks people in general what they think about the EU, some respondents might above all refer to the EU's political authorities, while others rather think about the EU's general principles or about the political community of all Europeans respectively. If citizens think about different elements of the European Union when judging it, however, they probably also do so for different reasons – which would explain the often contradictory results of empirical studies that deal with the explanatory factors of people's general EU support (for a review see Buecker 2009).

This problem of not knowing what people have in mind when talking about the EU points to a second and more fundamental weakness of most studies on public EU attitudes, because they do not seriously account for the actual process of people's attitude formation. But even without studying the numerous insights of social psychology in detail, it is evident that people have to *encounter* the respective object of attitudes in some way in order to evaluate it. In the case of a rather remote political system such as the European Union, a majority of citizens experience this encounter via communication processes as provided by

---

10 Most studies use the *Eurobarometer* surveys for their analysis of public EU support. In order to operationalize people's EU attitudes, many scholars employ the question on how people currently rate their country's EU membership (e.g. Hooghe and Marks 2005; McLaren 2006). Others combine this variable with the one capturing people's support for Europe's unification (Brinegar and Jolly 2005). Still another group of researchers merges the 'membership variable' with questions on how fast and intense people would like European integration to proceed in future (Ray 2004) or exclusively focus on people's desired speed of European integration now and in the coming years (Sánchez-Cuenca 2000).

the media. As a consequence, political debates on the EU and the process of European integration in general should be crucial for how citizens perceive the EU, what it means to them and how they evaluate it accordingly (Díez Medrano 2003: 5–7). Public discourses[11] thus put forward a specific interpretation of the EU and its most decisive elements, which might be its political community, but also any other object of political support. Hence, it becomes an empirical question which objects people endow with which type of support or objection. While not determining people's attitudes, public discourses still make some ways of perceiving and judging the EU more likely than others, which also strongly depends on the national context (ibid.: 6).[12]

But how can one analyse people's perceptions of the European Union? In recent years, the concept of frames has become a popular heuristic in order to examine the content and meanings of public discourses, and it has also been applied to people's accounts of the EU by Díez Medrano (2003). While this concept shares the fate of being rather ambiguous with many theoretical devices in the social sciences, most authors use it in the sense of a general 'interpretative scheme that helps people order new information meaningfully and process them efficiently' (Scheufele 2003: 46, own translation). Robert Entman defines the act of framing as '(selecting) some aspects of a perceived reality and (making) them more salient in a communicating text, in such a way as to promote a particular problem definition, causal interpretation, moral evaluation, and/or treatment recommendation for the item described' (Entman 1993: 52). Accordingly, a frame consists of a set of related arguments (Koenig *et al.* 2006: 153). For example, Díez Medrano (2003) has shown that many of his British interviewees argued against the European Union by pointing to its threat to their identity and sovereignty. On the other hand, his West German respondents frequently argued in favour of the European integration process by highlighting its positive impact on overcoming Germany's and Europe's problems after World War II.

The concept of framing thus enables us to find out more about citizens' perceptions of the EU and thereby to better understand their evaluation of this political entity. In the following, I present some of the empirical results of a study that I carried out in Eastern Germany and Poland in 2005.

Research design and methods

In summer and autumn 2005, I conducted 46 semi-standardized interviews in Poland and in Eastern Germany with citizens about their EU perceptions and

---

11 I define discourse as a network of texts 'that regulates the formation of statements' (Waever 2005: 199) and that constructs the objects it deals with according to specific rules (Diez 1999: 43).
12 Thus, diverging national discourses might not only explain the stable international differences in public EU support across the EU member states, but also why a person's nationality turns out to be the most powerful predictor of their EU attitude in many empirical studies (e.g. Eichenberg and Dalton 1993; Deflem and Pampel 1996; Gabel and Whitten 1997; Gabel 2001; McLaren 2002; Eichenberg and Dalton 2007).

evaluations. I chose to compare these two societies, because we still know relatively little about why citizens in post-communist countries support the EU and even less about their interpretations of this political system. In order to account not only for the impact of national discourses, but also of social milieu, I included five to six representatives of each of the following social groups in my sample: farmers, white-collar employees with and without university degree, blue-collar workers, students, pensioners and unemployed persons. Moreover, I aimed at sampling an equal share of men and women, as well as an equal number of young, middle-aged and old persons. In Eastern Germany, I interviewed people in Berlin, Rostock and Ribnitz-Damgarten; in Poland, I talked to respondents in Warsaw, Krosno Odrzańskie and Mońki.[13]

All interviews were recorded and transcribed. My qualitative content analysis, which I conducted with the software program Maxqda, was based on a two-fold coding process. First, I inductively coded those arguments that my respondents provided when answering questions on their reasons for supporting or objecting to the EU, their country's EU membership and the European integration process in general. Second, I deductively looked for frames that I had detected in my previous literature review of political discourses in both Eastern Germany and Poland as the most relevant interpretative schemes. If possible, the inductively coded arguments were then summarized with the deductively coded frames. In some instances, though, the inductive arguments constituted independent frames that had not been detected in the review of public discourses.[14]

Framing the European Union in Eastern Germany and Poland: empirical results

Although thinking about the EU is not 'people's favorite pastime' (Díez Medrano 2003: 22), most of my participants had many things to say about the European Union, their country's EU membership or their personal experiences with this political entity. Both Polish and Eastern German respondents turned out to be more Eurofriendly than their respective populations at large: 21 persons in each subsample supported their country's EU membership, while one Pole and one Eastern German expressed mixed attitudes in this respect. Only one Eastern German rejected Germany's membership in the EU.[15] On

---

13 Rostock and Ribnitz-Damgarten are cities located in the federal state of Mecklenburg-West Pomerania in the north-east of Germany. Krosno Odrzańskie belongs to the Voivodeship Lubuskie adjoining Germany, while Mońki is located in the Voivodeship Podlaskie, near the Belorussian border.
14 Due to the restrictions of this chapter, I cannot further elaborate on the linkage between national discourses and people's EU perceptions. Likewise, it is not possible to discuss other than national differences in framing that have occurred in this study. Suffice it to say that national ways of framing the EU have turned out to be more decisive than any other socioeconomic distinctions.
15 One Polish participant did not know how to answer this question. Altogether, 51.7 per cent of the Eastern German and 54 per cent of the Polish population declared in 2005 that their country's EU membership was 'a good thing' (Eurobarometer 63.4, own calculations).

the other hand, people evaluated the European Union itself slightly more negatively: 15 Eastern Germans and 18 Poles in general approved of the EU, while three Eastern Germans and four Poles said that it had both positive and negative aspects. Five Eastern Germans and one Pole expressed their negative attitude towards the EU.

In my analysis of people's ways of arguing against or in favour of the EU, I identified 26 different frames that turned up during the conversations. Of these, six were shared by an absolute majority of all participants; another six occurred in between 33 and 46 per cent of all interviews. Ten frames still manifested themselves in at least 20 per cent of all talks, while only a small group of respondents introduced the remaining four frames to their discussions. Table 2.3 displays the total number of respondents who mentioned a particular frame at least once, as well as the respective numbers of Eastern Germans and Poles who referred to this frame.

Table 2.3 EU frames in Eastern Germany and Poland

Frame	E. Germans (n)	Poles (n)	Total (n, %)
Solidary community	15	20	35 (76%)
People's Europe	15	18	33 (71.7%)
Beneficial single market	17	14	31 (67.4%)
Modernization	8	23	31 (67.4%)
Bad political system	18	10	28 (60.1%)
National discrimination	12	14	26 (56,5%)
Global player	15	6	21 (45.7%)
Protection and power	4	14	18 (39.1%)
Disastrous single market	9	6	15 (32.6%)
Threats of enlargement	13	2	15 (32.6%)
Positive lifeworld	7	8	15 (32.6%)
Threat to national identity/sovereignty	8	7	15 (32.6%)
Inherent necessity	11	2	13 (28.3%)
World War II	10	2	12 (26.1%)
Disappointment in solidary community	9	2	11 (23.9%)
Disappointment in people's Europe	9	2	11 (23.9%)
Unification	6	4	10 (21.7%)
Good governance	6	4	10 (21.7%)
European identity	1	8	9 (19.6%)
Chances of enlargement	5	4	9 (19.6%)
Negative lifeworld	5	4	9 (19.6%)
Economic solidarity	4	5	9 (19.6%)
Successful transformation	0	7	7 (15.2%)
Disappointment modernization	2	3	5 (10.9%)
Imperialistic world power	2	1	3 (6.5%)
Disastrous transformation	—	1	1 (2.2%)

The figures indicate the number of respondents who mentioned a particular frame at least once during the interview.

Altogether, 15 frames turned out to be shared by both Polish and Eastern German participants, while 11 frames were typical for only one of the national subsamples.[16] It thus becomes clear that the national context indeed influences how people perceive the EU, while at the same time an even bigger number of interpretative schemes is of transnational relevance. The next sections present both shared and national frames in more detail.

Transnational frames

The most widespread frame mentioned by both Poles and Eastern Germans was the one labelled *solidary community*. Altogether, 35 Polish and Eastern German participants, that is, 76 per cent of the complete sample, referred to this frame that above all presents the EU as a community of nation-states helping each other and bringing their peoples closer together. For a majority of respondents, an improved international understanding was the most important aspect of this frame:

> 'And if you think about the European Union, what comes spontaneously to mind?'
> 'Well, of course it depends on the context, but if I think about it in general terms, then I appreciate it very much that national borders are opened and peoples come closer together.'
> female Eastern German, A-levels, young

Closely related to the friendly exchange between the European nations were other dimensions of this 'community frame', such as the EU's peace-keeping in Europe. Additionally, many respondents also highlighted that the EU fostered political cooperation, mutual help and the exchange of knowledge between its member states.

This positive perception of the EU as a solidly united community is complemented by a second frame that also conveys a positive image of the European Union. This frame occurred in almost 72 per cent of all interviews and was labelled *people's Europe*. This interpretative scheme summarizes arguments that emphasize the various advantages ordinary citizens get from living in the European Union. Here, most participants mentioned the free travelling across borders and the possibility to study and work abroad:

> 'And if you think about the European Union, what comes automatically to mind?'
> 'Travel! (laughs) Anything else? Well, people looking for a job abroad, maybe not me personally, but I know a lot of people who go away and

---

16 One should note that three of the shared frames turned up in hardly more than 10 per cent of all interviews.

stay there, and very often they decided to stay there for the rest of their lives, especially in Great Britain right now.'

female Pole, studied, young

Apart from the free movement across the European continent, respondents discussed a number of further advantages for EU citizens. For instance, many Eastern Germans mentioned the comfort of using the Euro when travelling abroad, while a number of Polish participants highlighted people's chances to learn foreign languages or to get to know foreign cultures.

With almost 70 per cent of all participants employing the frame *beneficial single market*, this scheme constitutes the third most widespread one in the present study. Unlike the *people's Europe* frame's subcategories, arguments coded in this frame did not refer to the EU's benefits for ordinary people, but foremost to its economic advantages for people's own country. Thus, the reference point of this frame is rather the nation than the individual. Altogether, 32 respondents mentioned the various positive implications of the EU's economic integration, often without further specifying these advantages.

'(. . .) And why do you think the EU is overall rather positive?'
'Well, because of the economy, the exchange of products, this cooperation somehow (. . .) the free movement between countries, we don't have any borders, there is some exchange between countries, an exchange of jobs, tourists, and products.'

male Pole, studied, middle-aged

Additionally, a number of Eastern Germans and Poles highlighted the concrete economic benefits of their own countries, such as export markets for Germany or foreign investments in Poland.

The last frame that an absolute majority of all respondents shared was also the first major frame expressing an overall negative perception of the EU, namely the one on *national discrimination*. More than 56 per cent of all interviewees complained about their country's unfair treatment by the EU, either in economic or in political terms. Most frequently, the Eastern Germans criticized the high financial contributions of Germany. On the other hand, many Poles complained about the EU's economic protectionism, for example about the closed labour markets of many member states. Some of the Polish respondents also expressed a general feeling of not being accepted as an equal partner by the 'old EU'.

To sum up, four major frames were shared by between 57 and 76 per cent of all respondents in the present study, that is, the ones named *solidary community*, *people's Europe*, *beneficial single market* and *national discrimination*. Thus, the EU's transnational image was overall positive, although the impression of being treated unfairly by the EU was also prominent among participants.

Another three frames that were a little less widespread complement this transnational EU image: almost one-third of all respondents complained

Citizens' images of and support for the EU 47

about the *disastrous single market* and the EU's threat to their country's *national identity/sovereignty*. An equal number of respondents highlighted their personal EU advantages within the frame *positive lifeworld*. This common picture was supplemented by a number of typical Eastern German and Polish perceptions of the EU, as the following two sections demonstrate.

The Eastern German EU

Figure 2.1 displays all frames that were shared by more than 30 per cent of the Eastern German participants. The most widespread frame within the Eastern German sample was the one labelled *bad political system*, which occurred in 18 of the 23 Eastern German interviews. It demonstrates that the Eastern Germans frequently associated the EU with bad and lazy politicians, obscure political structures and, above all, with a useless and running wild bureaucracy.

> *'Are there also any disadvantages for Germany because of the European Union?'*
>
> 'Yes, this whole sluggish government that acts like a parallel government and that slowly becomes our true government. But somehow I don't really understand how this whole thing works, these weird party blocs and these elections that don't interest anybody, and all these standards and norms that only torture mankind (. . .).'
>
> male Eastern German, less than A-levels, middle-aged

Apart from the EU's desire to regulate people's lives in all details, many Eastern Germans requested above all more and better information on the

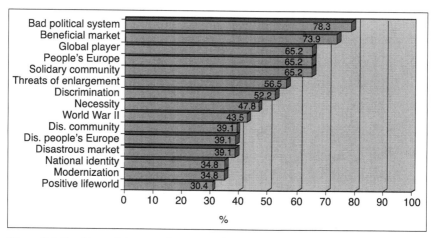

Figure 2.1 Ranking of the most important frames in the Eastern German sample

The figures indicate the percentage of respondents who mentioned a particular frame at least once during the interview.

EU and its policies. Additionally, 10 Eastern Germans (as compared with one Pole) also criticized the EU's lack of political competences and power vis-à-vis its member states, in other words they demanded a stronger political integration of the EU. On the other hand, several Eastern Germans also complained about the EU's exaggerated centralization.

The second frame that was significantly more widespread in the Eastern German sample than among the Polish participants was the one on globalization. Fifteen Eastern Germans, as compared with six Poles, described the EU as a *global player* that had to face both the economic and the political competition with other great powers in the world. The need for a common European voice in order to put through the European countries' interests on a global level was the most frequent topic in the respective argumentations, and often the US was portrayed as the EU's main opponent.

In addition to the political and economic power relations in a globalized world, some of the Eastern German respondents referred to the EU's better capacity to solve transnational or global problems, such as the protection of the environment or the fight against international crime and terrorism. Moreover, a smaller group of interviewees brought up the EU's task of protecting people's freedom and international peace worldwide.

The third most important frame that was typical for the Eastern German sample concerned the topic of the EU's past (and sometimes future) enlargement. Altogether, 13 of the Eastern German respondents emphasized the *threats of enlargement* as one reason for their disapproval of the European Union. A number of interviewees who argued within this frame referred to the EU's latest Eastern enlargement and its negative consequences for Germany, such as an increased inflow of cheap labour and an extended outsourcing of production facilities to Eastern European countries. Furthermore, many of the Eastern German respondents mentioned other risks and challenges of the EU's further expansion, such as its potential overstretching and subsequent breakdown, or the question of Turkey's EU accession.

Additionally, the 'Eastern German EU' comprised two more frames that more than 40 per cent of the Eastern German respondents referred to: the EU's *inherent necessity*, due to internal and external pressures for (further) integration, and the frame *World War II*, which points to Germany's historical responsibility for the European integration process, but also to the country's rehabilitation thanks to the European project. Little fewer participants expressed their disappointment about the failed *solidary community* and *people's Europe* respectively.

The Polish EU

The Eastern Germans' concern about the EU's deficient political system corresponds to the Poles' enthusiasm about their country's potential *modernization* in the European Union. In the present study, all of the 23 Polish participants introduced this frame at least once in the course of their interviews,

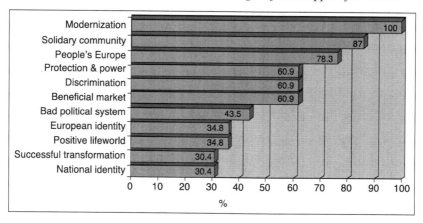

Figure 2.2 Ranking of the most important frames in the Polish sample

The figures indicate the percentage of respondents who mentioned a particular frame at least once during the interview.

as Figure 2.2 demonstrates.[17] Within this frame, the EU appeared as a catalyst that would trigger above all Poland's socioeconomic, but also its political, development and help the country close the gap towards the Western European countries.

The most important aspect of this frame constituted the financial aid Poland gets from the European Union, which altogether 17 Poles brought up.

> 'And do you see any economic advantages for Poland in the European Union?'
> 'Yes, I think that the EU helps us, and they show us how to do many things that we knew little of in the past! (laughs) (. . .) So they show us how to make things better, and they help us, they gave us money for many things, and it will be great.'
>
> female Pole, student, young

This quotation already alludes to a second aspect of the *modernization* theme that many Poles discussed, that is, the chance to learn and profit from the EU's expertise. Apart from the EU's technological and scientific know-how, several Poles also highlighted the political advice and guidance the EU might provide for their country, as well as its higher economic and legal standards that should contribute to Poland's further development.

The second frame that almost 70 per cent of the Polish interviewees brought up was the one comprising the issues of *protection and power* by and within the European Union. Altogether, 14 Poles mentioned these two aspects that

---

17 This figure presents all frames that were shared by more than 30 per cent of all Polish participants.

refer to Poland's international relations and its foreign policy options. While some respondents restricted themselves to a rather general discussion of Poland's protection by the EU, others made it very clear what kind of external threat they feared:

> *'How great is your interest in the European Union?'*
> 'I don't know, it's hard to tell. I guess that Poland should go West, not East, that's my opinion. It's good for us to join the Western part of Europe, because for the last 50 years, we have been dominated by the East. (. . .)'
> *'And why do you think it is important that Poland goes West and not East?'*
> 'That's obvious! (laughs) Russia – I hate Russia. Well, maybe I don't hate it, anyways I am talking about the country here, not about the Russian people. In my opinion, Russia is the biggest enemy ever of the Polish people. And therefore, we should try to protect ourselves better in future.'
>
> male Pole, A-levels, young

Thus, a number of Poles perceived the EU as a protective umbrella against Russia, but also more generally against any kind of military aggression from outside. The second aspect of this frame concerned above all the increased influence and power of Poland in Europe and within the European Union now that it had become a member of the latter.

Compared with the *protection and power* frame, and even more so to the *modernization* theme, a much smaller group of participants shared the last two frames that characterized the specific Polish way of European thinking. To begin with, eight of the Polish interviewees employed the frame *European identity* that, above all, contains a collective or national dimension. Most of the respondents who argued within this frame pointed out that the EU was an expression of their country's 'Europeanness', and that Poland's belonging to 'Europe' was one reason for its EU membership. Finally, the last frame that altogether seven Poles referred to concerns their country's *successful transformation*. Within this frame, the respondents described the European Union as helping their country to overcome the legacies of communism, foremost with regard to the economy, but also concerning the country's political structures and people's attitudes and values.

So far, the discussion has shown that Polish and Eastern German respondents share some major EU frames, but also employ several distinct interpretative schemes that often highlight the EU's specific meaning for their own country. In the Polish context, it is the EU's contribution to modernizing Poland that is most salient to participants, followed by an improved protection against external threats and the country's increased political power inside the EU. Furthermore, Poland's belonging to 'Europe' as well as the overcoming of communism are important national concerns where Polish people ascribe a positive role to the European Union. In a similar vein, a number of Eastern Germans perceive the EU against the background of Germany's martial past and accordingly emphasize their country's return to the community of European states, but also its historical responsibility for the European integration process. Likewise, several transnational frames represent the EU's positive and negative consequences that both Eastern Germans and Poles see for their own countries, such as the frames *beneficial single market* or *national discrimination*.

On the other hand, a number of frames do not primarily capture the EU's national relevance, but rather concern the European political system and the European integration process themselves. Among others, this holds true for the two most widespread shared frames *solidary community* and *people's Europe*, but also for a number of Eastern German frames, such as *bad political system* or *global player*. All of these interpretative schemes do not foremost refer to the nation-state, but to the different elements of the EU's political system. In the following section, I use the general model of people's EU attitudes put forward in Table 2.2 in order to demonstrate which objects the various frames refer to and which type of attitudes they express.

How citizens perceive the EU: frames, objects and political support

Table 2.4 summarizes all frames that a considerable number of participants shared according to their main objects and types of attitudes.[18]

To begin with people's diffuse EU support, it becomes clear that none of the major frames detected in this study deals with the political community of all Europeans. Apparently, the feeling of belonging to one European community was not salient for most of my participants when arguing in favour of the European Union.[19] At the same time, people expressed their general approval of the EU with regard to another two objects. First, a majority of participants supports the EU's ideals and principles, as the most important frame *international community* demonstrates. Apparently, many people view the EU as realizing core principles such as the peaceful cooperation between nation-states as well as an increased understanding between different nations and cultures. In this context, the EU's national meaning constitutes another source of citizens' general EU support. To many Poles, for example, the EU means above all modernization. While this frame also comprises people's specific support of the financial transfers Poland receives, it goes beyond this instrumental assessment and also expresses the general wish for catching up with the better developed Western European countries. Closely related, the frame *European identity* highlights that many Poles want to emphasize their

---

18 Some of the frames are multi-dimensional and thus refer to more than one object and/or express more than one type of EU attitude. These frames thus appear in several cells.
19 Still, one should mention that two Eastern Germans expressed a strong commitment to the community of all Europeans, which included their willingness to accept personal or national financial sacrifices for the sake of this community. These statements have been coded as part of the frame *economic solidarity* (see Table 2.3).

Table 2.4 A typology of EU frames

Types of EU attitudes	Objects of EU attitudes				
	Political community	Institutional structure	Ideals and principles	Political authorities	Policies
Diffuse support	—	beneficial market; global player; necessity	solidary community World War II; European identity; successful transformation; modernization	—	modernization
Specific support	people's Europe	beneficial market; global player; people's Europe; positive lifeworld; necessity; protection & power	—	—	people's Europe; modernization; successful transformation
Specific opposition (criticism)	—	disastrous market; bad political system; threat to national identity/sovereignty	—	bad political system	national discrimination; bad political system; threats of enlargement; disappointment people's Europe
Diffuse opposition	—	disastrous market; national discrimination; threat to national identity/sovereignty	disappointment solidary community	—	national discrimination

country's belonging to 'Europe' and its 'Europeanness' respectively. Many Eastern Germans, on the other hand, mention the EU's relevance against the background of World War II. Moreover, several Eastern Germans approve of the EU's institutional structure, providing more global power as well as borderless trade.

In a similar vein, participants displayed their specific support of the EU mainly with regard to their country's benefits. Here, it is above all the economic advantages of the single market that Eastern Germans and Poles mention. But in particular the Polish interviewees also legitimize the EU because of its political relevance for Poland and because of its positive impact on the country's transformation process. Additionally, two frames that capture citizens' positive output evaluations do not refer to their nation-state, but to the individuals' advantages within the EU's borderless space. Here, the frame *people's Europe* is most salient, expressing many participants' approval not only of free travelling and migration across the EU, but also of policy outcomes such as the Euro.

Turning to people's negative EU attitudes, we see that the frame *bad political system* primarily demonstrates respondents' criticism of the EU's authorities and policies. As mentioned above, many participants complained about exaggerated regulations, but also about a lack of information on the EU's policy process. Fewer Eastern Germans found fault with the EU's institutional structure. Concerning the EU's policies, a number of Eastern Germans and Poles perceived their nation-state as being discriminated against, be it with regard to its financial contributions or referring to economic protectionism. In several cases, the Polish participants' criticism of their own country's weakness inside the EU also comprised a general feeling of exploitation and unfair treatment, which expresses a rather general opposition to EU membership. Similarly, several Eastern Germans criticized the workings of the single market in principle. Still, the expression of general objection towards the EU's political system is considerably weaker than people's criticism of specific EU policies or institutions.

The results of this qualitative study are not representative for the Eastern German or Polish population at large, of course. It is possible to compare them to some survey data from *Eurobarometer*, however. In spring 2008, respondents were asked to give reasons for why they believed that their country did (not) benefit from its EU membership. While this question is obviously narrower than the ones posed in the present study, it still gives some insights into what people think to be most important about the EU and its consequences for their country. Table 2.5 and 2.6 display the results for Eastern Germany and Poland, but also for the whole EU and its old and new member states.[20] The three most important reasons that most respondents mentioned appear in bold.

---

20 The group of the new member states comprises the 12 countries that joined the EU in 2004 and 2007.

54   Nicola Bücker

Table 2.5 Our country's main benefits from EU membership

	Eastern Germany	Poland	EU27	EU15	EU new members
improved cooperation between countries	49.2%	22.3%	36.9%	39.9%	28.4%
maintaining peace/security	43.7%	16.1%	32.2%	34.4%	26.2%
stronger say in the world for our people	28.2%	16.4%	22.4%	25.2%	14.5%
new work opportunities	18.3%	50.4%	25.3%	18.4%	44.9%
economic growth	23.0%	33.6%	30.3%	28.0%	36.6%

Source: *Eurobarometer* 69.2, own calculations. The figures indicate the percentage of respondents who mentioned one reason.

Question: 'Which of the following are the main reasons for thinking that (our country) has benefited from being a member of the European Union?' (Maximum of three answers)

Table 2.5 demonstrates that the EU's image of a peace-keeping cooperative community is not only the most prominent interpretative scheme for Eastern Germans at large, but also for the EU27 and the old EU member states. In Poland and across the 'new EU', international cooperation still comes third, but national economic growth and in particular new job opportunities are more important EU benefits for the inhabitants of these countries. Both issues point to the modernization frame that was most prominent among my Polish respondents. To Eastern Germans, the third main advantage out of EU membership is a stronger say for Germans in the world. While not exactly reflecting the content of the *globalization* frame, this perception still indicates a more global understanding of the EU than the rest of the mentioned benefits.

With regard to the national drawbacks out of EU membership, the most important issue across all member states except for Eastern Germany is the small political influence that people see for their own nation. In Poland, this concern is followed by the conviction that important issues should be dealt with at the national and not at the European level. While many citizens living in the new member states share this belief, the danger of decreasing living standards is slightly more important to them. Across the EU27 and the EU15, people are almost equally worried about their living standards and their job safety. Both fears are extremely present among the Eastern German population and constitute the most important EU disadvantages people see for Germany. While these concerns as expressed in the frames *disastrous single market* and *threats of enlargement* were less salient in my study, the feeling of political weakness was part of the important frame *national discrimination*. People's belief in the primacy of the national political level also occurred in my study within the frame *threat to national identity/sovereignty*. Finally, one should emphasize that more than 16 per cent of the Polish respondents found it hard

Table 2.6 Our country's main disadvantages from EU membership

	Eastern Germany	Poland	EU27	EU15	EU new members
jobs in danger	**51.4%**	15.4%	**27.6%**	**28.4%**	23.0%
decreasing living standards	**44.6%**	15.4%	**27.8%**	**27.6%**	**29.1%**
important issues are best dealt with at the national level	**28.8%**	**23.1%**	26.0%	25.9%	**26.4%**
little influence of our people on decision-making	26.6%	**33.3%**	**36.4%**	**36.1%**	**38.5%**
don't know why country has not benefited	2.3%	**16.2%**	4.7%	4.5%	6.4%

Source: *Eurobaromter* 69.2, own calculations. The figures indicate the percentage of respondents who mentioned one reason.

Question: 'Which of the following are the main reasons for thinking that (our country) did not benefit from being a member of the European Union?' (Maximum of three answers)

to mention any disadvantage for their country out of its EU membership – a percentage that is much higher than in any other EU member state.

Discussion

The European Union is a political entity consisting of different political objects that its citizens might support or object to. The qualitative analysis has shown that people indeed refer to different objects of the EU and express attitudes of different quality when judging these objects. Overall, the participants of my study perceived the EU in a rather positive light. In particular, a majority of them supported the ideals and principles the EU stands for, such as a peaceful cooperation between nation-states. Another important source of people's general approval of the EU turned out to be its specific relevance for their own country, which often touched upon the national historical and cultural context. Especially the Eastern German participants also approved of the EU's institutional structure in principle.

Thus, the EU enjoys a considerable reservoir of people's diffuse support concerning its ideals and its symbolic national meaning, with the salience of the former dimension being confirmed by survey data.[21] My respondents did not express any European 'we' feeling when legitimizing the European Union, however. This does not mean that all of them lacked any feeling of belonging to 'Europe' or to the EU.[22] The result rather shows that people did not link

21 The EU's national meaning is more difficult to grasp in public surveys, as one needs detailed knowledge of the respective national contexts in order to pose the appropriate questions.
22 When asked directly about their attachment to their region, nation and 'Europe', 30 respondents expressed a feeling of belonging to 'Europe' in addition to their national and/or regional identity.

their European identity to their support for the EU's political system. Put differently, most of them did not perceive the EU as a legitimate political entity, because it acts upon the will of 'the Europeans'. Whether this result is as problematic as many social scientists assume depends on how resilient the other sources of people's diffuse and also specific support turn out to be if the national burdens out of European integration increase. For the time being, it seems that people's positive EU perceptions still outweigh the negative ones. Concerning the qualitative study, a majority of the Eastern German respondents supported the EU and their country's membership despite their harsh criticism of many of the EU's policies. The same holds true for the population of the EU27 at large.[23] On the other hand, one has to note that several of the unfavourable EU frames expressed both specific criticism and people's general disapproval of the EU, such as the frames *national discrimination* or *threat to national identity/sovereignty*. Together with fears of economic decline, the worries about a loss of national sovereignty turned out to be crucial for many EU citizens across all member states. This result indicates that a considerable number of citizens still regard the nation-state as the decisive political actor whose powers should not be restricted too much. It also corresponds with many respondents' understanding of the EU as a *solidary* community with positive implications for their respective nation in the first place. In contrast to this, the EU's political integration and its supranational institutions are much less present on people's minds, though one has to note that in particular Eastern Germans are also concerned about the EU's political authorities and its policies. Time will tell whether these and other concerns actually develop into a healthy scepticism of 'critical Europeans' who care about the EU's institutions and policies, or whether people rather articulate their general unease with the European integration process, which they finally reject for the benefit of regaining national sovereignty.

---

23 Although citizens mentioned a number of national disadvantages due to their country's EU membership, 52 per cent of them still evaluated this membership as 'a good thing' (*Eurobarometer* 69.2, own calculations).

References

Brinegar, A. P. and Jolly, S. 2005. 'Location, location, location: national contextual factors and public support for European integration', *European Union Politics* 6(2): 155–89.

Buecker, N. 2009. 'Legitimizing the European Union in different national contexts – the cases of Poland and East Germany', paper presented at the 5th ECPR Conference in Potsdam, 10–12 September.

Deflem, M. and Pampel, F. C. 1996. 'The myth of postnational identity: popular support for European unification', *Social Forces* 75(1): 119–43.

Delhey, J. 2007. 'Do enlargements make the European Union less cohesive? An analysis of trust between EU nationalities', *Journal of Common Market Studies* 45(2): 253–79.

Díez Medrano, J. 2003. *Framing Europe: attitudes to European integration in Germany, Spain, and the United Kingdom*. Princeton and Oxford: Princeton University Press.

Diez, T. 1999. *Die EU lesen: diskursive Knotenpunkte in der britischen Europadebatte*. Opladen: Leske & Budrich.

Dougan, M. 2008. 'The Treaty of Lisbon 2007: winning minds, not hearts', *Common Market Law Review* 45(3): 617–703.

Easton, D. 1965. *A systems analysis of political life*. New York: John Wiley & Sons, Inc.

Easton, D. 1975. 'A re-assessment of the concept of political support', *British Journal of Political Science* 5(4): 435–57.

Eichenberg, R. C. and Dalton, R. J. 1993. 'Europeans and the European Community: the dynamics of public support for European integration', *International Organization* 47(4): 507–34.

Eichenberg, R. C. and Dalton, R. J. 2007. 'Post-Maastricht blues: the transformation of citizen support for European integration 1973–2004', *Acta Politica* 42(2–3): 128–52.

Entman, R. M. 1993. 'Framing: toward clarification of a fractured paradigm', *Journal of Communication* 43(4): 51–8.

European Commission. 2010. 'EU enlargement', http://ec.europa.eu/enlargement/index_en.htm (25 May 2010).

Ferrara, F. and Weißhaupt, J. T. 2004. 'Get your act together: party performance in European parliamentary elections', *European Union Politics* 5(3): 283–306.

Fuchs, D., Roger, A. and Magni-Berton, R. 2009. 'European cleavage, Euroscepticism and support of the EU: a conceptual discussion', in: D. Fuchs, R. Magni-Berton and A. Roger (eds) *Euroscepticism: images of Europe among mass publics and political elites*. Opladen & Farmington Hills: Barbara Budrich Publishers, 9–32.

Gabel, M. 2001. *Interests and integration market liberalization, public opinion, and European Union*. Ann Arbor: The University of Michigan Press.

Gabel, M. and Whitten G. D. 1997. 'Economic conditions, economic perceptions, and public support for European integration', *Political Behavior* 19(1): 81–96.

Herrmann, R. and Brewer, M. B. 2004. 'Identities and institutions: becoming European in the EU', in: R. K. Herrmann, T. Risse and M. B. Brewer (eds) *Transnational identities: becoming European in the EU*. Lanham, MD: Rowman & Littlefield Publishers, 1–22.

Hooghe, L. and Marks, G. 2005. 'Calculation, community and cues: public opinion on European integration', *European Union Politics* 6(4): 419–43.

Kaina, V. 2009. *Wir in Europa: Kollektive Identität und Demokratie in der Europäischen Union*. Wiesbaden: VS Verlag für Sozialwissenschaften.

Kaina, V. and Karolewski, I. P. 2006. 'European identity – why another book on this topic?', in: V. Kaina and I. P. Karolewski (eds) *European identity: theoretical perspectives and empirical insights*. Berlin: LIT Verlag, 11–19.

Koenig, T., Mihelj, S., Downey, J. and Gencel Bek, M. 2006. 'Media framings of the issue of Turkish accession to the EU. A European or national process?', *Innovation* 19(2): 149–69.

Kopecky, P. and Mudde, C. 2002. 'The two sides of Euroscepticism. Party positions on European integration in East Central Europe', *European Union Politics* 3(3): 297–326.

Kriesi, H. 2007. 'The role of European Integration in national election campaigns', *European Union Politics* 8(1): 83–108.

Krouwel, A. and Abts, K. 2007. 'Varieties of Euroscepticism and populist mobilization: transforming attitudes from mild Euroscepticism to harsh Eurocynicism', *Acta Politica* 42(2–3): 252–70.

Kurpas, S. 2007. 'The Treaty of Lisbon – how much "constitution" is left? An overview of the main changes', *Central European Policy Studies Policy Brief* 147: 1–9.

Lindberg, L. N. and Scheingold, S. A. 1970. *Europe's would-be polity: patterns of change in the European Community*. Englewood Cliffs, NJ: Prentice-Hall.

Marks, G. and Steenbergen, M. R. 2004. *European integration and political conflict*. Cambridge: Cambridge University Press.

McLaren, L. 2002. 'Public support for the European Union: cost/benefit analysis or perceived cultural threat?', *The Journal of Politics* 64(2): 551–66.

McLaren, L. 2006. *Identity, interests and attitudes to European integration*. Houndmills and New York: Palgrave Macmillan.

Niedermayer, O. and Westle, B. 1995. 'A typology of orientations', in: O. Niedermayer and R. Sinnott (eds) *Public opinion and internationalized governance*. Oxford: Oxford University Press, 33–50.

Ray, L. 2004. 'Don't rock the boat: expectations, fears, and opposition to EU level policy making', in: G. Marks and M. Steenbergen (eds) *European integration and political conflict*. Cambridge: Cambridge University Press, 51–61.

Sánchez-Cuenca, I. 2000. 'The political basis of support for European integration', *European Union Politics* 1(2): 147–71.

Scheufele, B. 2003. *Frames – Framing – Framing-Effekte: theoretische und methodische Grundlegung des Framing-Ansatzes sowie empirische Befunde zur Nachrichtenproduktion*. Wiesbaden: Westdeutscher Verlag.

Schmidberger, M. 1997. *Regionen und europäische Legitimität: der Einfluss des regionalen Umfeldes auf Bevölkerungseinstellungen zur EU*. Frankfurt: Peter Lang.

Waever, O. 2005. 'Discursive approach', in: A. Wiener and T. Diez (eds) *European integration theories*. Oxford: Oxford University Press, 197–216.

Weßels, B. 2007. 'Discontent and European identity: three types of Euroscepticism', *Acta Politica* 42(2–3): 287–306.

3 Trust in co-Europeans and support for European unification
Extending the identity approach

Jan Delhey

Introduction

Why do citizens like or dislike supranational political integration? Different approaches have been developed for answering this question. Still a milestone of inspiration is Easton's (1965) theory of the difference between affective and utilitarian support for political institutions. Applied to the EU level, utilitarian support stresses the importance of economic and political gains when attitudes towards the European Union are formed – will I or my country benefit? Affective support, in contrast, assumes that citizens simply like the idea of a unified Europe, and that part of that emotional attachment comes from socio-psychological conceptions of group membership and sense of community – what is usually termed the *identity approach*. Other approaches have developed since then. Two recent reviews distinguish among three (Hooghe and Marks 2004) and five different explanatory approaches (Ray 2006), respectively. This plurality makes perfect sense, given the complexity of European integration. Ensuring mass citizen support is, eventually, a question of winning the minds *and* hearts of Europeans.

This chapter does not deal with the full range of approaches. Rather, its purpose is to add a new line of argumentation to those frequently summarized under the label 'identity approaches'. So far, this branch has focused either on feelings of collective identity and territorial attachment (Carey 2002; Hooghe and Marks 2004), or on cultural threat and xenophobia (McLaren 2002, 2004). The new line of argumentation introduced here is transnational trust: my main contention is that generalized interpersonal trust in people from other EU countries – which I propose to call *transnational trust*, or *trust in co-Europeans* – is impacting on mass support for European unification. The trust approach is seen as complementary to, rather than conflicting with, the existing identity approaches, which do not adequately account for how Europeans see each other. The idea is to broaden our understanding of which varieties of 'sense of community' (Deutsch *et al.* 1966) are involved when people make up their mind on supranational integration.

Since the European project is gradually moving towards a political union, it is perfectly possible that issues of sense of community become increasingly important for public opinion (Hooghe and Marks 2004). Another reason might be enlargements, which have greatly increased the Community's economic and cultural diversity (Bach 2000; Heidenreich 2003; Gerhards 2007). With eastward enlargement in particular, transnational trust has become an issue. Research has shown that the average level of trust in co-Europeans has plummeted in the EU25, compared with the social capital floating within the borders of the 'old' EU15 (Delhey 2007, 2009). One reason is that citizens from the old member states report to have only lukewarm trust in their new co-Europeans – another, that the new EU citizens do not trust each other very much either (for the general phenomenon of distrust in post-communist societies, see Rose 1994). Against this background, the question of whether individual support is driven by feelings of trust for fellow EU citizens (or the lack thereof) has become an important issue. Seen from a perspective of system legitimacy, declining trust in co-Europeans is rather unproblematic as long as it does not weaken mass support for the EU. Then, Eurocrats and politicians would not have to bother about the EU's composition in terms of countries and peoples. Yet if trust were to have an impact, this would mean that composition matters, and that enlargements can either strengthen or weaken mass support for the European project.

I proceed in three steps. In the first section, the main lines of theorizing of those approaches currently forming the identity approach are summarized. Then, transnational trust is introduced as a variant. Eventually, the latter approach is operationalized and tested against data using the European Elections Study from 2004. The final section draws some conclusions for further research.

The sense of community approaches: taking stock

The common denominator of the 'identity approaches', or probably better, 'sense of community approaches', is that emotional bonds of group membership are seen as important for citizens' support for European integration. Back in the 1950s, Deutsch and associates argued that sense of community between two peoples must *precede* measures of political amalgamation (Deutsch *et al.* 1966). Although the process of European integration, finally, was much more elite-driven than envisaged by this transactionalist school (Puchala 1981; Rosamond 2000), its rich definition of *sense of community* is extremely insightful; it includes mutual feelings of solidarity, trust, 'we' feeling, and perceived common interests among peoples. In a nutshell, sense of community can come in many guises – yet scholars have predominantly operationalized it in terms of 'we' feeling, i.e. as collective identity.

National and European identity

Whereas there is a small flood of publications on European identity in general (e.g. Kaina and Karolewski 2006), I confine myself here to those who have investigated the association between identity and mass support for European integration empirically. The strength of the identity approach is to highlight the importance of a 'we' feeling as an emotional capacity for group loyalty, which translates into loyalty to a political system and respective attitudes. Identities can refer to a group of people (e.g. 'Europeans'), a territory ('Europe') or a political community ('EU') and are not necessarily exclusive. Previous studies have been primarily concerned with two expressions of identity – European and national. There is more or less consensus about the salience of the former. In a number of studies, European identity has been found to increase support for the European project (Carey 2002; Fuchs 2002; Hooghe and Marks 2004; Karp and Bowler 2006). Identifying with Europe also increases the taste for specific European-level policies such as the common currency, regional policy or greater rights for the European parliament (Ray 2001).

In contrast, the impact of national identity is much more controversial. This is chiefly because the national and the European level can be conceptualized as friends or foes. If seen as friends, a supranational identity builds upon the national identity. If seen as foes, developing a European identity inevitably means an erosion of the national affiliation. Only under the latter condition, a strong national identity would be incompatible with unification support. Empirically, it has been found that strong feelings of national identity lead to less supportive attitudes (Carey 2002). Yet Carey further found that national attachment is only weakly detrimental for support if accompanied by a European attachment (hence forming a multiple identity). In the same vein Marks and Hooghe (2004) found that an *exclusive* national identity is much more problematic than an inclusive one, i.e. one which combines a national with a European layer. An exclusive national identity turned out to be an even more potent force in forming individuals' opinions than utilitarian concerns.

Bruter's qualitative research helps further in understanding the content of European identity (Bruter 2005). Apparently, it carries two components, cultural and civic. The cultural component is primarily related to Europeans as a group of peoples, bonding citizens horizontally. In contrast, the civic component bonds citizens vertically to the EU as a political system, pushing collective identity toward a *political* identity. Equipped with this knowledge, the main flaw of the identity approach for understanding mass support becomes obvious – its conceptual ambiguity. It is unclear in which mix the usual measures of collective identity capture the horizontal and the vertical component. In other words: the power of identity as an explanatory concept for public opinion does not necessarily stem from a high degree of identification with the other people that together form the political community of 'Europe' (the cultural identity); it might primarily stem from an identification with the political system (the civic identity). Moreover, there remains some ambiguity about what collectivity of people respondents exactly have in mind when reporting their attachment to 'Europe'. Some Western Europeans may think of Western Europe only, while for others the 'imagined community' (Anderson 1983) may include the Eastern parts of Europe as well, or Turkey. Another criticism can be derived from postmodern social theories which generally question the applicability of notions of 'unity' and 'identity' for contemporary advanced societies; if they are right, these concepts might be even more questionable in the heterogeneous, multinational and multicultural political community the EU represents (Beck and Grande 2004; Delanty and Rumford 2005).

Cultural threat

A distinct variant within the broader family of identity approaches is the *cultural threat model* (McLaren 2002, 2004). A general antipathy towards other cultures, this approach goes, is a powerful source of attitudes against European integration. Many citizens aim at protecting what they assume to be their national culture – their language, way of living, currency – against foreign influences in general. Europeanization puts national cultures under stress by opening borders and undermining national sovereignty. This puts citizens that want to conserve their national culture in opposition towards any supranational project. 'This is because the EU is not just a free trade zone, but rather is making policies that were formerly within the prerogative of the nation-state, and it is likely to be seen as having a homogenizing effect on the member states' (McLaren 2002: 554). By voting against Europe, citizens are supposed to aim at protecting the culture and identity of their in-group that is at stake. In her research, McLaren has split the concept of perceived threat into two components, realistic and symbolic threat. Whereas the former perceives minorities primarily as competitors for economic resources formerly exclusively devoted to the in-group of nationals, the latter highlights the threat to national culture and lifestyle. From the analysis she concludes that attitudes towards the European Union tend to be based in great part on a general hostility towards other cultures.

The open question this approach can hardly answer is who these threatening others precisely are. McLaren writes: 'The questions are very likely *not* to be measuring perceptions of other Europeans at all' (McLaren 2002: 559). Rather, when perceiving cultural threat, EU citizens might imagine 'Muslims from Turkey, North Africa, or Pakistan, Chinese Buddhists, or Hindus from India, not Basques living in Spain or Catholics in Northern Ireland' (ibid.). This suspicion is strengthened by the finding that in the 1990s most EU citizens imagined Eastern Europeans or non-Europeans, rather than EU nationalities from Western or Southern Europe, when distinguishing between 'us' and 'them' (Fuchs *et al.* 1993). In the same vein, Bruter (2003) reported experimental evidence that EU citizens tend to feel closer to fellow European citizens than to non-Europeans.

The strength of the cultural threat model is to remind us that lust for supranational integration is, among other things, related to general positive feelings towards other cultures, and lack of support to feelings of xenophobia. Its weakness, however, is its failure in informing us by whom exactly EU citizens feel culturally threatened, and to what extent co-Europeans play a role in this. This again demonstrates that one avenue of understanding attitudes towards European integration has been largely unexplored yet – the friendly or hostile feelings Europeans have *towards each other*. Both the identity approach and the cultural threat approach fail to account adequately for this. But the transnational trust approach does, and I turn to this approach now.

Extending the sense of community approaches: transnational trust

The phenomenon of trust has received considerable attention from a variety of disciplines, both in its own right and as a core component of social capital (Putnam 1995). A working definition is that trust is the belief that, at worst, others will not knowingly or willingly do us harm and, at best, they will act in our interest (cf. Gambetta 1988; Warren 1999; Delhey and Newton 2003). Trusting others means viewing them in a positive way and expecting them to behave in a predictable and friendly manner (Inglehart 1991). What I am here concerned with is interpersonal (or social) trust – the kind of trust that flows *horizontally* between persons and groups, in stark contrast to political trust that flows vertically, linking ordinary citizens on the one hand and political elites or political institutions on the other (cf. Newton 2007). Moreover, I am concerned with *generalized* social trust, a 'thin' form of trust, which is usually differentiated from the 'thick', particularistic trust prevailing within small communities or kinships. Unlike the latter, generalized social trust does not rest on acquaintance. This feature makes it a valuable synthetic force for modern, large-scale societies (cf. Simmel 1950), and probably even more valuable for the pan-European space with its 450 million inhabitants. I define *transnational* trust as the level of generalized trust citizens of a given nationality vest in people from other EU member countries ('co-Europeans'). The radius of this sort of trust is certainly larger than for trust in co-nationals, but narrower than trust in humankind in general. According to the logic of the European project, exactly those peoples are relevant objects of trust which are assembled together in the supranational polity 'EU' – not those who are outside its borders.

Eric Uslaner (2002) sees generalized trust as 'the chicken soup of social life'. Social scientists have again and again suggested that good things tend to happen in settings where people trust each other. Trust seems to serve two main functions (Philips 2006). As a lubricant, it ensures that people and groups interact smoothly – 'metaphorically oiling the wheels of society' (Philips 2006: 133). As social glue, trust holds together social groups by means of its moral qualities and implications. It is precisely these qualities which are of interest from a mass support perspective. Trusting strangers means accepting them into our 'moral community' (Uslaner 2002), based on the belief that fundamental values are shared. This inclusive view, Uslaner argues, is capable of building bridges across groups, since people who trust are more tolerant, more cosmopolitan-minded and more inclined to welcome those who are different from them. Part and parcel of this are sentiments of mutual obligation and solidarity:

> When we perceive a shared fate with others, we reach out to them in other ways. We feel bad when those we trust have difficulties not of their own making. So people who trust others will seek to better the lives of those who have less, either by favouring government programs to redress grievances or, even more critically, by giving of their own time and money.
>
> Uslaner 2002: 2

In a nutshell, trust is a 'thin' form of sense of community, based on reputation and sympathy and implying feelings of loyalty, concern and solidarity. Distrust, in contrast, signals a considerable social distance, which can take the mild form of indifference or the severe form of hostility. True, one can trust others without an urgent longing for political unification. Yet it is very unlikely that people who dislike their partner nationalities welcome a unified Europe with open arms. Arguably, mutual trust is part of the affiliational integration story which Wallace named as being equally important for making Europe work than measures of functional and territorial integration (Wallace 1999).

It is plausible on general grounds that the very idea of a supranational community demands that citizens feel positively about each other. Moreover, there is a string of more specific arguments for why trust might turn politically relevant for the European project: first, the EU is a deliverer of collective goods from which all member states' populations benefit. Second, membership implies solidarity, one concrete manifestation of which is the redistribution of financial resources from richer to poorer areas. Third, EU citizenship opens up the legal boundaries of what were once relatively closed national political and welfare communities to mobile people from other member states, who are provided with a status of quasi-nationals (Bartolini 2005; Ferrera 2005). Finally, the European project involves handing over a good deal of national sovereignty to European bodies, which brings with it the risk of decisions being taken that are perceived to be against national interest. Thus it is safe to say that it shall be much easier to favour or at least accept these by-products of the European project if citizens regard their co-Europeans as trustworthy.

It is an established claim of both the political culture school and the social capital school that, generally, high levels of horizontal trust within nation-states go together with supportive attitudes for national political regimes and trust in its basic institutions (Inglehart 1990, 1997; Zmerli and Newton 2008). Yet there is also evidence that social trust is related to political attitudes beyond national matters. Surveying foreign policy preferences of US students, Rosenberg found a linkage between the students' preferred solution to international problems and their view of humanity (Rosenberg 1957). Distrusters voted for coercion and force as methods of settling international disputes, whereas trusters (i.e. those with strong faith in other people) were more likely to place their reliance upon cooperation and mutual understanding. He concluded that 'people appear more likely to be "peacelike" if they love and trust their fellow men' (345). Brewer *et al.* studied international trust, measured as the belief that the US can trust 'most countries'. They found that 'international trust helps dictate whether citizens approach international politics with fear of a bad world or faith in working together for a better one' (Brewer *et al.* 2004: 106).

I conclude this section with summarizing the main differences between the trust approach and the two approaches introduced above. Transnational trust is about how Europeans as members of national collectivities view each other. It avoids the conceptual ambiguity of European identity, which taps simultaneously a cultural and a political dimension. Moreover, trust does not necessarily imply feelings of unity or 'sameness'. Like the cultural threat model, the trust approach is horizontal, linking citizenries. The main difference is that the targets of trust (or distrust) are more clearly named, whereas in the cultural threat model a lot of ambiguity remains about which other culture(s) exactly are perceived as threatening. Hence both European identity and cultural threat do not allow straightforward conclusions to be drawn about how much mutual acceptance and liking there is *among Europeans* and how salient this specific aspect of sense of community is for loving or hating supranational integration. As a consequence, for these approaches it hardly makes a difference which nationalities are assembled together in a supranational community, whereas the transnational trust approach is sensitive to composition.

Testing the social trust approach against data

Database

The subsequent analysis is based on data from the European Election Study (EES) 2004. The European Election Studies (EES) mainly help scientists to analyse electoral participation and voting behaviour in European Parliament elections. But it also covers other issues such as the EU as a political community, the European public sphere, perceptions of and preferences about the EU as a political regime, and evaluations of the EU's political performance. Between 1979 and 2004, five election studies were realized. The strengths of the EES 2004 for my purpose are considerable. First, it provides measures on mutual trust and collective identity, as well as on support for the European project. Second, as a post-enlargement survey, old and new member states of the EU25 are covered. Whereas all of them, Malta apart, did participate, the trust question has not been fielded in the United Kingdom, Sweden, Belgium and Lithuania, so that I am left with 21.792 respondents from 20 countries. The surveys are representative of the electorates of the respective member states, i.e. the EU citizens aged 18-plus. The sample size ranges between 500 in

Cyprus and Greece and 1,606 in Estonia. Data and documentation (Schmitt and Loveless 2004) are available through the webpage of the EES project.[1]

Dependent variables

The dependent variable is a measure of supranational unification support, for which the EES provides two pertinent questions. One concerns further political integration (unification):

> *Some say European unification should be pushed further. Others say it already has gone too far. What is your opinion? Please indicate your views using a 10-point-scale. On this scale, 1 means unification 'has already gone too far' and 10 means it 'should be pushed further'. What number on this scale best describes your position?*

Although it is left in the eye of the beholder how far European unification has moved already, and what further unification might entail, this question seems useful to measure a *general* readiness to support political integration. The question is similar to the *Eurobarometer*'s speedometer question, but has the advantage of addressing the depth of unification rather than its speed.

A second question concerns EU membership. The wording is very similar to one of the core questions of the *Eurobarometer* which is often taken to measure citizens' stance towards integration:

> *Generally speaking, do you think that [Country's] membership of the European Union is a good thing, a bad thing, or neither good nor bad?*

For this chapter I combined both indicators into one index, 'amalgamation support'. The blending allows for a more valid measurement of the underlying construct than any single-indicator approach. The answers to both items were rescaled to a 0–1 format, summated, and eventually divided by 2, so that the range of the index is 0–1. '1' means the maximum possible support for amalgamation, whereas '0' means the maximum possible rejection. The index construction is justified on theoretical grounds, but on statistical as well, as factor analysis revealed (not displayed). In a previous study (Scheuer 2005), very similar questions ('pro unite Western Europe'; 'membership is a good thing', among others) have been shown to belong to a common attitudinal dimension as well. This parallelism makes me extremely confident that the index constructed indeed reveals how citizens think about European unification.

Independent variables

The main independent variable is trust in fellow EU citizens. It is measured in a format where the extent of trust in each of the 25 EU nationalities is surveyed

---

[1] http://www.ees-homepage.net/.

separately (see 'Appendix' at the end of this chapter for the full question wording).[2]

> *Now I would like to ask you a question about how much trust you have in people from various countries. Can you please tell me for each, whether you have a lot of trust of them or not very much trust? If you do not know a country well enough, just say so and I will go on to the next.*

The separate trust ratings were summated (only by leaving out trust in co-nationals), so that the sum indicates how many fellow EU nationalities the respondent reports to trust 'a lot' (range from 0–24). For the final computations, the trust index was re-scaled to a 0–1 format. '1' stands for the maximum possible trust in fellow EU citizens, i.e. people from all member states are trusted 'a lot'; '0' means that people from all countries are 'not trusted very much'; all nuances between 0 and 1 are possible. In a collapsed version of the trust index, individuals are classified in three groups – low trust (less than one-third of co-Europeans are trusted 'a lot'); medium (between one-third and two-thirds are trusted); high trust (more than two-thirds).

Do survey questions on trust deserve our confidence? Experimental research has shown that customary dichotomous trust questions are indeed related to trustful behaviour (Fehr *et al.* 2002). Moreover, the EES instrument has advantages over the standard trust question frequently employed in other surveys ('Do you think that most people can be trusted, or that you can't be too careful in dealing with people?'). Whereas there remains some ambiguity about what is meant by 'most people', in the EES the target group is clearly named, which increases cross-national comparability. A weakness, however, is the dichotomous scale, which is a rather unsubtle measure. Finally, it would be preferable to have more than just one trust measure for each target group (Rost 2005), although multiple approaches to trust are not unproblematic either (Jagodzinski and Manabe 2005).

The second key independent variable relates to European identity. Here, the survey provides two items: whether respondents see themselves as European or national citizens, and how proud they are of being an EU citizen:

> *Do you ever think of yourself not only as a [Nationality] citizen, but also as a citizen of the European Union? [often; sometimes; never]*
>
> *Are you personally proud or not of being a citizen of the European Union? Would you say you are . . . very proud, fairly proud, not very proud, not at all proud?*

Although these questions refer explicitly to the European Union, I use the term 'European identity' as a shortcut. Similar to all other variables, the answers to both identity questions are re-scaled to a 0–1 format.

---

2 Plus a small number of additional target nations, which have not been used for the analysis.

Results: trust in co-Europeans and taste for European integration

Does trust matter? At a bivariate level there is indeed a relationship with political attitudes. In Figure 3.1, for each country the collapsed trust index – low, medium (denoted as '0.5' in the figure), high – is used.[3] If we break down average amalgamation support by trust levels, the graphical result is almost always a stairway. The more the respondents regard people from other EU countries as trustworthy, the more they like unification. Take France as an example: in the lowest trust group the French support European integration with an average score of roughly 0.4, hence being slightly against. For the middle trust group the score is 0.6, slightly pro. And for the highest trust group the score is 0.7, slightly more supportive (recall: on a scale from 0–1). A similarly pronounced stairway pattern can be seen, e.g., for the Netherlands, Austria, Germany, Finland, the Czech Republic and Slovakia. Elsewhere the stairway is less pronounced, yet visible. An exception is Spain, where there is no monotonous relationship. In all countries, including Spain, the individual-level association between trust and amalgamation support is significant (at a 0.05 level or higher). Yet the strength of association varies considerably: in the old member states between 0.38 in Austria and 0.08 in Spain, in the new member states between 0.29 in the Czech Republic and 0.09 in Cyprus. A common pattern within both country groups is the relatively low strength of association in the Mediterranean countries, a pattern to which we will return later.

This descriptive picture is of course not a proof of a causal relationship. In order to make a statement about causality, we need to control two sets of individual characteristics: first, one needs to control for demographic and socioeconomic characteristics which may simultaneously influence social trust (Whiteley 1999; Delhey and Newton 2003) and attitudes towards the EU (Hix 1999; Ehin 2001; Alvarez 2002; Caplanova et al. 2004; Mau 2005). These controls are included in the 'trust model'. Second, collective identity motives on which mass support may be based alternatively need to be taken into account additionally. This extension is done in a second step, labelled the 'trust + identity model'.

For all respondents the dataset provides information on sex, education, employment/unemployment status, subjective class position and religious denomination (see 'Appendix' at the end of this chapter for details). It was not possible to account for age directly, since no age information was provided for Luxembourg. It is well established that younger cohorts are more pro-European than older ones (Inglehart 1971). This applies also to the EES, as further analyses show (not displayed). Since the information whether respondents are still in education/vocational training is available, we can consider age at least indirectly; it's in the nature of things that, with very few exceptions, those who are still in the educational system are younger than those who have left it.

---

3 In all tables and figures in this chapter, the countries are arranged according to length of membership, from founding to most recent members.

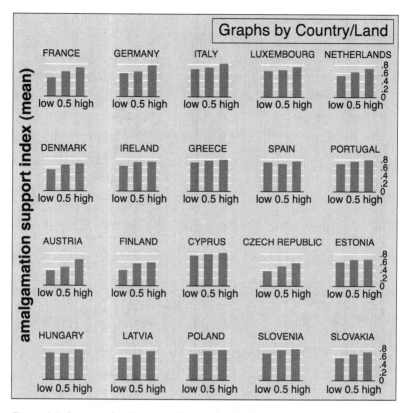

Figure 3.1 Support for European integration by level of trust

Table 3.1 shows the results for the 'trust model'. The three columns refer to the entire EU25 ('all countries', i.e. those 20 member states in which the trust question has been fielded), the old members states ('EU15'), and the eight new member states ('AC10'), respectively. The dependent variable is, as always, the amalgamation support index. The independent variables in this model are transnational trust plus the respondents' demographic and socioeconomic profile as controls. Additionally, country dummies have been used to control for country effects (not displayed in the table). Each of the columns shows the average effect of the various independent variables on support in the respective set of countries, based on OLS regressions. Needless to say that for single countries, these effects can well be stronger or weaker.

Turning directly to the coefficient for trust in co-Europeans, the key message is that after controlling for a number of individual characteristics, generalized trust in co-Europeans matters for how citizens think about political integration. Trust seems to be, on average, more salient in the old member states, as the larger coefficient indicates. The general results for the control variables correspond pretty much to those of previous studies: men (see Liebert 1997;

70 Jan Delhey

Table 3.1 Determinants of support for European integration – 'trust model'

	All countries b/t	EU15 b/t	AC10 b/t
Sex (men)	0.021***	0.030***	0.002
	(5.21)	(6.12)	(0.35)
Education	0.004***	0.004***	0.004***
	(8.28)	(6.88)	(4.24)
Still studying	0.040***	0.043***	0.032
	(4.75)	(4.36)	(1.90)
Unemployed	–0.012	–0.005	–0.020
	(–1.15)	(–0.34)	(–1.36)
Subjective class	0.032***	0.034***	0.028***
	(14.50)	(12.57)	(7.29)
Catholic	0.005	0.010	–0.001
	(1.00)	(1.50)	(–0.15)
Trust in co-Europeans	0.176***	0.197***	0.146***
	(25.30)	(21.98)	(13.11)
_cons	0.379***	0.358***	0.492***
	(24.16)	(21.09)	(21.25)
r2	0.152	0.163	0.137
N	14,996	9,866	5,130

OLS regressions.
Dependent variable: amalgamation support.
Results for country dummies not reported.

Nelsen and Guth 2000), the younger cohorts/still in education, the educated and higher classes are more enthusiastic about the EU. In contrast, being unemployed and being a Catholic are not shaping attitudes, unlike in previous studies. In the old member states, integration support is more clearly structured along respondents' demographic and socioeconomic profile, whereas in the new member states only education and subjective class make a difference.

Next I account additionally for feelings of European identity ('trust + identity model'). Only then can we be sure that how Europeans view each other adds a layer of understanding to the conventional identity approach. In the computations reported in Table 3.2, both identity items provided by the EES are included. As in previous studies, issues of European identity are indeed strong predictors of public support. Taking pride in EU citizenship in particular increases the taste for amalgamation. This comes not as a big surprise, given the conceptual proximity between the object of support – European-level political integration – and emotional attachment to one of its major institutions, EU citizenship. The second key result is that trust in co-Europeans significantly influences citizens' support as well. How comfortable Europeans are with each other exerts an influence on its own, over and above any expressions of collective identity. However, the inclusion of identity items clearly decreases the impact of trust (roughly by 50 per cent), which

Table 3.2 Determinants of support for European integration – 'trust + identity model'

	All countries b/t	EU15 b/t	AC10 b/t
Sex (men)	0.016***	0.024***	–0.002
	(4.23)	(5.34)	(–0.31)
Education	0.003***	0.002***	0.003***
	(6.07)	(4.65)	(3.59)
Still studying	0.018*	0.020*	0.013
	(2.24)	(2.18)	(0.86)
Unemployed	–0.004	–0.002	–0.008
	(–0.48)	(–0.18)	(–0.59)
Subjective class	0.017***	0.021***	0.011**
	(8.39)	(8.22)	(2.96)
Catholic	–0.007	–0.004	–0.011
	(–1.37)	(–0.70)	(–1.24)
Trust in co-Europeans	0.087***	0.101***	0.066***
	(12.99)	(11.78)	(6.07)
Feeling as EU citizen	0.102***	0.113***	0.070***
	(16.77)	(15.87)	(5.99)
Proud being EU citizen	0.326***	0.319***	0.346***
	(42.20)	(33.86)	(25.55)
_cons	0.301***	0.284***	0.373***
	(20.63)	(17.98)	(16.86)
r2	0.325	0.336	0.310
N	14,017	9,362	4,655

OLS regressions.
Dependent variable: amalgamation support.
Results for country dummies not reported.

indicates a certain overlap between the two. Presumably, this overlap is chiefly with the cultural component of European identity, which, like social trust, bonds people horizontally. Moreover, including the identity items doubles the explanatory power of the whole model (the explained variance), as compared with the previous 'trust model'. There is no doubt that collective identity is the stronger driver of mass support. Yet the fact that trust remains a significant predictor demonstrates that identity and trust should not be equated. Both constitute related, but different, dimensions of the same overarching construct, sense of community.

When looking at old and new member states separately (columns 2 and 3, respectively, of Table 3.2), it is obvious that in the former social trust is more salient for mass attitudes than in the latter. The average coefficient is about 50 per cent larger. This finding lends some support to the idea that *diffuse* support has a stronger home base in the old member states. This interpretation would be in line with research on why citizens support their *national* political systems; specific support is of particularly high importance for citizens in post-communist countries, compared with Western Europe (Bartolome Peral 2007). This line of argumentation is indeed strengthened by further analysis (not displayed here) with the EES, revealing that utilitarian considerations like the country's benefit from EU membership (as a measure of specific support) is the strongest driver of unification support among citizens of the accession countries. However, as we will see in a moment, old versus new member states is not the true dividing line.

Figure 3.2 shows the average effect of trust in co-Europeans on amalgamation support, for each country separately. The coefficients are picked out from OLS regressions done for each country separately, using the 'trust and identity model' introduced above. Thus the *additional* impact of trust on support is captured, over and above the effect of European identity. There is considerable cross-national variation in how sensitive unification support is to transnational trust. Sensitivity is clearly above average in Germany, Austria, France, the Netherlands and Latvia (the only new member state in this group), whereas it is clearly below average in Spain, Cyprus, Greece, Hungary, Italy and Portugal. In the latter six countries plus Estonia, trust is not significantly related to unification support in addition to identity feelings. Obviously, in

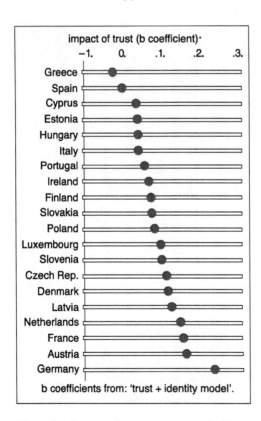

Figure 3.2 Impact of trust on support for European integration

the Mediterranean countries in particular attitudes towards the EU are *not* a matter of trust in co-Europeans. Here, citizens are enthusiastic (or not) about the EU regardless of how they view the partner nationalities. In the remaining plurality of 13 countries (out of 20 for which we have data), however, trust matters. Hence it makes sense to enlarge the sense of community approaches by the trust approach introduced here.

Although it is not the main purpose of this chapter, the remainder seeks to establish more rigorously cross-national differences in the salience of trust. Particular attention is paid to the geographic pattern and to membership (new versus old member states; length of membership). For this purpose, a two-step multi-level analysis is conducted, in which the b-coefficients indicating the salience of trust for unification support obtained from the individual level (step 1) are averaged for each country and then correlated with, or regressed against, country characteristics (step 2). This can be done for 20 cases, the member countries which have fielded the trust question. Note that in this second step, the salience of trust for support (as indicated by the averaged b coefficient) is the dependent variable.

Beginning with geography, countries are classified into broad regions: north, east, south and west. When using the largest group of Eastern European countries as the reference group and including the other three regions as dummy variables, one can see from the country-level regression that two regions are clearly different: trust in co-Europeans is significantly *less* important among the *southern* citizenries, and significantly *more* important among the *western* citizenries. The northern citizenries do not differ in this respect from the Eastern Europeans (Table 3.3).

This geographical pattern already suggests that it is not a story about insiders and newcomers. Indeed, the distinction between old and new member countries does not yield a significant association. In the old member states, trust matters not more for supportive attitudes than in the new member states (r=0.15, p=0.52, with old member states coded as '1' for the dummy variable). Likewise, it is not a question of *how long* citizenries belong to the club: there is no significant relationship with membership years, although there is a mild tendency of increasing salience of trust with length of Community membership (r=0.33, p=0.15). Hence there is no automatism that enduring membership makes citizens increasingly receptive for the idea that horizontal feelings of community are a necessary condition for supranational integration. Yet the puzzling finding is that in this respect the founding members are indeed significantly different from the rest (r=0.48, p=0.03, with founding members coded as '1' for the dummy variable). Hence the founding members – bar Italy, in which trust plays a minor role for EU support – seem to share some traits which make issues of transnational trust important. Trust is also hugely important for Austrians, who joined in the 1990s, and generally unimportant for southerners. Further research should focus on finding out why two groups of countries – western continental and southern Mediterranean – are exceptional in this respect. Presumably, this has to be qualitative research,

74 Jan Delhey

Table 3.3 The salience of trust for support – geographical differences

Geographic region (Eastern = reference)	b/t
Southern countries (dummy)	–0.062*
	(–2.41)
Western countries (dummy)	0.065*
	(2.67)
Northern countries (dummy)	0.012
	(0.35)
_cons	0.079***
	(4.75)
r2	0.590
N	20

Country-level OLS regression.
Dependent variable: aggregated individual-level salience of transnational trust on amalgamation support (b coefficient, averaged by country).

since what we need now is to *understand* citizens' deeper reasoning about trust, community and political integration.

Conclusion

This chapter has addressed the role of trust in co-Europeans for citizens' taste for European integration. The main contestation was that the transnational trust approach represents a unique, so far unexplored, variation of the broader theme of sense of community. Previous research has almost exclusively focused on collective identity and cultural threat. Trust captures a different layer of sense of community for which the other two approaches do not adequately account: how Europeans see each other. The empirical analysis has, first, shown that supportive attitudes are strongly driven by collective identities. Hence, 'feeling European' is certainly the key source of affective support. However, transnational trust provides an *additional* source of mass support in the majority of countries. Thus it is justified to enrich the existing approaches by the approach introduced here, transnational trust. As rules of thumb, trust matters most in the western continental countries and very little, if at all, in the Mediterranean countries, for reasons that are still to be explored.

With respect to enlargements and its detrimental impact on the EU's stock of social trust, the results provide bad news and good news at the same time. The bad news (seen from the perspective of those who would love to see Europe politically fully united) is that integration support is not unrelated to trust in co-Europeans. To put it differently: composition matters. It matters which nationalities are assembled together, and unpopular enlargements can result in dwindling support for the European project. In this context it is instructive that EU citizens are not very enthusiastic about those countries currently queuing for membership (Gerhards and Hans 2008). Moreover, enlargement support varies considerably by applicant country, which means that citizens feel much closer to some Europeans than to others.

The good news, on the other hand, is that trust is not of paramount importance for unification support. As long as citizens trust key European institutions such as the Commission and the European Parliament and continue to see EU membership as beneficial, an offensive enlargement strategy will not vastly threaten the popularity of the European project as a whole. On the other hand, it is obvious that 'calculated inclusions' (Vobruba 2003) of poorer and politically less consolidated countries – exactly those who inspire only little trust (Delhey 2007) – do not strengthen public support either, and the dwindling sense of community has to be compensated for elsewhere if the level of support should be maintained. Hence, to a limited extent, there *is* a trade-off between widening the club and mass support for deepening it, in particular in the core EU countries.

The implication for opinion research is as follows: since transnational trust provides an additional layer of understanding public support, over and above European identity, our set of explanatory approaches should be enlarged by the transnational trust approach. The policy implications are equally straightforward: how Europeans see each other is not only of interest as a descriptive indicator of EU-level social cohesion (Delhey 2007), but has measurable consequences for how popular the idea of European integration is among ordinary citizens.

Appendix

1: The trust question (taken from English master questionnaire)

Trust in co-Europeans

Q26 Now I would like to ask you a question about how much trust you have in people from various countries. Can you please tell me for each, whether you have a lot of trust of them or not very much trust? If you do not know a country well enough, just say so and I will go on to the next. How about the Austrians: do you have a lot of trust of them or not very much trust? And the Belgians?

	a lot of trust	not very much trust	dk	na
Austrians	( )	( )	( )	( )
Belgians	( )	( )	( )	( )
British	( )	( )	( )	( )
Bulgarians	( )	( )	( )	( )
Cypriots	( )	( )	( )	( )
Czechs	( )	( )	( )	( )
Danes	( )	( )	( )	( )
Dutch	( )	( )	( )	( )

	a lot of trust	not very much trust	dk	na
Estonians	( )	( )	( )	( )
Finns	( )	( )	( )	( )
French	( )	( )	( )	( )
Germans	( )	( )	( )	( )
Greeks	( )	( )	( )	( )
Hungarians	( )	( )	( )	( )
Irish	( )	( )	( )	( )
Italians	( )	( )	( )	( )
Latvians	( )	( )	( )	( )
Lithuanians	( )	( )	( )	( )
Luxembourgers	( )	( )	( )	( )
Maltese	( )	( )	( )	( )
Poles	( )	( )	( )	( )
Portuguese	( )	( )	( )	( )
Romanians	( )	( )	( )	( )
Slovaks	( )	( )	( )	( )
Slovenes	( )	( )	( )	( )
Spaniards	( )	( )	( )	( )
Swedes	( )	( )	( )	( )
Turks	( )	( )	( )	( )

2: Socioeconomic and demographic control variables

Sex of respondent	Dummy variable, 1 = men
Still in educational system	Dummy variable, 1 = yes
Unemployed	Dummy variable, 1 = yes
Education	Continuous variable, age when stopping education
Subjective class position	Scale from 1 to 4, 1 = 'working class' to 4 = 'upper middle class' + 'upper class'
Religious denomination	Dummy variable, 1 = Catholic

References

Alvarez, R. 2002. 'Attitudes toward the European Union: the role of social class, social stratification, and political orientation', *International Journal of Sociology* 32(1): 58–76.

Anderson, B. R. 1983. *Imagined communities*. London: Verso.

Bach, M. 2000. 'Die Europäisierung der nationalen Gesellschaft? Problemstellungen und Perspektiven einer Soziologie der europäischen Integration', in: M. Bach (ed.) *Die Europäisierung nationaler Gesellschaften. Sonderheft 40, Kölner Zeitschrift für Soziologie und Sozialpsychologie*. Opladen: Westdeutscher Verlag, 11–35.

Bartolini, S. 2005. *Restructuring Europe: centre formation, system building and political structuring between the nation-state and the European Union*. Oxford: Oxford University Press.

Bartolome Peral, E. 2007. 'Apoyo Politico y Confianza Social en Europa, 1999–2005: Factores Explicativos en Perspectiva Comparada', Faculdad de Ciencias Politicas y Sociologica, Universidad de Deusto, Bilbao.
Beck, U. and Grande, E. 2004. *Das kosmopolitische Europa. Gesellschaft und Politik in der Zweiten Moderne.* Frankfurt/M.: Suhrkamp Verlag.
Brewer, P. R., Gross, K., Sean, A. and Willnat, L. 2004. 'International trust and public opinion about world affairs', *American Journal of Political Science* 48(1): 93–109.
Bruter, M. 2003. 'Winning hearts and minds for Europe: the impact of news and symbols on civic and cultural European identity', *Comparative Political Studies* 36(10): 1148–79.
Bruter, M. 2005. *Citizens of Europe? The emergence of a mass European identity.* Houndmills: Palgrave Macmillan.
Caplanova, A., Orviska, M. and Hudson, J. 2004. 'Eastern European attitudes to integration with Western Europe', *Journal of Common Market Studies* 42(2): 271–88.
Carey, S. 2002. 'Undivided loyalties: is national identity an obstacle to European integration?', *European Union Politics* 3(4): 387–413.
Delanty, G. and Rumford, C. 2005. *Rethinking Europe: social theory and the implications of Europeanization.* London: Routledge.
Delhey, J. 2007. 'Do enlargements make the European Union less cohesive? An analysis of trust between EU nationalities', *Journal of Common Market Studies* 45(2): 253–79.
Delhey, J. 2009. 'Die osterweiterte EU – ein optimaler Integrationsraum?', in: M. Eigmüller and S. Mau (eds) *Gesellschaftstheorie und Europapolitik. Sozialwissenschaftliche Ansätze zur Europaforschung.* Wiesbaden: VS Verlag für Sozialwissenschaften, 300–318.
Delhey, J. and Newton, K. 2003. 'Who trusts? The origins of social trust in seven societies', *European Societies* 5(2): 93–137.
Deutsch, K. W., Burrel, S. A., Kann, R. A., Lee, M., Lichtermann, M., Lindgren, R. E., Loewenheim, F. L. and Van Wagenen, R. W. 1966. 'Political community and the North Atlantic area', in: K. W. Deutsch, S. A. Burrel, R. A. Kann, M. Lee, M. Lichtermann, R. E. Lindgren, F. L. Loewenheim and R. W. Van Wagenen (eds) *International political communities: an anthology.* Garden City: Anchor Books, 1–91.
Easton, D. 1965. *A systems analysis of political life.* New York: Wiley and Son.
Ehin, P. 2001. 'Determinants of public support for EU membership: data from the Baltic countries', *European Journal of Political Research* 40(1): 31–56.
Fehr, E., Fischbacher, U., von Rosenbladt, B., Schupp, J. and Wagner, G. G. 2002. 'A nation-wide laboratory: examining trust and trustworthiness by integration behavioral experiments into representative surveys', *DIW Discussion Papers.* Berlin: German Institute for Economic Research (DIW).
Ferrera, M. 2005. *The boundaries of welfare: European integration and the territorial restructuring of social protection.* Oxford: Oxford University Press.
Fuchs, D. 2002. 'Das Demokratiedefizit der Europäischen Union und die politische Integration Europas: Eine Analyse der Einstellungen der Bürger in Westeuropa', in Wissenschaftszentrum Berlin für Sozialforschung (WZB) *Discussion Paper*, Berlin.
Fuchs, D., Gerhards, J. and Roller, E. 1993. 'Wir und die Anderen. Ethnozentrismus in den zwölf Ländern der europäischen Gemeinschaft', *Kölner Zeitschrift für Soziologie und Sozialpsychologie* 45(2): 238–53.
Gambetta, D. 1988. 'Mafia: the price of distrust', in D. Gambetta (ed.) *Trust: making and breaking cooperative relations.* Oxford: Blackwell, 158–75.

Gerhards, J. 2007. *Cultural overstretch? Differences between old and new member states of the EU and Turkey*. London: Routledge.
Gerhards, J. and Hans, S. 2008. 'Die Grenzen Europas aus der Perspektive der Bürger', *Aus Politik und Zeitgeschichte* 35–36: 8–13.
Heidenreich, M. 2003. 'Regional inequalities in the enlarged Euroland', *Journal of European Social Policy* 13(4): 313–33.
Hix, S. 1999. *The political system of the European Union*. Houndmills: Macmillan.
Hooghe, L. and Marks, G. 2004. 'Does identity or economic rationality drive public opinion on European integration?' *PSOnline*, 2005.
Inglehart, R. 1971. 'Changing value priorities and European integration', *Journal of Common Market Studies* 10(1): 1–36.
Inglehart, R. 1990. *Culture shift in advanced industrial society*. Princeton: Princeton University Press.
Inglehart, R. 1991. 'Trust between nations: primordial ties, societal learning and economic development', in: K. Reif and R. Inglehart (eds) *Eurobarometer: the dynamics of European public opinion: essays in honour of Jacques-René Rabier*. Houndmills: Macmillan, 145–86.
Inglehart, R. 1997. *Modernization and postmodernization: cultural, economic, and political change in 43 societies*. Princeton: Princeton University Press.
Jagodzinski, W. and Manabe, K. 2005. 'Warum auch Mehrfachindikatoren manchmal nicht helfen: Überlegungen zu einem multiplen Indikatorenmodell für interpersonales Vertrauen im Anschluss an die Anmerkung von Jürgen Rost', *ZA-Informationen* 56: 8–17.
Kaina, V. and Karolewski, I. P. 2006. *Theoretical perspectives and empirical insights*. Münster: LIT-Verlag.
Karp, J. A. and Bowler, S. 2006. 'Broadening and deepening or broadening vs. deepening: The question of enlargement and Europe's "hesitant Europeans"', *European Journal of Political Research* 45(3): 369–90.
Liebert, U. 1997. 'The gendering of euro-scepticism: public discourse and support to the EU in a cross-national comparison', *Institute for European Studies Working Paper no. 97.2*. Cornell University.
Mau, S. 2005. 'Europe from the bottom: assessing personal gains and losses and its effects on EU support', *Journal of Public Policy* 25(3): 289–311.
McLaren, L. M. 2002. 'Public support for the European Union: cost/benefit analysis or perceived cultural threat?', *The Journal of Politics* 64(2): 551–66.
McLaren, L. M. 2004. 'Opposition to European integration and fear of loss of national identity: debunking a basic assumption regarding hostility to the integration project', *European Journal of Political Research* 43(6): 895–912.
Nelsen, B. F. and Guth, J. L. 2000. 'Exploring the gender gap: women, men and public attitudes toward European integration', *European Union Politics* 1(3): 267–91.
Newton, K. 2007. 'Social and political trust', in: R. J. Dalton and H.-D. Klingemann (eds) *The Oxford handbook of political behaviour*. Oxford: Oxford University Press.
Philips, D. 2006. *Quality of life: concept, policy and practice*. London and New York: Routledge.
Puchala, D. J. 1981. 'Integration theory and the study of international relations', in R. L. Merritt and B. M. Russett (eds) *From national development to global community: essays in honour of Karl W. Deutsch*. London: George Allen & Unwin, 145–63.
Putnam, R. D. 1995. 'Bowling alone: America's declining social capital', *Journal of Democracy* 6(1): 65–78.

Ray, L. 2001. 'The ideological structure of mass opinion about European policymaking', in *Annual meeting of the American Political Science Association*, San Francisco.

Ray, L. 2006. 'Public opinion, socialization and political communication', in K. E. Jorgensen, M. A. Pollack and B. Rosamond (eds) *Handbook of European Union politics*, London: Sage, 263–81.

Rosamond, B. 2000. *Theories of European integration*. Houndmills: Palgrave.

Rose, R. 1994. 'Postcommunism and the problem of trust', *Journal of Democracy* 5(3): 18–30.

Rosenberg, M. 1957. 'Misanthropy and attitudes towards international affairs', *The Journal of Conflict Resolution* 1(4): 340–45.

Rost, J. 2005. 'Messen wird immer einfacher!', *Zentralarchiv-Informationen* 56: 6–7.

Scheuer, A. 2005. 'How Europeans see Europe: structure and dynamics of European legitimacy beliefs', Universität Amsterdam, Amsterdam.

Schmitt, H. and Loveless, M. 2004. 'European Election Study 2004: design, data description and documentation', Mannheimer Zentrum für Europäische Sozialforschung, European Election Study Research Group.

Simmel, G. 1950. *The sociology of Georg Simmel*. Translated and edtited by Kurt Wolff. Glencoe: The Free Press.

Uslaner, E. 2002. *The moral foundation of trust*. Cambridge: Cambridge University Press.

Vobruba, G. 2003. 'The enlargement crisis of the European Union: limits of the dialectics of integration and expansion', *Journal of European Social Policy* 13(1): 35–62.

Wallace, W. 1999. 'Whose Europe is it anyway? The 1998 Stein Rokkan lecture', *European Journal of Political Research* 35(3): 287–306.

Warren, M. E. 1999. 'Democratic theory and trust', in M. E. Warren (ed.) *Democracy and trust*. Cambridge: Cambridge University Press, 310–45.

Whiteley, P. F. 1999. 'The origins of social capital', in J. van Deth, M. Maraffi, K. Newton and P. Whiteley (eds) *Social capital and European democracy*. London: Routledge, 25–44.

Zmerli, S. and Newton, K. 2008. 'Social trust and attitudes toward democracy', *Public Opinion Quarterly* 72(4): 706–24.

4 'In the Union we trust'?
Institutional confidence and citizens' support for supranational decision-making

Viktoria Kaina

Introduction

Europe is gripped by a post-Maastricht blues. This diagnosis (Eichenberg and Dalton 2007) refers to an erosion of citizen support for European integration following the ratification of the Maastricht Treaty in 1992. Although citizen attitudes towards European integration are far from being in a 'mood indigo', several studies have confirmed a downward trend in public support for European integration since the early 1990s (see the introduction to this volume). However, the scholarly literature on Euroscepticism did not only reveal variations among the EU member states but also disclosed a rather complex pattern of reasons for a declining 'permissive consensus' among EU citizens (e.g. Fuchs *et al.* 2009; Weßels 2007, 2009a). We are accordingly advised to be careful not to confuse criticism with rejection or concerns with opposition. Furthermore, we should differentiate between citizen attitudes towards the *aim* of European unification on the one hand and the *way* of integration on the other. While Eichenberg and Dalton (2007: 133) argued that 'endorsing (EU) membership is (. . .) endorsing the process of integration itself', I suggest to analytically distinguish citizen attitudes towards the 'if' of European integration and 'how' or 'to what extent' this process should proceed. This distinction is helpful to understand the colours and shades of public opinion towards European integration since people may appreciate their country's EU membership and be sceptical about the current integration process at the same time.

One reason for such conflicting assessments is that citizen attitudes towards European integration may refer to different integration modes, namely European integration as *deepening* the unification process and European integration as *enlargement* by admitting new member states to the EU. Both aspects of European integration are needed for analysing the dynamics of the European unification process (Vobruba 2003, 2007) as well as the trends and patterns of public opinion on the European Union. In this context, enlargement and deepening are generally considered as parts of a dialectic and sometimes conflicting relationship. The potential for conflict between both modes of integration is partly caused by the fact that they unfold different ramifications for the scope of legitimate supranational governance. The enlargement of the European Union has an impact on the *territorial scope* of legitimate European governance by defining the group of people who are affected by European decision-making. In contrast, deepening the European unification process has a bearing on the *substantial scope* of legitimate European governance by shifting policy competence from the national to the supranational level. Since a transfer of policy competence to the EU is tantamount to willingly assign national sovereignty and allow a European harmonization of policy standards, the broadening of the EU borders may easily come into conflict with citizens' willingness to accept a policy shift to the European level. This is all the more probable the more citizens believe that the newcomers are economically and culturally too different from the community members and consequently pose a challenge to national achievements.

Against this background, this chapter is focused on the deepening mode of European unification and the substantial scope of legitimate European governance. Referring to the aim of this volume, I want to empirically explore the role of institutional trust for citizens' approval for a transfer of policy competence from the national to the European level. My main hypothesis is that European citizens tend to support European decision-making in several policy areas only if they also tend to trust European institutions. I will justify my assumption in the next section by outlining the theoretical background of my empirical analysis. In the third section, I present some preliminary empirical findings. In the concluding section, I will briefly discuss the key results in view of the volume's research interest in civic resources for a European Union in trouble.

Theoretical considerations

Scholars dealing with the landmarks of European unification (Laffan 1998; Thomas 2006) agree that today's European Union is quite different from the functional agency (Mitrany 1966: 145) and the economic *Zweckverband* (Ipsen 1972) of preceding integration years. Intensified by the Maastricht Treaty of 1993, the European unification path has developed a power structure of supranational authority and a new type of governance (e.g. Marks *et al.* 1996; Stone Sweet and Sandholtz 1997; Bach 1999, 2000; Kohler-Koch 1999; Jachtenfuchs 2000; Stone Sweet *et al.* 2001; Hooghe and Marks 2009). Thus, the question arises: what are the good reasons for rule, since every sort of governance limits the self-determination and individual freedom of people? This question describes the core problem of political legitimacy in that the answers may explain why people even willingly accept political decisions detrimental to their own benefit.

The long tradition of democratic thinking makes clear that *democratic* governance has to be based not only on certain core principles but also on the citizens' consent. Put differently, governance is democratic inasmuch as binding political decisions are legitimized 'as a manifestation of collective self-determination' (Scharpf 1999: 6). In normative democratic theory, however, there are two key perspectives emphasizing different but complementary dimensions for realizing collective self-determination. Fritz W. Scharpf (1999: 6) called the first dimension 'input-oriented' legitimacy beliefs emphasizing 'government *by* the people'. Therefore, political decisions are legitimate 'if and because (...) they can be derived from the authentic preferences of the members of the community' (ibid.). The second dimension was named 'output-oriented' legitimacy beliefs emphasizing 'government *for* the people' (ibid.). According to the output perspective, 'political choices are legitimate if and because they effectively promote the common welfare of the constituency in question' (ibid.). While both dimensions rest on different preconditions and unfold distinct implications for political legitimacy, they normally go hand in hand in democratic nation-states. When it comes to the European Union, however, Scharpf and other scholars are rather sceptical whether the EU can be legitimized by input-legitimacy in the foreseeable future (for an overview: Kaina 2009; Kaina and Karolewski 2009). This scepticism is theoretically justified by two important challenges for democratic governance in large-scale communities. The first issue is known as the *community problem*, the second one as the *congruence dilemma*.

The *community problem* refers to the specific 'burdens' of democracy. The 'imposition' of democracy chiefly results from the fact that democratic decision-making generates winners and losers by using majority rule and producing policies with redistributive consequences. Therefore, a shared sense of togetherness is supposed to be the indispensable precondition that makes group members consider the results of democratic decision-making as an expression of self-determination, even though the consequences of this process conflict with one's own interests (Decker 2002: 263). Numerous researchers accordingly believe that strengthening the EU's input-legitimacy requires the gradual development of a resilient sense of community among European citizens. At the same time, many of these scholars are sceptical about the conditions and prospects for an emerging sense of community among EU citizens (Kaina and Karolewski 2009).

The *congruence dilemma* describes a tense relationship between citizen participation and system effectiveness (Dahl 1994). It can be traced back to a twofold meaning of 'democracy' (Kaina 2009: 153–66). On the one hand, 'democracy' means a certain idea of a good political order where citizen participation is said to be essential for realizing collective self-determination. On the other hand, democracy is also a type of government which has to be effective in order to endure. In decision processes of modern large-scale democracies, the double meaning of democracy regularly provokes a collision between the call for citizen influence on decisions they are affected by and functional requirements of effective government. Robert Dahl (1994: 23f.) depicted this problem as a 'democratic dilemma' since citizens and political leaders have to choose between two options: on the one hand, they could choose to preserve governance authority of a smaller political unit within which citizens can more effectively participate in political decision-making, even though the matter in question is 'beyond the capacity of that government to deal with effectively' (Scharpf 1999: 24). On the other hand, they might choose to increase system effectiveness by transferring policy competence to a larger political unit, even though citizens' ability to influence decision-making substantially decreases in large political units. At any rate, both choices bring about a potential lack of congruence: the first option is inclined to reduce congruence between effective citizen participation and the scope of political issues. The second option tends to abolish the congruence between decision-taker and decision-receiver.

The European Union is a prominent example for both the community problem and the congruence dilemma in large political units. Hence, many scholars argue that the EU's legitimacy is and has to be mainly based on its output, at least as long as there is no convincing solution to the community problem and the congruence dilemma. Accordingly, the transfer of policy authority to the European level is mainly justified by the European Union's capacity to solve problems that single EU member states cannot effectively deal with. However, whether European citizens accept the transfer of policy authority to the supranational level – and, therefore, the deepening of European integration – is not only a question of how citizens evaluate the EU's problem-solving capacity, but also a matter of trust.

Although there is a large amount of interdisciplinary literature on trust, the concept is still fuzzy (Levi and Stoker 2000; Hardin 2006). Most of the various conceptions and explications at least agree on the functional connotation of trust (Schmalz-Bruns 2002: 16). According to the prominent proposition by Niklas Luhmann (1979, 1989), for example, trust is an indispensable social resource in modern societies because it helps to reduce social complexity and coordinate collective action. James Coleman (1988) described trust as a *transfer of control* of actions, resources and events to others (Schneeberger 1982: 302). Trust, however, is always based on expectations of the one who abstains from acting personally by delegating her/his control to someone else. These expectations are not safe from disappointment. The one who trusts will not know before tomorrow whether her/his expectations of today will have been met.

According to Coleman's idea of trust as a transfer of control, there also has to be a kind of trust when EU citizens endorse a shift of policy authority from the national to the supranational level. However, this kind of trust is subject to several citizens' expectations such as efficiency, effectiveness, fairness or integrity. In other words, whether EU citizens accept a transfer of policy authority to the EU level should – among others – depend on their belief that European institutions are capable of coping with this responsibility. I assume, therefore, European citizens tend to support European decision-making in several policy areas only if they also tend to trust European institutions. Conversely, EU citizens who do not trust European institutions should be rather reluctant to support a shift of policy authority to the European Union. In the next section, I will empirically test this hypothesis by using the bi-annual standard *Eurobarometer*.

Empirical results

The following empirical analysis consists of three main steps. *First*, I will deal with EU citizens' trust in European institutions. *Second*, I shall offer the main findings regarding the Europeans' attitudes towards a policy shift from the national to the European level. *Finally*, I will test my main hypothesis at both the aggregate and individual level of analysis using the standard *Eurobarometer* data from autumn 2008, the most updated dataset at my disposal when I have finished this book chapter.

Taking the first step, Figures 4.1–4.5 show the average net trust in five European institutions between 1999 and 2008. The net trust results from subtracting the negative answers ('tend not to trust') from the positive statements ('tend to trust'). Especially for longitudinal analyses of public opinion on European integration, the advantage of this net measure is to be sensitive to the amount of 'don't know' answers and, therefore, to public opinion mobilization (Niedermayer 1995; Kaina 2009: 18). This is all the more important as we continuously observe a great deal of 'don't know' answers when it comes to citizens' trust in European institutions.

After subtracting the negative answers from the positive ones, I have built an index ranging from –1 up to +1 (see also Niedermayer 1995: 56). A value of +1 would indicate that all respondents state that they tend to trust the European institution in question; a value of –1 would accordingly signify that all respondents declare that they tend not to trust this institution. A special note is needed for the Court of Justice of the European Communities (in the following: European Court of Justice). Here, the longitudinal trend goes only from 1999 to 2007 due to a lack of data for 2008.

Looking at Figures 4.1–4.5, three findings are noteworthy. First, the average net trust is always in the positive field of the index range, which means that

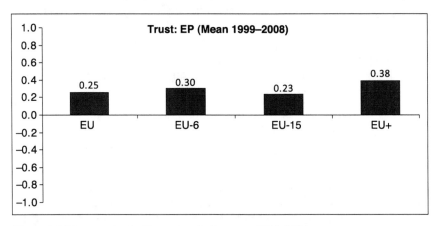

Figure 4.1 Net trust in the European Parliament, 1999–2008

Data source: EB 51.0, EB 54.1, EB 56.2, EB 57.1, EB 60.1, EB 62.0, EB 64.2, EB 66.1, EB 68.1, EB 70.1.

Citizens' support for supranational decision-making 85

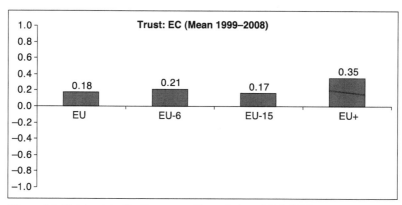

Figure 4.2 Net trust in the European Commission, 1999–2008

Data source: EB 51.0, EB 54.1, EB 56.2, EB 57.1, EB 60.1, EB 62.0, EB 64.2, EB 66.1, EB 68.1, EB 70.1.

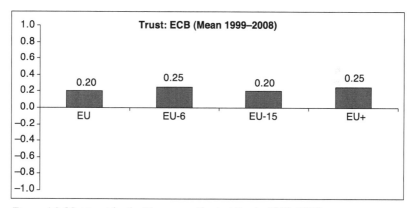

Figure 4.3 Net trust in the European Central Bank, 1999–2008

Data source: EB 51.0, EB 54.1, EB 56.2, EB 57.1, EB 60.1, EB 62.0, EB 64.2, EB 66.1, EB 68.1, EB 70.1.

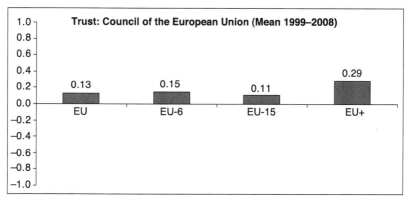

Figure 4.4 Net trust in the Council of the European Union, 1999–2008

Data source: EB 51.0, EB 54.1, EB 56.2, EB 57.1, EB 60.1, EB 62.0, EB 64.2, EB 66.1, EB 68.1, EB 70.1.

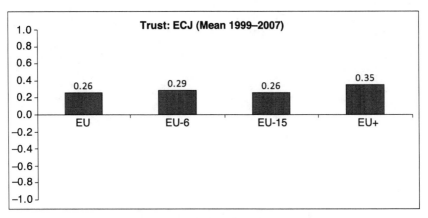

Figure 4.5 Net trust in the European Court of Justice, 1999–2007

Data source: EB 51.0, EB 54.1, EB 56.2, EB 57.1, EB 60.1, EB 62.0, EB 64.2, EB 66.1, EB 68.1, EB 70.1.

EU citizens more tend to trust than not to trust these EU institutions. The sole exception from this trend is the UK, where the mean net trust is always in the negative field of the index range, except for citizens' trust in the European Court of Justice (not shown). Second, the Europeans' trust varies between the five institutions. The European Parliament (EP) and the European Court of Justice (ECJ) are the most trusted European institutions, whereas the Council of the European Union is the least trusted one. The latter finding probably mirrors a lack of information and poor knowledge about the duties and responsibilities of the Council of the European Union, since the percentage of the 'don't know' answers is particularly high in many EU member states. Third, there are great differences between the EU member states. The publics of the new member states which joined the European Union in 2004 and 2007 are on average more trusting than those of the older member states. This result is in line with previous research (Weßels 2009b).

In the following, I have reduced the data complexity by developing an index of 'trust in EU institutions'. For this purpose I have initially computed a factor analysis, using the principal component analysis method. Since I wanted to use this index in order to test my main hypothesis with the most current data, I have based the factor analysis on the standard *Eurobarometer* data of autumn 2008. For this reason, I had to omit the European Court of Justice from the analysis. Furthermore, I have added two national trust variables, namely trust in national government and trust in national parliament. This choice is justified by two arguments. On the one hand, previous research has revealed that citizens' trust in national and European institutions significantly differs in that the populace of many EU member states repeatedly shows more trust in European institutions than in national ones (Weßels 2009b). On the other hand, given the Euroscepticism phenomenon, it is also

Table 4.1 Factor analysis: trust in European and national institutions, 2008 (principal component analysis: varimax rotation)

	F I	F II
Trust in Council of the European Union	0.918	0.198
Trust in European Commission	0.914	0.200
Trust in European Parliament	0.896	0.181
Trust in European Central Bank	0.819	0.226
Trust in national parliament	0.197	0.911
Trust in national government	0.215	0.904
Eigenvalue	3.24	1.81
Explanation of variance per factor (in %)	53.9	30.2
Total explanation of variance (in %)	84.1	
KMO	0.826 (p = 0.000)	
Cronbach's alpha	0.93	0.84

Data source: EB 70.1.

plausible to assume that some EU citizens – in particular those who express a strong exclusive attachment to their nation state – are less trustful towards European institutions than other citizens (McLaren 2007). Both aspects, however, suggest a difference in citizens' institutional trust at the national and European level. In order to get a clear result, I also omitted the 'don't know' answers from the factor analysis even though the number of valid cases was considerably reduced in some countries.[1] Table 4.1 contains the results of the factor analysis for the average of the EU27. The analysis generated a stable structure of two factors. Together, both factors are able to bind 84 per cent of variance.

This two-factor-structure could be reproduced for almost all 27 EU countries (not shown in table form). The deviant cases are Germany and Malta. In these countries, the factor analysis has produced only a single-factor structure. All in all, the results of the factor analysis strongly support my decision to scale an additive index, which I have named 'trust in EU institutions'. It includes citizens' trust in four European institutions – the European Commission (EC), the Council of the European Union (Council), the European Parliament (EP) and the European Central Bank (ECB). For the pooled data of all 27 EU member states, the reliability of this index is high (see Cronbach's alpha in Table 4.1). As for the single-factor structure in the case of Germany

---

1 I have also tried two alternatives. For the first variant I have dichotomized the trust variables so that the 'don't know' answers were collated to the group of people who stated that they tend not to trust. For the second alternative I have recoded the original trust variables as follows: +1 = 'tend to trust', 0 = 'don't know', –1 = 'tend not to trust'. Both alternatives, however, generated a less stable factor structure, which has also shown a lower binding of variance.

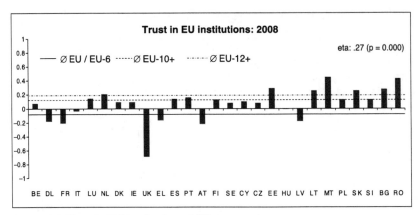

Figure 4.6 Trust in EU institutions, 2008 (z-scores)

Data source: EB 70.1.

and Malta, there is also a good reliability given a Cronbach's alpha of 0.89 for Germany and 0.96 for Malta.

Figure 4.6 reveals that citizens' trust in EU institutions significantly differs between the 27 member states. The EU institutions are most trusted in Malta and Romania. But also Bulgaria, Estonia, Lithuania and Slovakia show high levels of citizen trust in EU institutions. In contrast, public trust in EU institutions is below EU average in Austria, Germany, Greece, France, Latvia and, most notably, the UK. Hence, Figure 4.6 provides a preliminary reference point for testing the main hypothesis of this chapter at the aggregate level of analysis: if citizens' trust in EU institutions actually has a bearing on citizens' willingness to accept a transfer of policy authority from the national to the supranational level, we should find that Austrian, German, Greek, French, Latvian and UK citizens are more reluctant to support a shift of policy authority to the EU than other EU citizens. In contrast, the publics from Bulgaria, Estonia, Lithuania, Malta, Romania and Slovakia should tend to be more open-minded than other EU citizens when it comes to endorse a transfer of policy authority from the national to the EU level. This suggestion, however, does not say anything about how institutional trust does affect the preferred policy authority of individual EU citizens.

Before I examine the main hypothesis, however, I will take the second step I have named at the outset of this section. The bi-annual standard *Eurobarometer* regularly comprises EU citizens' attitudes on a policy transfer from the national to the European level. In autumn 2008, for instance, people could say for 20 policy areas whether decisions in these fields should be made by their national government or jointly within the European Union. The latter is tantamount to a shift of policy authority to EU institutions, and the EU citizens seem to have a certain idea about which level should be responsible for several policy areas. This interpretation holds, at least, when we take the

Table 4.2 Factor analysis: preferred policy authority at the national and European level, 2008 (principal component analysis: varimax rotation)

	F I	F II
Fighting terrorism	0.799	0.044
Protecting the environment	0.675	0.201
Scientific and technological research	0.674	0.141
Defence and foreign affairs	0.667	0.179
Energy	0.647	0.270
Fighting crime	0.613	0.271
Immigration	0.612	0.239
Pensions	0.133	0.808
Social welfare	0.205	0.776
Health	0.238	0.756
Taxation	0.194	0.740
The educational system	0.247	0.696
Eigenvalue	3.38	3.15
Explanation of variance per factor (in %)	28.1	26.3
Total explanation of variance (in %)	54.4	
KMO	0.910 (p = 0.000)	
Cronbach's alpha	0.82	0.84

Data source: EB 70.1.

number of 'don't know' answers as an indicator for the mere existence of an opinion. In contrast to the results on trust in EU institutions I have reported above, citizens have far more seldom given a 'don't know' answer.[2]

Again, I have computed a factor analysis using a principal component analysis in order to reduce the data's complexity. Table 4.2 offers the results of an optimized factor analysis which generated the most stable factor structure. Given the two-factor structure, EU citizens obviously distinguish between several policy areas. This result confirms previous research, which not only classified diverse policy fields according to their degree of Europeanization, cross-border scope and distributional relevance, but also found several dimensions of policy areas in Europeans' minds (Eichenberg and Dalton 2007: 141; Trüdinger 2009: 139, 141; Weßels 2004). Hence, the interesting question arises whether I will find evidence for my main hypothesis regardless of the specific character of different policy domains.

2 Certainly, the number of 'don't know' answers is not sufficient to reliably assess the level of sophistication of public opinions. That is, high proportions of valid answers might also result from so-called non-attitudes (Converse 1974). Comparing the 'don't know' answers regarding citizens' trust in EU institutions and the level of policy authority nonetheless suggests that EU citizens' attitudes are far more present in the latter case. One reason might be that the question on policy authority does not solely refer to the European level but also to the national one, which is generally closer to the people's mind.

Based on the results of the factor analysis, I have scaled two additive indices. The first index includes the following policy areas: fighting terrorism, protecting the environment, scientific and technological research, defence and foreign affairs, energy, fighting crime and immigration. Given the character of most of these policy fields, I have labelled this index 'cross-border problems'. The scale has been recoded with value labels from 1 up to 7. The lower the value, the more people want to conserve policy authority at the national level; the higher the value, the more citizens believe that cross-border problems should be governed jointly within the EU.

The second index I have scaled comprehends five policy areas, namely pensions, social welfare, health, taxation and the educational system. It is typical for these policy areas that they unfold distributive and redistributive consequences. Furthermore, the educational system is tangent to issues of national collective identity. Simplifying, I have named the second index 'welfare and identity issues'. After recoding the value labels from 1 up to 5, lower values mean that people favour national policy authority for this policy bundle while higher values indicate a preference for supranational decision-making.

Figure 4.7 illustrates the preferred policy competence for both groups of issues across all 27 member states. At least three results are striking. First, Europeans' attitudes clearly vary between the 27 EU countries. This holds for both the cross-border problems (eta: 0.26, p=0.000) and the welfare and identity issues (eta: 0.24, p=0.000), even though the variance is somewhat stronger in the former case. Concerning cross-border problems, however, there is only a minor country variance in the EU6 (eta: 0.08, p=0.000) and the group of the 12 newcomers (eta: 0.10, p=0.000). The strongest variance across countries can be found in the EU15. Here, Europeans more strongly disagree about the preferred policy authority for cross-border problems (eta: 0.28, p=0.000) as well as welfare issues (eta: 0.25, p=0.000).

Second, the public's support for EU harmonization of the distinct packages of issues reveals a disparate rather than a clear picture across the 27 EU

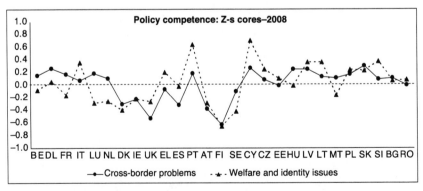

Figure 4.7 Preferred policy competence, 2008

Data source: EB 70.1.

countries. In eight member states, the populace tends to show more approval for supranational decision-making in policy areas of cross-border problems than for EU harmonization of welfare and identity issues. In nine EU countries it is the converse case and in ten member states it makes no or hardly any difference. Hence, the increased heterogeneity of the European Union is once again reflected in these results. It is notable, however, that I cannot observe a specific gap between the old member states and the newcomers of the enlargement rounds in 2004 and 2007. Instead, there seems to be a complicated pattern of cross-cutting divides across old and new 'club members'. As for the welfare and identity issues, for example, the new member states – with the exception of Malta – tend to be more supportive of supranational decision-making than many of the old EU countries. However, the populace of Greece, Italy and especially Portugal similarly tends to prefer EU decisions in welfare politics. These findings suggest that the level of Europeans' support for supranational governance is partly influenced by context effects such as the countries' economic prosperity, social development and overall living conditions. Since it is not my concern in this chapter to explain country differences of this kind (see, however, Weßels 2004: 260–5), I cede this finding to future research on this topic.

The third insight of Figure 4.7 refers to my main hypothesis. As for the aggregate level of country analysis, the descriptive results raise some doubts that the hypothesis holds in general. Remembering the findings on country levels of citizen trust in European institutions, we should see that Austrian, German, Greek, French, Latvian and UK citizens are more reluctant to support a transfer of policy competence from the national to the European level than their fellow EU citizens. In contrast, the populace from Bulgaria, Estonia, Lithuania, Malta, Romania and Slovakia should endorse supranational decision-making more than other EU publics. These assumptions, however, are not confirmed for each country. Actually, the Austrian and UK populations are among the most reluctant EU publics concerning a shift of policy competence to European institutions. The Danish and Finnish publics are similarly sceptical, though. Furthermore, the German, Greek and French populations do not generally reject supranational decision-making more often than other EU citizens. As for the highest levels of citizen trust in European institutions, the populace of Malta is relatively reluctant to accept supranational decision-making in welfare politics.

Hence, I come to the final step of my empirical analysis. Starting with the aggregate level of analysis, I only partially found evidence that citizens' willingness to accept a shift of policy authority to the supranational level is contingent upon their trust in EU institutions. With regard to cross-border problems, there is a fair correlation ($r=0.41$, $p<0.05$) while citizen trust in European institutions does not significantly affect the public's support of supranational decision-making in welfare politics ($r=0.23$, not significant). These results confirm the impression from the descriptive aggregate data analysis whereupon the main hypothesis does not seem to hold in general.

Table 4.3 Bivariate correlation between preferred level of policy competence and citizen assessment of the EU's democraticness (r; n=29)

Cross-border problems	0.60**
Welfare and identity issues	0.53**

Data source: EB 70.1.

That is, a country's level of citizen trust in EU institutions does not necessarily have a bearing on the public's approval for supranational decision-making. Instead, the widespread citizen belief in the democratic character of the EU seems to play a greater role (see Table 4.3). That is, the more the population of an EU country perceive the European Union as democratic, the more prevalent is the willingness in the populace to accept supranational decision-making for cross-border problems as well as welfare and identity issues.

This result is important for two reasons: first, it makes clear that the discussion on the 'democratic deficit' of the European Union is no longer a mere academic debate. To the contrary, the results of Table 4.3 demonstrate that citizens' perception of the EU as democratic does matter. Second, the results also suggest that, in future, it might be increasingly difficult to ensure the EU's 'output legitimacy' without improving the preconditions for its 'input legitimacy'. The EU's problem-solving capacity rests on the functional need for transferring policy competence to the EU in order to effectively cope with certain problems. However, implementing a shift of policy authority to the supranational level against the will of the people is not possible without the risk of high political costs, such as a rise in Eurosceptical moods, the rejection of important treaty revisions by popular vote or a loss of voter support in national elections. Hence, as long as a population's approval for transferring policy authority to the EU correlates with the common assessment of the EU's 'democraticness', the EU's system effectiveness also depends on its democratic legitimacy.

A shift to the individual level of analysis brings about findings akin to the aggregate level of analysis. That is, also at the individual level of analysis the evidence for my main hypothesis is rather mixed across the 27 EU countries. Table 4.4 documents the correlation coefficients for both policy domains. Starting with the cross-border problems, in almost all 27 member states citizens' trust in European institutions significantly correlates with people's willingness to accept supranational decision-making. The sole exception is Spain. In Austria, Greece, Ireland and the UK, there is a particularly strong correlation, while in Belgium, Finland, Estonia and Luxembourg the relationship is rather weak. As for the welfare and identity issues, the picture is somewhat different again. In five member states, namely in Belgium, Estonia, Finland, Luxembourg and Portugal, citizens do not significantly tend to endorse supranational decision-making in welfare politics when they also tend to trust EU institutions. In contrast, I found the strongest correlation of this kind in Cyprus, Austria, Greece, Slovenia and the UK.

Table 4.4 Bivariate correlation between preferred level of policy competence and citizens' trust in European institutions (trust index) (r)

	Cross-border problems	Welfare and identity issues		Cross-border problems	Welfare and identity issues
Belgium	0.09*	n.s.	Cyprus	0.28***	0.24***
Germany	0.20***	0.21***	Czech Republic	0.30***	0.24***
France	0.30***	0.08*	Estonia	0.11**	n.s.
Italy	0.15***	0.09*	Hungary	0.19***	0.08*
Luxembourg	0.11*	n.s.	Latvia	0.14***	0.11**
The Netherlands	0.25***	0.11**	Lithuania	0.16***	0.15***
Denmark	0.30***	0.16***	Malta	0.16**	0.18**
United Kingdom (UK)	0.40***	0.33***	Poland	0.28***	0.14**
Ireland	0.38***	0.13**	Slovakia	0.26***	0.14**
Greece	0.35***	0.30***	Slovenia	0.33***	0.21***
Portugal	0.19***	n.s.	Bulgaria	0.31***	0.14**
Spain	n.s.	0.09*	Romania	0.24***	0.19***
Austria	0.47***	0.27***	EU27	0.25***	0.17***
Finland	0.13***	n.s.	EU6	0.20***	0.12***
Sweden	0.21**	0.09	EU+	0.25***	0.15***

Data source: EB 70.1.

***p<0.001; **p<0.01; *p<0.05.

Although there is some evidence corroborating the main hypothesis, the results are based on bivariate correlations so far. In order to test the robustness of this finding, I finally present the results of an optimized OLS-regression model for both issue areas (see Tables 4.5 and 4.6). Accordingly, I have added four control variables. The first indicator measures whether citizens think that their country has benefited from its membership in the European Union. I assume people tend to support supranational decision-making only if they also tend to believe that their country has benefited from being an EU member. In other words, Europeans tend to support a shift of policy authority to the European level only if they positively evaluate the EU's output in terms of advantages for their own nation state.

As I have argued in the introduction of this chapter, there is a tense, often conflicting relationship between deepening the European unification and the EU's enlargement process. Accordingly, I have added a second variable referring to the statement that the EU has grown too rapidly. Given a potential conflict between the two distinct modes of integration, I suppose that people are rather reluctant to support supranational decision-making if they tend to agree with this statement.

The third variable refers to how citizens assess the extent of EU policy competence. The citizens could choose between two options: (a) 'There are too many areas where the EU can take decisions;' and (b) 'There are not enough areas where the EU can take decisions.' Another spontaneously formulated statement was as follows: 'The number of areas where the EU can take decisions is about right.' I assume that the more people think that there are not enough areas governed by the EU, the more they also tend to accept supranational decision-making.

The final variable refers to citizens' idea of the European Union concerning its democratic character (see the Appendix at the end of this chapter). As I have argued above, trust is always based on certain expectations of the one who trusts. Since Europeans are citizens of democratic nation states, it would not be plausible to expect that they do not care about the 'democraticness' of the European Union when it comes to a transfer of policy authority from the national to the European level. Put differently, I argue that people expect EU institutions – among others – to be democratic. I therefore assume that citizens who question the democratic character of the EU tend to be reluctant concerning supranational decision-making.

Table 4.5 documents the results referring to cross-border problems. In the average of all 27 member states, trust hardly affects citizens' support for their preference of supranational decision-making. However, this effect is stronger for the average of the 12 newcomers. In the average of the older member states it is more important whether people think that their country has benefited from being an EU member, how they assess the extent of the EU's decision competence and whether they believe that the European Union is democratic. Looking at country differences, I will not go in detail. It is interesting, however, that also at the individual level of analysis the main hypothesis was falsified in 9 out of 27 member states, including Belgium, Estonia, Finland, Germany, Italy, Latvia, Luxembourg, Malta and Sweden. I have again found a strong effect in Austria, Greece and the UK, but also in Bulgaria, Poland and Slovenia. In many countries, however, citizens' evaluation of the EU's output is far more important for their willingness to accept supranational decision-making. That is, if people are convinced that their country has benefited from being an EU member, they also tend to willingly accept a transfer of policy competence to govern cross-border problems at the supranational level. Hence, citizens' attitudes towards supranational decision-making concerning cross-border problems are frequently instrumentally driven. Trust in EU institutions is nonetheless *indirectly* important since it strongly correlates, in general, with output evaluation (not shown in table form). In fact, Barroso's idea of a 'Europe of results' seems to be partly suited for strengthening Europeans' trust in EU institutions. Yet, in several countries, such as Luxembourg and Sweden or Cyprus, Hungary and Slovakia, citizens' willingness to accept supranational decision-making also depends on their belief in the 'democraticness' of the EU. Here, people are less willing to support a policy transfer to the European level when they question the democratic character of the European Union. This result confirms the argument above that the scholarly discussion on the EU's democratic deficit is not a sheer academic debate any more.

Table 4.5 Preferred level of policy competence for cross-border problems (OLS regression model; entries are B-coefficients)

	Trust in EU institutions	EU membership: country benefit	Building Europe: grown too rapidly	Assessing degree of EU's decision competence	EU concept: democratic	Constant	R^2	N
Belgium	n.s.	−0.22**	n.s.	n.s.	−0.09*	6.92***	0.07	741
Germany	n.s.	−0.18***	n.s.	n.s.	−0.10**	6.62***	0.08	817
France	0.16**	−0.14**	n.s.	0.11**	−0.11*	5.85***	0.15	564
Italy	n.s.	−0.10*	0.18***	0.13**	n.s.	4.18***	0.10	467
Luxembourg	n.s.	−0.25***	n.s.	n.s.	−0.18***	7.47***	0.11	265
The Netherlands	0.19***	n.s.	n.s.	0.11**	n.s.	4.71***	0.08	630
Denmark	0.12*	−0.22***	0.14**	0.15***	n.s.	5.08***	0.19	614
UK	0.21***	−0.15**	0.11*	0.15***	n.s.	4.24***	0.25	539
Ireland	0.18***	−0.19***	0.16**	0.10*	n.s.	4.54***	0.19	423
Greece	0.24***	−0.13**	0.12***	n.s.	n.s.	4.18***	0.15	926
Portugal	0.11*	−0.11*	n.s.	n.s.	−0.11*	6.85***	0.07	437
Spain	−0.11*	−0.16**	n.s.	n.s.	−0.11*	7.71***	0.13	423
Austria	0.32***	−0.17***	n.s.	0.26***	n.s.	4.08***	0.26	588
Finland	n.s.	−0.20***	0.10*	n.s.	n.s.	3.81***	0.06	662
Sweden	n.s	−0.14*	n.s.	n.s.	−0.24***	6.47***	0.14	294
Cyprus	0.19**	n.s.	n.s.	n.s.	−0.17*	6.14***	0.12	254
Czech Republic	0.16***	−0.14**	n.s.	n.s.	−0.10*	5.34***	0.13	677
Estonia	n.s.	n.s.	n.s.	n.s.	−0.11*	5.44***	0.02	501
Hungary	0.12*	n.s.	n.s.	−0.11*	−0.17**	5.92***	0.06	546
Latvia	n.s.	n.s.	n.s.	n.s.	−0.11*	5.80***	0.06	492
Lithuania	0.11*	−0.11*	n.s.	n.s.	−0.11*	5.58***	0.06	409
Malta	n.s.	−0.25**	n.s.	n.s.	n.s.	7.99***	0.10	197
Poland	0.19**	n.s.	0.12*	n.s.	n.s.	4.20***	0.10	363
Slovakia	0.14**	−0.19***	n.s.	n.s.	−0.16***	6.70***	0.14	665
Slovenia	0.19***	−0.16***	0.11**	0.10*	−0.10*	5.24***	0.19	695
Bulgaria	0.31***	n.s.	0.14**	n.s.	n.s.	2.82***	0.03	322
Romania	0.18**	n.s.	n.s.	0.12*	n.s.	4.03***	0.09	301
EU27	0.10***	−0.14***	0.05***	0.11***	−0.11***	5.78***	0.12	1,2894
EU6	0.07***	−0.15***	0.05***	0.07***	−0.10***	6.15***	0.08	2,982
EU+	0.18***	−0.06**	0.07***	n.s.	−0.06***	4.60***	.07	4,647

Data source: EB 70.1.

***p<0.001; **p<0.01; *p<0.05.

Table 4.6 Preferred level of policy competence for welfare and identity issues (OLS regression model; entries are B-coefficients)

	Trust in EU institutions	EU membership: country benefit	Building Europe: grown too rapidly	Assessing degree of EU's decision competence	EU concept: democratic	Constant	R^2	N
Belgium	n.s.	n.s.	0.10**	0.17***	n.s.	1.52***	0.05	741
Germany	0.15***	−0.15***	n.s.	0.07*	n.s.	2.02***	0.08	823
France	n.s.	n.s.	n.s.	0.16***	n.s.	1.62**	0.05	567
Italy	n.s.	n.s.	0.17***	0.12*	n.s.	1.88**	0.06	472
Luxembourg	n.s.	n.s.	0.13*	n.s.	n.s.	n.s.	0.03	269
The Netherlands	0.11*	n.s.	n.s.	0.19***	n.s.	n.s.	0.06	634
Denmark	n.s.	n.s.	n.s.	0.18***	−0.10*	0.80*	0.08	620
UK	0.22***	n.s.	n.s.	0.22***	n.s.	n.s.	0.18	547
Ireland	0.11*	n.s.	n.s.	0.26***	0.15**	n.s.	0.11	425
Greece	0.17***	−0.10*	0.15***	n.s.	n.s.	1.52	0.12	930
Portugal	n.s.	n.s.	n.s.	n.s.	n.s.	3.02***	0.00	437
Spain	n.s.	−0.13*	n.s.	0.16**	n.s.	2.43	0.04	429
Austria	n.s.	n.s.	0.14**	0.13**	−0.10*	1.26**	0.15	598
Finland	n.s.	−0.10*	n.s.	n.s	n.s.	0.68**	0.03	673
Sweden	n.s.	n.s.	n.s.	0.32***	n.s.	1.51**	0.13	299
Cyprus	0.17*	n.s.	n.s.	0.14*	n.s.	3.40***	0.08	236
Czech Republic	0.14**	n.s.	n.s.	0.15***	−0.11**	2.37***	0.09	677
Estonia	n.s.	n.s.	n.s.	0.12**	n.s.	2.18***	0.02	499
Hungary	n.s.	n.s.	n.s.	0.10*	n.s.	1.59***	0.01	541
Latvia	n.s.	n.s.	n.s.	n.s.	−0.10*	2.47***	0.03	494
Lithuania	0.11*	n.s.	n.s.	n.s.	n.s.	2.17***	0.05	413
Malta	n.s.	n.s.	n.s.	0.23**	n.s.	n.s.	0.08	199
Poland	n.s.	n.s.	n.s.	n.s.	n.s.	2.63***	0.03	368
Slovakia	n.s.	n.s.	n.s.	n.s.	−0.10*	2.80***	0.03	670
Slovenia	0.11**	n.s.	n.s.	n.s.	−0.16***	2.76***	0.09	701
Bulgaria	n.s.	n.s.	n.s.	n.s.	−0.14*	1.91**	0.04	327
Romania	0.15**	n.s.	n.s.	n.s.	n.s.	n.s.	0.04	310
EU27	0.08***	−0.08***	0.08***	0.12***	−0.05***	1.71***	0.07	13,013
EU6	0.05*	−0.07***	0.11***	0.13***	n.s.	1.53***	0.06	2,999
EU+	0.06***	−0.06***	0.04**	0.06***	−0.06***	2.16***	0.03	4,688

Data source: EB 70.1.

***p<0.001; **p<0.01; *p<0.05.

Given the results of Table 4.6, the picture is fundamentally different when it comes to welfare and identity issues. Based on the averages of all 27 EU states as well as the groups of older and newer member states, there is just a slight impact of citizens' institutional trust on citizens' approval for supranational policy competence in welfare politics. It is also of minor importance how people think about their country's benefit from being an EU member and how they perceive the democratic quality of the European Union. Instead, I have found the strongest influence for citizens' assessment of the current degree of supranational decision-making. If people think that there are not enough areas where the EU can take decisions, they also tend to accept a shift of policy authority to the EU level in the domain of welfare and identity issues. To my interpretation, this is also a kind of output evaluation stemming from citizens' positive experiences with supranational decision-making. Accordingly, it makes absolute sense to think that there are not enough areas where the EU can take decisions when I have generally made a positive experience with supranational decision-making. In this case, I might even accept a shift of policy authority to the European level when it comes to policies with redistributive consequences. This interpretation is also supported by the data. In almost all countries where I found the aforementioned correlation, there is also a correlation between how citizens evaluate their country's benefit from EU membership and how they assess the current degree of the EU's decision competence (not shown in table form). That is, if people tend to believe that their country has benefited from being an EU member they also tend to think that the EU's room for decision-making is not broad enough. I have found the strongest correlation of this kind in the UK ($r=0.32$, $p=0.000$) and Sweden ($r=0.26$, $p=0.000$); the exceptions are Spain and Malta.

Finally, in three countries, namely in Austria, Greece and Italy, some people tend to be against supranational decision-making in welfare politics when they also believe that the building of Europe has grown too rapidly. These citizens apparently see a conflict between deepening the integration process and enlarging the European Union, at least when it comes to problems of national identity and issues with distributive and redistributive consequences.

Summing up the main results of the empirical analyses, I would like to highlight four insights. First, based on the standard *Eurobarometer* data from 2008, I did not observe strong confirmation for the main hypothesis of this chapter. Even though there is some evidence at the aggregate level of analysis that the extent of citizen trust in EU institutions affects the degree of citizen approval for supranational decision-making concerning cross-border problems, it did not hold for welfare and identity issues. Second, the overall impression of the European Union as democratic has shown a far stronger effect on people's willingness to accept a shift of policy authority to the European level for both issue domains. Third, at the individual level of analysis, there is a mixed corroboration for the main hypothesis across countries and depending on the problems in question. I found quite strong evidence for the main hypothesis with regard to cross-border problems in some countries, especially in Austria, Greece and the UK. In 9 out of 27 member states, however, the hypothesis was falsified. When it comes to welfare and identity issues, it was hardly significant for someone's acceptance of supranational decision-making whether she or he tends to trust EU institutions. Instead, attitudinal dissimilarities were based on a clash between supporter and objectors of deepening European integration furthermore. Fourth, the results generally suggest that citizens' support for supranational decision-making is first and foremost instrumentally driven.

Conclusion

What can we learn from the presented empirical findings with regard to the book's main interest in civic resources? At first glance, it seems that citizens' trust in EU institutions is of minor importance or even irrelevant for people's willingness to accept a shift of policy authority from the national to the supranational level. According to these findings, Europeans' trust in EU institutions is hardly able to serve as a civic resource for strengthening the output-legitimacy of the European Union in that citizens willingly accept further policy transfer to the supranational level. I argue, however, that the poor results of the third section do not necessarily prove a falsification of the trust hypothesis and that we need further research on this question. First of all, we need to improve the operationalization and measurement of trust in institutions.

Trust – understood as a transfer of control to others – is always contingent upon expectations and experiences. When we do not expect anything from others or a given institution, we cannot be disappointed. Otherwise, transferring control to others or an institution without any expectation or despite bad experiences is foolish since we knowingly accept betrayal. The empirical evidence of the third section suggests that many European citizens do have expectations concerning EU institutions. They expect from EU governance, for example, some benefit for their country and that they are on the winning side of the European integration process. Another expectation, at least for some publics in various member states, is that the European Union is democratic in character. That is, if a populace commonly questions the EU's 'democraticness', it also tends to be against supranational decision-making.

According to these results, I suggest finding another way to operationalize institutional trust, above all, trust in institutions which are so far from citizens' awareness, interest and knowledge. By asking people whether they tend to trust or not trust EU institutions, we do not know at all what they have in mind when they give their answers. In order to learn more about institutional trust I therefore propose to look for answers to at least three questions (see also Kaina 2008: 423): first, what do people expect from the institutions in question? Second, which principles, norms and values justify those expectations? And finally, in what way do people consider these expectations unfulfilled, and how do these disappointments affect people's confidence in the given institutions?

Appendix

EU membership: country benefit

Question wording: 'Taking everything into account, would you say that (OUR COUNTRY) has on balance benefited or not from being a member of the European Union?'

1 = benefited, 2 = not benefited. Don't know = missing value.

Building Europe: grown too rapidly

Question wording: 'Can you tell me whether you agree or disagree with the following statements regarding the building of Europe? – The EU has grown too rapidly.'

1 = totally agree, 2 = tend to agree, 3 = tend to disagree, 4 = totally disagree. Don't know = missing value.

Assessing degree of EU's decision competence

Question wording: 'Personally, regarding the areas where the European Union can take decisions, which opinion comes closest to your view?'

The original variable was recoded as follows: −1 = there are too many areas where the EU can take decisions; 0 = the number of areas where the EU can take decisions is about right (spontaneous); +1 = there are not enough areas where the EU can take decisions. Don't know = missing value.

EU concept: democratic

Question wording: 'Please tell for each of the following words if it describes very well, fairly well, fairly badly or very badly the idea you might have of the European Union – democratic.'

1 = describes very well, 2 = describes fairly well, 3 = describes fairly badly, 4 = describes very badly. Don't know = missing value.

References

Bach, M. 1999. *Die Bürokratisierung Europas. Verwaltungseliten, Experten und politische Legitimation in Europa*. Frankfurt/M.: Campus Verlag.

Bach, M. 2000. 'Die Europäisierung der nationalen Gesellschaft? Problemstellungen und Perspektiven einer Soziologie der europäischen Integration', in: M. Bach (ed.) *Die Europäisierung nationaler Gesellschaften*. Opladen: Westdeutscher Verlag, 11–35.

Coleman, J. S. 1988. 'Social capital in the creation of human capital', in: C. Winship and S. Rosen (eds) *Organizations and institutions: sociological and economic* approaches to the analysis of social structure, special issue of the American Journal of Sociology 94(supplement): 95–120.

Converse, P. E. 1974. 'Comment: the status of non-attitudes', *American Political Science Review* 68(2): 650–60.

Dahl, R. A. 1994. 'A democratic dilemma: system effectiveness versus citizen participation', *Political Science Quarterly* 109(1): 23–34.

Decker, F. 2002. 'Governance beyond the nation-state: reflections on the democratic deficit of the European Union', *Journal of European Public Policy* 9(2): 256–72.

Eichenberg, R. C. and Dalton, R. J. 2007. 'Post-Maastricht blues: the transformation of citizen support for European integration, 1973–2004', *Acta Politica* 42(2–3): 128–52.

Fuchs, D., Magni-Berton, R. and Roger, A. (eds) 2009. *Euroscepticism: images of Europe among mass publics and political elites*. Opladen and Farmington Hills, MI: Barbara Budrich Publishers.

Hardin, R. 2006. *Trust*. Cambridge and Malden, MA: Polity Press.

Hooghe, L. and Marks, G. 2009. 'A postfunctionalist theory of European integration: from permissive consensus to constraining dissensus', *British Journal of Political Science* 39(1): 1–23.

Ipsen, H. P. 1972. *Europäisches Gemeinschaftsrecht*. Tübingen: Mohr.

Jachtenfuchs, M. 2000. 'Die Problemlösungsfähigkeit der EU: Begriffe, Befunde, Erklärungen', in: E. Grande and M. Jachtenfuchs (eds) *Wie problemlösungsfähig ist die EU? Regieren im europäischen Mehrebenensystem*. Baden-Baden: Nomos, 345–56.

Kaina, V. 2008. 'Declining trust in elites and why we should worry about it – with empirical evidence from Germany', *Government and Opposition* 43(3): 405–23.

Kaina, V. 2009. *Wir in Europa. Kollektive Identität und Demokratie in der Europäischen Union*. Wiesbaden: VS Verlag für Sozialwissenschaften.

Kaina, V. and Karolewski, I.P. 2009. 'EU governance and European identity', *Living Reviews in European Governance*, 4(2) [online article], http://europeangovernance.livingreviews.org/Articles/lreg-2009-2/ (accessed 13 December 2010).

Kohler-Koch, B. 1999. 'The evolution and transformation of European governance', in: B. Kohler-Koch and R. Eising (eds) *The transformation of governance in the European Union*. London: Routledge, 14–35.

Laffan, B. 1998. 'The European Union: a distinctive model of internationalization', *Journal of European Public Policy* 5(2): 235–53.

Levi, M. and Stoker, L. 2000. 'Political trust and trustworthiness', *Annual Review of Political Science* 3(1): 475–507.

Luhmann, N. 1979. *Trust and power: two works by Niklas Luhmann*. Chichester: John Wiley and Sons.

Luhmann, N. 1989 [1968]. *Vertrauen. Ein Mechanismus der Reduktion sozialer Komplexität*. Stuttgart: Ferdinand Enke.

Marks, G., Hooghe, L. and Blank, K. 1996. 'European integration from the 1980s: state-centric v. multi-level governance', *Journal of Common Market Studies* 34(3): 341–78.

McLaren, L. M. 2007. 'Explaining mass-level Euroscepticism: identity, interests, and institutional distrust', *Acta Politica* 42(2–3): 233–51.

Mitrany, D. 1966. *A working peace system*. Chicago: Quadrangle Books.

Niedermayer, O. 1995. 'Trends and contrasts', in: O. Niedermayer and R. Sinnott (eds) *Public opinion and internationalized governance: beliefs in government, Vol. 2*. Oxford and New York: Oxford University Press, 53–72.

Scharpf, F. W. 1999. *Governing in Europe: effective und democratic?* Oxford: Oxford University Press.
Schmalz-Bruns, R. 2002. 'Vertrauen in Vertrauen? Ein konzeptioneller Aufriss des Verhältnisses von Politik und Vertrauen', in: R. Schmalz-Bruns and R. Zintl (eds) *Politisches Vertrauen. Soziale Grundlagen reflexiver Kooperation.* Baden-Baden: Nomos, 9–35.
Schneeberger, A. 1982. 'Vertrauen als Eigenschaft von Interaktionssystemen. Entwurf eines theoretischen Bezugsrahmens', *Angewandte Sozialforschung* 10(3): 301–7.
Stone Sweet, A. and Sandholtz, W. 1997. 'European integration and supranational governance', *Journal of European Public Policy* 4(3): 297–317.
Stone Sweet, A., Sandholtz, W. and Fligstein, N. (eds) 2001. *The institutionalization of Europe.* Oxford and New York: Oxford University Press.
Thomas, D. C. 2006. 'Constitutionalization through enlargement: the contested origins of the EU's democratic identity', *Journal of European Public Policy* 13(8): 1190–210.
Trüdinger, E.-M. 2009. 'Have they gone too far? Attitudes towards the transfer of politics on the EU level', in: D. Fuchs, R. Magni-Berton and A. Roger (eds) *Euroscepticism: images of Europe among mass publics and political elites.* Opladen and Farmington Hills, MI: Barbara Budrich Publishers, 135–55.
Vobruba, G. 2003. 'The enlargement crisis of the European Union: limits of the dialectics of integration and expansion', *Journal of European Social Policy* 13(1): 35–62.
Vobruba, G. 2007. *Die Dynamik Europas.* 2nd ed. Wiesbaden: VS Verlag für Sozialwissenschaften.
Weßels, B. 2004. 'Staatsaufgaben: gewünschte Entscheidungsebene für acht Politikbereiche', in: J. W. van Deth (ed.) *Deutschland in Europa.* Wiesbaden: VS Verlag für Sozialwissenschaften, 257–73.
Weßels, B. 2007. 'Discontent and European identity: three types of Euroscepticism', *Acta Politica* 42(2–3): 287–306.
Weßels, B. 2009a. 'Spielarten des Euroskeptizismus', in: F. Decker and M. Höreth (eds) *Die Verfassung Europas. Perspektiven des Integrationsprojekts.* Wiesbaden: VS Verlag für Sozialwissenschaften, 50–68.
Weßels, B. 2009b. 'Trust in political institutions', in J. Thomassen (ed.) *The legitimacy of the European Union after enlargement.* New York: Oxford University Press, 165–83.

Part II
Civic resources, recognition and citizenship

5 Civic resources for European democracy in Central and Eastern Europe

Matthew Loveless

Introduction

As of 2007, Bulgaria and Romania have joined the European Union (EU) following the 2004 eastern enlargement that brought Central, Eastern and Baltic Europe in as members. Yet, studies of popular support for the EU have struggled with the nagging perception that it suffers from a 'democratic deficit', in new and old member states alike (Rohrschneider 2002; Rohrschneider and Loveless 2010). While a large literature exists to understand this, an emerging strand concerns itself with the nature and extent of national democratic culture as a resource for maintaining long-term EU support. This chapter seeks to deepen our understanding of this process by focusing on trust and solidarity as both core elements of democratic political values and potential resources for EU support. This inquiry is underpinned by the notion that trusting, inclusive citizens are the foundation for social cohesion and community and thus are more likely to extend optimism and goodwill beyond themselves, their country and beyond (Almond and Verba 1963; Putnam 1993), including the ongoing European experiment.

I seek to address three specific questions here. First, do more trusting and inclusive societies and individuals demonstrate higher support for the EU? Second, if so, what are the sources of this trust and inclusiveness? And finally, do these sources of trust and inclusiveness directly influence support for the EU? In asking these questions, we hope to identify national, civic resources of political cultures that can provide a bulwark to the ebb of support for EU membership in Central and Eastern Europe (CEE).

The question of support for the EU is an important question, particularly for the newest member states. However, for CEE, the literature associated with this question has largely limited itself to narrow, economic self-interest or broad ideological congruence to explain individuals' support. While significant and worthy of continued investigation, we should be curious as to alternative sources, such as broader democratic political values, that also bring support to the EU. As such, this research looks at the large literature on social capital as the starting point for identifying some of these alternative sources.

The appreciation of social capital is neither new nor groundbreaking; however, just as political cultures vary across countries, so do the content and volume of social capital. The discussion below is a brief survey of the most relevant work on social capital, considering civic resources specifically as candidates for EU support. Further, I return to the original conceptualization from Coleman (1988) to reconsider what might have been overlooked.

Taken together, this contributes to our understanding of both social capital and the bases of support for the EU. For Eastern Europeans, trust is arguably a larger leap of faith than citizens of more mature democracies. Citizens wanting to participate in the political action space must trust the function of the institutions and the actions of the other citizens in their community. Each attempt to participate is crucial to the lessening or deepening of social capital as successful contact with both the community and institutions promotes iterated action, and broader democratic support (Boix and Posner 1998). Thus, this chapter attempts to identify the 'homegrown' sources of democratic political culture that extend to support for the EU.

However, using new mass public surveys from 2007 in CEE, the findings here suggest that while various forms of civic engagement play important, if differential, roles in explaining social capital and that social capital exerts an independent influence on support for the EU, the findings also demonstrate a lack of empirical linkage between these forms of civic engagement and support for the EU in CEE. The implication is twofold. On the one hand, the increased theoretical precision of social capital theory finds empirical support as trusting and inclusive societies are more supportive of the EU at both the aggregate and individual levels. On the other hand, however, 'schools of democracy', as civic resources, fail as candidates for the potential mechanism through which trust and inclusiveness – as indicators of social capital – translate support for the EU.

This chapter first introduces the theory of support for the EU and social capital as they pertain to CEE. It then merges these with research on these topics in the region to create a set of testable hypotheses. These hypotheses are then tested against new survey data from the European Union member states in CEE. I then conclude as to the effect of enlarging our search for determinants of social capital and cohesion as they pertain to support for the EU in CEE.

Social capital as civic resources

Analyses of pre-EU membership CEE have resulted in conflicting findings that contrast the utilitarian approach with ideological congruency on the free market and democracy as determinants of EU support. Utilitarianism is an extension of individuals' social location and the perceptions of their own economic experience and expectations in their respective market economies to support for EU membership (Tucker *et al.* 2002). Others present evidence that this approach is not only misplaced but not reproducible in other analyses (Rohrschneider and Whitefield 2004, 2006), suggesting instead that ideological congruence between individuals and the underlying principles of the EU, namely democratic governance and market economies, are the mechanism of support. However, if we broaden our search of determinants of EU support beyond general economic concerns and ideological congruence, what other sources of democratic political values are candidates for consideration?

At the broadest level, congruence between the form of governance and mass opinion is paramount, although a multifaceted relationship. An aggregation of individuals' political attitudes (whether positive or negative) is a substantial component of political culture and political culture includes the diffuse support of political institutions or the political system as a whole. Within the literature, the empirical referents for these attitudes vary widely and support may require both the behavioural and attitudinal components to be combined. It is here that social capital research can contribute to our conceptualization of this relationship. Individuals' engagement with groups and others outside the home (as behaviour) as a means to develop both collective orientations and trust (as attitudes) serves as an example of how social capital links the relationship between political culture (as attitudes and behaviours) and regime support.

Putnam has asserted that associational membership is closely linked to interpersonal trust and that civic engagement and social trust are strongly correlated (1993, 2000). He further argues that social capital accumulates from social interaction, shared norms and networks that allow citizens to solve collective action problems, but has many democratic value/attitudinal benefits as well, including appreciation for both the ideals and practice of democracy. Thus, in a search for civic resources as the basis for EU support, social capital provides fertile ground from which to draw.

Explanations of social capital originate, at the core, from two sources. Social explanations include the notion that social capital is produced by the day-to-day interaction between citizens while institutional explanations include the related political, social and economic institutions that facilitate these social interactions. This research will concern itself with the former. Of the examined social explanations, two have garnered the most attention and empirical evidence, group participation and social interaction (Putnam 1993, 2000; Uslaner 1999). To the former, this includes individuals' participation in groups outside of the home in the form of membership in professional, political or social groups. To the latter, inasmuch as individuals interact and intermingle with others is sufficient. In either case, these presumably bring about trust and community-mindedness. However, both rest on the bedrock – albeit broad – notion that exposure to and interaction with others, particularly a diverse group of 'others' (Uslaner 2002), is conducive to the development of trust and collective-mindedness.

The current manifestation of social capital (e.g. Putnam 1993, 2000) demonstrates this relaxed connotation. In this literature, social capital is a component of democratic culture that emerges from the interactions of individuals within its domain. This component serves to support institutions (a causal and influential relationship also being pursued but not discussed here) and shape interaction among individuals in a community at large. Putnam suggests it is the features of social organization rather than the mere presence of the organizations themselves (1993: 167).[1] This implies that these organizations hold some latent instructions for their members for the unconscious implementation of social capital, and this may be true. He further argues that trust, norms of reciprocity and horizontal engagement (interaction of actors within a social structure) are the components of a political culture that supports normative democratic governance. By 2000, Putnam had landed on the notion that voluntary group activity (VGA) was a core social activity that produced social capital.

Recent criticism has suggested that membership in VGAs and civic attitudes are not related (Mutz and Mondak 1997; Stolle 2003), are at best related weakly (Brehm and Rahn 1997) or are even possibly reversed in their causal relationship (Uslaner 1998). This empirical evidence, however, does not undermine social capital theory but better defines its edges. For example, more recent works have countered that in contrast to Putnam's general membership/attitudes argument, not all organizations are alike (Stolle 2001) or more specifically, the nature of the group matters (Bowler *et al.* 2003) such that the *type* of group individuals participate in is pivotal. This distinction is instructive and one that develops social capital theory by pointing towards a more nuanced understanding of VGA for investigation.

However, social capital *is* social relationships such that dense networks in society (inasmuch as they are related to norms of generalized trust and reciprocity) allow citizens to overcome collective problems more effectively (Hooghe and Stolle 2003). Coleman's original conceptualization of social capital (1988) suggests social capital is some aspect of social structure that facilitates actions by actors within that structure. As it resides in and amongst actors, the obligations and expectations, information channels and social norms of a community are a public good that can be drawn from (and lost); such that changes of the quantity of social capital in a community are changes in the relations between people in that community. He includes an important, and often passed over, concept of closure, which provides the opportunity to enforce norms (rewards and sanctions) within a social grouping. He asserts specifically that social capital pertains more to 'closed' networks of social relationships than to others (see also Ostrom and Ahn 2003).

Therefore, if Coleman intended it to represent the social constraints in which individuals interact, why does the current social capital literature include interactions with strangers but fail to consider families, schools, neighbourhood or work environments that serve as social networks (like VGAs; see Hooghe 2003: 92) and include an ability to reinforce norms through their 'closed' nature? If social capital extends outward from individuals and comprises individuals' networks of relationships worthy of being

---

1 Although some suggest that passive membership might also be as effective as active membership (Wollebak and Selle 2003).

cultivated and maintained, it can also be conceptualized as a horizontal association of persons and activities with them, including more *familiar* networks. These networks, in particular, are likely to be ones in which rewards are generated and norms maintained more easily due to their 'closed' nature than in participation outside the home.

Finally, the level of broad social cohesion is also theoretically salient. At the core of individuals' attitudes about conflict and cooperation is the perception of threat. Individuals' concerns about 'others' (i.e. feeling threatened) exacerbate intolerance such that both tolerance and threat perceptions are buttressed by an individual's psychological insecurity. Individuals' feelings that their own economic and/or personal situations are tenuous, that social uncertainties (e.g. civil unrest) are probable, or that they are under 'cultural attack' (particularly as it relates to the EU, see McLaren 2002) are likely to reinforce the feeling of being threatened by others, in turn reinforcing attitudes inconsistent with cooperation.

Thus, the literature on social capital provides a variety of specific sources of social capital that are increasingly under investigation and may provide further insight into the export of social capital to broader democratic objects. Therefore, using 'closed' networks (e.g. friends and family), a general perception of psychological security and increased specificity of various types of voluntary group activity do more to define the edges of individuals' social capital. Considering social capital as a meso-level component of successful democratic political culture, this, in turn, suggests sources from which EU support might be harboured in the region.

Literature review

As discussed briefly above, while most of the literature associated with support for the EU in CEE is economically grounded, newer research suggests that broader attitudes of fairness and egalitarianism underpin EU support in CEE (Loveless 2010). This corresponds to social capital as it is grounded in a societal rather than individualistic view. Individuals within a society that demonstrate civic disengagement find themselves isolated and it would not be unreasonable to argue that increased political atomization stems from the lack of connectedness in a community or society. Successful experiences with democratic institutions (positive socialization) share a reciprocal relationship with social capital, network robustness and civil society (Putnam 2000). Given the lasting effects of atomization in CEE (Howard 2002; from the effect of Communism specifically see Inglehart and Catterberg 2002[2]), it is remarkable to see evidence of (albeit limited) trust in CEE (Mishler and Rose 1997a, 1997b).

However, maintaining a focus on social explanations, how exactly that has been and continues to be generated – and how it influences democratic political

---

2 History has also been argued to be a determinant of social capital (Putnam 1993), however that is not taken up here.

institutions – has undergone limited cross-national testing. As for the effect of trust and/or collective thinking on EU support, there has been no direct testing of this hypothesized relationship. However, and from an earlier period in CEE (1993–4), Letki tests the effect of trust and group membership on political engagement (2004). Centrally, she argues that membership in voluntary associations is an important 'school of democracy' and as such an important predictor of political involvement; yet groups vary in their ability to provide this service. Secondly, she tests whether more trusting individuals are more politically active. Significantly, she finds that membership in VGAs is related to socialization for political participation but that the type of group matters, favouring community associations over professional, lifestyle and labour groups. Although Letki finds that interpersonal trust is weakly connected with political involvement (ibid.: 675), this research corresponds to the more resent social capital literature in that it uses membership in VGAs as a predictor of trust.[3]

In sum, we find broad theoretical support for the underlying notion that trust and collective thinking can serve as bases for support for the EU, particularly as these can serve as the basis for democratic political culture and thus political institutions, such as the EU. However, we find little recent empirical evidence. Therefore, this chapter sets out to test three elements of social capital theory as a basis for EU support in CEE: activity in different types of groups, the 'closed' nature of groups (from Coleman) and insecurity as a broader measure of social cohesion. We arrive at the following hypotheses:

H_1: Individuals' participation in voluntary group associations are likely to have higher levels of trust and collective thinking (i.e. social capital); although, the type of group is relevant.

H_2: Individuals' 'closed' networks are likely to exert a positive effect on their level of trust and collective thinking (i.e. social capital).

H_3: Individuals' perception of insecurity is likely to exert a negative effect on their level of trust and collective thinking (i.e. social capital).

H_4: Not only do trust and collective thinking (i.e. social capital) positively influence support for the European Union, their determinants are also significant contributors in the directions hypothesized above.

Support for the first three hypotheses would help us to further define the edges of social capital and contribute to the growing empirical precision of the sources of social capital and support for the fourth hypothesis would buttress the claim of civic resources – in the form of various forms of social capital building – as important 'schools of democracy' in the region.

---

3 I again note the dates of the analysis (1993–4). These countries' memberships in the EU and arguable political and economic consolidation are likely to manifest, in addition to nearly 15 additional years between surveys, a significant difference.

Methodology

The data that we use in this chapter come from mass pubic surveys conducted in 2007 in nine Central and Eastern European countries.[4] The analysis is in two steps. First is to understand how both trust and collective thinking – as indicators of social capital – are generated in CEE given the more recent theoretical and empirical work on the subject. The second step is to determine whether these empirical referents of social capital as well as their determinants correlate with higher support for the EU.[5]

For research in Eastern Europe, social capital has simply been operationalized as trust (see Rose 1994; Mishler and Rose 1995; Edwards and Foley 1998; Kunioka and Woller 1999). As social capital is a non-individual-level characteristic, it is more accurately conceived of as an inter-individual characteristic; however, as Jackman and Miller note, social capital requires evidence at the micro level (1996). As interpersonal trust within a community lends itself to a less competitive political action space, it is manifested in a lower threshold for collective action, such as conventional (and unconventional) political engagement and participation (see Mishler and Rose 1997a, 1997b). Trust affects the social norms of interaction as individuals assess the members of in- or out-groups with their own relative perceptions of generalized risk (i.e. members' trustworthiness). This is not to imply that trust in other people within the community and even nation-state is evenly distributed, but rather that it varies according to individuals' groupings of other individuals, allowing us to extrapolate from the concentric boundaries of trust that radiate from individuals. This variable is the response to the question of whether respondents feel that they can generally trust another person. There is competing evidence on the relationship between trust in institutions and individuals. Muller and Seligson assert that trust in others and democratic institutions goes together (1994), while Mishler and Rose would suggest, especially in the new democratizing states of CEE, they do not (2001; see also Seyd and Whitely 2002).

Given the notion of networks and social capital, individuals' attitudes regarding the primacy of individuals over the community at large may reveal a *collective thinking* component. Conversely, individuals that place preferences on personal attainment and personal matters are less likely to have cooperative beliefs and attitudes. This variable is a combined response to questions

---

4 Data collection for this chapter was carried out as part of the EUREQUAL project 'Social Inequality and Why It Matters for the Economic and Democratic Development of Europe and Its Citizens: Post-Communist Central and Eastern Europe in Comparative Perspective', funded by the European Commission under contract No. 028920 (CIT5), Framework 6. Fieldwork was conducted by national survey/polling institutes in each country (face-to-face interviews) on the basis of stratified national random probability samples. The number of observations for each country is Bulgaria 1,000, the Czech Republic 994, Estonia 1,057, Hungary 1,030, Latvia 1,001, Lithuania 1,002, Poland 1,463, Romania 1,492 and Slovakia 1,032. Details of the main variables used in the analysis can be found in the Measurement Appendix.

5 All indicators and measurements are in the Appendix.

regarding social organization (i.e. the best way for people like me to improve our situation is to join together with others to promote our interests) and competition (i.e. the best way for people like me to improve our situation is to look after ourselves and not be concerned about what others are doing). Together with trust, this broadly captures individuals' attitudes towards conflict and cooperation and thus social capital.In order to operationalize the theorized determinants of social capital, I include voluntary group membership, 'closed' networks and psychological insecurity. The literature asserts that participation in VGAs brings individuals together and fosters the socialization to democratic norms. Organizations function as low-level 'schools of democracy', or more aptly, provide latent instructions for the norms of democracy. So, in the context of this research, by examining citizens' attitudes towards participation and the aggregate sum of their behaviours, we can begin to gauge the level of social capital. Conversely, the loss of civic-ness is the loss of social capital (Putnam 1993). In this research, membership in VGAs is captured by individuals' responses to questions about groups that they are members of or do not belong to.

In order to examine the effect of the *type* of group activity, groups have been separated into three types (see Stolle 2001). The 'professional group' includes membership in: a business association (chamber of industry/trade), a professional association, a trade union, a farmers' association, a factory committee or an armed forces association.[6] The 'political group' includes membership in either a political party or civic organization (NGO, social movement).[7] For 'social group', membership includes a church or religious group, a local/community group, a sports or social club, an ethnic organization, a neighbourhood watch or other.[8]

To investigate the effect of 'closed' networks, I employ measures that capture individuals' perceptions of the networks available to them. These variables attempt to capture the added empirical product of the importance of 'closed' networks. Beliefs on the importance of familial and non-family but immediate relationships give a preliminary view of the nature of communal integration and interaction. These are simply the responses to questions about the level of contact with respondents' family, friends and tertiary relationships (e.g. work colleagues). A high placement of family, friends and colleagues should indicate beliefs about the importance of close networks, contributing to social capital. One way to conceptualize this would be concentric circles of trust radiating from the most 'closed' (in which norms can most easily be enforced) to the

---

6 While some may be members of more than one group (such as business and professional associations), the majority (82.3 per cent) claim membership in only one. An additive version of professional group membership was also run with nearly the exact results. Substantively, the results are the same.
7 Again, this was run as an additive variable but, substantively, the results are the same.
8 Social group membership can easily include more than one, and both forms of the analysis (including a respondent with a minimum of only one membership) produced the same substantive results. The additive version is used in this analysis as this makes more intuitive sense.

least. Therefore, our expectation – while uniformly positive – is that family, then friends, then colleagues will exert a decreasing effect on trust and collective thinking.

Finally, psychological insecurity is captured by combining the questions about the respondent's economic and life satisfaction levels, such that a high score indicates a high level of security and subsequently a higher likelihood of social capital. The reverse is also expected to be true.

There are clear limitations to this research. The region has produced conflicting results as to the level and influence of trust as well as a limited understanding of support for the EU. Similarly, like the vast majority of social capital research, we are unable to unravel the order of social capital and its theorized determinants but correlations should manifest in expected ways (i.e. for specific groups, for closed networks and psychological insecurity). The interest here is widening the search for determinants of support for the EU.

Results

What do these countries look like in terms of trust and collective thinking? We can see in Table 5.1 that while there is variation in the levels of both, none seem to deviate significantly (except possibly Latvia and collective thinking). Estonia and Poland rank as the highest trusting countries on the whole and Bulgaria and Slovakia seem to have the highest level of collective thinking.

The primary question of this investigation revolves around the sources of trust and collective thinking to explain support for the European Union. There are two ways of asking this question: (1) are more trusting and collective thinking societies more likely to be supportive of the EU? This is an appropriate question to investigate societies with various levels of social capital (as an aggregate attribute); and (2) do those who trust and have collective orientations have a higher evaluation of the EU than those who do not? Once this link has

Table 5.1 Trust and collective thinking

	Trust			Collective thinking		
	Mean	Std dev	N	Mean	Std dev	N
Bulgaria	2.16	0.77	985	3.72	1.27	994
Czech	2.41	0.79	973	3.49	1.14	988
Estonia	2.67	0.74	1,019	3.22	1.30	1,057
Hungary	2.48	0.89	1,023	3.30	1.22	1,030
Latvia	2.40	0.84	992	2.82	1.32	1,001
Lithuania	2.48	0.77	973	3.32	1.30	1,002
Poland	2.54	0.76	1,458	3.54	1.31	1,498
Romania	2.34	0.67	1,463	3.27	1.34	1,492
Slovakia	2.52	0.85	1,011	3.68	0.95	1,032

Data source: *EUREQUAL* surveys in CEE 2007.

114 *Matthew Loveless*

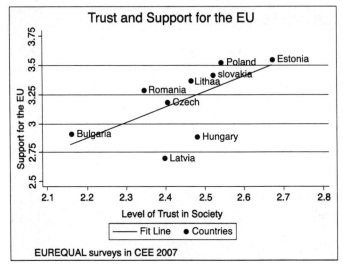

Figure 5.1 Trust and support for the European Union

been established, we can then investigate whether the contributors to social capital also contribute to support for the EU.

If we begin at the aggregate level, are states with higher levels of trust and collective thinking, i.e. higher levels of social capital, more likely to be supportive of the EU than those with lower levels? Aggregating both the level of trust, collective thinking and support for the EU by country, the correlations bear this out (see Figures 5.1 and 5.2).

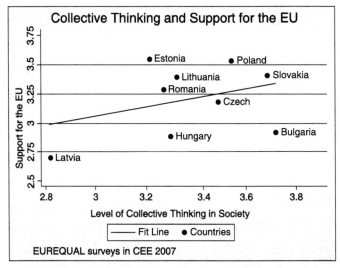

Figure 5.2 Collective thinking and support for the European Union

EU support and trust are correlated at r=0.63 (p≤0.07, N=9) and EU support and collective thinking at r=0.36 (p≤0.35, N=9). While neither are strictly statistically significant and given the central question of this research, we can argue that we are not interested in extrapolating beyond CEE and take both the correlation of trust and collective thinking with EU support to be in the former case quite convincing and, in the latter, somewhat less so. What the figures demonstrate is that, in general, countries with higher levels of social capital have higher support for the EU. However, to avoid ecological fallacy, we need to examine this relationship at the individual level and, correlating individual-level responses, we find that trust and EU support (r=0.12, p≤0.001, N=9,893) and collective thinking and EU support (r=0.16, p≤0.001, N=10,092) are in fact correlated – although somewhat weakly. In either case, we have preliminary support for the idea that trust and collective thinking (as proxies for social capital) do more together – in both the aggregate and at the individual level – with support for the EU.

The next question is whether social capital affects support for the EU and, further, whether the determinants of social capital (the hypothesized 'schools of democracy', 'closed' networks and psychological insecurity) are also influential. In doing so, we would be able to assert a claim to civic resources for the EU in CEE.

In Table 5.2, we see the output of the hypothesized relationships. For trust, and most significantly, political group membership maintains a positive and significant relationship. Surprisingly, the only 'closed' network to have any effect is 'colleagues' (relationships beyond direct friendship) as both family and friend networks are statistically insignificant. However, psychological insecurity has a negative effect such that increased perceptions of insecurity drive trust levels down. For collective thinking, we find instead that all forms of VGA are statistically significant as is the 'closed' network of 'friends' (but not family and colleagues).

For the expectations of *types* of group participation (H_1), we find that political groups are important to trust and all groups are important to collective thinking. While political group participation makes intuitive sense, that all forms of VGA are salient to collective thinking is somewhat surprising. The disparity is likely a function of the proxies for social capital, although the significance of the political group participation for both indicators of social capital is one that corresponds with the larger literature given both its likely structure (reflecting a democratic *zeitgeist*), suggesting a strong 'school of democracy' effect.

For 'closed' networks (H_2), we are presented with evidence that does not lend itself to easy theorizing. However, it might be possible to posit that extended relationships (such as work colleagues) might be a relevant predictor of trust as the most 'closed' relationships of family and friends might be too narrow or too immediate for extending trust. As for collective thinking and the 'closed' network of friends, this might signal a middle range theory of non-individualistic thinking.

Table 5.2 Trust and collective thinking: VGAs, 'closed' networks, and psychological insecurity [9]

	Trust			Collective thinking		
Voluntary group membership						
Professional	0.0602*	0.0510*	0.0350	0.174***	0.148***	0.140***
	(2.56)	(2.12)	(1.40)	(4.64)	(3.82)	(3.44)
Social	−0.0065	−0.0193	−0.0227	0.103***	0.0802**	0.0832**
	(−0.41)	(−1.16)	(−1.29)	(4.09)	(2.98)	(2.91)
Political	0.141***	0.142***	0.160***	0.324***	0.292***	0.287***
	(3.85)	(3.74)	(4.09)	(5.53)	(4.78)	(4.50)
'Closed' networks						
Family		0.003	0.003		0.017	0.017
		(0.53)	(0.57)		(1.93)	(1.80)
Friends		−0.005	−0.007		0.024**	0.027**
		(−0.99)	(−1.27)		(2.96)	(2.96)
Colleagues		0.018**	0.017**		0.021*	0.014
		(3.22)	(2.96)		(2.33)	(1.44)
Insecurity			−0.031**			0.002
			(−3.06)			(0.13)
Country dummies						
Bulgaria	−0.173***	−0.165***	−0.161***	0.456***	0.443***	0.494***
	(−5.34)	(−4.93)	(−4.51)	(8.82)	(8.19)	(8.48)
Czech Rep.	0.0621	0.082*	0.097**	0.182***	0.201***	0.200***
	(1.90)	(2.42)	(2.75)	(3.49)	(3.71)	(3.49)
Estonia	0.333***	0.371***	0.386***	−0.105*	−0.115*	−0.095
	(10.10)	(10.42)	(10.15)	(−2.01)	(−2.01)	(−1.55)
Hungary	0.145***	0.188***	0.213***	0.028	0.040	0.034
	(4.53)	(5.04)	(5.36)	(0.55)	(0.67)	(0.52)
Latvia	0.060	0.090**	0.098**	−0.471***	−0.470***	−0.437***
	(1.86)	(2.66)	(2.73)	(−9.14)	(−8.67)	(−7.50)
Lithuania	0.147***	0.171***	0.190***	0.011	0.053	0.000
	(4.41)	(4.84)	(4.91)	(0.21)	(0.94)	(0.00)
Poland	0.211***	0.218***	0.205***	0.285***	0.290***	0.308***
	(7.25)	(7.09)	(6.25)	(6.17)	(5.90)	(5.81)
Slovakia	0.159***	0.171***	0.201***	0.348***	0.340***	0.355***
	(4.69)	(4.94)	(5.53)	(6.43)	(6.10)	(6.01)
Constant	2.325***	2.219***	2.322***	3.221***	2.805***	2.835***
	(111.10)	(46.11)	(36.72)	(96.79)	(36.29)	(27.57)
Number of Obs.	9,745	8,423	7,412	9,939	8,561	7,505
R-sq	0.030	0.034	0.037	0.046	0.052	0.052

t statistics in parentheses; *p<0.05, **p<0.01, ***p<0.001. Romania is the reference category.

9 EUREQUAL surveys in CEE 2007.

Finally, psychological insecurity's clear importance (H_3) to trust and failure to reach significance to collective thinking is rather straightforward. Individuals' perceptions of threat is a clear impediment to extending general trust as trust is inherently about expectations of others whereas collective thinking is related to collective action solutions in the sense of Putnam-esque social capital (1993). Central to the claim of the social capital literature is the notion that these attributes of individuals are developed and can expand beyond individuals to include societies and even the nation-state. Thus, are trust and collective thinking related to support for the EU and, more specifically, are the determinants of those elements of social capital also elements of support for the EU (H_4)?

As discussed above, this literature has produced competing views of what drives EU support in these countries, the utilitarian approach (Tucker *et al.* 2002) versus the ideological or values approach (Rohrschneider and Whitefield 2004, 2006). Therefore, these are included to test the viability of trust and collective. In Table 5.3, we can see that, in fact, controlling for the variables most commonly associated with both the utilitarian approach (individuals' social location and the perceptions of their own economic experience and expectations in their respective market economies) and the ideological or values approach (ideological congruence between individuals and democratic governance and market economies), both trust and collective thinking show statistical significance (Model 1).

Table 5.3 Support for the European Union in CEE[10]

European institutions have been helpful and supportive of our country

Trust	**0.0831*****		
	(4.46)		
Collective thinking	**0.107*****		
	(9.58)		
Group participation			
Professional	–0.0137	–0.0180	–0.0334
	(–0.34)	(–0.43)	(–0.78)
Social	–0.0038	–0.0168	–0.0128
	(–0.13)	(–0.55)	(–0.41)
Political	0.0138	0.0191	0.0211
	(0.22)	(0.30)	(0.32)
'Closed' networks			
Family	0.0006	0.0002	
	(0.05)	(0.02)	
Friends	0.0084	0.0076	
	(0.79)	(0.70)	

10 EUREQUAL surveys in CEE 2007. The EU question – found in the Measurement Appendix – speaks to legitimacy as it represents a congruency between the extant institutions of the region, in this case the EU, and the values of its constituents.

Table 5.3 (Continued)

Colleagues		−0.0032	−0.0065	
		(−0.31)	(−0.62)	
Insecurity			−0.0153	
			(−0.67)	
Country financial situation	**0.0756*****	**0.0814*** **	**0.0808*** **	**0.0799*** **
	(7.89)	**(8.39)**	**(7.80)**	**(6.51)**
Experience with democracy	**0.0499****	**0.0589*** **	**0.0567****	**0.0525****
	(2.90)	**(3.40)**	**(3.05)**	**(2.76)**
Experience with markets	**0.123*** **	**0.124*** **	**0.123*** **	**0.125*** **
	(6.67)	**(6.69)**	**(6.17)**	**(6.18)**
Democratic ideal	**0.0315***	**0.0337***	**0.0360***	**0.0400***
	(2.06)	**(2.19)**	**(2.16)**	**(2.35)**
Market ideal	**0.0966*** **	**0.102*** **	**0.0992*** **	**0.0967*** **
	(5.47)	**(5.70)**	**(5.16)**	**(4.93)**
Ideology	**0.0180****	**0.0156***	**0.0235****	**0.0228****
	(2.71)	**(2.33)**	**(3.24)**	**(3.07)**
Age	−0.0016	−0.0010	−0.0014	−0.0014
	(−1.62)	(−0.94)	(−1.22)	(−1.11)
Education	0.0141	**0.0201***	**0.0360***	**0.0329***
	(1.61)	**(2.25)**	**(2.49)**	**(2.24)**
Income	0.0270	0.0317	0.0183	0.0115
	(1.47)	(1.71)	(0.91)	(0.55)
Gender (1=male)	−0.0056	−0.0136	−0.0157	−0.0231
	(−0.20)	(−0.47)	(−0.50)	(−0.73)
Employed	−0.0093	−0.0035	−0.0009	0.0100
	(−0.27)	(−0.10)	(−0.02)	(0.25)

Country dummies

Bulgaria	**−0.192****	**−0.142***	**−0.155***	**−0.163***
	(−3.24)	**(−2.38)**	**(−2.47)**	**(−2.55)**
Czech Rep.	−0.0826	−0.0554	−0.0255	−0.0292
	(−1.44)	(−0.95)	(−0.42)	(−0.46)
Estonia	**0.216*** **	**0.219*** **	**0.219****	**0.219****
	(3.38)	**(3.32)**	**(3.06)**	**(2.97)**
Hungary	−0.0427	−0.0153	−0.0303	−0.0220
	(−0.68)	(−0.24)	(−0.41)	(−0.29)
Latvia	**−0.551*** **	**−0.598*** **	**−0.607*** **	**−0.606*** **
	(−9.45)	**(−10.15)**	**(−9.77)**	**(−9.53)**
Lithuania	**0.241*** **	**0.259*** **	**0.283*** **	**0.324*** **
	(3.53)	**(3.67)**	**(3.76)**	**(4.18)**
Poland	**0.233*** **	**0.279*** **	**0.288*** **	**0.296*** **
	(4.29)	**(5.09)**	**(5.00)**	**(4.99)**
Slovakia	0.0356	0.125	**0.146***	**0.139***
	(0.59)	(1.94)	**(2.22)**	**(2.06)**
Constant	**1.108*** **	**1.513*** **	**1.438*** **	**1.552*** **
	(9.06)	**(13.00)**	**(9.32)**	**(8.34)**
Number of obs.	6,454	6,427	5,700	5,455
R-sq	0.161	0.146	0.147	0.149

t statistics in parentheses; *p<0.05, **p<0.01, ***p<0.001. Romania is the reference category.

However, we can see in the additional models (Models 2, 3 and 4) that by replacing the determinants for both trust and collective thinking into the model, all fail to achieve statistical significance in the presence of the other hypothesized determinants of EU support in CEE.[11] This suggests that the development of trust and collective thinking through these 'schools of democracy' (i.e. 'closed' networks and psychological insecurity) fail to translate into support for the EU.

Discussion/conclusion

We have seen that both trust and collective thinking positively influence support for the EU in CEE, both at the aggregate and individual levels. This is not entirely unexpected as preferences for democratic politics, democratic culture and positive orientation towards democratic national institutions have been determinants of EU support in the 'old' member states for some time (Schmitt and Thomassen 1999). We also find that indicators of social capital derive from specific and, as these findings suggest, different sources of group participation, 'closed' networks and insecurity. However, these activities, networks and orientations – as civic resources for the development of trust and collective thinking (i.e. social capital) – do not explain individuals' support for the EU.

In accordance with our expectations and the most recent developments in social capital theory, the *type* of group membership informs our understanding of the relevant sources of social capital. Both trust and collective thinking respond similarly to individuals' group membership in political groups (and collective thinking benefits from *any* VGA participation). This adds to the growing evidence that suggests, for political activity in particular, VGAs can serve as 'schools of democracy'. Secondly, 'closed' networks seem to be differentially effective, possibly a spill-over effect that does not extend as far as trust, although the collective thinking question (as constructed) implies the actual solving of a problem which may be facilitated by in-group interaction. One major limitation here is the ability to assess Coleman's original conceptualization of 'closed' networks. To capture an individual's 'mental map' of his/her own network would require a great deal of and different data collection and the reconstruction of the interactions, relationships and happenchance occasions that make up an individual's life. Here, we have been constrained by estimated individual's *perception* of the network available to him/her which might have shaped the evidence presented here.

However, both trust and collective thinking are positively related to support for the EU, suggesting that, if the past literature is a good guide, cultural 'goods' such as higher levels of social capital do translate positive social values and attitudes into broader political support. Yet, as specified, these specified determinants of social capital do not seem to convert into broader political

---

11 These models were also run as instrumental variable models and resulted in the same substantive findings.

support (for the disconnect between personal and institutional trust in CEE, see Mishler and Rose 2001). Given the preliminary nature of this examination, I hesitate to suggest that this undermines the potency of civic resources in CEE, preferring instead to consider that other, unexamined determinants of trust and collective thinking drive support for the EU. More simply, the mechanism linking civic resources to support for the EU lies elsewhere.

To be certain, trust and collective thinking are different concepts. Are they part of social capital? Arguably yes, but how remains an interesting question worth more effort. We see similarities (e.g. political group membership) and disparities (e.g. psychological insecurity and 'closed' networks) that inform our understanding of these; however, closer and continued inspection is required to unravel these concepts to determine what part of social capital they are and how they drive political support. Similar, and possibly of greater importance to the study of the 'democratic deficit', is the notion that individuals' support for the EU is conceptually simplistic such that the assumption is that EU institutions are democratic *and perceived as so*. This may be an under-examined question and the lack of conceptual and empirical specificity may hamper our ability to connect the determinants of individuals' support to individuals' perceptions of the EU as a set of democratic institutions.

Finally, Putnam (1993 and 2000) suggests that, like all forms of capital, social capital is cumulative and self-reinforcing. In contrast to other forms of capital (human and physical), the return on investment of social capital has broader ramifications than other self-interested, short-term motivations. It inherently modifies the incentive structures of actors as the effects are shared among community members and their orientations to politics. It would seem here that while these beneficial effects do not extend further to include broad support for the ongoing engagement with the EU, they are nonetheless relevant to durable democratic political culture (Paxton 2002).

Appendix

Interpersonal trust: 'Please choose one of the phrases from this card to tell me how much you agree with the following statements: Most people can be trusted.' *Response categories*: strongly agree, somewhat agree, somewhat disagree, strongly disagree. (DK). Reverse-coded so that a high response equalled agreement.

Collective thinking: 'Consider the following pairs of statements: which one comes closest to your own views? (1) The best way for people like me to improve our situation is to join together with others to promote our interests. OR (2) The best way for people like me to improve our situation is to look after ourselves and not be concerned about what others are doing.' *Response categories:* definitely the first opinion; the first opinion rather than the second; in between; the second opinion rather than the first; definitely the second opinion, (DK). Recoded so agreeing with the first sentence (solidarity) is the higher score.

Civic resources in Central and Eastern Europe 121

Support for European Union: 'Consider the following pairs of statements: which one comes closest to your own views? (1) European institutions have been helpful and supportive of our country. OR (2) European institutions have been interfering in our affairs and using our difficulties for their own advantage.' Definitely the first opinion; the first opinion rather than the second; in between; the second opinion rather than the first; definitely the second opinion. Recoded so support is higher (DK to the middle category).

Professional group membership: A dummy variable including respondents' memberships in any of the following: a business association (chamber of industry/trade), a professional association, a trade union, a farmers' association, a factory committee or an armed forces association. A member of any one of these was coded '1'. None was coded '0'.

Social group membership: Includes a church or religious group, a local/community group, a sports or social club, an ethnic organization, a neighbourhood watch or other. Any membership is a '1' and the variable is cumulative.

Political group membership: A dummy variable including membership in either a political party or civic organization (NGO, social movement). Membership in either coded '1', otherwise '0'.

Closed networks: Additive of 'How often do you speak to [family/friends] on the phone?' and 'How often do you meet up with [family/friends] who are not living with you?' *Colleagues (tertiary networks):* 'And how often do you speak to neighbours (face-to-face)' and 'How often you meet up with work colleagues outside of work times?' *Response categories:* on most days; once or twice a week; once or twice a month; less often than once a month; never; (DK). Reverse-coded

Psychological insecurity: 'And looking ahead over the next five years, do you think that your household's standard of living will fall a great deal from its current level, fall a little, stay about the same as it is now, rise a little, or rise a lot from its current level?' Reverse-coded so a high score is high insecurity.

Socioeconomic status

Age: open-ended response

Education: all countries were adjusted to the ISCED 1997.

Pre-primary level of education (0), Primary level of education (1), Lower secondary level of education (2), Upper secondary level of education (3), Post-secondary, non-tertiary level of education (4), First stage tertiary education (5), Second stage of tertiary education (leading to an advanced research qualification) of education (6).

Income: Which of the following statements best describes your household's financial circumstances? *Response categories*: We do not have enough money even to buy food; We have enough money to buy food but we cannot afford to buy clothes and shoes; We have enough money to buy food, clothes and shoes and have some savings but not enough to buy more expensive goods such as a TV set and fridge; We can buy some expensive goods such as a TV set and fridge but we cannot afford all things we would want; We can afford everything that we would want; (DK recoded to missing).

Gender: Male is '1' and female is '0'.

Employment: Is the respondent currently in paid work? Employed is '1', unemployed is '0'.

Ideology: 'Many people think of political attitudes as being on the "Left" or the "Right". This is a scale stretching from the Left to the Right. When you think of your own political attitudes, where would you put yourself?' Left =1 — Right=10, (DK).

Attitudes about the market economy and democracy

Democracy as ideal: 'Tell us, please, what do you think about the idea that a democracy, in which multiple parties compete for power, is the best system for governing [*country*]?'

Market economy as ideal: 'And what do you think about the idea that a market economy, in which there is private property and economic freedom to entrepreneurs, is the best system for [*country*]?'

- For *both*: strong supporter; supporter; opponent; strong opponent; neither supporter nor opponent.
- Recoded so that very positively is highest. 'Neither' and 'DK' are a middle, neutral category.

Experience with market economy: 'And how would you evaluate the *actual experience* of the market economy so far?'

Experience with democracy: 'And how would you evaluate the *actual practice* of democracy here in *[country]* so far?'

- For *both*: very positively; positively; negatively; very negatively; neither positively nor negatively.
- Recoded so that very positively is highest. 'Neither' and 'DK' are a middle, neutral category.

Economic evaluations

Country financial situation: Additive variable of, 'Thinking now of the country as a whole, do you think that compared with five years ago, standards of living have fallen a great deal, fallen a little, stayed about the same, risen a little, or risen a lot?' and 'And looking ahead over the *next five years*, do you think that standards of living will fall a great deal from their *current* level, fall a little, stay about the same as now, rise a little, or rise a lot from their current level?' DK coded as missing.

References

Almond, G. A. and Verba, S. 1963. *The civic culture*. Princeton, NJ: Princeton University Press.

Boix, C. and Posner, D. N. 1998. 'Social capital: explaining its origins and effects on government performance', *British Journal of Political Science* 28(4): 686–93.

Bowler, S., Todd, D. and Hanneman, R. 2003. 'Art for democracy's sake? Group membership and political engagement in Europe', *The Journal of Politics* 65(4): 1111–29.

Brehm, J. and Rahn, W. 1997. 'Individual-level evidence for the causes and consequences of social capital', *American Journal of Political Science* 41(3): 999–1023.

Coleman, J. S. 1988. 'Social capital in the creation of human capital', *American Journal of Sociology* 94(supplement): 95–120.

Edwards, B. and Foley, M. 1998. 'Civil society and social capital beyond Putnam', *American Behavioral Scientist* 42(1): 124–40.

Hooghe, M. 2003. 'Voluntary associations and democratic attitudes: values congruence as a causal mechanism', in: H. Marc and S. Dietlind (eds) *Generating social capital*. New York: Palgrave Macmillan, 89–112.

Hooghe, M. and Stolle, D. 2003. 'Introduction: generating social capital', in: H. Marc and S. Dietlind (eds) *Generating social capital*. New York: Palgrave Macmillan, 1–18.

Howard, M. M. 2002. 'The weakness of postcommunist civil society', *Journal of Democracy* 13(1): 157–69.

Inglehart, R. and Catterberg, G. 2002. 'Trends in political action: the developmental trend and the post-honeymoon decline', *International Journal of Comparative Sociology* 43(3–5): 300–16.

Jackman, R. and Miller, R.A. 1996. 'A renaissance of political culture', *American Journal of Political Science* 40(3): 632–59.

Kunioka, T. and Woller, G. 1999. 'In (a) democracy we trust: social and economic determinants of support for democratic procedures in Central and Eastern Europe', *Journal of Socio-Economics* 28(5): 577–97.

Letki, N. 2004. 'Socialization for participation? Trust, membership, and democratization in East-Central Europe', *Political Research Quarterly* 57(4): 665–79.

Loveless, M. 2010. 'Agreeing in principle: perceptions of social inequality and support for the European Union in Central and Eastern Europe', *Journal of Common Market Studies* 48(4): 1083–106.

McLaren, L. 2002. 'Public support for the European Union: cost/benefit analysis or perceived cultural threat', *Journal of Politics* 64(2): 551–66.

Mishler, W. and Rose, R. 1995. 'Trajectories of fear and hope: support for democracy in post-communist Europe', *Comparative Political Studies* 28(4): 553–81.

Mishler, W. and Rose, R. 1997a. 'Trust, distrust and skepticism: popular evaluations of civil and political institutions in post-communist society', *The Journal of Politics* 59(2): 418–51.

Mishler, W. and Rose, R. 1997b. 'Social capital in civic and stressful societies', *Studies in Comparative International Development* 32(3): 84–111.

Mishler, W. and Rose, R. 2001. 'What are the origins of trust?', *Comparative Political Studies* 34(1): 30–63.

Muller, E. N. and Seligson, M. A. 1994. 'Civic culture and democracy: the question of causal relationships', *American Political Science Review* 88(3): 635–52.

Mutz, D. C. and Mondak, J. J. 1997. 'Dimensions of sociotropic behavior: group-based judgements of fairness and well-being', *American Journal of Political Science* 41(1): 284–308.

Ostrom, E. and Ahn, T. K. (eds) 2003. *Foundations of social capital*. Northampton, MA: Edward Elgar.

Paxton, P. 2002. 'Social capital and democracy: an interdependent relationship', *American Sociological Review* 67(2): 254–77.

Putnam, R. D. 1993. *Making democracy work: civic traditions in modern Italy*. Princeton, NJ: Princeton University Press.

Putnam, R. D. 2000. *Bowling alone*. New York: Touchstone.

Rohrschneider, R. 1999. *Learning democracy: democratic and economic values in unified Germany*. Oxford: Oxford University Press.

Rohrschneider, R. 2002. 'The democratic deficit and support of an EU-wide government', *American Journal of Political Science* 46(2): 463–75.

Rohrschneider, R. and Loveless, M. 2010. 'Macro-salience: how economic and political contexts mediate popular evaluations of the democracy deficit in the European Union', *The Journal of Politics* 74(4): 1029–45.

Rohrschneider, R. and Whitefield, S. 2004. 'Support for foreign ownership and integration in Eastern Europe: economic interests, ideological commitments, and democratic contexts', *Comparative Political Studies* 37(3): 313–39.

Rohrschneider, R. and Whitefield, S. 2006. 'Political parties, public opinion, and European integration in post-communist countries: the state of the art', *European Union Politics* 7(1): 141–60.

Rose, R. 1994. 'Postcommunism and the problem of trust', *Journal of Democracy* 5(3): 18–30.

Schmitt, H. and Thomassen, J. (eds) 1999. *Political representation and legitimacy in the European Union*. Oxford: Oxford University Press.

Seyd, P. and Whiteley, P. 2002. 'Is Britain still a civic culture?', Annual Meeting of the British Group of the American Political Science Association Meetings, Boston, MA.

Stolle, D. 2001. 'Clubs and congregations: the benefits of joining an association', in: K. S. Cook (ed.) *Trust in society*. New York: Russell Sage Foundation, 202–44.

Stolle, D. 2003. 'The sources of social capital', in: M. Hooghe and D. Stolle (eds) *Generating social capital*. New York: Palgrave Macmillan, 19–42.

Tucker, J. A., Pacek, A. C. and Berinsky, A. J. 2002. 'Transitional winners and losers: attitudes toward EU membership in post-communist countries', *American Journal of Political Science* 46(3): 557–71.

Uslaner, E. M. 1998. 'Social capital, television, and the "mean world": trust, optimism, and civic participation', *Political Psychology* 19(3): 441–67.

Uslaner, E. 1999. 'Democracy and social capital', in: M. Warren (ed.) *Democracy and trust*. Cambridge: Cambridge University Press, 121–50.

Uslaner, E. 2002. *The moral foundations of trust*. Cambridge: Cambridge University Press.

Wollebak, D. and Selle, P. 2003. 'The importance of passive membership for social capital formation', in: M. Hooghe and D. Stolle (eds) *Generating social capital*. New York: Palgrave Macmillan, 67–88.

6 Mobilizing civic resources through e-participation in the European public sphere
Problem-solving, re-legitimizing or decoupling?

Simon Smith

Introduction

There appears to be a secular trend towards more participative styles of governance. Part of this trend may be bottom-up: the continuation of several centuries of struggle by groups and social movements for democratic rights and inclusion in decision-making processes. But not always is it evident that governments and other public authorities who invite citizens to participate are responding to pressure from society to re-legitimize the dominant social contract in a polity. There is also a top-down explanation for the advent of more participative governance, which seems to be linked to the increasing complexity of social problems. More participation, in other words, may be part of a response to the limitations on the state's capacity to direct society and redistribute resources to the same extent that was the norm in the twentieth century. Twenty-first-century states confront indeterminate issues and risks, and – in a context of unclear rules, unintended consequences and uncertain payoffs – they may be more inclined to seek a different 'division of labour' between state, market and society in order to achieve collective goals and create public goods and values (Jessop 2003; Peters 2006).

For these reasons, participation is increasingly demanded of us by modern states. The pursuit of governmental objectives involves attempts to mobilize the self-governing capacities of individuals, groups and communities, such that 'active citizenship' is normalized as a responsibility as well as a right. Thus it has been argued that 'advanced liberal government' reserves a major role for the 'technologies of agency' (Dean 1999: 1678), or that empowering people to co-govern and self-govern has become a key governance strategy because 'unless they are prepared to assume responsibility for and participate actively in solving their own everyday problems, the system stands little chance of being able to connect with them and deliver them the welfare goods they demand' (Bang 2003: 243).

At the same time we are witnessing changes in the nature of citizenship, from a political to a cultural citizenship, expressed through people's everyday participation in popular culture (Hermes 2006), and from a bounded to an unbounded citizenship, expressed through participation in communities of interest and action extending beyond the nation state (Cammaerts and Van Audenhove 2005). It follows that there is always likely to be an underlying tension between system-oriented participation (what we might call co-governance) and self-governance as the practice of political freedoms on an actor's own terms. Bang's concept of culture governance implies that to utilize people's self-governing capacities to the full extent, rulers must 'pay heed to the irreducibility of the "small tactics" of lay people in the political community for making a difference' (Bang 2003: 248) and link this popular creativity to goal-setting, if only indirectly. This means guaranteeing a space for participation within what Goffman would call back regions of the social system. Participation, as a specific form of social integration, can be thought of as 'regionalized' according to the locales in which it takes place. Each locale acts as a power container, and there exists a hierarchy of locales, through which social and system integration are articulated across time–space (Giddens 1984). Back regions – essentially locales which are distant from power centres – resemble Habermas' literary public sphere in the sense of being insulated from dominant power relations, both governmental and commercial (Habermas 1989).[1] Here, participation may be driven by a search for cognitive reassurance rather than the pursuit of interests.

Summarizing, an analytical distinction can be made between three different rationales for the participation of civic actors in politics:

- mobilizing knowledge resources for problem-solving
- re-legitimizing the polity through political debate
- creating space for autonomous collective action and alternative discourses, decoupled from formal policy processes.

The purpose of this chapter is to assess which of these rationales was dominant during an online debate linked to participative policymaking, a style of policymaking in which governments, and in particular the European Union, are investing considerable resources. It also aims to assess whether the intended rationale of the organizer was matched by the enacted rationales of participants.

Participation in the governance of the European Union

Until recently, the dominant rationale for participation in European Union governance was the first of the above: a deliberately depoliticized mode of policymaking in which 'strong publics'[2] were engaged in participation (for

---

1 Discursive practice in the literary public sphere is insulated from determination by power relations, which is not the same as saying that the two are completely unconnected: the public sphere, as a component of civil society, is always in a fundamental sense in opposition to the power of the state.
2 The key distinction between strong publics and general publics is that the former are arenas with direct links to centres of decision-making power, although they do not actually take decisions; the latter are arenas for opinion formation (Eriksen and Fossum 2002: 405).

example via expert advisory groups and committees), not for reasons of legitimacy but because the Union (principally the Commission) required external expertise due to the limitations of its own legal competences, administrative capacities and knowledge resources. Participation of this type continues to play a central role in the governance of the EU, in keeping with its predominantly 'network' mode of governance (Smith 2009a). Indeed, participation in expert groups has been growing in quantitative terms: the number of expert groups organized by the EC increased from around 600 in 1990 to over 1,200 in January 2007 (Gornitzka and Sverdrup 2008). Such arrangements were and remain appropriate to the preponderance of regulatory over redistributive policymaking, where specific interests rather than society as a whole are frequently the key stakeholders (affected parties).

More recently, however, the rationale for participation in European policymaking has partially shifted towards the second type of securing democratic legitimacy. The EU is a political entity whose mode of operation and in particular whose policymaking is criticized by many as lacking legitimacy. The term 'democratic deficit' is increasingly used to capture this legitimacy failure, defined on the Europa website as 'a concept invoked principally in the argument that the European Union and its various bodies suffer from a lack of democracy and seem inaccessible to the ordinary citizen because their method of operating is so complex'.[3] A concern for their own democratic legitimacy has therefore been a factor of growing importance in the communication policies of European institutions, and has led many of them to attempt to communicate not only with their habitual 'strong publics' but with the general public(s) and with loosely organized 'issue publics' – citizens' networks that coalesce around particular issues, sometimes in the form of campaigns, but also less tangible currents of opinion and platforms for the discussion of particular issues – to stimulate broad-based participation in framing policy objectives.

The third rationale for participation – autonomous collective action and discourse – almost by definition cannot be planned or even made explicit by authorities, but occurs spontaneously to the extent that collective actors are able to create independent spaces or (as will be seen) 'invade' institutional spaces to organize around autonomously defined projects and discourses.

These three rationales for participation can be associated with different sectors, or levels, of the public sphere. A multi-level public sphere has been proposed by numerous authors (e.g. Keane 2000, Eriksen 2007, Fraser 2005, Haug 2008) as either a normative or empirical model for Europe. Table 6.1 illustrates these conceptions, bearing in mind that the correspondences between them are not exact. It also suggests how they can be related to different genres of participation and citizenship and different types of regionalization and integration according to structuration theory. Given that the weakness or fragmentation of a European public sphere is often cited as an inhibiting factor for both

---

3 http://europa.eu/legislation_summaries/glossary/democratic_deficit_en.htm

Table 6.1 Properties of a multi-tiered European public sphere

Tier	Micro level	Meso level	Macro level
Locale / power container	Localization (not necessarily location)	Nation	Europe
Public situation (after Haug 2008)	Encounter or assembly public	Mass media	Socio-technical system
Type of public (after Eriksen 2007)	Enclaves and issue publics	General publics	Strong publics
Regionalization (structuration theory)	Back region	Front region	Front region
Integration (structuration theory)	Social	System	System
Participation rationale	Intrinsic and autonomous	Instrumental and re-legitimizing	Instrumental and problem-solving
Citizenship	Localized and cultural	Bounded (by the nation-state)	Unbounded (transnational or cosmopolitan)

deliberation and democratic legitimacy (Eriksen 2007), it has been suggested that, while the EU itself seems to conceptualize the European public sphere in a rather simplistic unitary and linear manner, we ought instead to consider the hypothesis that 'the public sphere follows the EU's existing governance system by also developing a multi-level structure in which, at each level, citizens relate to different institutions of governance' (Bärenreuter *et al.* 2008: 21).[4] Thus Table 6.1 can be read as indicating the type(s) of public sphere required for the effective governance of the EU, in which strong publics play the dominant role as communication partners for political authorities at the European scale, but in which there is also an increasing imperative to engage other types of public, including 'general' publics and 'issue' publics, which may manifest themselves primarily at a smaller scale of action. This therefore requires that the opinion of these publics is somehow 'sluiced' into the institutional channels through which strong publics operate, viewing the multi-tiered public sphere as a hierarchical structure, or that other mechanisms are found for translating participation and citizenship performed at lower levels in different types of public into signals that can be understood by political authorities at the macro-level.

Evolution of European policy on participation

Politics and policymaking in the EU have witnessed a number of innovations designed to increase and expand public participation. In terms of official policy, this process dates from around 2000, although conceptual work on a

---

4 See the Eurosphere working papers series for a rich and growing repository of research on the European public sphere: http://www.eurosphere.uib.no/2010/07/30/workingpapers/

more participative mode of governance and on the related concept of the European public sphere began some years earlier, both within the Commission's Forward Studies Unit and in academia. Coinciding with the gradual shift in emphasis from a problem-solving to a re-legitimizing rationale has been an increasing use of ICTs, and in particular the Internet, as a means of mobilizing the wider public(s) whose participation European institutions seek. Described in more detail in Smith and Dalakiouridou (2009), this evolution had the following milestones:

2001: publication of the White Paper on European Governance. During the preparation of this key Commission policy statement there were calls for better coordination of consultation processes between sectors/Directorate-Generals (DGs) (Working Group 2a 2001: 18) and better linking with the estimated 1–2 million Europeans involved in networks linked to European policies (Working Group 4b 2001: 22). The document itself expressed a general aspiration to 'reach out' to citizens, identifying four channels: local and regional development, civil society organizations, looser citizens' networks and the EUROPA website as 'an interactive platform for information, feedback and debate, linking to parallel networks across the Union' (EC 2001: 11) – the first real commitment to e-participation in EU policy. Later on it called for European institutions to connect with, recognize and incorporate existing business, community or research networks, 'to enable them to contribute to decision shaping and policy execution' (ibid.: 18). To a large extent this activity was still framed by the depoliticized mode of policymaking characteristic of the Community method: consultation was to become more extensive, but was seen primarily as a means of engaging the capacities of external actors for problem-solving and mobilizing their resources for policy implementation.

2005: that situation changed following the referenda on the proposed European Constitution in the Netherlands and France, since which time more politicized forms of participation have grown in significance. The 2005 policy Plan D for Democracy, Dialogue and Debate took up the idea of the European public sphere and initiated both a series of decentralized events (the 'going local' strategy focusing on creating local 'European public spaces') and further development of the EUROPA website as a communication tool, including online debate on the Debate Europe page, launched in March 2006 under Plan D's Internet objective, which stated 'the Commission will use state-of-the-art Internet technology to actively debate and advocate its policies in cyberspace': Commission officials are said to use Debate Europe to 'feel what matters to the participants', though generally not through direct participation but through monthly summaries compiled by the moderators (response to a questionnaire in the European e-participation study, see Panopoulou *et al.* 2009). Both of these types of initiative represent attempts to generate democratic legitimacy through ongoing dialogue with the public rather than to mobilize distributed problem-solving capacities for specific purposes.

2008: Plan D was rechristened Debate Europe (after the discussion website) with an emphasis on a 'listening' Commission. In practical terms, a number of European projects supported by Plan D have envisaged or actually tried to bridge a gap between the institutionalized settings of formal participation processes and civil society settings, including the 'social web'. For example, one project team funded under the Commission's eParticipation Preparatory Action plans to use Facebook for future regional e-participation events in order to publicize them, to discuss the same broad issues in a more informal atmosphere, and then invite members of the relevant Facebook groups to a more formal discussion on the project website (Smith 2009b: 17). This would resemble the 'staged interventions' advocated by Hermes as a means of translating abundant contemporary expressions of 'cultural citizenship' into political citizenship, and which should be framed as temporary, purpose-specific and transactional events (Hermes 2006). The 'Tell Barroso' web-based consultation, run by the European People's Party-associated Centre for European Studies prior to the 2009 European elections as an ideas-gathering exercise, was also linked to a Facebook group. The group grew to about 1,000 members by May 2009, the consultation itself received 12,000 citizen proposals, and each proposer evaluated on average 10 other proposals. For an initiative headed by the Commission President himself during a period of campaigning for the European elections, this is quite a modest return, although the level of involvement by each participant is impressive. There was apparently little Facebook 'multiplier' effect, however: in fact, the Facebook group was rather clumsily constructed as an add-on to the official consultation page, and certainly does not represent a civic or social space with its own participation rationale, separate from the political purpose of the consultation.

At this point in time we can only really speak of intentions by government to use the social web. At European, as at national level, the day is still a long way off when civil servants engage the public on user-generated e-participation websites 'as a matter of course', as recommended by the UK Power of Information taskforce (Cabinet Office 2009). Similarly, there is a disconnect between European institutions and e-participation processes hosted by third parties, notably media organizations, notwithstanding EU sponsorship of initiatives such as the Cafe Babel European portal for participative journalism. A considerable amount of debate among citizens, politicians and journalists about European political affairs occurs on the websites of public service broadcasters and leading national newspapers, for example, with much higher participation rates than any official e-participation processes (see Dalakiouridou *et al.* 2009). Yet the Commission still generally seems to prefer to 'listen' to civil society through its own channels and events, expecting citizens to be informed enough to know how and where to address policymakers.

Interactive policymaking

The remainder of this chapter will focus on an example that at one level remains a highly institutionalized form of e-participation, but which, it will be argued, has been deployed in ways that have allowed civic actors to find new ways of engaging with European policymakers according to different rationales, and whose long-term consequences remain unclear.

The case study concerns a policymaking process carried out by the European Commission's Directorate-General for Education and Culture using the Interactive Policy-Making (IPM) tool. This online tool, launched in 2001, was intended for collecting and analysing public opinion for use in EU policymaking, and it included both consultation and discussion platforms. Primarily it is used for managing online consultation processes with existing 'strong publics'; but, when deployed for open public consultations, it acts as a certain corrective to corporatist tendencies since it combines disintermediating and re-intermediating components which ought to be more open to unorganized interests.[5] In particular it may have rendered consultations more susceptible to the mobilization of issue publics such as temporary public mobilizations emerging from the hidden networks of social movements and latent inter-organizational networks taking advantage of the networking possibilities of online communication. The underlying principle was that high-quality, electronically enabled interaction between citizens and enterprises on the one hand, and the Commission on the other, including the facility for the former to give spontaneous feedback on issues affecting them, would lead to benefits such as better responsiveness to stakeholder demand, improved efficiency in analysing and sorting relevant data, better predictive knowledge about the likely impacts of policies, and more inclusive policymaking (TEEC 2005). Thus IPM is interesting because it combines the problem-solving and re-legitimizing rationales for participation.

In addition, the consultation process analysed here used IPM in association with an online discussion forum, which introduces the possibility – maybe even the likelihood – that autonomous actor-driven forms of participation will occur. Under certain circumstances participation processes can take on user-determined meanings that bear little relation to the intended purposes of authorities but fulfil autonomous needs not directly linked to the search for political influence. This has been described as a 'decoupling' of top–down and bottom–up participation processes, and implicitly involves contesting the very way in which the participation process has been officially framed (Bang and Dryberg 2003). Some online tools seem to favour decoupling because they reduce the ability of organizers to stage-manage a process. For example, in a consultation about the site of a new airport for Paris, the environment of an online discussion forum 'favoured a redefinition of the subjects [of debate] that actors find pertinent' such that fundamental questions about a political issue, which had been 'organized out' of the official terms of debate, reappeared as participants appropriated the tool (Monnoyer-Smith 2006: 12). Such

---

5 Some applications, notably the Feedback Mechanism, positioned institutions such as European Information Centres in a data-gathering and data-processing role, which the mid-term evaluation report interpreted as a failure to utilize the Internet's capacity and ubiquity to create direct linkages with stakeholders (TEEC 2005: 12).

redefinitions did not occur, at least to the same extent, during a parallel offline participation process, whose less flexible structure left participants with the choice to either play by the rules or reject the process out of hand. At best they could stage protests outside the venues for public meetings, but these did not necessarily appear 'on the public record' (unless they attracted media coverage), whereas the online public discussions did.

Multilingualism

The case has been selected within a policy sector – education and culture – in which the European Commission has weak competences, merely supporting policy formation and implementation at lower levels. Hence neither direct regulation nor the standard Community method is possible. Influencing policy on the ground takes place primarily through the Open Method of Coordination, and national, regional and local authorities are responsible for providing the bulk of the funding. If it wants to steer education and culture policy, the Commission may need to build coalitions with actors in civil society, either through expert groups or newer forms of participation.

In general there are more expert groups in policy sectors where competences are shared between European and national/sub-national authorities, and fewest in sectors of exclusive European competence. In sectors where there is very limited or no treaty basis for Commission action, there is no clear pattern to the number of expert groups established by the relevant DG, but DG Education and Culture has about as many as could be expected under a shared competence regime (Gornitzka and Sverdrup 2008). In the case described here, the expert group established to make recommendations on an emerging policy theme interpreted its remit far more broadly than the limits of Commission competences and put forward political arguments as well as more 'technical' recommendations. Arguably, expert groups like this could play a role in a strategy to maximize the scope for action by the Commission in spite of limited formal competences. This case study concerns a consultation on multilingualism, an issue likely to become a surrogate for wider public debates about identity and integration in Europe, since 'multilingualism is a value' (HLGM 2007: 17) and how it is understood and defined has far-reaching implications for how Europe itself is constructed. For example, it can be defined in terms of individual abilities to speak more than one language or in terms of the coexistence of different language communities in the same space. Such choices have practical implications (whether to prioritize language learning or translation/interpretation/intermediation services, for example) but above all they have political implications because they affect fundamental political issues such as social cohesion (one of the key themes of the Lisbon strategy). Moreover, multilingualism is seen as a prerequisite for active citizenship at European level (European Parliament and Council of the European Union 2006: 13) and is part of the response by the EC to the 'democratic deficit' because it is identified as a key enabling factor in the creation of a 'European public sphere' whether by means of transnational public service broadcasting or by means of transnational e-participation (HLGM 2007: 13, 17). Therefore political attention to multilingualism itself signals a shift to a more participative mode of governance.

Although an active European policy to promote multilingualism within the education sector can be dated from the Maastricht Treaty in 1992, it was not until the advent of the Barroso Commission that the first comprehensive framework was developed, gaining momentum after 2007, when multilingualism was made a separate portfolio (HLGM 2007: 5). Even if this decision may have been motivated in part by the need to find a job for the new Romanian Commissioner (Leonard Orban), a series of wider social, political and institutional trends had given the issue greater 'policy relevance' for European institutions and created a double rationale for soliciting public participation: firstly, migration and globalization have increased the urgency of finding solutions to the 'problem' of multilingualism as a daily reality of communities across Europe (a problem-solving rationale); secondly, resistance to the increasing dominance of English as the de facto European *lingua franca*, together with the resurgence of regional identities over recent decades, have politicized multilingualism (a re-legitimizing rationale). In practice, the heavy involvement in the process by the 'Esperanto community' also introduced an autonomy rationale to the public discussion of multilingualism, which became particularly apparent as the threads of the online discussion forum 'unravelled'.

The multilingualism consultation

In the course of preparing a policy initiative on multilingualism, the Commission launched a consultation process in autumn 2007, inviting organizations and individuals to give their views and expectations concerning language policy. The whole process consisted of several different elements: the formal online public consultation, a report from a high-level group on multilingualism (an expert group set up in September 2006), a report from a 'group of intellectuals' (a group of 10 personalities set up for the 2008 European Year of Intercultural Dialogue, chaired by the Lebanese writer Amin Maalouf), a report from a business forum (an advisory group with representatives from small and large companies set up in 2007), a public hearing held on 15 April 2008 in Brussels with 167 stakeholders, mainly representing educational and cultural organizations, and the 'suggestions and critical assessment' (in the Commissioner's words) received via a 'Have Your Say' discussion forum on multilingualism. The next section of the chapter focuses on the latter.

The online discussion forum

The 'Have Your Say' discussion forum on multilingualism was not directly linked from the consultation webpages, but from the Commissioner's homepage (it was actually built into his homepage, so that the menu options display around the edge of the discussion area).⁶ Apart from the press release cited, no other official publicity was found for the forum, but a few other organizations picked up on it. In particular, it was advertised in the Esperanto magazine *Libera Folio* in October 2007 and readers were encouraged to use it. In the social web, it had a very modest presence, although it was slightly more visible than the consultation page itself: for example, there are two links to the forum in blogs indexed on Technorati.com, and two Delicious.com users have bookmarked the forum, whereas there were no traces of the consultation webpage on either of these platforms when a search was performed in August 2009. Low visibility is not necessarily a disadvantage for this type of online discussion: Wright (2007) has suggested that lack of advertising was a factor explaining the 'success' (in terms of deliberative quality) of the debates on the European constitution on the Futurum discussion forum, since it meant that 'generally, only interested people would have gone to the website and come across the discussion'.

The structure of the forum was unusual. Only one discussion thread was open at a given time, and there was no possibility for users to start new threads. Each one was introduced by the Commissioner, and there followed a series of replies displayed un-nested in reverse chronological order – thus more like a blog than a standard forum. This structure might have been expected to encourage vertical debate, but as will be seen, this was only the case during certain phases.

Altogether there were three threads on the forum. Each thread began with a few paragraphs of commentary from Commissioner Orban, followed by a specific question. The first question, dated 24 September 2007, was: 'Why do you think it is important to learn languages?' The second question, dated 6 February 2008, was: 'Do you experience problems in your everyday life that are due to language difficulties: to inadequate or unavailable translation for example of product descriptions or user manuals?' The third question, dated 15 August 2009, was: 'Did languages influence your business or your career?' It is clear, however, from the way in which the questions are framed, that these are essentially prompts, and that discussion of all language-related topics was welcome. The following sections summarize the content of the second discussion thread, which followed the online consultation and which included the period in which the official Communication was published. This thread has been chosen because it captures a critical moment in the ongoing dialogue between Commissioner Orban and the public: Orban used his opening remarks to respond at some length to issues raised in the first thread, claiming to have 'followed your views with great interest' but noting that 'many answers went well beyond this first question, anticipating other areas of debate', the implication being that he welcomed the expansion of the topic of debate. He claimed to have seen a consensus around the importance of 'keeping the

---

6 Since the new European Commission assumed office in late 2009, the forum is no longer available.

meaning' of the Union's motto of Unity in Diversity. He then addressed a sizeable number of contributors who were using the forum to advocate for an enhanced status for Esperanto within EU language policy, prefacing his own opinions by stressing the limited scope of the policy review under way due to the nature of Community law on languages (in particular the political impossibility of giving official status to languages other than those of member states). He tried to convey a sense of respectful disagreement with most of the arguments for Esperanto. Finally, he encouraged further use of the forum for discussion among citizens: 'the Multilingualism Forum should be a discussion forum for you and not just an exchange between you and me.' There were 200 contributions between 6 February 2008 and 11 August 2009, submitted in numerous different European languages.[7]

The following analysis does not attempt to evaluate discursive or deliberative quality, but tries to identify the dominant participation rationales during different phases of the discussion.

Phase 1 (6–19 February 2008, 80 contributions)

The first 50 responses came in within a week, with another 30 in the second week. Almost all were from advocates of Esperanto, with a majority writing in French (often also with an Esperanto translation or vice versa), which is indicative that a relatively well-organized issue network had mobilized.[8] The majority of contributions were addressed to Mr Orban in the second person (always the 'vous' form in languages which have this distinction, and only one contributor – an Iranian – addressed him by his first name, Leonard). Towards the end of the period there were more frequent contributions commenting on the Commissioner's words in the third person. Many of these were more confrontational in tone, but only one contribution could be called offensive, even though the majority opposed the Commissioner's views on Esperanto. Many adopted a polite, dialogical tone, often explicitly welcoming the opportunity for exchange, the establishment by the Commission of a discussion forum which welcomed contributions in any EU language, the Commissioner's declared interest in discussion with the general public, and his recognition of Esperanto. The typical response could be summed up as rational counter-argumentation, which took one of two forms: either it adopted a *problem-solving rationale* and presented factual corrections or technical arguments in favour of adopting Esperanto as the EU's common language, often adding practical suggestions; or it adopted a *re-legitimizing rationale* and presented political claims (or counterclaims), usually referring to the injustice of adopting English as the de facto *lingua franca* of the EU. The former type of

---

7 The author was able to analyse the content of contributions in English, French, Polish, Czech and Slovak, which covered nearly 60 per cent of the total.
8 In France the Esperanto community is politically organized, having fielded candidates in recent European elections as Europe Démocratie Espéranto.

contributions often challenged the Directorate General to commission more scientific research or properly review the evidence about the feasibility of different ways in which the EU could use or promote Esperanto. Many scientific studies were cited, typically with links. Also falling within this category were numerous personal narratives about the advantages of knowing Esperanto or the ease of learning the language. The latter type of contributions often expressed frustration at the Commissioner's self-professed competence limits (which some saw as alibiism) and called for the EU to exercise its powers (change the law, ensure genuine multilingualism exists at least in the institutions, intervene against allegedly discriminatory national language policies).

Thus there were countervailing attempts to either depoliticize or politicize the issue of multilingualism – on the one hand, to mimic traditional community methods like expert groups, and on the other, to link the issue to wider value-laden debates about the nature of Europe as a political, social and cultural entity. What both had in common was an insistence that participants had a right to be involved in problem definition, something which they suspected was not the case. One participant expressed cynicism about the whole process: 'There's a big difference between investigating a problem without any preconceptions about the "best solution" and formulating a problem with the solution already in your mind' [my translation from French].

Two contributions took issue with the Commissioner's comment that the forum should be a place for horizontal debate, stressing that they wanted to address him in the first instance, and that horizontal debate was difficult in any case because of the multitude of languages used in the forum. There were only three direct references to other contributions in the first 50 posts, emphasizing the predominantly vertical structure of the dialogue in this phase.

In addition to the discussion on Esperanto, there were a few 'position statements' from interest groups such as the Conseil Européen des Associations de Traducteurs Littéraires and some regional language communities, likewise addressed directly to the Commissioner.

Phase 2 (20 February – mid-September 2008, 57 contributions)

The intensity of exchange fell off markedly after the first few weeks, as is typical of threads in most online discussion forums. The nature of the discourse also changed in a number of respects. Participants more frequently referred to the Commissioner (if at all) in the third person, and addressed or referred to one another's contributions more often. To aid the discussion, it became quite common practice to translate others' contributions, especially those in less commonly spoken languages, into French, English or Esperanto.[9] The dialogue thus became more horizontal in structure. The sense

---

9 According to Wodak and Wright (2007) spontaneous translation also occurred in the Futurum discussion forum, although in that case users tended to translate their own contributions rather than those of others.

of frustration became increasingly evident in relation to the consultation exercise, and to Commission policymaking on multilingualism as a whole. A number of participants cast doubts on the sincerity of the Commission's professed openness to public debate and input (e.g. 'It's clear that the facade of multilingualism aims to create an illusion . . . when English has long since been the unique language practised exclusively by the Commission' [my translation from French]) or expressed cynicism about the Community method of policymaking ('When one wants to kill an idea, one sets up a commission to silence the demands' [my translation from French]). The Commissioner was portrayed as distant and unapproachable, partly because his office's interventions in the forum were rare, but also because, according to one contributor whose words were then translated by a second from Polish into French, his responses to emails were 'evasive' and he had refused to be interviewed by the Esperanto magazine *Libera Folio* (although he did eventually agree, and an extensive interview with him was published on 28 March 2008). Despite users' frustrations, a *re-legitimizing rationale* was still dominant at this point.

As forum contributors began to sense their own lack of influence, however, the rationale for participation shifted a second time from the *re-legitimizing rationale* to a *rationale of autonomy*. Participants questioned the utility of the forum as a means of participating in policymaking, but they continued to use it both to criticize power and to share ideas and opinions. Discussion assumed a value of its own, and correspondingly there was a growing sense of community, camaraderie and solidarity among forum participants. Several of them exchanged email addresses in order to continue networking activities 'off-forum', although they had to be inventive to subvert the forum's automated censoring of email addresses. Solidarity was also expressed between representatives of different minority (regional) language communities who used the forum to express their sense of victimization by discriminatory national language policies. The type of arguments advanced about the role of Esperanto in Europe also changed subtly. For example, there were gradually fewer demands for the EU to use its powers to promote Esperanto as a *lingua franca*, with some contributions going as far as to argue that this would be contrary to the ethos of the language:

> Esperanto is about equality and direct human to human contact. Esperanto does not seek to replace one imperial language with another . . . But these are imperialist times, and you, [Commissioner Orban] an official representative, cannot directly oppose imperialism. So, maybe it's better that your office is against Esperanto. Perhaps more open-minded Europeans will look into Esperanto and find a useful tool with which to talk to their neighbors.

The politics of Esperanto were presented as a non-violent politics, antithetical to the exercise of state power: 'to put an end to the domination of culture and of the dominant language in order to give back the people their speech rights' [my translation from French]. One participant suggested that the forum itself had perfectly illustrated the principles of linguistic democracy which Esperanto stands for: thanks to the organic emergence of the practice of translating each other's contributions, and of using Esperanto in addition to one's native tongue, (s)he had been able to communicate with fellow Europeans across language barriers. This illustrates the autonomy rationale: the forum had become a space for the *practice* of a certain discursive politics of multilingualism rather than a discourse about (the politics of) multilingualism.

During phase 2 of the discussion there were only occasional references to other elements of the policy development process on multilingualism such as the work of the group of intellectuals, whose report became available during this period (two contributions criticized its recommendations for a 'personal adoptive language' as too timid or too elitist 'to stem the march of English'), and the forthcoming publication of the Commission's communication in the autumn. Phase 2 can therefore be characterized as an increasingly horizontal, self-sustaining discussion taking place in the shadow of – with a background awareness of, but distanced from – a policymaking process.

Phase 3 (mid-September 2008 – August 2009, 63 contributions)

In this phase the intensity of exchange was lowest, although not markedly lower than in phase 2. In fact it is surprising that the same thread continued being used for over a year and a half despite little active moderation. In phase 3 the *rationale of autonomy* ceded ground once again to a mixture of the *problem-solving and re-legitimizing rationales*, in that there was less of a sense of community among participants. The pattern was for brief, isolated claims and suggestions to trickle in. The discourse was disconnected, as if the Esperanto 'issue public' (as manifest in this space) was in the process of demobilization. In April 2009, however, there was a brief mobilization of a second 'issue public', when several members of the Spanish-speaking community in Catalonia described their experience of linguistic discrimination by the Catalan regional authorities.

The dialogue was mostly vertical, with the bulk of contributions addressed directly to the Commissioner. Many of them had a petitioning nature, advocating on behalf of particular causes or constituencies. Others provided personal narratives, or made specific complaints about the gap between policy and practice in the EU's implementation of multilingualism, for example on the Europa website. Paradoxically, this was the most 'on-topic' phase of the discussion, in which around half of contributions actually addressed the question posed by the Commissioner at the start of the thread.

The most surprising feature of phase 3, however, was the lack of any discussion of the Communication on Multilingualism published by the Commission on 18 September 2008, since this was the key outcome of the consultation itself. The fact that the moderator did not announce its publication in the forum, or even place a link there, and that participants did not pick up on it spontaneously either, implies that both sides saw the purpose of this freer discussion space as independent of the formal consultation process.

Discussion

In the resulting policy on multilingualism, announced by the Commission in its Communication of 18 September 2008, the consultation process is invoked essentially to legitimize the existing policy direction on multilingualism: the analysis of the situation contained in the previous 2005 Communication, 'A new framework for multilingualism' ('the value of linguistic diversity' and 'the need for a broader policy to promote multilingualism') had been 'confirmed by a broad consultation in 2007–08 which included an online consultation attracting over 2 400 replies, and two advisory groups [the high-level group and the business forum]' (EC 2008: 3). There is no acknowledgement in the Communication of the strident opposition to current policy directions in the Have Your Say discussion forum, which Commissioner Orban nevertheless claimed had been 'very important in the elaboration of the strategic communication'.

Although the Communication claims to initiate 'a qualitative shift' in multilingualism policy (EC 2008: 4), its wording is cautious and self-limiting, reflecting the strictly limited competences of European institutions in this area. The main policy instrument for taking things forward is a 'structured dialogue' with identifiable stakeholders, and giving a prominent role to expert groups (a business forum and a civil society forum have since been set up as permanent advisory bodies). The dominant rationale remained one of problem-solving. The actions set out for European institutions steer clear of any regulatory instruments, and concentrate on facilitation and incentivization: monitoring, developing metrics, setting up platforms for sharing good practice, promoting student mobility through existing EU programmes, disseminating, awareness-raising, linking intelligently with policies in other sectors, and making recommendations to the member states, which are acknowledged as 'the key decision-makers on language policy' (ibid.: 4).

How might we explain the evident tension in the Commission's approach to this consultation and to the political use of its outcomes? Participation was invited on the basis of both the problem-solving and the re-legitimizing rationales, but the official policy that resulted only appears to have taken into account the former. Thus, for example, the press release announcing the launch of the consultation and the Have Your Say forum on 26 September 2007 gave three examples of the types of issues the consultation was to explore: safeguarding lesser spoken languages against the trend towards one *lingua franca*, integrating migrants into society and the value of maintaining a multilingual EU administration. Yet these essentially political questions, which attracted a lot a feedback, are given only marginal attention in the Communication. The Commission's apparent disingenuity in stressing aspects of the process which were later 'organized out' of the policy output should be seen in the context of the politics of multilevel governance. It evidently felt obliged to defer to the right of member states to determine their own policy on the status of regional languages and to respect the rule that only national languages can be designated as official EU languages. But in creating a more open space for policy development at European scale it had arguably altered the balance of power, since the stating of positions and raising of arguments in an official public space indicated a demand for European action. Members of the high-level expert group noted that 'the link between language policies or language education policies and political power is somewhat of a taboo subject' (HLGM 2007: 21), and the consultation process itself went some way towards removing such taboos. De jure, the outputs of the participation process were a series of technical recommendations on promoting multilingualism, but de facto it enabled citizens and organizational stakeholders to participate in problem (re)definition. In other words, rather than just mobilize knowledge for problem-solving, the process mobilized arguments which began to redefine the problem and created a space for more autonomous collective action and discourse, raising alternative scenarios, politically unthinkable in the present, but not necessarily so in the much longer term. These scenarios implicate the Commission's own competences and the EU's democratic legitimacy.

In relation to the European public sphere and the purported need for spaces of transnational deliberation which would add a missing layer to European democracy, a number of insights follow from a comparison of this case with those studied by Wright (2007) and Cammaerts and Van Audenhove (2005). In the case of Futurum, Wright argued that its hosting by a political authority detracted from deliberative quality. Cammaerts and Van Audenhove studied three forums hosted by organizations affiliated to transnational social movements, which they found to be spaces relatively well suited to the performance of a cosmopolitan or 'unbounded' citizenship, but the hosting by a member organization tended to promote information and mobilization at the expense of 'real debate'. Coleman and Gotze (2001) have suggested that the ideal host for democratic deliberation might be a public service broadcasting organization such as the BBC, whose neutrality is widely respected. The problem for the European public sphere, of course, is that there is no highly visible and universally trusted mass media outlet operating on the same scale as the polity of the European Union. If this suggests that Europe will inevitably lack any 'master forum' for public deliberation, it is all the more important to observe how different publics take shape and act in the various kinds of more 'compromised' spaces that are made available. This study suggests, however counterintuitive it may seem, that there are openings within policymaking processes themselves for expressions of cultural citizenship that achieve their communicative power by decoupling these spaces from the policymaking cycle, although the issue publics that emerge may well have been attracted initially by the prospect of influence. In this case, the political institutions did not succeed in recoupling cultural citizenship to the formal consultation process. Yet localized and unbounded citizenships resemble one another insofar as they are socially constructed rather than empirically given (Cammaerts and Van Audenhove 2005), and in that they are linked to long-term cultural change rather than short-term decision-making. In that case a listening, supporting and translating approach on the part of political authorities such as the EU may be a more appropriate response than one which treats online discussion simply as an input to a consultation process.

Conclusion

Having argued that the online discussion on multilingualism saw forms of participation inspired by all three rationales – problem-solving, re-legitimizing and autonomy – with a progressive 'decoupling' of the community from the policy process itself (followed by a partial return to a mixture of problem-solving and re-legitimizing action in the later stages after the Esperanto community had demobilized), the question remains how public authorities could improve their ability to listen to these kinds of public debate: how can they recouple the sort of autonomous actor-driven participation that flourished during phase 2 of the online discussion with the political system? Coupling will never be a perfect fit, since it involves the connection of network structures of the public sphere(s) to the hierarchical systems of political and legal institutions 'with specified media and codes' (Bader 2008: 4). There is a risk of introducing fundamental conflicts to policymaking which, according to proponents of a strictly regulatory EU, has hitherto been relatively successful because policymaking is deliberately under-politicized (Majone 2002). There is also a trade-off between autonomy and influence, meaning that participation in the public sphere will always produce some knowledge that is redundant, in the sense that it cannot be used by the political system, at least in the short term: some part of the efforts of participants will always be 'wasted' from a purely instrumental perspective. But it is important to find ways of preserving the benefits of the redundant knowledge produced in participatory processes, since their validation may not only increase the rewards of participation for individuals but also contribute to society's stocks of knowledge and hence to its long-term sustainability, as well as to its governability, recalling that 'not all and everything depends on "politics"' (Bader 2008: 23).

Technical problem-solving with obvious 'strong publics' may have little to gain from mobilizing civic resources via the social web: there is little need to involve new actors, because the affected parties are clearly identifiable and their outputs are 'appropriately formatted', whereas those from other publics may not be. On this point the present analysis concurs with Wright (2007), as it does on the limitations of a discussion forum as a medium for surveying public opinion within a 'general public' in response to a re-legitimizing rationale, given the small and unrepresentative participation and the apparent capture of the discussion by particular groups. The notion of an 'issue public', however, may be more pertinent to the types of collective organization and communicative action that occurred within the multilingualism discussion forum. These can be understood as forms of collective action that emerge from the micro-level public sphere, and retain most of their characteristics, but which can coalesce temporarily and – crucially – leave traces of their existence in the meso-level or macro-level public sphere. The process is not quite analogous to the crystallization of temporary public mobilizations of 'hidden networks' in the manner predicted by new social movement theory (Melucci 1989), because in the latter case the public manifestation of social movements occurs precisely to make concrete demands to the political system. Issue publics such as the Esperanto public that took shape within the multilingualism discussion forum did not formulate political demands so much as replicate a cultural politics that has its roots in the everyday practice of a micro-level public sphere. What is unusual is that it took place within a heavily institutionalized space apparently close to the centre of power. Winkler and Kozeluh made a similar observation about the discussion on Your Voice in Europe, which worked best (in terms of interactivity and rationality) among a small group of 'expert' regular contributors replicating a form of communication more typical of a 'micro-public sphere' (2005: 45). This partially contradicts Bärenreuter et al.'s hypothesis that the European public sphere may develop a multi-level structure that correlates to the framework of multi-level governance in the EU. Here we do not see a straightforward mapping of the public sphere onto formal governance mechanisms so much as an appropriation of a 'sphericule' within the macro-level public sphere for civic action more appropriate to the micro-level public sphere. This reflects the fact that contemporary structures of governance, when the term is understood in its broadest sense, are highly complex and overlapping.

If this analysis is accurate, then recoupling may depend less upon the 'sluicing' of information generated by online discussion back into a policymaking process and more on the success of translations between political and cultural citizenship. In replicating micro-level forms of participation at the macro level in a form which leaves a permanent trace in a space linked to a power centre, the collective actors here termed 'issue publics' were translating political into cultural citizenship. An equally effective mechanism for translating cultural citizenship back into political citizenship is still to be found. Such a mechanism would require that actions construed from a system perspective as nonparticipation could be recognized and incorporated into the long-term reproduction of political systems and thereby increase their capacity for experimentation and renewal. If we push the translation metaphor a bit further, the key issue is one of commensurability (Callon 1991). E-participation was an intermediary that permitted the establishment of an effective local translation regime, based on a negotiated commensurability between an issue public's desire to express cultural citizenship and the Commission's desire for stronger civic input to policy consultations. The more difficult next step is to configure a wider chain of interactions, encompassing intermediaries as varied as the conventions that define EU citizenship rights and the social practices of local groups of Esperanto speakers, with a view to ensuring commensurability across a chain of translations linking each of these realms into a network while avoiding the creation of a single obligatory passage point that could infringe the sense of agency of all but the strongest of publics.

References

Bader, V. 2008. 'Eurospheres? Fragmented and stratified or integrated and fair? A conceptual and pretheoretical mapping exercise', *Eurosphere working paper 9*. Available at: http://eurospheres.org/files/2010/08/Eurosphere_Working_Paper_9_Bader.pdf

Bang, H. 2003. 'A new ruler meeting a new citizen: culture governance and everyday making', in: H. Bang (ed.) *Governance as social and political communication*. Manchester: Manchester University Press, 241–66.

Bang, H. and Dyrberg, T. 2003. 'Governing at close range: demo-elites and lay people', in: H. Bang (ed.) *Governance as social and political communication*. Manchester: Manchester University Press, 222–40.

Bärenreuter, C., Brüll, C., Mokre, M. and Wahl-Jorgensen, K. 2008. 'An overview of research on the European public sphere', *Eurosphere working paper 3*. Available at: http://eurospheres.org/files/2010/08/Eurosphere_Working_Paper_3_Barenreuter_etal.pdf

Cabinet Office. 2009. *Power of Information Taskforce Final Report*. Available at: http://poit.cabinetoffice.gov.uk/poit/

Callon, M. 1991. 'Réseaux technico-économiques et irréversibilité', in: H. Dumez, J. Girin, H. Laroche, J.-G. Padioleau and E. Szuyskya (eds) *Actes du Séminaire Contradictions et Dynamique des Organizations CONDOR*. Paris: CRG/ESCP, 205–32.

Cammaerts, B. and Van Audenhove, L. 2005. 'Online political debate, unbounded citizenship, and the problematic nature of a transnational public sphere', *Political Communication* 22(2): 179–96.

Coleman, S. and Gotze, J. 2001. *Bowling together: online public engagement in policy deliberation*. London: Hansard Society.

Dalakiouridou, E., Tambouris, E., Tarabanis, K. and Smith, S. 2009. *Mapping the state of play in eParticipation in the EU*. European eParticipation study, Deliverable 1.4c. Available at: http://islab.uom.gr/eP/

Dean, M. 1999. *Governmentality: power and rule in modern society*. London: Sage.

Eriksen, E. 2007. 'Conceptualising European public spheres: general, segmented and strong publics', in: J. Fossum and P. Schlesinger (eds) *The European Union and the public sphere: a communicative space in the making?* London: Routledge, 23–43.

Eriksen, E. and Fossum, J. 2002. 'Democracy through strong publics in the European Union', *Journal of Common Market Studies* 40(3): 401–24.

European Commission. 2001. *European Governance. A White Paper*. COM (2001) 428 final. Brussels: Conference of European Churches.

European Commission. 2007. *Outcomes of the European Commission's public consultation on multilingualism 14 September – 15 November 2007*. Brussels: DG Education and Culture. Available at: http://ec.europa.eu/languages/documents/sumnews_en.pdf

European Commission. 2008. *Multilingualism: an asset for Europe and a shared commitment*. COM (2008) 566 final. Brussels: Conference of European Churches.

European Parliament and Council of the European Union. 2006. *Recommendation of the European Parliament and of the Council on key competences for lifelong learning* (2006/962/EC), Official Journal of the European Union L394: 10–18.

Fraser, N. 2005. *Transnationalizing the public sphere*. Vienna: European Institute for Progressive Cultural Policies. Available at: http://republicart.net/disc/publicum/fraser01_en.pdf

Giddens, A. 1984. *The constitution of society: outline of the theory of structuration*. Cambridge: Polity Press.

Gornitzka, A. and Sverdrup, U. 2008. 'Who consults? The configuration of expert groups in the European Union', *West European Politics* 31(4): 725–50.

Habermas, J. 1989/1962. *The Structural transformation of the public sphere: an inquiry into a category of bourgeois society*. Cambridge: Polity Press.

Haug, C. 2008. 'Public spheres within movements: challenging the (re)search for a European public sphere', *RECON Online Working Paper* 2008/02. Available at: http://www.reconproject.eu

Hermes, J. 2006. 'Hidden debates: rethinking the relationship between popular culture and the public sphere', *Javnost – The Public* 13(4): 27–44.

High Level Group on Multilingualism (HLGM). 2007. *Final report*. Brussels: DG Education and Culture. Available at: http://ec.europa.eu/languages/documents/doc1664_en.pdf

Jessop, B. 2003. 'Governance and meta-governance: on reflexivity, requisite variety and requisite irony', in: H. Bang (ed.) *Governance as social and political communication*. Manchester: Manchester University Press, 101–16.

Keane, J. 2000. 'Structural transformations of the public sphere', in: K. Hacker and J. van Dijk (eds) *Digital democracy: issues of theory and practice*. London: Sage, 70–89.

Maalouf, A. et al. 2008. *A rewarding challenge: how the multiplicity of languages could strengthen Europe: Proposals from the Group of Intellectuals for Intercultural Dialogue*. Brussels: DG Education and Culture. Available at: http://ec.europa.eu/languages/documents/report_en.pdf

Majone, G. 2002. 'Delegation of regulatory powers in a mixed polity', *European Law Journal* 38(3): 319–39.

Melucci, A. 1989. *Nomads of the present: social movements and individual needs in contemporary society*. Philadelphia: Temple University Press.

Monnoyer-Smith, L. 2006. *Être créatif sous la contrainte. Une analyse des formes nouvelles de la délibération publique. Le cas DUCSAI*, *Politix* 75(3): 75–101.

Panopoulou, E., Tambouris, E. and Tarabanis, K. 2009. *eParticipation good practice cases and diffusion*. European eParticipation study, Deliverable 4.2c. Available at: http://islab.uom.gr/eP/

Peters, B. 2006. 'Forms of informality: identifying informal governance in the European Union', *Perspectives on European Politics and Society* 7(1): 25–40.

Smith, S. 2009a. *Main benefits of eParticipation developments in the EU – a contextualisation with reference to the EU governance regime and the European public sphere*. European eParticipation study, Deliverable 1.3c. Available at: http://islab.uom.gr/eP/

Smith, S. 2009b. *Key actors in eParticipation developments in the EU*. European eParticipation study, Deliverable 1.2c. Available at: http://islab.uom.gr/eP/

Smith, S. and Dalakiouridou, E. 2009. 'Contextualising public (e)Participation in the governance of the European Union', *European Journal of ePractice* No. 7, March.

The European Evaluation Consortium (TEEC). 2005. *Mid-term evaluation of the Interactive Policy-Making (IPM) programme. Final report.* Brussels: DG MARKT.
Winkler, R. and Kozeluh, U. 2005. *Europeans have a say: online debates and consultations in the EU. Final report.* Vienna: Institute of Technology Assessment, Austrian Academy of Sciences.
Wodak, R. and Wright, S. 2007. 'The European Union in cyberspace', in: B. Danet and S. Herring (eds) *The multilingual internet: language, culture and communication online.* Oxford: Oxford University Press, 385–407.
Working Group 2a. 2001. *Consultation et participation de la société civile.* Report of working group for the White Paper on Governance. Available at: http://ec.europa.eu/governance/areas/group3/report_fr.pdf (accessed 28 November 2008).
Working Group 4b. 2001. *Networking people for a good governance in Europe.* Report of working group for the White Paper on Governance. Available at: http://ec.europa.eu/governance/areas/group9/report_en.pdf (accessed 28 November 2008).
Wright, S. 2007. 'A virtual European public sphere? The Futurum discussion forum', *Journal of European Public Policy* 14(8): 1167–85.

7 Conceptualizing (and tentatively mapping) the EU's social constituency

John Erik Fossum and Marit Eldholm

> 'Recognition' has become a keyword of our time. A venerable category of Hegelian philosophy, recently resuscitated by political theorists, this notion is proving central to efforts to conceptualize today's struggles over identity and difference ... Hegel's old figure of 'the struggle for recognition' finds new purchase as rapidly globalizing capitalism accelerates transcultural contacts, fracturing interpretative schemata, pluralizing value horizons, and politicizing identities and differences ... recognition's salience is now indisputable ...
>
> Fraser and Honneth 2003: 1

Introduction[1]

The purpose of this chapter is to heighten our understanding of the nature of the EU's social constituency. With *social constituency* is meant the structure of demands and expectations that citizens and groups place on the EU. The EU is widely held to be a functional-type organization. If this is a correct assessment, it would mean that its social constituency would be made up of utility-oriented, economic interest organizations and be much narrower than that of a state.[2]

Is such a conception of the EU consistent with citizens' demands and social movement involvement in, and engagement with, the EU? Is it consistent with the EU's self-conception, and how it defines its social constituency? Many studies note that the social contingent that approaches the EU exceeds well beyond the realm of functional interest organizations (Greenwood and Aspinwall 1998; Greenwood 2003). The EU also presents itself as a polity with a far more committing relationship to its social contingent,

---

1 This is an extended version of the article 'Conceptualising the EU's Social Constituency', by John Erik Fossum, published in *European Journal of Social Theory*, vol. 8, no. 2, 2005. The authors are grateful to the publishers for permission to reprint material from the article.
2 Many analysts argue that the EU is democratically legitimate because it derives its democratic legitimacy from the member states. Some concede that the EU addresses a wide range of issues, but they argue that the types of issues it handles lack the salience to spark deep social involvement and public participation (see for instance Moravcsik 2004).

through its embrace of democratic norms and its instituting of a European citizenship.

But although the EU is approached by a broad range of actors, this does not in itself prove that it is more than a functional organization. Actors may still approach it for material gains or in a narrow, instrumental sense. Or they may approach it so as to curtail it and prevent it from touching on issues of fundamental importance to them. Further, that the EU seeks to portray itself as different from a functional-type organization does not necessarily mean that it really is so. In other words, for it to be meaningful to talk of an EU social constituency that is something more and different from that of a functional organization we *also* need to look at the nature of concerns that the actors bring to the EU. Are these so salient as to revolve around the actors' identities, their senses of self and their conceptions of right and wrong? If we relate this to the above quotation from Fraser and Honneth, the issue is whether actors conceive of the EU as a relevant site for *recognition* of identity and for rectification of injustice.

The politics of recognition has entered centre political stage, not only nationally, but also, and increasingly so, *transnationally* (Fraser and Honneth 2003; Fraser 2003; Hobson 2003). Given such a development, those that hold that the EU is a mere functional-type organization, with a narrow social contingent of economic interest organizations, also claim that the EU and its social constituency are *exceptional*, in that they both have escaped entanglement with recognition politics. Those that claim that the EU is legitimate similarly imply that it is made up of a range of national recognition-oriented structures of demands and expectations and that these have not been transnationalized and (re)directed at the EU.

If, however, the EU makes up an important site for recognition politics, the question remains as to *how* – given its special non-state character – the struggle for recognition would unfold within the EU. What kind of a social constituency would emerge within an EU engulfed in recognition struggles? Would it be made up foremost of the new social movements?[3] Would the concerns be mainly those of *cultural* recognition (cf. Taylor 1994; Fraser 2003)? Would the focus be on *post-material* values (cf. Inglehart 1977, 1990)? Would instead *states* figure as the central actors so that the dominant demands would be those of recognition of *national difference and uniqueness*? These questions bring up the larger conceptual issue of what is meant by recognition. They also bring up the empirical issue of who the relevant actors are, what their claims are and how the EU relates to these. And not the least, they bring up the methodological issue of *how* to properly map the EU's social constituency.

This chapter seeks to develop a conceptual-methodological framework that will help us to identify the EU's social constituency and spell out its specific traits. To this end, we seek to fuse elements of a modified version of Axel

---

3 New social movements are generally identified with the women's movement, sexual liberation, ecologists, the peace movement, and ethnic and linguistic minorities.

Honneth's (1995a, 1995b, 2003) approach to recognition (*the what*) with the contentious politics approach (*the how*) associated with Charles Tilly (1978) and associates (see for instance McAdam *et al.* 2001). The latter apply this to the EU but not from a recognition perspective (Imig and Tarrow 2001).

Recognition, notes Honneth, 'is of central importance today . . . because it has proven to be the appropriate tool for categorically unlocking social experiences of injustice as a whole' (2003: 249). A core feature here is the notion of a *recognition order*: 'a framework within which individuals and groups are learning to see themselves as recognized with respect to certain characteristics.' Honneth's project is to establish the characteristic features of the modern recognition order.

This framework (appropriately modified and extended) can serve as a useful heuristic tool for the conceptualization of the EU's social constituency.[4] First, it underlines that any polity generates recognition expectations. The notion of recognition has not only a social, but also a critical legal-institutional component. A person's or group's experience of injustice and disrespect relates to a set of institutionalized principles of recognition.

Second, the framework is useful not only to determine whether the EU establishes such expectations, but also what types they are, and whether the EU can be construed as a novel or unique recognition order.

Third, the framework can accommodate the alleged uniqueness of the EU also because of its inclusiveness: it provides us with a set of analytical categories whose purpose it is to encompass the entire range of motivations that could prompt people to act to rectify injustice. As such it can also capture the *enlarged EU's social constituency*. If we had developed a framework that focused on new social movements only, we would most likely have inserted an unwarranted bias in favour of Western Europe.

In the following section, we spell out the recognition framework in further detail and assess its relevance to the EU. Then, we present a framework that helps us to map and assess the structure of claims-making in the EU and undertake a first attempt to apply this framework to minorities in Europe. These three sections demonstrate that it takes a very major research effort to establish with precision the structure of demands and expectations that are directed at the EU. A recognition-theoretical perspective underlines that such a mapping should also be seen in light of the type of recognition expectations that the EU establishes. In the subsequent section, such a brief sketch is provided. It is placed after the mapping so as to make clear that there might be discrepancies between the social demands that are oriented at the EU on the one hand and the nature of the recognition expectations that the EU seeks to establish on the other. An assessment of the EU's social constituency requires proper attention *both* to the recognition expectations that the EU

---

4 We do not consider the normative problems in Honneth's framework. For these consider Fraser's numerous objections to Honneth's approach. See Fraser (1997, 2003); Fraser and Honneth (2003).

establishes *and* to the structure of social demands that is oriented at it. The latter is clearly informed by the former but cannot be derived from it. The final section holds the conclusion.

The recognition framework: presentation and assessment

The term recognition has roots in Hegelian philosophy, in Hegel's phenomenology of consciousness and

> designates an ideal reciprocal relation between subjects in which each sees the other as equal and also as separate from it. This relation is deemed constitutive for subjectivity; one becomes an individual subject only in virtue of recognizing, and being recognized by, another subject.
> Fraser 2003: 10

Recognition is therefore critical to identity. It speaks to how identities are constructed, sustained and how they may be violated. Recognition is about the moral sources of social discontent. What subjects expect from society above all is recognition of their identity claims, in other words,

> subjects perceive institutional procedures as social injustice when they see aspects of their personality being disrespected which they believe have a right to recognition. What is called 'injustice' in theoretical language is experienced by those affected as social injury to well-founded claims to recognition.
> Honneth 2003: 114

Recognition speaks to matters moral because of people's expectations: 'every society requires justification from the perspective of its members to the extent that it has to fulfil a number of normative criteria that arise from deep-seated claims in the context of social interaction' (Honneth 2003: 129). Recognition is a social phenomenon because individuals (and groups) direct their expectations and concerns at society.

To claim that people have a strong need for recognition is akin to saying that human beings are something more than, and different from, a mere collection of atomistic actors who pursue their self-interests. Claims and issues revolve around conceptions of the good life, and what is just and valuable; and they are therefore very difficult to reconcile. They can spark extremely intense and upsetting conflicts, and can as easily break as make a fledgling entity (such as the EU). Struggles for recognition can bring with them demands for attitudinal changes, for changes in institutions and socialization patterns, and for changes in sociocultural valuations.

Honneth's notion of the modern recognition order consists of three sets of principles. The first principle relates to 'self-confidence' and is based on needs and emotions generally found in love, the notion of 'being oneself in another'.

This notion of recognition as self-confidence highlights trust, as it is based on love. It refers to the individual's basic trust in itself and others – a taken-for-granted trust in one's own control of one's body. This is deeply harmed when the individual is deprived of basic control of his or her body, through abuse, rape and torture.[5] A person who is unable freely to control his or her body will suffer a lasting loss in basic self-confidence because of reduced trust in their own ability to control their own body, and that others will respect his or her physical integrity. Violation deeply affects the victims' emotive state, as it also produces a deep sense of humiliation and social shame.

The second recognition principle is termed 'self-respect'. It refers to the moral responsibility that derives from legal rights. Legal rights also have a clear recognition aspect because:

> we can only come to understand ourselves as the bearers of rights when we know, in turn, what various normative obligations we must keep vis-à-vis others: only once we have taken the perspective of the 'generalized other', which teaches us to recognize the other members of the community as the bearers of rights, can we also understand ourselves to be legal persons, in the sense that we can be sure that certain of our claims will be met.
>
> Honneth 1995a: 108

Legal relations highlight the general and universalizable aspect of the recognition relationship because what is recognized is the person as a holder of rights, not the particular personality traits or attributes of the person. Rights provide their bearers with the reassurance of a standardized form of entitlement and provide rights-bearers with the opportunity 'to exercise the universal capacities constitutive of personhood' (Anderson in Honneth 1995a: xv). They also offer a measure of protection against negative social evaluations. Legal recognition does not refer to a given set of human abilities which are fixed once and for all:

> It will rather turn out to be the case that the essential indeterminacy as to what constitutes the status of a responsible person leads to a structural openness on the part of modern law to a gradual increase in inclusivity and precision.
>
> Honneth 1995a: 110

Failure of recognition occurs when people are excluded from possession of rights, or when they are denied certain rights. Such denial affects a person's moral self-respect. This of course refers to the sense of loss of whatever entitlements were associated with the rights. But since rights are also expressions of the social structure of belief in a given community, exclusion or denial of rights is also a sign that the person is not recognized as a full and equal

---

5 See Young (1990) for an excellent account of such different forms.

member of the community. The person's sense of individual autonomy is weakened or even undermined because its ability to form moral judgements is restricted.

The third and final recognition principle is 'self-esteem'. It highlights a person's or group's sense of what makes someone special, unique and (in Hegel's terms) 'particular'. Self-esteem highlights those distinct features or personality traits that are socially significant and valued. It is always oriented at a social setting or context in which the values are communicated and assessed. The social setting provides a framework that serves as a reference for the appraisal of particular personality features and where the social 'worth' of such is measured in relation to societal goals and to the personality features' contribution to their realization.[6]

Denial of recognition is under this principle associated with the denigration and insult that emanate from experiences in which one's own form of behaviour and manner of belief are regarded as inferior or even deficient. Those affected suffer a loss in self-esteem, as they recognize that their mode of life is not considered to offer anything of positive value to the community.

There is a tension in the third recognition principle between one notion of self-esteem that is ultimately settled through legal equality and another that seeks measures to ensure communal protection and preservation. The latter 'cultural' type prompts Honneth to ask whether it might make up a fourth recognition principle.

Preliminary European application and evaluation

What implications might we draw from this for the study of the EU's social constituency? As noted above, this framework is not confined to the new social movements, although they of course matter, as is for instance the case with the women's movement in Europe.[7] But *confining* the framework to new social movements could mean failing to capture the nature and extent of the politically salient human suffering that is relevant to the politics of recognition. In the post-socialist era, it has become more difficult to reach agreement on what are the core social ills and injustices (as the debate between Fraser and Honneth over redistribution versus recognition brings out very clearly). Honneth consequently underlines the need to be on the constant lookout for social ills.

> A critical social theory that supports only normative goals that are already publicly articulated by social movements risks precipitously affirming the

---

6 'Unlike the sphere of rights, solidarity carries with it a "communitarian" moment of particularity: which particular values are endorsed by a community is a contingent matter, the result of social and cultural struggles that lack the universality that is distinctive of legal relations' (Anderson in Honneth 1995a: xvii).
7 On the role of women in the EU, see for instance Hoskyns (1996); Ackers (1999); Shaw (2000); Williams (2003).

prevailing level of political-conflict in a given society: only experiences of suffering that have already crossed the threshold of mass media attention are confirmed as morally relevant, and we are unable to advocatorially thematize and make claims about socially unjust states of affairs that have so far been deprived of public attention.

Honneth 2003: 115–16

This observation is relevant to the mapping of the EU's social constituency. We must develop a framework that can adequately caption the most important types of injustice. In other words, we must avoid falling into the trap that Offe spells out, namely that each society has a '"hegemonic" configuration of issues that seem to deserve priority and in respect to which political success or progress is primarily measured, while others are marginal or "outside" of politics' (1987: 66).

Second, the recognition framework does not approach the question of the EU's social constituency exclusively 'from below', i.e., from the structure of citizens' demands and social movement involvement in the EU. Rather, it highlights how citizens' demands are shaped by the structure of expectations that the society or community creates. The law and, in particular, rights are of central importance to the framing of such expectations. The recognition relation could thus be seen to have a 'triadic character': it involves the relation between individuals (and groups/collectives), i.e., the expectations that they place on each other, and that these relations are steeped within a set of institutions that make up the framework of expectations.

Third, we need a framework that is open-ended also because the process of European integration could generate new injustices, foster new actors and create new and different conflict configurations.[8] European integration need not replicate nation-building. European integration can provide a new arena for claims, such as for instance for the recognition of Europe's Christian identity,[9] and for the recognition of national language minorities (Trenz 2004). But it can also make dominant national frames more visible and reflexive, as nationals in one state have to relate to the concerns of non-nationals within and without their state.[10]

Fourth, the Honneth framework does not confine recognition struggles to the realm of culture, but is meant to include issues of distributional injustice.[11] This is, however, a problematic assertion (cf. Fraser 1997, 2003; Fraser and

---

8 A prominent finding is that European integration fosters Europeanization of domestic politics over transnationalization of politics (Imig and Tarrow 2001: 48).
9 Consider in particular the struggle for having a reference to Europe's Christian heritage inserted into the Draft Treaty establishing a Constitution for Europe (European Convention 2003).
10 Consider in this connection Weiler's (2001, 2002) notion of constitutional tolerance.
11 Honneth's strong thesis is that 'even distributional injustices must be understood as the institutional expression of social disrespect – or, better said, of unjustified relations of recognition' (Honneth 2003: 114). Fraser argues that this may serve to displace issues of redistribution (Fraser 2003; Fraser and Honneth 2003).

Honneth 2003). The issue is not *whether* recognition and redistribution are imbricated, as both Fraser and Honneth agree that they are, but rather whether we can rely on one intellectual framework steeped in recognition, or whether we need two frameworks, one steeped in recognition and the other in redistribution. The critical issue is what is lost in relying on one framework. Fraser argues that reliance on recognition alone poses two core problems: that of *displacement* and that of *reification*. With displacement is meant that cultural conflicts can overshadow, marginalize and replace redistribution struggles. The second problem, that of reification, speaks to how groups involved in a recognition struggle retain and defend entrenched identities and ways of life rather than relate to, adapt to and reflect on those of its adversaries. Reification relates foremost to Honneth's third recognition mode, that of self-esteem. When reification occurs, reflexivity, learning and transformation are inhibited.

These are important objections. In a sense, the first problem, when related to the EU, might be the opposite of displacement, a *reverse displacement*, so to speak, as those who see the EU as a functional-type organization do not consider questions of recognition to be very relevant to the EU. Therefore, it seems important first to establish that the EU is a relevant site for recognition politics, and *thereafter* consider the role of displacement. This chapter is only concerned with establishing whether recognition politics is relevant to the EU.

The problem of reification is of direct relevance to the EU setting, with one possible case being national identity. If we consider the recognition order associated with the nation-state, we find that it holds both a domestic and an international dimension. The domestic order is based on a complex mixture of self-confidence, self-respect and self-esteem. The *democratic* nation-state, very simply put, reins in and makes group-based notions of self-esteem subject to legal-institutional controls, foremost through the medium of individual rights. But in its relations to other states, it can still largely rely on *national auto-recognition*, which is an assurance that the state can appeal to and be recognized as an entity with a distinct national identity entrenched in the doctrine of national sovereignty and upheld by international law.

What this entails in recognition terms has nevertheless been reined in through developments in international law which have modified the doctrine of national sovereignty through a strengthened commitment to human rights. This development has been particularly pronounced in Europe, through the European Court of Human Rights and, increasingly so, through EU law. These (and other) developments point to the prospect of a *post-national* constellation (cf. Habermas 2000).[12] Such a recognition order – whether of a cosmopolitan or of a state-based kind – would privilege the second mode: self-respect. It is steeped in individual rights and can render the other two modes reflexive. The relevant mode of allegiance would be different from that

---

12 See also Delanty (1995) on the importance of post-national citizenship.

of the nation-state, as it would be based on a post-national constitutional patriotism (cf. Habermas 1994, 1996, 2000).

The question then is whether the EU represents a recognition order that is distinctly different from that of the nation-state. To get at this we both need to understand the nature of claims directed at the EU and the nature of recognition expectations that the EU generates. On the identification of claims, Honneth's recognition framework has been critiqued for being static and perhaps even deterministic in terms of privileging presumed over actual claims and for being overly concerned with pre-political suffering. In other words, Honneth's socio-psychological framework does not provide adequate mechanisms for *whether* and *how* a sense of grievance is converted into action. The Honneth framework lacks attention to the political-organizational conditions that convert a sense of social injustice into remedial action. Hence, it cannot account for which forms of unthematized suffering, wrongdoing and injustice that *actually organize* and act. Further, this framework also lacks the means to spell out how the very act of politicization affects the nature of recognition, as

> recognition struggles name, interpret, and make visible histories of discrimination and disrespect, and thus not only motivate an aggrieved person to become politically active or to resist, but are a crucial part of the process of self-realization of mis- and nonrecognition.
>
> Hobson 2003: 5

In the following, we present a methodological strategy for mapping the EU's social constituency that seeks to take into account both Honneth's notion of unthematized suffering, and the limitations built into the Honneth recognition order. We do so first by trying to outline the possible range of claims and claimants in a European setting. Thereafter we spell out a methodology for studying the EU, with a view to capture the EU's 'recognition order', i.e., to highlight the range of expectations that people derive from and place on the EU.

Identifying claims and claimants

The EU has emerged within a setting with well-entrenched recognition expectations. It is built on top of nation-states, all of which are democratic and the majority of which are welfare states. If the EU were to copy the arrangements of its member states or somehow duplicate them, it would establish a recognition structure that would encourage citizens to have equally high expectations. What kind of recognition expectations the EU shapes will be the subject of the next part. Here we will try to identify the relevant actors – the claims-seekers or the claimants – by drawing on the contentious politics perspective.[13] This perspective has three traits that permit its combining

---

13 By contentious politics is meant 'episodic, public, collective interaction among makers of claims and their objects when (a) at least one government is a claimant, an object of claims,

with the recognition framework presented above. First, it permits a focus on identity. Second, it is inclusive and not confined to a specific set of actors such as social movements. And third, it highlights institutional and social *interaction* (Imig and Tarrow 2001: 4). Nevertheless, this framework must also be modified to suit the recognition framework. In light of the concern expressed above pertaining to reification, the framework must permit us to distinguish between different modes of recognition, with the core distinction between self-confidence/self-respect on the one hand and self-esteem on the other.

Recognition theorists emphasize the political salience of characteristics that are for the most part *not* self-chosen, such as gender, race, class, physical handicap, sexual orientation, age and nationality. A mapping of the EU's social constituency should therefore start with mapping these. But each such category is not an exclusive container: many people belong in several. To capture this, we can use Tilly's (1978) notion of *catness* because it sees category as a variable component, that is, the categories may be more or less complete and exclusive.

But if we use category as the main criterion for selection, that would exclude all voluntary groups. Further, there is no automatic link between category and action. A category of people that suffers enormous wrongdoing and injustice (as have women and homosexuals for centuries) may go on enduring it, or they may suddenly rise to action. It is therefore imperative to consider the organizational dimension, including conditions that either facilitate or stymie mobilization and sudden and episodic bursts of action.

Tilly's definition of organization is largely compatible with the recognition framework. Organization is defined as 'the extent of common identity and unifying structure among the individuals in the population; as a process, an increase in common identity and/or unifying structure . . .' (1978: 54). A particular category can give the organization its identity, such as a women's organization. The group may be loosely structured, as a network, or it may be a tightly integrated organization. An organization is a *catnet*, as it is made up of category(ies) and network(s). 'This notion of organization stresses the group's inclusiveness: how close it comes to absorbing the members' whole lives' (Tilly 1978: 64). To caption the dynamic character of organizing, we can use Tilly's notion of *netness*. Organization is then the function of:

CATNESS × NETNESS

Catnet, as reflected in 'catness' and 'netness', can be both inclusive and exclusive, depending on the nature and range of categories involved, as well as the nature and density of the networks involved. But however relevant and useful this notion of *catnet* is, it does not determine the particular orientation of a group and the types of demands that a group will set forth. It is not possible

or a party to the claims and (b) the claims would, if realized, affect the interests of at least one of the claimants' (McAdam *et al.* 2001: 5). See also Aminzade *et al.* (2001).

to infer from a particular *catnet* or organization whether it will be foremost concerned with claims relating to self-confidence, self-respect or self-esteem. In the extension of this, it is also not clear whether its overall orientation will be to the promotion and protection of equal dignity, or to the promotion and protection of difference/uniqueness.[14] Groups may seek all of these, which means that it is necessary to clarify the objectives of a given group. In addition, several other steps must be taken if the notion of *catnet* is to be used to map the scope and magnitude of concern with recognition in a given setting. In principle, such an effort involves *to go through all of the following steps of identification*:

Step 1

To clarify the *catness*, we need to know the nature and extent of relevant categories in the entities under study. Such categories, as noted, can be gender, sexuality, ethnicity, race, nation, age, region, religion, province and class. Public statistics are useful, insofar as they contain information on the relevant categories. A complete mapping has to take into account, on an ongoing basis, changes caused by immigration and emigration, and births and deaths, and is therefore extremely resource-demanding. In principle, this initial mapping says nothing about subjective identification with a category, the relation between and among categories, i.e., whether they converge or diverge, coincide or compete, or the political salience of the category. For that we need additional information.

Step 2

The next step is to clarify *netness*, to know the nature and extent of networks within which people involve themselves. A network is made up of people with some kind of an interpersonal bond – weak or strong. To map this we need to know the type and the degree of contact, and whether this firms up into an organization. Modern societies are dynamic, are marked by great mobility and also increasingly by technology that facilitates contact and interaction among large numbers of people, at very different levels of personal contact and intimacy. In the European setting, with the supra and transnational EU institutions imposed on the nation-states, there is great potential for network formation.

Networks are often formed around categories, or the latter are embedded in specific networks.

Step 3

In the next step, we assess the *catness* and *netness* of these, in order to get a sense of their organizational status. This includes an assessment of the degree

---

14 Some theorists underline this distinction more than do others. Consider for instance Taylor (1994); Young (1990); versus Fraser (1997, 2003); Fraser and Honneth (2003).

Conceptualizing the EU's social constituency 157

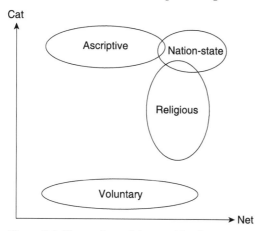

Figure 7.1 Illustration of the combined *catnet* strength of the nation-state

of inclusiveness and exclusiveness of each *catnet*, as well as an assessment of their organizational status, such as the resources they command, as well as how they are structured.

A further indicator of *netness* is the group or organization's mobilizing potential, which ranges from action taken by a group *in response to* an outside threat to a group's identity or sense of self (defensive), to action taken to capitalize on opportunities that have arisen (offensive) and to that of preparatory mobilization, where a group 'pools resources in anticipation of future opportunities and threats' (Tilly 1978: 74). Organizational characteristics pertaining to goal, ideology, structure, technology and 'task environment' clearly matter to the establishment of overall *netness* in a society. The same applies to the nature of inter-organizational relations and the particular constellation of social costs versus opportunities involved.

As Figure 7.1 shows, groups and collectives place themselves differently within the two-dimensional catnet grid.

Step 4

The next step is to sort out *which catnets*, from the whole range of possible ones, that would be the most important for us to establish the relevant claimants. This task requires theory because we need to establish criteria for sorting out the ones that are the most important.

The recognition framework cited above can serve such a theoretical purpose. The question is whether it yields sufficiently clear indicators to select claimants. We can start from any one of the following angles:

- Identify all those groups that are directly involved in the generation, maintenance and also rectification of the basic conditions that ensure self-confidence in any given society.

- Identify the type and range of rights that are available to citizens in a society with the aim of sorting out those groups that are particularly involved in ensuring the conditions that underpin self-respect.
- Identify those groups most closely associated with the 'hegemonic' values in any given society and then look at all those dependent on the 'hegemons' so as to establish the conditions that underpin self-esteem.
- Supplemental investigations, such as, for instance, to obtain information on the prison population, on the presumption that disadvantaged groups tend to be more frequently incarcerated – are there particular groups that dominate here?

Step 5

Step 5 is to clarify the *reasons* that groups give to seek recognition. One take is to look for the explanations that groups give to account for *why* they are concerned with recognition, and try to ascertain which mode of recognition they are most concerned with. We could interview members of the groups, study the information they produce, the interventions they make, the claims they set forth, and how they are addressed by other groups and by public authorities.

Step 6

The next step is to sort groups by explicit reference to the notion of *denial of recognition*. This has the advantage of focusing explicitly on those groups that subjectively see themselves as in need of recognition, and who will also be able and prone to refer to experiences of *denial of recognition* or who refer to some form of *denigration* or *insult*. This strategy is fraught with danger, as its success depends on all those with such experiences *actually using* this particular language. Conversely, widespread public debate on and concern with recognition can have a strong mobilizing and educative effect. This could improve a society's collective ability to handle recognition problems. But societies can cement into the reification of group identities. Such societies may also experience negative 'learning' processes, where the authenticity of claims is sacrificed in a competitive quest for positional advantage: groups may learn from each other what to claim, how to voice their complaints and how to frame their claims. This can lead to improved ways of expressing grievances, but the expressions need not be authentic in the sense that they can come to reflect the learning of the socially most effective ways of expressing dissatisfaction. In that sense, resourceful groups and individuals can use the language of recognition strategically to promote their interests and concerns.

Step 7

The final step is to establish how and the extent to which those actors that can be categorized under the label of recognition approach the EU. Four possible ways in which claims and claimants may relate to the EU can be identified:

1 They focus *exclusively* on the EU as the addressee for claims.
2 The EU is seen as *supplemental*, meaning that there is an equal focus on the EU and on another entity, such as an organization's home state.
3 The EU is a *subsidiary* addressee, meaning that there is another addressee that matters more to the groups or the organizations.
4 The relevant claim-seekers *do not focus* on the EU at all.

This classification permits us to sort out claims and claimants in terms of degree of focus on and interest in the EU. It is important to establish which mode of recognition predominates under each category, in particular whether those in (1) and (2) are concerned with self-confidence/self-respect or with self-esteem.

In line with what researchers have found on the nature of contentious politics in the EU (cf. Imig and Tarrow 2001), this set of indicators should distinguish between organizing to participate in EU affairs versus channel demands to the EU versus channel demands dealing with EU issues through their respective national bodies.[15]

On the last category (4), the larger this category of claims and claimants that do not have the EU as their addressee, the weaker the EU's social constituency. But, as noted, even if there are few claims-seekers directly addressing the EU, the EU could still figure as an issue within the member states, which might either put forth claims or be used to *curtail* the role of the EU.

The framework set out above makes clear that to properly establish the nature, scope and salience of the politics of recognition in the recently enlarged EU requires a very comprehensive research effort. This framework helps us to spell out the specific character of this constituency from a recognition perspective, through our effort to distinguish between different modes of recognition, with self-confidence/self-respect versus self-esteem as the most important distinction. Further, such a comprehensive mapping 'from below' is also useful precisely because it does not take as its point of departure the EU's own definition of its social constituency. How the EU defines its social constituency, i.e. the nature of the expectations that the EU generates, is the theme of the last section. It is the combination of these two sets of investigations, when conducted to the full, that will yield the most complete picture as to the uniqueness of the EU's recognition order.

But first, we will provide a mapping of some of the relevant categories. This effort will also illustrate some of the problems – pertaining to data availability and data collection; research methodology; and research ethics – that such an undertaking involves.

Tentative mapping of the EU's social constituency

The first step to take to clarify the scope and magnitude of the EU's social constituency is to identify the nature and extent of relevant categories across

---

15 Our second and third categories would contain Imig and Tarrow's (2001) collective transnationalism and our third would also cover what they refer to as domestication of conflict 'in which national actors protest at home against policies of the European Union'.

the EU's territory. The most recent EU enlargement to Bulgaria and Romania on 1 January 2007 is not included in the following, as these two countries were not EU members at the time of data collection.[16] The mapping thus covers 25 member states. This is already a large number of entities, with great variations as to the availability of descriptive population statistics, as well as with regard to the legal constraints on the collection of such data. As the below parts will show, it is close to impossible to establish exact numbers for the vast amount of minority groups in Europe. This means that the main concern of this first step of the analysis, to ensure as exact a stipulation of groups based on objective categories as possible, is extremely hard to come by. It is thus extremely difficult to devise a study that is wholly capable of addressing this problem.

We first present some of the main challenges as regards the collection of data, and then turn to a tentative mapping of four of the most relevant categories: ethnicity, immigration, religion and language minority in the pre-2007 25 EU member states.

Such a mapping raises important methodological issues. We will point to some of these here, as we go through examples of how the different countries gather the data. We will show that even the first apparently simple step in the effort to map Europe's social constituency – statistical mapping – is fraught with danger, as it brings up methodological as well as important ethical issues and concerns. As the relevant groups themselves know, the act of placing someone in a given group or category is also to locate the person or group in the given society's status hierarchy. This can also intervene with the very definition of a category of people and enter into the way the data is collected. Further, the sociocultural salience of a given category may weigh differently in one setting from another because the relevant categories interact differently. For instance, a particular ethnic identity may in one setting or country be closely linked with wealth and influence, whereas in another with poverty and social estrangement. The number belonging to the ethnic group may be the same in each place but how they are regarded – and regard themselves – in each country may vary greatly. James D. Fearon notes that

> what the ethnic groups in a country are depends on what the people in the country think they are at a given time [. . .] it cannot be assumed, without argument, that ethnic distinctions are wholly exogenous to other political, economic, and social variables of interest.
>
> Fearon 2003: 199

One problem is that this may shape the way ethnic distinctions are coded in a given setting; another is that this greatly limits the scope for 'recognition data' to have the same meaning and significance across different contexts. The implication is that we need to consider the statistical data in relation to the other steps in the analysis before we start comparing across contexts.

---

16 The data in this section was collected in the period February–May 2005.

It should also be added that historical factors affect both the definition of groups and a given group's propensity to be reported, notably when this registration involves active participation from the group(s) in question. For European Jews, to cite a group whose experiences have been particularly horrific, the availability and efficient use of such registers clearly facilitated the Nazi regime's extermination efforts.[17] Hence, Jews may still be likely to underreport their ethnic status.

Data (non-)availability

The processing of data on racial origin, religious or philosophical affiliation, health (disability) or sexual orientation is subject to particularly strict conditions in the EU, as the use of such data involves a risk of discrimination (CFR-CDF 2004: 98). The EU Data Protection Directive[18] states that 'Member States shall prohibit the processing of personal data revealing racial or ethnic origin, political opinions, religious or philosophical beliefs, trade union membership, and the processing of data concerning health or sex life' (Article 8 §1). Thus, in some member states the registration of disaggregated sensitive data is prohibited by privacy and personal data protection legislation. In Denmark, such sensitive information may not be processed with reference to the Danish Personal Data Protection Act – which implements the above-mentioned EU directive on the protection of individuals. Danish authorities argue that the necessary requirements of anonymity would lead to considerable uncertainty in the material, and have 'no plans for carrying out a census with a view to gathering information on ethnic groups, religions or languages'.[19] This stands in contrast to the policy of Slovenia, whose constitution explicitly states that any person has the right to declare his or her ethnic affiliation.[20]

The European Monitoring Centre on Racism and Xenophobia (EUMC) makes ongoing efforts to collect descriptive statistics in order to highlight different aspects of racial discrimination in Europe, and recognizes the challenges encountered in the search for data disaggregated by ethnicity or race,

---

17 The Nazi bureaucracy registered individuals in 'Jewish Registers' (*Judenkartei*), based on the September 1935 Nuremberg racial laws, local registers and the 1939 census. Systematic registration of Roma and Sinti as well as of disabled (including homosexuals) provided a means to identify and locate victims of compulsory sterilization, incarceration in concentration camps and, for the latter, the so-called euthanasia programme. The German effort to accumulate precise statistical population data also extended to Czechoslovakia, Poland and the Netherlands (Milton 1997).
18 Directive 95/46/EC of the European Parliament and of the Council of 24 October 1995 on the protection of individuals with regard to the processing of personal data and on the free movement of such data. *Official Journal of the European Communities*, L 281, 23 November 1995.
19 Sensitive information may only be processed by non-profit organizations relative to their 'members and other persons who by virtue of the object of the organization are in regular contact with this, however, with the proviso that the processing of such information lies within the framework of the organization's activities' (Danish Government 2004: 27–8).
20 Constitution of the Republic of Slovenia, OJ RS 33/91-I, Article 61.

as well as religion, in order to identify the different minority groups (see also Alesina *et al.* 2003). The EUMC calls specifically on 'all Member States to collect, compile and publish yearly such statistics' (EUMC 2003/2004: 193). CompStat is an EU-funded project aimed at overcoming some of these difficulties in the study of integration of immigrants and their descendants in Europe. The project gives a comprehensive account of the availability and comparability of relevant datasets – based on registers, counts, censuses or surveys – and has developed a meta-database with full descriptions of micro-datasets (Gächter 2003). However, only eight member states are covered, and this illustrates the difficulties involved in comparing national data sources in the field of migration and integration.[21]

Another source of information on minority groups is the *Council of Europe Framework Convention for the Protection of National Minorities*. Of the EU25 countries, 21 have signed and ratified the Convention.[22] Signatories of the Convention are committed to reporting on their national minorities; however, the reports vary considerably both in scope and accuracy. Some of the reports give estimated numbers for their 'recognized' national minorities, thus excluding immigrants and other minorities that are not granted such status. Again, Denmark provides an example of the problem, reporting only on the one German-speaking minority living close to the German border. No other minority group residing in the country is mentioned. Furthermore, in the Italian legal system the concept of 'minority' is linked exclusively to that of language, and the Roma, Sinti and travellers are referred to as a 'Gypsy linguistic minority' (Italian Government 2004: 37). As a consequence, foreign ethnic minorities are not reported to the Framework Convention. The usefulness of the national reports to the Convention in establishing the number of national minorities is thus limited.

One further challenge when collecting data from a vast number of national statistical sources is language constraints. Much of the statistical data from the different national bureaus is only available in national language(s), requiring extensive language skills as well as a certain effort of translation, when collecting the data.[23] The problems related to data comparability due to the 'absence or very limited existence of English translations of legislation and

---

21 The countries are Austria, Belgium, Germany, Hungary, Italy, the Netherlands, the Czech Republic and Poland. The six former countries are surveyed in detail, while the two latter only in outline.
22 The remaining four countries are Belgium, Greece, Luxembourg (who have signed but not yet ratified the Convention) and France (the only country that has not signed). See the Chart of signature and ratifications, available at http://conventions.coe.int/Treaty/Commun/Cherche Sig.asp?NT=157&CM=8&DF=09/11/2011&CL=ENG (accessed 9 November 2011).
23 For example, the main official statistical institution in Belgium, *Institut National de Statistique (INS)*, mainly offers information in French, and to a certain extent Dutch, despite German being one of three official language communities. Also, the official statistical bureaus in the Netherlands, the Czech Republic, Italy, France and Luxembourg have limited public information in other languages than their national ones, although information may be provided upon request.

Conceptualizing the EU's social constituency 163

other relevant material' are also emphasized by the EUMC (Chahrokh *et al.* 2004: 4).

Bearing the above constraints in mind, we have attempted to number some of the minority groups in the EU according to four criteria: ethnic, immigrant, religious and linguistic. For each of them, the particular conceptual and methodological challenges encountered are outlined. Data have been collected predominantly from national statistical bureaus. In the first instance, data were gathered from online databases and statistical volumes published by the various national offices, providing population statistics based on censuses, registers and surveys. Complementary information on available disaggregated data was given by officials when such were not accessible online. Further, national reports submitted to the Council of Europe's Framework Convention for the Protection of National Minorities were consulted, where estimates of national minorities are found for several countries, although restricted to a small part of all the groups in question. These data were supplemented by secondary sources, such as the annual country-specific International Religious Freedom Reports published by the US Bureau for Democracy, Human Rights and Labor (on religious minorities), the Euromosaic study (on language minorities) and information from other research projects and intergovernmental organizations.[24]

The purpose of this tentative mapping is to demonstrate the lack of coherent, comprehensive data across EU member states, and that the disaggregated data on the populations that are available must be derived from a variety of sources, concepts and definitions. The presentation is meant to be illustrative and the main intention is to highlight which data are available, as well as to show the extent to which figures for minority groups actually exist in the various member states. It is not our aim to collect data that can be used for statistical analysis, nor is it to assess which definitions are best suited for the categorization of various minorities. We rather aim to highlight the issues and concerns that need to be taken into account when attempting to map the current minorities in the EU – as seen from a recognition perspective.[25]

Ethnic minorities in the EU

When identifying the first category – ethnic minorities – we encounter the most challenging conceptual problems. 'Ethnic identity' refers to membership of a particular cultural group, defined by shared cultural practices, language and custom. The UN Recommendation for 2000 censuses of population gives the following definition:

---

24 See e.g. Compstat, the European Monitoring Centre on Racism and Xenophobia (EUMC) (as of 1 March 2007 the EU Agency for Fundamental Rights, FRA), the International Centre for Migration Policy Development (ICMPD), EUREL.
25 We wish to thank Lars Tore Rydland at the Norwegian Social Science Data Services (NSD) for constructive comments on this part of the chapter.

Ethnic groups (and/or national groups) are made up of persons who consider themselves as having a same origin and/or culture, which may appear in linguistic and/or religious and/or other characteristics which differ from those of the rest of the population. It depends on the historical and political circumstances whether countries consider such groups as ethnic groups and/or national groups.[26]

This category includes both citizens (nationals) and non-citizens (non-nationals) of the EU member states who consider themselves as having identifiable group characteristics (such as language, culture and religion). From a data collection perspective, problems arise when member states define ethnicity differently, and when there are severe restrictions on the data collection in several countries.

The very concept of 'ethnicity' is highly controversial, and represents as such a further obstacle when trying to identify the groups of different ethnic origin in Europe. Some member states do not use concepts such as 'national minority', 'race' or 'ethnic origin' in legal terms, and more than half of the member states have no official registers of ethnic minority populations.[27] Only 10 of the 25 member states collect census data on 'ethnic origin', and with the exception of the UK, they are all among the new member states in Central and Eastern Europe.[28] Most of the censuses asked the respondents to write a nationality or national identity of his or her choice, hence the data is not based on 'category' but on self-identification.

This is of course understandable for numerous reasons, but from a statistical mapping perspective, it raises several methodological problems. It is frequently observed that the true ethnic group is not recorded or stated by the respondent. People might be reluctant to report his or her belonging to an ethnic minority group, which will result in under-reported figures.

The complex character of this issue is illustrated by the Czech 2001 census. The number of people reporting 'other than Czech' identity decreased considerably for several groups from the 1991 census to the 2001 census.[29] Moravian national identity, for example, was reported by 13.2 per cent of the covered population in the 1991 census and only by 3.6 per cent in the 2001 census. The discrepancy between census results and the real size of a minority group was also very obvious in the case of the Roma community. According to 'informed estimates, there are about 200,000 Roma in the Czech Republic'. However,

---

26 United Nations Economic Commission for Europe and the Statistical Office of the European Communities, Statistical Standards and Studies No. 49, *Recommendations for the 2000 Censuses of Population and Housing in the ECE Region*, UN, New York and Geneva, 1998, p. 21.
27 Austria, Belgium, Denmark, Finland, Germany, Greece, France, Ireland, Italy, Luxembourg, Malta, the Netherlands, Portugal, Spain and Sweden.
28 The member states that collect data on ethnic origin are: Cyprus, the Czech Republic, Estonia, Hungary, Latvia, Lithuania, Poland, Slovenia, Slovakia and the United Kingdom.
29 The percentage decreases for the main groups were Moravian 72.6 per cent, Silesian 74.7 per cent, Slovak 41.6 per cent and Roma 64.4 per cent.

only 11,746 reported Roma national identity in their census forms (Czech Government 2004: 46). Among the explanatory factors are societal developments, such as the increasing homogeneity of the population after the split of the Czechoslovak federation, and advancing integration or assimilation of persons belonging to national minorities. However, part of the discrepancy is believed to be caused by mere methodological factors. Claims were put forward before the 2001 census that personal data might be misused, and this negative publicity is believed to have affected the final result (ibid: 44). An additional methodological explanation is held to be the confusion of 'nationality' with 'citizenship', and the fact that it was optional to report on nationality in the census.

The character of the wording used may also affect the result when collecting sensitive personal data. The Hungarian 2001 census aimed at identifying 'traditional' ethnic minorities only. The first question asked was: 'Which of these nationalities do you think you belong to?' and included an 'exhaustive list of nationalities'. Respondents were allowed to give three answers; however, apart from the 13 officially registered ethnic groups, only one could be named. The subsequent question was: 'which of these nationalities' cultural values and traditions do you feel affinity with?' The *total* number of people reporting 'other than Hungarian' on the latter question does not differ considerably from the former; however, there are large variations *within* the ethnic groups. For instance, a total of 189,984 (1.9 per cent) regarded themselves as Gypsy and Roma, but only 129,208 (1.3 per cent) felt affinity with Gypsy (Roma) cultural values and traditions.[30]

Table 7.1 gives the *estimated* size of ethnic minorities in 25 EU countries. The figures are based on a variety of sources and are not comparable, but serve to illustrate the various conceptions used and the quality of the 'raw data' available. Where disaggregated data exist, figures are reported by national statistical offices. As discussed above these data are of varying quality. In some cases, such as for instance Slovenia, Table 7.1 lists the 'most reliable' figures stemming from the census, and thus *under-reports* the size of ethnic minority groups.[31] For the remaining countries, reports from national governments to the Framework Convention for the Protection of National Minorities have been used to include some groups that are considered to be 'national minorities', a concept that to a certain extent overlaps with 'ethnicity'. However, the signatories use different definitions of such groups, with some countries limiting the framework convention to their language minorities, and others reporting only on the Roma community. Table 7.1 provides rough

---

30 It is generally difficult to estimate the size of the Roma community in Europe. According to a Slovenian national minority report, an estimated 7,000 to 10,000 Roma live in the country, but only 3,246 persons declared themselves as Roma in the 2002 census (Slovenian Government 2004).
31 According to estimates from local elections in November 2002, the real numbers of the members of the Italian and Hungarian minorities are 3,388 and 8,328, respectively, while the census figures listed in Table 7.1 only count 2,970 and 6,243, respectively.

Table 7.1 Ethnic minorities in 25 EU member states

	Definition used for data collection	Absolute numbers	Total population	% of total population	Reference date
AT[1]	National minorities	169,500	8,000,000	2.1	2000
BE[2]	—	—	—	—	—
CY[3]	Ethnic group	119,200	741,000	16.1	1996
CZ[4]	Nationality/national identity	980,283	10,230,060	9.6	1 March 2001
DE[5]	Ethnic groups	240,000	82,300,000	0.3	21 September 2004
DK[6]	—	—	—	—	—
EE[7]	Ethnic nationality	439,833	1,370,052	32.1	31 March 2000
EL[8]	—	—	—	—	—
ES[9]	Roma community	650,000–700,000	44,108,530	1.6	1 January 2005
FI[10]	National minority	67,000	5,219,732	1.3	31 December 2003
FR[11]	Nationality	6,396,740	59,229,090	10.8	1 July 2004
HU[12]	Nationality	345,611 No answer: 543,317	10,198,315	3.4 No answer: 5.3	1 February 2001
IE[13]	Indigenous minority	23,509	3,917,203	0.6	28 April 2002
IT[14]	National minorities	2,785,533	56,000,000	4.9	2004
LV[15]	Ethnicity	939,941	2,288,923	41.1	16 August 2006
LT[16]	Ethnicity	576,679	3,483,972	16.6	5 April 2001
LU[17]	—	—	—	—	—
MT[18]	—	—	—	—	—
NL[19]	Allochthonous	3,088,152	16,258,032	19.0	1 January 2004
PL[20]	Nationality	471,475 Unknown: 774,885	38,230,080	1.2 Unknown: 2.0	2002
PT[21]	—	—	—	—	—
SE[22]	National minority	580,000	8,883,590	6.5	31 December 2000
SI[23]	Ethnic affiliation	Declared: 135,619 Other: 197,054	1,964,036	Declared: 6.9 Other: 10.0	31 March 2002
SK[24]	Nationality	710,099 Unknown: 54,502	5,379,455	13.2 Unknown: 1.0	26 May 2001
UK[25]	Ethnic group	4,635,296	58,789,194	7.9	29 April 2001

1 No official data on ethnic minorities is available. Estimates of the five autochthonous minorities of Austrian citizenship (Croats, Hungarians, Slovenes, Czechs and Slovaks) are largely drawn upon information from the respective national minorities' organizations. Also includes the Roma community as reported by the Austrian Government (2000).

2 No data available. The 2001 census does not include variables such as ethnicity or race. Belgium has not ratified the Framework Convention for the Protection of National Minorities, thus no reports on national minorities are issued by the government.
3 Numbers are given for the 'ethnic groups' living on the island, as reported by the Cypriot Government (1999). The Turkish-Cypriots represent the largest minority group, around 12 per cent of the total population (89,200). The 2001 census results are *not* used, as the census was carried out in the government-controlled area only, thus counting only 361 Turkish-Cypriots. Furthermore, it is noted on the census results of other ethnic groups that 'the number of persons recorded [...] does not represent the actual figure. Due to the small percentage of persons belonging to these ethnic groups, what is frequently observed in Censuses is that the true ethnic group is not recorded or stated by the respondent' (Republic of Cyprus, *Census of population 2001, Volume I General Demographic Characteristics*, at p. 144).
4 Czech Statistical Office, Census 2001.
5 Statistics based on ethnic criteria are not available in Germany. The numbers are estimates of some national minorities (Danes, Sorbs, Frisians, and German Sinti and Roma) reported as 'ethnic groups' to the Framework Convention for the Protection of National Minorities (German Government 2005). The reference date for the total population size is 31 December 2001.
6 No data available.
7 Statistical Office of Estonia, Population Census 2000.
8 No data available.
9 No official statistics on ethnic origins available. The Spanish minority reports only include estimates of the Roma community (Spanish Government 2006).
10 No statistical data exist on ethnic minorities. The numbers are estimates from the second national minority report and include the Sami, Roma, Jewish, Tatar, Russian and Estonian population (Finnish Government 2004). The Swedish-speaking Finns are not considered to be an ethnic minority group by the Finnish government and are not included in the table.
11 No data is available on ethnic minorities in France. The table gives the number of the French population born outside France, which to a certain extent might overlap with the concept of 'ethnicity'. INSEE, *Enquêtes annuelles de recensement 2004 et 2005*.
12 Hungarian Central Statistical Office, Census 2001. Information on ethnicity is collected on a voluntary basis.
13 No data available. Central Statistics Office Ireland, Census 2002. Only the traveller community is registered and included in the table.
14 In the Italian legal system, the concept of 'minority' is linked exclusively to that of language, and data on ethnicity or origin are not available. The above figures are indicative only and based upon studies and publications (Italian Government 1999: 31–4).
15 Population Registry, Office of the Citizenship and Migration Affairs (Latvian Government 2006: 3).
16 Statistics Lithuania, Population Census 2001.
17 No data available.
18 No data available.
19 Statistic Netherlands. No data is available on ethnic minorities, the table only includes the so-called '*allochthonous*', referring to persons of immigrant origin (defined by at least one parent born abroad).
20 Central Statistical Office, Poland, Census 2002. According to a national minority report, the number of persons belonging to national minorities is between 841,200 and 1,286,000 (2–3 per cent of the total population) (Polish Government 2002).
21 No data available.
22 It is not allowed to collect data on ethnicity in Sweden. Estimates of the five national minorities that are recognized within the Framework Convention for the Protection of National Minorities are given: Sami, Swedish Finns, Tornedalers, Roma and Jews (Swedish Government 2001).
23 Statistical Office of the Republic of Slovenia, Census 2002. The category 'other' includes 22,141 undeclared persons (Yugoslavs, Bosnians, regionally declared, and people who preferred to be ethnically undeclared), 48,588 persons who did not wish to reply, and 126,325 unknown (6.4 per cent of the total population).
24 Statistical Office of the Slovak Republic, Population and Housing Census 2001. The category 'unknown' covers those who did not declare their nationality, and constitutes 7.1 per cent of the non-Slovak population.
25 Office for National Statistics, UK, Census 2001. The respondents' own perception of belonging to an ethnic group and cultural background. A total of 677,117 persons who replied 'mixed' are included in the figure.

estimates only, and smaller ethnic minority groups in several countries are excluded as no reliable data were found.

In order to provide a more comprehensive and coherent mapping, we would first of all need to elaborate a definition of 'ethnic minorities' that best serves our purpose, and then adjust the various numbers systematically according to this definition. Due to the contested concept of ethnicity, this first step alone requires careful assessment. Furthermore, due to legal constraints as well as conceptual and practical problems, extensive data are missing and any attempt to construct a list of ethnic groups requires an important research effort and still runs the risk of low consistency and comparability.

Immigrant minorities in the EU

The second category we have sorted out for illustrative purposes, that of immigrant minorities, also turns out to be difficult to assess – both in terms of availability of data and comparability across member states. The conception of 'foreign' varies considerably. Most member states largely rely on *citizenship* in determining 'foreign persons'; however, some also have information on the *country of birth*, and/or the *country of origin* in their population statistics.

Immigrants are often defined as the foreign-born population, regardless of acquisition of citizenship, and the notion is often associated with that of ethnic origin. For instance, the definition of immigrants in Slovenia is 'people who had their first residence outside Slovenia and have been living in Slovenia for at least a year'. However, the duration of residence is usually only present in sample surveys, if at all (Gächter 2003: 14). Descendants, understood as children born in an EU member state by immigrant parents, are registered in few member states, as *country of origin*. One of them is the Netherlands, which has a long history of recording parents' place of birth with the notion '*allochthonous*'. In Denmark, three different concepts are used in the Central Personality Register: '*foreign origin*' (immigrants and their descendants, regardless of citizenship), '*immigrants*' (foreign-born population whose parents are foreign citizens or foreign-born) and '*descendants*' (persons born in Denmark but whose parents are not Danish citizens born in Denmark).

The only category that can be found in the population statistics of all member states is *citizenship*. Nevertheless, the value of this data is limited when seeking to map the immigrant minorities in Europe. This is due to discrepancies between the countries as regards laws and procedures for granting citizenship, the extent of mass (labour) migration and/or immigration, and history of former colonies or overseas territories, which for some results in a large presence of colonial/post-colonial immigrants.[32]

---

32 The EUMC makes a distinction between three groups of countries in the former EU15 on the background of their immigration history as well as their concepts of migrants and minority population. The first group consists of France, the Netherlands and the UK, which have a history of 'relatively significant immigration from former colonial territories'; the second of

In the Netherlands, for instance, naturalization is fairly 'easy', and among immigrants born in Turkey, more than half are Dutch nationals. Acceptance of dual citizenship is high. This is illustrated by the fact that 10 per cent of the population have more than one citizenship, and 5.8 per cent have Dutch in addition to one or two other nationalities. Most people of Surinamese descent, people from the Antillean Islands and Aruba are also Dutch nationals, and are not counted if only foreign citizenship is recorded. Table 7.2 clearly illustrates the discrepancy between figures on foreign *citizenship* and foreign *origins*. The Kurd minority in Germany represents another example of the problems related to the concept of citizenship. According to 1998 estimates, there were approximately 500,000 Kurds in the Federal Republic.[33] But German statistics are based on citizenship rather than ethnic identity, and the recorded number of persons with Turkish citizenship gives no possibility to establish the number of Kurds within this group. In the case of Hungary, 'citizenship' includes those with multiple citizenships, without distinguishing them. As a result, these persons are counted *twice*; both as Hungarian and foreign citizens. In Finland, on the other hand, a person with both Finnish and foreign citizenship is recorded as a Finnish national only.

The method for collecting data on citizenship also *varies* across countries. In some instances, such as the Italian 2001 census, citizenship is declared by the respondent. As a consequence, it does *not* necessarily reflect the number of persons actually holding a particular citizenship. Children born in Italy by foreign citizens might have been declared as Italian citizens even though this is not correct according to Italian law. Furthermore, Italy experienced mass labour migration in the late 1950s and 1960s, and many sons of emigrants born abroad have later returned to Italy. This blurs the distinction between country of birth and that of citizenship.[34] More common, however, is to establish the data on citizenship from registers, sometimes linked with immigration border control offices. The CompStat project identifies 37 of the 223 datasets for six selected member states as containing information on immigrants and/or persons with foreign citizenship. Among these, 14 are registers (38 per cent) and 23 are sample surveys (62 per cent). None of them is counts, censuses or panel surveys (Gächter 2003: 17). In an EU of 27 member states, mainstreaming immigrants statistically is still an unaccomplished task.

Austria, Belgium, Denmark, Germany, Luxembourg and Sweden have systematically practised the recruitment of migrant workers; and the third group includes the six remaining, so-called 'new immigration' countries, who experienced long-time emigration and only recently are subject to significant immigration (Greece, Italy, Portugal and Spain since the late 1980s, Finland and Ireland since the early 1990s) (Chahrokh et al. 2004: vi).

33 'EU: Kurds, smuggling,' *Migration News* 5(2). 2 January 1998. Available at http://migration.ucdavis.edu/mn/more.php?id=1454_0_4_0 (accessed 9 November 2011). The EFMS (*Europäisches forum für migrations-studien*) Migration Report 1995 estimated the number to be between 400,000 and 450,000.

34 See '*Gli stranieri residenti in famiglia e in convivenza*', 16. June 2004. Available at http://dawinci.istat.it/daWinci/jsp/MD/download/com_stranieri_res.pdf (accessed 9 November 2011).

Mapping the immigrant minorities on the basis of official statistics and registers also falls short of identifying large groups of stateless persons and persons with unknown citizenship. The Baltic countries have a particular history in this regard. In Latvia, 73 per cent of all foreign nationals are citizens of the former USSR and have never obtained any other nationality. Close to another 19 per cent of the foreign nationals are from the Russian Federation. The country's citizenship laws have been stringent and relatively few non-Latvians have sought or gained citizenship – even after the relaxing of some requirements in order for the country to become an EU member (Kent 2000). The category 'country of birth' can also be a contested concept, as is the case of Estonia. Russia was recorded as the country of birth for persons born before 1945 within the area between the national border of the Republic of Estonia and the temporary control line. Three-quarters of the foreign-born population are born in Russia (a total of 190,599 persons). Furthermore, in 2000, as much as 12.4 per cent of the total population was recorded as having undetermined citizenship.[35] The lion's share was Russians holding an 'aliens passport'. Lithuania, on the other hand, has had a less restrictive citizenship policy, as Table 7.2 clearly indicates. The Law on Citizenship of 1989 made possible, upon request, for any non-Lithuanian, irrespective of the time, purpose and duration of his or her residence in the country, to be granted Lithuanian citizenship. As a consequence, 'a majority of the Lithuanians expressed their wish to become Lithuanian citizens, including over 90 per cent of all the inhabitants who were of different nationality' (Lithuanian Government 2001: 5). Also in Lithuania, however, 30 per cent of the non-Lithuanian citizens are stateless.

The various immigrant groups in 25 EU member states are outlined in Table 7.2. Due to the variations in the statistical material and the availability of data, Table 7.2 distinguishes between three categories in order to provide a more complete overview: people with foreign *citizenship*, foreign *country of birth*, and foreign *origin* (normally defined as one or two parents born in a foreign country). OECD (2006) contains comparable figures on long-term international migration flows, but not for all the member states. We have at this stage chosen to use the raw data that is available from the national bureaus.

Religious minorities in the EU

When turning to the mapping of religious minorities in the EU, the member states are again split as regards the availability of such population data.[36] In almost half of the countries, censuses ask citizens to state their religious or

---

35 The group of 'undetermined' also includes persons who asserted that they had not received the document and did not know their citizenship.
36 There is a clear distinction between old and new member states: only four of the former EU15 report such data (Austria, Finland, Ireland and the UK), while eight of ten new members do the same (Cyprus, the Czech Republic, Estonia, Hungary, Lithuania, Poland, Slovenia and Slovakia).

Table 7.2 Immigrant minorities in 25 EU member states

	Definition used for data collection	Absolute numbers	% of total population	Total population	Reference date
AT[1]	Citizenship	710,926	8.9	8,032,926	15 May 2001
	Country of birth	1,003,399	12.5		
BE[2]	Citizenship	850,077	8.2	10,355,844	1 January 2003
CY[3]	Citizenship	64,810	9.4	689,565	1 October 2001
	Country of birth	60,024	8.7		
CZ[4]	Citizenship	124,608	1.2	10,230,060	1 March 2001
DE[5]	Citizenship	7,341,800	9.8	82,531,700	31 December 2003
DK[6]	Citizenship	271,211	5.0	5,397,640	1 January 2004
	Country of origin	442,036	8.2		
EE[7]	Citizenship	103,960	7.6	1,370,052	31 March 2000
	Country of birth	252,266	18.4		
	Undetermined	170,349	12.4		
EL[8]	Citizenship	762,191	7.0	10,934,097	18 March 2001
	Country of birth	1,122,894	10.3		
ES[9]	Citizenship	2,664,168	6.2	42,717,064	1 January 2003
	Country of birth	3,302,440	7.7		
FI[10]	Citizenship	107,003	2.0	5,219,732	31 December 2003
	Country of birth	158,867	3.0		
FR[11]	Citizenship	3,258,539	5.6	58,520,000	8 March 1999
	Country of origin	4,306,094	7.4		
HU[12]	Citizenship	110,598	1.1	10,198,315	1 February 2001
IE[13]	Nationality	273,520	7.1	3,858,495	28 April 2002
	Country of birth	400,016	10.4		
IT[14]	Citizenship	1,334,889	2.3	56,995,744	21 October 2001
	Immigrants	1,446,697	2.5		
LV[15]	Foreign nationality	504,000	21.2	2,377,400	2000
	Country of birth	435,000	18.3		
LT[16]	Citizenship	35,094	1.0	3,483,972	6 April 2001
	Country of birth	246,609	7.1		
LU[17]	Aliens	174,200	38.6	451,600	1 January 2004
MT[18]	Permanent foreign residents	11,000	2.8	399,867	2003
NL[19]	Nationality	591,205	3.6	16,258,032	1 January 2004
	Foreign background	1,602,730	9.9		
PL[20]	Citizenship	40,661	0.1	38,230,080	2002
	Unknown	659,668	1.7		
PT[21]	Citizenship	232,695	2.2	10,356,117	12 March 2001
	Country of birth	651,472	6.3		
SE[22]	Citizenship	484,076	5.4	8,975,670	31 December 2003
	Country of birth	1,077,596	12.0		
	Country of origin	1,393,207	15.5		

(Continued)

Table 7.2 (Continued)

	Definition used for data collection	Absolute numbers	% of total population	Total population	Reference date
SI[23]	Citizenship	44,591	2.2	1,995,718	31 December 2002
	Immigrants	169,605	8.6	1,964,036	31 March 2002
SK[24]	Nationality	710,099	13.2	5,379,455	26 May 2001
UK	Citizenship[25]	2,450,000	4.1	59,623,406	1 January 2000
	Country of birth[26]	4,896,551	8.3	58,789,194	29 April 2001

Unless otherwise specified, the figures for foreign citizenship include stateless persons, persons with undetermined citizenship and unknown.

1 Statistik Austria, Census of Population 2001.
2 Institut National de Statistique, Bruxelles 2003.
3 Republic of Cyprus, Census of Population 2001.
4 Czech Statistical Office, Census 2001.
5 Federal Statistical Office, 2005.
6 Danmarks Statistik, 2004.
7 Statistical Office of Estonia, Population Census 2000.
8 National Statistical Service of Greece, Census 2001.
9 Spanish Statistical Office, INEbase, 2005.
10 Statistics Finland, Population Census 2000.
11 INSEE, Population census 1999.
12 Hungarian Central Statistical Office, Census 2001. The number includes 17,593 persons carrying multiple citizenship.
13 Central Statistics Office, Ireland, Census 2002. The number on citizenship includes 48,412 persons who did not state their citizenship as well as 103,476 persons with British citizenship. A total of 49,299 persons carrying Irish in addition to another citizenship are not included. The number on country of birth include 248,515 persons (or 62.1 per cent of the persons born outside Ireland) born in the UK.
14 Istat, Census 2001.
15 Central Statistical Bureau of Latvia, Census 2000, Population Statistics Division. See the Press Release of 21 February 2003, 'Country of birth and nationality of the Latvian population according to the 2000 population census'.
16 Statistics Lithuania, Population Census 2001. A total of 10,351 stateless persons are included in the number of people with foreign citizenship, constituting 30 per cent of the group. In addition to the number indicating foreign country of birth, a total of 42,512 persons did not answer.
17 Estimations, 1 January 2004, 'Luxembourg in Figures', STATEC, September 2004.
18 Demographic Review 2003, National Statistics Office, 2004.
19 Statistics Netherlands, 2005. In addition to the number of foreign citizenship, a total of 110,980 are stateless or have unknown citizenship. The category 'foreign background' denotes all persons of first generation with a foreign background (while the category 'allochthonous', which is reported in Table 7.1, includes all with a foreign background also of second generation).
20 Central Statistical Office, Poland, Census 2002. In addition to the number of persons with foreign citizenship, a total of 444,930 (1.2 per cent) carry a second citizenship in addition to Polish. For 62.9 per cent of this group the second citizenship is German.
21 National Statistical Institute of Portugal (INE), Census 2001.
22 The Swedish Integration Board, see http://www.integrationsverket.se (the office was closed on 30 June 2007 and the statistical service taken over by Statistics Sweden).
23 Statistical Office of the Republic of Slovenia. Figures on citizenship from 31 December 2002, while on immigrants from the 2002 census. 'Immigrants' are defined as 'people who had their first residence outside Slovenia and have been living in Slovenia for at least a year'.
24 Statistical Office of the Slovak Republic, Census 2001. No data on citizenship is available; the number is the same as Table 7.1, giving the respondents' own declaration in the census.
25 Council of Europe Demographic Yearbook 2001.
26 Office for National Statistics, UK, Census 2001.

philosophical affiliation, while other countries have no official records. In the latter case, numbers can only be estimated very roughly. There are also internal variations in this group, as some member states provide official statistics at an aggregated level, or on the number of congregations present in the country. However, all the above methods may give a misleading account of the size of religious minorities.

Where disaggregated data exist, they are mainly based upon censuses that vary considerably with regard to the formulation of the questions. The population asked may also differ. For instance, the Estonian 2000 census recorded religion only for persons aged 15 or older. Furthermore, the question was voluntary and registered the faith that the person regarded as his or her own. The person did not need to be member of a church or congregation, and whether he or she was baptized was irrelevant.

For our purposes data on self-identification is of course very useful. A person's self-identification matters and is an important trigger for claims for recognition. However, from a data-gathering perspective, if the only source of data is based on persons' self-identifications, we have no 'objective' data based on category to contrast the data on self-identification with. If for instance oppressed groups tend to *under-report* their religious affiliations, our data will not capture the full extent of unthematized oppression.

Some of the problems encountered in the case of self-reporting of ethnic or racial origin as discussed above also come into play when recording data on religious affiliation on the basis of self-identification. People might fear suppression and/or the misuse of data and prefer not to state their minority religion when asked in a census. In the Slovenian 2002 census, for instance, as many as 15.7 per cent of the total population did *not* wish to state their religion,[37] while another 3.5 per cent stated that he or she was a 'believer but belongs to no religion', and 7.1 per cent remains 'unknown'.

This matter of conviction is clearly a very sensitive issue. This can be illustrated by the Czech 2001 census. According to 'informed estimates', there are about 3,500 Jews living in the Czech Republic, while only 1,515 persons stated that they belonged to the Jewish society in the census (Czech Government 2004). Still, this represented an important increase from the 1991 census, when only 218 persons classified themselves as Jewish. Interestingly, the category was changed from Jewish 'identity' in the 1991 census to be a matter of religious denomination in 2001, and the number of people who stated their affiliation with Judaism multiplied by almost seven.

It is even more challenging to establish the number of people affiliated with minority religions when relying on aggregated data. When no official data is collected at the micro level, the size of the main religious groups may be estimated based on information provided by the religious or philosophical organizations themselves, sometimes with surveys completing

---

37 This number increased considerably – it was almost multiplied by four – from the 1991 census, when 4.2 per cent did not wish to state their religion (81,302 persons).

the data.[38] The US Bureau of Democracy, Human Rights, and Labor release annual reports on religious freedom worldwide. The reports outline the religious demography for each country and are the main source of information for several countries in Table 7.3. All reports draw upon available statistics, as in the case of France, where the numbers are based on survey data, press reports and polls. Another source of information is the EUREL project, which provides 'accurate and up-to-date information on the social and legal status of religion in Europe', but which to this date covers only 16 EU member states.[39]

The problems related to such aggregated data are also manifold. Firstly, it could be in a congregation's own interest to *overestimate* the number of affiliated people. This would be particularly relevant if it receives some form of economic support based on its membership, or simply wishes to appear more significant than it really is.

On the other hand, such data collection might also *under-report* the actual number of adherents to a religion. In Germany, an estimated 87,500 persons are members of Jewish congregations; however, the size of the Jewish population is believed to be considerably higher. Since 1990, approximately 100,000 Jews have arrived from the former Soviet Union, and smaller numbers from other countries. The discrepancy between population numbers and the number of congregation members is due to the fact that *people do not necessarily join congregations*. The same discrepancies are found in Latvia, where figures are based upon membership as reported to the Ministry of Justice. The Jewish community, for instance, is estimated to encompass around 6,000 persons, while only 685 persons are reported as formally members.[40] The largest discrepancy is found in Poland, where the formal membership list of the Jewish congregation counts 2,500 persons, while the Jewish community is estimated to include between 20,000 and 30,000 persons.

From the point of view of our scheme, it is problematic that the size of categories is established through *catnets*, and not the reverse, which is how we have set up the investigation. Again, if we were to see the full extent of unthematized oppression, we would need to have data on categories, then on organizing, so as to see how much of a given category is actually part of a given *catnet*.

Furthermore, in several member states only figures for the largest groups are registered, and smaller religious and/or philosophical communities are thus ignored.[41] In Italy, for instance, several groups that are considered to be significant religious communities are left out from the statistics, as no estimates are available (Orthodox churches, small Protestant groups, Japanese Buddhists, the Baha'i Faith and South Asian Hindus). The actual number of persons

---

38 This has been the main procedure for establishing the numbers for Belgium, Denmark, France, Germany, Greece, Italy, Latvia, Luxembourg, the Netherlands, Spain and Sweden.
39 See EUREL at http://eurel.u-strasbg.fr/ (accessed 12 February 2007). Data are provided and checked by a network of correspondents, specialists of law or social sciences.
40 The Central Statistical Bureau of Latvia only keeps figures for registered religious congregations by denomination, listing more than 1,100 congregations in 2003.
41 This is the case in Luxembourg, Italy, Malta, the Netherlands and Spain.

belonging to religious minorities is thus considerably higher than what is reported in Table 7.3.

Adding to the complexity of mapping the various minorities is the *overlap* between categories. In many EU member states, the largest groups affiliated with minority religions tend to be foreign born. This is the case in Sweden, where the exact number of Muslims, for instance, is difficult to estimate and has increased rapidly in the past several years,[42] and Greece, where the majority of those affiliated with minority religions are not Greek citizens.[43] In Italy, where 87 per cent of native-born citizens are nominally Roman Catholics, the large group of non-Christian residents has increased in size as a result of continuous immigration. This group mainly consists of Muslims from North Africa, South Asia, Albania and the Middle East and numbers an estimated 1 million. Further, 'Buddhists include approximately 40,000 adherents of European origin and 20,000 of Asian origin'.[44] In the Netherlands, more than half of the Muslim community are non-Western, with the largest groups originating from Morocco and Turkey.[45]

Table 7.3 Religious minorities in 25 EU member states

	Main religion(s) and % affiliated	Affiliated minority religions	% of total population	Other[A]	Reference date[B]
AT[1]	Roman Catholic	993,580	12.4	U: 12.0	15 May 2001
BE[2]	Roman Catholic 80%	645,000–670,000	6.3–6.5	A: 8.5	2001
CY[3]	Christian Orthodox	33,437	4.8	A: 0.2	1 October 2001
CZ[4]	Roman Catholic	547,308	5.3	U: 59.0 NI: 8.8	1 March 2001
DE[5]	Reformed Protestant 33% Catholic 33.4%	5,310,000–5,710,000	6.5–7.0	U: 26.6	2004
DK[6]	Evangelical Lutheran 84%	252,000	4.7	U: 5.4 A: 1.5	2002
EE[7]	Lutheran/Orthodox	30,151	2.7	U: 27.9 A: 6.1	31 March 2000
EL[8]	Greek Orthodox 97%	1,178,000	10.8		2004
ES[9]	Roman Catholic 87%	2,200,000	5.2		2002

(Continued)

---

42 US Bureau of Democracy, Human Rights and Labor, *Sweden – International Religious Freedom Report 2004*. Available at http://www.state.gov/g/drl/rls/irf/2004/35486.htm (accessed 9 November 2011).

43 US Bureau of Democracy, Human Rights and Labor, *Greece – International Religious Freedom Report 2004*. Available at http://www.state.gov/g/drl/rls/irf/2004/35458.htm (accessed 9 November 2011).

44 US Bureau of Democracy, Human Rights and Labor, *Italy – International Religious Freedom Report 2004*. Available at http://www.state.gov/g/drl/rls/irf/2004/35462.htm (accessed 9 November 2011).

45 There are some 296,000 Muslims from Morocco and 328,000 from Turkey, constituting 1.8 and 2.0 per cent of the total population, respectively.

Table 7.3 (Continued)

	Main religion(s) and % affiliated	Affiliated minority religions	% of total population	Other[A]	Reference date[B]
FI[10]	Evangelical Lutheran 84%	117,116	2.2	U: 13.5	31 December 2003
FR[11]	Roman Catholic 62%	6,000,000–8,000,000	10–13.5	U: 6.0	2003
HU[12]	Roman Catholic 51.9%	2,321,092	22.8	U: 14.5 N: 10.8	1 February 2001
IE[13]	Roman Catholic 88.4%	235,711	6.0	U: 3.5	28 April 2002
IT[14]	Roman Catholic 83.1%	1,640,000	2.9	A: 14.0	2004
LT[15]	Roman Catholic 79%	213,991	6.1	U: 9.5	6 April 2001
LU[16]	Roman Catholic 90%	12,000	2.7		2004
LV[17]	Lutheran, Orthodox, Roman Catholic 58.1% (total)	93,852	4.1		2003
MT[18]	Roman Catholic 95%		1.0		2004
NL[19]	Roman Catholic 30%	4,550,000	28.0	U: 42,0	2003
PL[20]	Roman Catholic 89.7%	901,542	2.4	NI: 7.9	31 December 2003
PT[21]	Roman Catholic 80%	489,700	4.8	A: 2,9 NI: 12.3	July 2003
SE[22]	Protestant 80%	965,000–1,018,000	10.7–11.3		2004
SI[23]	Catholic 57.8%	113,091	5.8	U: 3.5 A: 10.2 N: 15.7 NI: 7.1	31 March 2002
SK[24]	Roman Catholic 68.9%	813,429	15.1	U: 13.0 A: 3.0	26 May 2001
UK[25]	Anglican 35%	19,057,000	32.3	U/A: 33.0	2000

A The 'other' category distinguishes between unaffiliated (**U**), atheists/agnostics (**A**), persons who have explicitly chosen 'no answer'/'not wish to answer' (**N**) and persons who have provided 'no info' (**NI**).
B Date of reference is set to 2004 when no date is specified in the US Religious Freedom Reports 2004.
1 Statistik Austria, Census 2001.
2 Survey-based estimates. US Bureau of Democracy, Human Rights and Labor, *Belgium – International Religious Freedom Report 2004*. Available at http://www.state.gov/g/drl/rls/irf/2004/35444.htm (accessed 9 November 2011).
3 Republic of Cyprus, Census of population 2001.
4 Czech Statistical Office, Census 2001.
5 Estimates. US Bureau of Democracy, Human Rights and Labor, *Germany – International Religious Freedom Report 2004*. Available at http://www.state.gov/g/drl/rls/irf/2004/35456.htm (accessed 9 November 2011).
6 Estimates. US Bureau of Democracy, Human Rights and Labor, *Denmark – International Religious Freedom Report 2004*. Available at http://www.state.gov/g/drl/rls/irf/2004/35451.htm (accessed 9 November 2011).
7 Statistical Office of Estonia, Population Census 2000.
8 Estimates. US Bureau of Democracy, Human Rights and Labor, *Greece – International Religious Freedom Report 2004*. Available at http://www.state.gov/g/drl/rls/irf/2004/35458.htm (accessed 9 November 2011). Members of the several religious minorities are mostly non-citizen residents, thus the total percentage exceeds 100.

Conceptualizing the EU's social constituency 177

9 Estimates of the largest religious groups only (Protestants, Muslims, Jews and practising Buddhists). US Bureau of Democracy, Human Rights and Labor, *Spain – International Religious Freedom Report 2004*. Available at http://www.state.gov/g/drl/rls/irf/2004/35485.htm (accessed 9 November 2011).
10 Statistics Finland, 2005.
11 Estimated figures, based on survey data. US Bureau of Democracy, Human Rights and Labor, *France – International Religious Freedom Report 2004*. Available at http://www.state.gov/g/drl/rls/irf/2004/35454.htm (accessed 9 November 2011).
12 Hungarian Central Statistical Office, Census 2001.
13 Central Statistics Office, Ireland, Census 2002.
14 Estimates for the main groups, the percentage of atheists and agnostics is poll based. US Bureau of Democracy, Human Rights and Labor, *Italy – International Religious Freedom Report 2004*. Available at http://www.state.gov/g/drl/rls/irf/2004/35462.htm (accessed 9 November 2011).
15 Statistics Lithuania, Population Census 2001.
16 Purely indicative figures. US Bureau of Democracy, Human Rights and Labor, *Luxembourg – International Religious Freedom Report 2004*. Available at http://www.state.gov/g/drl/rls/irf/2004/35469.htm (accessed 9 November 2011).
17 Estimates. US Bureau of Democracy, Human Rights and Labor, *Latvia – International Religious Freedom Report 2004*. Available at http://www.state.gov/g/drl/rls/irf/2004/35465.htm (accessed 9 November 2011).
18 Estimates. US Bureau of Democracy, Human Rights and Labor, *Malta – International Religious Freedom Report 2004*. Available at http://www.state.gov/g/drl/rls/irf/2004/35472.htm (accessed 9 November 2011).
19 Statistics Netherlands, 2003. Although there is an important group of Protestants in the country, they amount to only 14 per cent of the population and are thus listed as adherents to a minority religion.
20 Central Statistical Office, Poland, Census 2002. The number of Roman Catholics corresponds to baptized persons.
21 Estimates. US Bureau of Democracy, Human Rights and Labor, *Portugal – International Religious Freedom Report 2004*. Available at http://www.state.gov/g/drl/rls/irf/2004/35478.htm (accessed 9 November 2011).
22 Estimates. US Bureau of Democracy, Human Rights and Labor, *Sweden – International Religious Freedom Report 2004*. Available at http://www.state.gov/g/drl/rls/irf/2004/35486.htm (accessed 9 November 2011).
23 Statistical Office of the Republic of Slovenia, Census 2002.
24 Statistical Office of the Slovak Republic, Census 2001.
25 The 2001 census included a question on religion, but 'Christian' was used as a category covering all Christian denominations. Thus, no disaggregated data on Anglican, Roman Catholic, Protestant and other sub-categories were recorded (Office for National Statistics, UK, Census 2001). The data here are estimates provided by the National Centre for Social Research, available at the EUREL website, http://eurel.u-strasbg.fr/. Other numbers are reported in the US Bureau of Democracy, Human Rights and Labor, *United Kingdom – International Religious Freedom Report 2004*. Available at http://www.state.gov/g/drl/rls/irf/2004/35492.htm (accessed 9 November 2011).

The lion's share of the persons belonging to the much smaller Hindu community, counting 99,000 people, is of Surinamese descent (83.3 per cent). Only 1,000 of the Hindus are of Western origin. The same patterns are found in Portugal. The Muslims are 'largely from Portuguese Africa, who are ethnically sub-Saharan African or Asian' while the Hindu community 'largely traces its origins to South Asians who emigrated from Portuguese Africa and the former Portuguese colony of Goa in India'.[46] Many of these minority communities are not organized formally, and numbers are difficult to estimate.

46 US Bureau of Democracy, Human Rights and Labor, *Portugal – International Religious Freedom Report 2004*. Available at http://www.state.gov/g/drl/rls/irf/2004/35478.htm (accessed 9 November 2011).

The overlap of religious groups with immigrant communities entails that the mapping of this category must also take into account the flux of immigration. Continuous updates would be necessary in order to provide a full picture, and the size of the various groups can be subject to important changes in relatively short time-perspectives.

With the above reservations in mind, Table 7.3 presents a schematic overview of religious minorities in 25 EU countries.

Language minorities in the EU

Finally, mapping the many different language minorities in the EU is no less of a challenge than mapping the ethnic, immigrant and religious minorities. Also here, there are considerable variations between the member states as regards language policies, the definitions of language and mother tongue, and the availability of disaggregated data.

Only nine[47] of the 25 countries in this study collect census data on language. The most common term used is 'mother tongue', while the Austrian 2001 census asked for 'colloquial language' ('*Umgangssprache*'), defined as 'the language spoken at home', and more than one language could be given. However, as with other sensitive data, such self-declaration might not capture in full a group that speaks a minority language, as people might fear the misuse of data or have a desire to integrate. Other countries have official counts of their language minorities, but in many cases such numbers are believed to under-report the actual size of the groups. Three member states are mentioned in particular to illustrate the problems involved.

In Finland, the registration of data on language is based on statutory reports by citizens and authorities. The official numbers are self-declared and based on the principle that each person has only one language of his or her free choice. The result of this is that Statistics Finland reports 1,704 as having Sami as their mother tongue,[48] while, according to the country's national minority report, there are 7,956 Sami-speaking (Finnish Government 2004: 20–1). Moreover, the official registers inform that only 122 persons have Tatar as their mother tongue, while the actual number of Tatars is more than seven times as high – 900 persons – according to the above report. The official statistics also give no figures for Romany-speaking people, while there are estimated to be 10,000 Roma in Finland.

In Belgium, the collection of data on language is not legal, and estimates must be based on data from political or educational institutions, identity cards and driver's licences, and the like. The inhabitants of the federal entities Wallonia and Flandern are mainly French- and Flemish-speaking, respectively, and the population size provides information on the size of the two main

---

47 Austria, the Czech Republic, Estonia, Hungary, Latvia, Lithuania, Poland, Slovenia and Slovakia.
48 Statistics Finland, 'Mother tongue of the population by age 31.12.2003'.

groups. The bilingual region of Brussels, however, is more complicated, as people can declare different languages as their 'administrative', 'educational' and 'electoral' language. The country's complex federal system allows each person to choose a language community of his or her own choice. However, the respective membership numbers of the three communities (Flemish, French and German) do not reflect the language demography of the country, as any other minority language is excluded. As there are no reliable figures for these groups, Table 7.4 only reports the size of the German community. We consider both French and Flemish to be majority languages, as they are fairly balanced in terms of recognition, legal framework and use, and are main languages in their respective regions.

As for Italy, the language minorities are recognized as national minorities; however, 'no census of the members of minority groups is provided for in the existing national legislation (law No.482/99)' (Italian Government 2004: 5). The available figures have 'a purely indicative value' and are based on a survey 'in the municipalities hosting minority groups with the purpose of identifying the real number of minority language speakers' (ibid.). Other sources are studies and publications, and surveys on the use of Italian language, dialects and foreign languages have been carried out. One survey asked for the respondent's knowledge of minority languages, and the numbers are thus *overestimated* as compared with the people who have minority languages as their mother tongue. Moreover, the survey asked for the 'language usually spoken' with family and friends, respectively. The results show that 44.1 and 48.0 per cent speak 'only' or 'mainly' Italian, 19.1 and 16.0 per cent speak 'only' or 'mostly' dialect, and 32.9 and 32.7 per cent speak both Italian and dialect. Apparently, the use of other languages than Italian is widely diffused.[49] Nevertheless, this does not necessarily lead to claims for recognition.

Again, it is quite clear that this approach does not offer reliable information on the relevant category of people.

The member states follow different language policies and a majority of them recognizes particular 'national' language minorities. Such minorities rely on the same rights as the main national language(s) in terms of education, public information and the like. The 'co-official' status of a minority language is often regionally based, such as Catalan, Galician and Basque in Spain, and French, German, Friulian and others in Italy. However, accurate data on the size of these groups are missing. Different policies further contribute to creating a complex picture when mapping possible recognition structures in the EU. Members of a recognized minority group in one country might enjoy full rights to use their mother tongue, while the same language group might struggle for recognition in another country if the language is not officially recognized.

The EU is concerned with the protection of regional and minority languages and several studies have been conducted to identify the use of such languages

---

49 Istat, *Letture e linguaggio – Indagine multiscopo sulle famiglie – anno 2000*, 18 December 2002. Available at http://www.istat.it/dati/catalogo/20021218_00 (accessed 9 November 2011).

in the member states.[50] However, they are usually confined to the dominant or officially recognized minority languages in the various countries and are not exhaustive with regard to language minorities. Moreover, the onus is on the present state of the language groups and the legal, institutional and social structures that condition the use of minority languages, and they must rely on the same incomplete sources and data as regards the linguistic demography. Up until 2010, the European Bureau for Lesser-Used Languages (EBLUL)[51] represented the regional and minority language communities of the EU. The fourth minority group covered in this study was thus provided with a channel for promoting their common interest at the EU level, but this was closed down in 2010.

Table 7.4 outlines the total members of language minority groups in 25 EU member states.

Lack of data and further implications

To sum up this far, it is clear that there are important ethical and methodological as well as conceptual and practical problems when seeking to undertake a reliable mapping of the relevant categories. Legal constraints and different procedures for collecting disaggregated data do not permit such a mapping to be complete. We simply do not have fully reliable data on the relevant categories; the first step of the overall mapping is thus incomplete. This will have effects on the entire mapping exercise because we will not have a wholly reliable benchmark of statistical data that the subsequent steps can be assessed in relation to. This in no way renders the remaining steps irrelevant (although we have not had capacity to do this), but it is likely to affect the problem of unthematized oppression and the issue of displacement (addressed above).

Thus far we have shown how we might start the work to undertake a comprehensive 'from below' mapping. We found that this was fraught with problems. How serious is this problem? If the EU does not generate recognition expectations, then there is no real problem. As a rule of thumb, let us assume that the greater the recognition expectations generated by the EU, the more serious the data lacunae are.

The EU – instigator of a new recognition order?

Recognition theorists have not discussed the EU in any systematic manner. Most also take the existing democratic nation-state framework as their point of departure and spend little time on developing *alternative polity frameworks*.[52]

---

50 See the Euromosaic study. Available at http://www.uoc.edu/euromosaic (accessed 9 November 2011). See also European Commission (1996).
51 The non-governmental organization EBLUL was founded in 1985 but closed in 2010, allegedly due to lack of continued funding.
52 Honneth's recognition framework is largely derived from the democratic constitutional state (but not necessarily the nation-state). It would likely be that of a welfare state, or a state with

Table 7.4 Language minorities in 25 EU member states

	Definition used for data collection	Absolute numbers[A]	% of total population	Total population	Reference date
AT[1]	Colloquial language	O: 119,667 U: 797,479	O: 1.5 U: 9.9	8,032,926	15 May 2001
BE[2]	Language community	O: 100,000	1.0	10,263,414	1 January 2003
CY[3]	Best spoken language	56,147	8.1	689,565	1 October 2001
CZ[4]	Mother tongue	522,663	5.1	10,230,060	1 March 2001
DE[5]	National minority	142,000–157,000	0.2	82,300,000	21 September 2004
DK[6]	—	—	—	—	—
EE[7]	Mother tongue	448,235	32.7	1,370,052	31 March 2000
EL[8]	Minority language	750,000	6.9	10,934,097	18 March 2001
ES[9]	Language spoken	O: 14,380,000 U: 833,814	O: 36.0 U: 2.1	40,000,000	1998
FI[10]	Mother tongue	O: 289,868 U: 126,521	O: 2.4 U: 5.6	5,147,349	31 December 2003
FR[11]	Language spoken	3,792,000	6.5	58,000,000	—
HU[12]	Mother tongue	167,780	1.6	10,198,315	1 February 2001
IE[13]	First/main language	180,000	5.0	3,600,000	1991
IT[14]	Language spoken	5,572,553	9.8	57,000,000	2000
LV[15]	Mother tongue	994,278	41.8	2,377,383	2000
LT[16]	Mother tongue	506,362	14.5	3,483,972	5 April 2001
LU[17]	—	—	—	—	—
MT[18]	—	—	—	—	—
NL[19]	National minority	400,000	2.5	16,258,032	—
PL[20]	Language used most often	563,499	1.5	38,230,080	2002
PT[21]	Minority language	10,000	0.1	10,356,117	12 March 2001
SE[22]	National minority	580,000	6.5	8,883,590	31 December 2000
SI[23]	Mother tongue	240,602	12.3	1,964,036	31 March 2002
SK[24]	Mother tongue	801,182	14.9	5,379,455	26 May 2001
UK[25]	Speaker of language	717,079	1.3	57,000,000	1991

A Where relevant, minority language speakers are divided in two groups: those speaking an officially recognized minority language (**O**) versus non-official/unrecognized ones (**U**).
1 Statistik Austria, Census 2001. Officially recognized languages (O) are Burgenland-Croatian, Czech, Hungarian, Roman, Slovak, Slovenian and Windisch ('*anerkannten österreichen Volksgruppen*').
2 Disaggregated data does not exist and the table only includes the estimated size of the group speaking the officially recognized German language. See 'German in Belgium', Research Centre of Multilingualism, available at http://www.uoc.edu/euromosaic/web/document/alemany/an/i1/i1.html (accessed 9 November 2011). Members of the French and Flemish communities are around 40 per cent and 60 per cent, respectively (http://en.wikipedia.org/wiki/Belgium, accessed 9 November 2011).

(cont.)
3   Republic of Cyprus, Census of population 2001. The Cypriot 2001 census did not collect data on mother tongue but on 'best spoken language'. The census was conducted in the government-controlled area, excluding some 89,200 Turkish Cypriots (Cypriot Government 1999). Only 340 persons are registered as Turkish speakers.
4   Czech Statistical Office, Census 2001. Respondents were asked to give the language spoken to him or her in childhood by his or her mother or other people who brought him or her up.
5   No statistics are established on the basis of linguistic criteria. The numbers are estimates of the language minority groups speaking Danish, Sorbian, Frisian and Romany, as reported to the Framework Convention for the Protection of National Minorities (German Government 2005). The reference date for the total population size is 31 December 2001.
6   No data available. Authorities do not intend to gather data on languages (Danish Government 2004).
7   Statistical Office of Estonia, Population Census 2000.
8   Estimates based on data from the Euromosaic study (http://www.uoc.edu/euromosaic/), covering five language minority groups: Albanese/Arvanite (200,000), Bulgarian/Pomak (30,000), Macedonian (200,000), Turkish (120,000) and Walachian (Aromanian/Megleno-Romanian) (200,000). Official census data do not exist and Greece has not ratified the Framework Convention on National Minorities.
9   There are eight language groups of considerable size in Spain: Aragonese, Asturian, Basque, Berber, Catalan, Galician, Occitan and Portuguese. However, no statistics are available and estimates of many of the groups are difficult to find. Numbers are from the 'Worldwide language framework', Jacques Leclerc (CIRAL, le Centre international de recherche en aménagement linguistique de l'Université Laval, Quebec). Available at http://www.tlfq.ulaval.ca/axl/europe/espagneetat.htm (accessed 9 November 2011).
10 Statistics Finland, 2003 (figures provided upon request). The officially recognized Swedish language (O) is spoken by more than two-thirds of the population belonging to a minority language group.
11 No statistics available, purely indicative estimates from the Euromosaic study of seven language groups: Basque (85,300), Breton (320,000), Catalan (92,000), Corsican (25,000), Dutch (20,000), German (1,250,000) and Occitan (2,000,000). See outlines by the Institut de Sociolingüística Catalana, Research Centre of Wales and Research Centre of Multilingualism. Available at http://www.uoc.edu/euromosaic (accessed 9 November 2011)
12 Hungarian Central Statistical Office, 2004, Census 2001. An additional 5 per cent did not wish to answer. A slightly larger group reported other than Hungarian as the 'language spoken' (170,377, or 1.7 per cent).
13 In the 1991 Census a total of 1,095,830 persons (32 per cent) reported being Irish speakers. However, according to recent surveys, only about 5 per cent of the population use Irish as their first or main language. See 'Irish in Ireland', Research Centre of Wales. Available at http://www.uoc.edu/euromosaic/web/document/irlandes/an/i1/i1.html (accessed 9 November 2011).
14 Disaggregated data on language does not exist. The figures are survey-based and thus purely indicative (Italian Government 1999).
15 Central Statistical Bureau of Latvia, Census 2000.
16 Statistics Lithuania, Census 2001. In addition to the persons who reported any other mother tongue than Lithuanian, as many as 121,830 persons (3.5 per cent) did not answer.
17 STATEC does not provide statistics on language. The national language Luxembourgian (Letzeburgesh) is spoken by some 350,000 persons (75.2 per cent). French and German are also official languages. See 'Letzeburgesh in Luxembourg', Research Centre of Multilingualism. Available at http://www.uoc.edu/euromosaic/web/document/luxemburgues/an/i1/i1.html (accessed 9 November 2011).
18 No data available.
19 Statistics Netherlands do not provide statistics on language. The number is an estimate of the Frisian-speaking group; see 'Frisian ('Frysk') in the Netherlands', Research Centre of Multilingualism, at http://www.uoc.edu/euromosaic/web/document/friso/an/i1/i1.html (accessed 9 November 2011).
20 Central Statistical Office, Poland, Census 2002. According to the national minority report submitted in July 2002, the real number lies between 830,000 and 1,276,000 (2.1–3.3 per cent) (Polish Government 2002).
21 No statistics available. The number is an estimate of the group of the Romance language Mirandese, see 'Mirandese in Portugal', Institut de Sociolingüística Catalana. Available at

(cont.)
    http://www.uoc.edu/euromosaic/web/document/mirandes/an/i1/i1.html (accessed 9 November 2011).
22 Data on language is not collected in Sweden, as it is considered sensitive information connected to a person's ethnicity. The figure is an estimate of the five national minorities recognized by Sweden within the Framework Convention for the Protection of National Minorities; Sami, Swedish Finns, Tornedalers, Roma and Jews (Swedish Government 2001).
23 Statistical Office of the Republic of Slovenia, Census 2002.
24 Statistical Office of the Slovak Republic, Census 2001. It is worth noting that 8.2 per cent of the population that do not have Slovak as their mother tongue did not specify their mother tongue (66,056 persons, 1.2 per cent of the total population). Hungarian was reported as the mother tongue by almost three out of four who do not have Slovak as their mother tongue (71.5 per cent).
25 The census 2001 did not include any question for language, and the UK Office for National Statistics does not provide data for this subject. The above estimate includes four language minorities: Cornish (1,000), Gaelic (65,978), Welsh (508,098) and Irish (142,003). The three latter numbers are from the 1991 census and include persons reporting to be speakers of the languages, not those using it as their first language. See outlines by the Research Centre of Wales. Available at http://www.uoc.edu/euromosaic/web/document/cornic/an/i1/i1.html (accessed 9 November 2011).

These lacunae are amplified by the fact that the EU has not spelled out a clear conception of itself *qua polity*.

Our assessment should establish whether the EU generates recognition expectations and as part of this should also try to make explicit what kind of 'recognition order' the EU represents. There are three options, at least:

1 The EU *does not* form an independent recognition order.
2 The EU copies or emulates the recognition order we associate with the democratic nation-state.
3 The EU makes up a distinct recognition order – clearly different from that of the nation-state.

With regard to (1), the EU *does* establish recognition expectations. As will be further developed below, such pertain to individuals, groups and movements, regions and member states. There is, however, considerable opposition to the EU establishing itself as an *independent recognition order*.[53] One important component of the politics of recognition that is unfolding in Europe consists in ideological and (national) identity-based efforts to *curtail* the role and scope of the EU, and to scale it down to a narrow, functional-type organization. These efforts have not precluded the EU from developing into an independent recognition order, however.

    a social-market economy. Taylor's framework could be akin to a 'community of communities', based on 'deep diversity' (for this term, see Taylor 1993) but Taylor does not spell out the polity requirements. From Iris Young, we may think of a pyramidal-type polity, where groups serve as vital actors. In political-institutional terms, the polity may be based on the principle of subsidiarity, in a society-encompassing and secular form (and quite unlike how the EU applies this principle).
53 TEAM – The European Alliance of EU-critical groups, co-ordinating 47 organizations from 18 countries. Available at http://www.teameurope.info (accessed 9 November 2011).

But the EU has only partly emulated the state-based recognition order (2). The EU is not a state but is a complex polity with a mixture of supranational, transnational and intergovernmental traits. It does subscribe to a set of basic principles that cohere with those of the democratic constitutional state,[54] but it nevertheless makes up a distinctive recognition order. One aspect of this consists in the strong presence of states as core actors in identity politics. The EU holds numerous provisions on the need for protection of national identities and emphasizes diversity. But the politics of identity that is conveyed through state actors in the EU is not a mere defence of national identity. Consider the case of Germany. The Second World War and the Nazi atrocities had deeply discredited German national identity. In response, Germany embraced an inclusive European identity as a means to restore a measure of self-respect and international recognition as a democratic nation (cf. Lipgens 1982: 60–1),[55] and this has worked.[56] One driving force behind the states' reneging of their sovereignty can be to obtain international recognition. Further, a distinctive trait of the EU is that it reduces the ability of states to pose as uniform actors who present one coherent national position. In the EU, state and societal actors contend for space and recognition, in a setting that is no doubt more permissive of national identity protection than is the case *within* established states, such as the US and – albeit less so – in Canada (where much of the theoretical literature on recognition and identity politics has emanated[57]), but which is also far less permissive of national identity protection than is the *international* setting. The EU setting weakens or undermines national auto-recognition.

To shed further light on this, we will (a) try to clarify what is the core relation to the citizens and the social actors that the EU seeks to establish; (b) assess the extent to which the EU is set up to handle claims; and (c) shed light on the EU's recognition order by looking at the conditions for obtaining EU membership.

The EU and its conception of its social constituency

The recognition framework presented above places great emphasis on self-respect, and a critical instrument for generating such, is rights. Thus, it is important to establish whether the EU is a mere derivative of the member

---

54 Article 6(1) TEU states that 'The Union is founded on the principles of liberty, democracy, respect for human rights and fundamental freedoms and the rule of law, principles which are common to the Member States.'
55 The same argument, albeit in obviously different form, can be extended to Italy and other former non-democratic states, such as Portugal and Spain. These states, all of which have had discredited political regimes in the post-war period, seized upon integration as a means of attaining international respectability.
56 A *Eurobarometer* survey reveals that Germany had the lowest score among 15 West European countries on questions aimed at tapping national pride. *Eurobarometer* 42 (1994), 1. Germany also had the highest score on the question 'National pride is dangerous' (13.9 per cent).
57 The most prominent ones in Canada are: Taylor (1985, 1986, 1989, 1993); Tully (1995), but see also Kymlicka (1995, 1998); Kymlicka and Norman (2000). In the US the most prominent is Young (1990); but see also Benhabib (2002); Gutmann (2003). In Europe the most prominent one is Honneth (1995a, 2003).

states or an independent granter of rights. If the latter, the range of rights granted matters a lot to the nature of the expectations produced.

The EU is an independent granter of rights. What type of recognition relation does it establish through rights? Does it relate to its social constituency as a collection of functional interest organizations and does it consider its citizens as narrowly based *economic citizens*? Are the citizens referred to foremost as producers, consumers, users and customers? Or are they considered in *social and cultural* terms as members of a European value community? Or are they considered as *political* citizens, as holders of a set of common civil and political rights?

If we consider the Charter of Fundamental Rights of the European Union (2000), which as the consolidation of the existing rights of Europeans (as culled from EU law, the constitutional traditions common to the member states, the European Convention for Human Rights and the European Social Charter) represents the most explicit statement of the rights of European citizens, we find that the set of rights is quite comprehensive in terms of range; it is no less encompassing than other bills of rights (Eriksen *et al.* 2003). The Charter, in line with EU law, recognizes European citizens, not only as economic rights-holders, but also as civil, political, social and cultural rights-holders. In this sense the EU establishes a relation to its citizens through the Charter that is no different from that which any democratic state establishes in relation to its citizens. The Charter holds numerous provisions for ensuring private autonomy, as well as provisions to ensure citizens' *public autonomy*.[58] There are also many provisions in the Charter on social rights that speak to solidarity and which are suggestive of a commitment to the welfare state (Chapter IV, Articles 27–38).

The very invocation of the terminology of European citizenship, and its institutional manifestation in civil and political rights, conveys the impression to European citizens that they live under a set of legal and political institutions that permit them to mutually recognize each other as the self-legislating citizens of a European political order.

A further distinctive trait of the EU's recognition order is that citizenship is separated from national identity. Although the EU has emulated nation-type symbols, it seeks its justification foremost in universal principles (democracy, the rule of law, justice and solidarity). The type of allegiance that the EU seeks to elicit is that of a post-national kind.

To conceptualize the EU's social constituency from a recognition perspective it is not enough to establish which principles the EU subscribes to; the principles also have to be entrenched in institutional form, so as to have binding character, as well as to establish their 'social take' or acceptance. Significant gaps between principles and statements on the one hand, and actual arrangements and practice on the other, can generate significant recognition problems.

---

58 For instance, Articles 39 and 40 provide for voting rights and rights to stand as a candidate in European and municipal elections.

If we take the Charter as our point of departure, does it ensure as legal fact that the EU is a strong rights-based entity? The European Charter was a codification of existing law and it was solemnly proclaimed at Nice in December 2000, but was not a part of the Nice Treaty. The very invocation of the term Charter was bound to generate expectations. But if its status would remain that of mere political declaration this could be construed as a case of *recognition denied*. Note that the process of forging the Charter did serve to mobilize aspects of Europe's civil society, and a very significant proportion of NGOs sought a rights-based EU (Kværk 2003: Table 5.6; see also Kværk 2007). Citizens who were concerned with their rights and saw that governments *refused* to incorporate the Charter into the treaties could easily construe this as proof of the EU *not* prioritizing rights. The core EU institutions declared that they would act as if the Charter were binding, but the EU was barred from incorporating the Charter in the treaties because of opposition from some of the member states. From this we can conclude that the EU has sought to establish a recognition order very strongly entrenched in rights, but these rights have been challenged and their role curtailed by opposition from some of the member states.

How and to what extent is the EU set up to handle claims?

The Charter case suggests that there is a considerable gap between the EU's standards and principles on the one hand and its actual ability to deliver on the other. This is borne out in citizenship terms. In the EU, there are clear institutional and procedural limits on the citizens' ability to consider themselves as self-legislating citizens. First, the provisions for ensuring *public* autonomy in the Charter reflect the *weakly* developed political rights of the EU. A person must be a citizen of a member state to qualify as a citizen of the Union, where each state's rules of incorporation vary considerably[59] (although they have still contributed to a degree of Europeanization of national citizenship norms). At the same time there are also provisions that ensure economic and social rights to third-country nationals who do not hold national citizenship.

Second, in institutional terms, the Union suffers from deficiencies in representation and representativeness, accountability, transparency and legitimacy, all of which serve to stymie the Union's effectiveness in ensuring self-confidence and self-respect. Just to cite some aspects, consider for instance the pillar structure of the treaties, the still weak role of the European Parliament (EP), the closed and secretive manner of the Council's operation, the appointed character of the Commission and the limits on individual access to the European Court of Justice.[60] The EU also, underlines Weiler, lacks a *human*

---

59 For an overview, see for instance Soysal (1994).
60 See Francis Jacobs, 'Necessary changes to the system of judicial remedies', Working Document 20 of Working Group II (Charter) of the European Convention. Available at http://european-convention.eu.int/docs/wd2/3222.pdf (accessed 9 November 2011).

rights policy apparatus that can enhance rights protection (2002: 577; see also Alston 1999). The net upshot is that there is a considerable gap between the commitment to provisions to ensure self-confidence and self-respect, and the legal-institutional apparatus that has been set up to realize these.

Third, the general principle guiding Union action is that the Union's competences are 'governed by the principle of conferral'. This means that 'the Union shall act within the limits of the competences conferred upon it by the Member States to attain the objectives set out in the Treaties, and competences not conferred upon the Union remain with the Member States', a provision clearly aimed at national protection. This has not served as a very strong constraint on the scope of action, however, as new tasks have been almost constantly added so that few, if any, areas remain unaffected by the EU and completely within the remit of the member states. The precise realm of Union competence is not easy to establish in the way it is set out in the complex treaties architecture. If for guidance we look at the Convention's draft, we find that most areas are within the category of complementary competences (European Convention 2003). In other words, there is a strong interweaving of Union and member state action. At the same time, the Union's fiscal resources are limited and essentially controlled by the member states, and the EU's redistributive ability is quite limited. The Union is far more of a regulatory agent than that of a redistributive one, although its contributions to the poor regions of Europe through the cohesion funds should not be underestimated, and the Union has consistently shown that it does not pursue a social 'race-to-the bottom' (Moravcsik 2004).

Fourth, recognition theorists underline the role of access. Access can help to settle claims, and conversely, denial of access or strong biases in access can exacerbate recognition problems, as claimants can come to see lack of access as a denial of recognition. The EU encourages the formation of a European social constituency through support to organization formation at the European level. It also seeks to ensure them access to the institutions. The two main channels go through (a) the national governments and the institutions of each member state to the EU; and (b) the complex of EU institutions and arrangements, such as the Commission, the European Parliament, the Council, the system of comitology, the European Court of Justice, and the Committee of the Regions. The EU is a complex multi-level system, where member governments have privileged access to many of the institutions at EU level. Social actors have access to some of the EU institutions, and to their respective governments (national and regional). This adds up to a system of 'multiple arenas, venues, and points of access' (Greenwood 2003: 29). If we look at how this system is used, Imig and Tarrow conclude that

> our evidence strongly suggests that the largest proportion of contentious political responses to the policies of the European Union takes domestic rather than transnational form. In other words, although Europeans are

increasingly troubled by the policy incursions of the EU, they continue to vent their grievances close to home – demanding that their national governments serve as interlocutors on their behalf.

Imig and Tarrow 2001: 47

Does this suggest that the EU is after all effectively closed? The general trend over time has been for the EU to heighten transparency and openness.[61] It also has institutions, in particular *strong publics*[62] such as the EP, that foster transparency. The EP serves as an important forum of debate, conducts hearings, sets up committees of inquiry, receives petitions from citizens and appoints an ombudsman, all to heighten accountability and transparency and stimulate the development of a European public sphere. The strong publics (such as the EP) also ensure inclusion in a deliberative process where claims are presented, justified and seen in relation to possible and available solutions. Here claims are assessed against each other and the relative merits of each can be tested. According to Honneth (2003) and Benhabib (2002), this is an essential ingredient for the handling of recognition claims, although as noted, the EP's ability to translate claims into actions is more limited than that of any national parliament.

Another widely critiqued instance of lack of access is to the process of treaty-making/change. Up to recently formal treaty changes were conducted by elites and experts, in relative insulation from Europeans. In other words, citizens were only very indirectly included in this process and were only called upon to ratify what had already been wrought. In the last four years, however, this process has been opened up dramatically through the two Conventions, on the Charter and on the Constitution. These bodies have been unprecedentedly open and have provided avenues for a wide range of social actors in Europe to express their claims. As such, these processes represent not only channels for social inputs into the EU, but also arenas where the EU's social constituency reflexively comes into existence, and obtains a sense of self. They are also critical venues for constitutional reflexivity.

From the vantage point of democracy, the problem in both Convention cases has been that their deliberations and outputs have not had a direct decisional effect. They have elicited responses from organized and unorganized European society, but after having heard them the governments have gone back and decided among themselves what to do. In a sense this can be construed as a *denial of recognition*, as the governments, not the citizens, decide on the rights that accrue to citizens. Citizens are consulted (directly or indirectly) in the ratification stage, not in their capacity as European citizens, but in their capacity as national citizens.

---

61 The Treaty of Amsterdam established a general principle of openness and citizen access to documents. On the Commission, and its efforts to foster openness and transparency, see Imig and Tarrow (2001: 51–2).
62 For this term applied to the EU, see Eriksen and Fossum (2002).

In sum, when we consider the recognition expectations raised by the EU, for instance through such powerful terms as European citizenship, and contrast these with institutional reality, we find a *recognition gap*, because the provisions and the institutions set up to realize citizenship are not consistent with the expectations raised by this term. The democratic deficit, as an acknowledgement of a gap between standards and practice, is also a case of a recognition gap. A similar argument applies to the social rights in the Charter, which are accorded a less prominent role than property rights and whose substance the EU is not equipped to realize (Menéndez 2003). The EU's weak institutional and fiscal capacity, its dependence on the member states, raise serious questions as to its ability to ensure self-confidence and self-respect – with deep implications for the actual community of values that Europeans can realistically relate to.

Enlargement – as viewed from a recognition perspective

The EU has developed through several major bouts of enlargement. The conditions for membership yield information on the recognition expectations that the EU generates. Further, the EU's actual handling of the (often lengthy) enlargement process also affects and shapes such expectations.

With every enlargement an altered social constituency emerges. The recent enlargements to the east and south entail a great increase in the EU's social constituency, as a whole range of new claimants have entered the EU. These citizens, groups, social movements and states come with expectations and hopes, and with a history of structured expectations of recognition and of recognition denied.[63]

How, then, does the EU frame the recognition relation with regard to the enlargement process? It has set out very specific conditions for enlargement and these have emerged and firmed up over time. Those guiding the latest bout of enlargement were set out at the Copenhagen European Council (1993). To qualify as an applicant it must: (a) have a functioning market economy with the capacity to cope with competitive pressures and market forces within the EU; (b) have achieved stability of institutions guaranteeing democracy, the rule of law and human rights; and (c) be able to take on the obligations of EU membership, including adherence to the aims of economic and political union. If we relate these criteria to the recognition framework, we see that they highlight self-confidence and self-respect: membership is conditioned on every state complying with democratic norms and regarding each person as equal under the law. In addition to these conditions, there is an additional one that dates back to the Treaty of Rome, namely that 'any European state may apply to become a member of the Community'.

---

63 Minister of Foreign Affairs of Slovakia, Eduard Kukan, notes that enlargement represents the 'fulfilment of desires of many generations of Slovak citizens to become equal, rightful and respected actors on the European scene'. When entering the EU Slovakia is 'no longer just a small country from the heart of Europe' (Zagreb 2003).

Application is voluntary but membership is restricted to European states in the way the EU defines 'European'. In other words, a question of relevance to the recognition relation that the EU establishes to its future membership is whether Europeanness is defined through universal or through Europe-specific, contextual and 'ethical' referents. If the latter is used, it brings up the issue of self-esteem, and that some states are more authentically European than others. Research has shown that the EU, which formally relies on a set of uniform criteria, in its actual justifications for enlargement, does distinguish between European states. The Central and Eastern European countries are referred to as 'us', as an intrinsic part of a shared European destiny, and the EU as having a duty to let them in, whereas Turkey, also recognized as European, is not considered in such kinship or duty terms, but rather as a strategically important partner to Europe (Sjursen 2002: 504). In other words, Eastern and Central Europeans are considered the same kin and part of a European community of common values, whereas Turkey is not. The decision on whether to admit Turkey is therefore also a decision on Europe as a community and how it conceives of itself, including whether it upholds recognition expectations that are ultimately founded on self-respect and self-confidence, or whether these are confined by religious affiliation.

Differences in framing, which relate to self-esteem-based categories such as 'kinship', can generate differences in the applicant countries' actual recognition expectations. Further, since such a framing of the issue diverges from the formal criteria, it also brings up the issue of double standards and hypocrisy.

The EU, in line with its membership requirements, presupposes that applicants become full-fledged members, which is underlined by the need for them to accept the entire *acquis*. Thus, whatever the justifications for including a state, once a member, it has to be treated equally. But this also means that a new member state has no recourse to special treatment. Nevertheless, several existing member states *have* obtained exemptions. Further, the EU *has* introduced minority protection conditions that only apply to applicants. Finally, some member states have also introduced entrance conditionality to Eastern/Central Europeans. Note that these are the same people that were addressed in kinship terms and that were told that Western Europeans had a duty to help them. Here lies a considerable recognition gap.

In sum, the EU has established a set of entrance requirements that the applicants must accept to be included. This might look like an imposition since there is no reciprocity, but the requirements are intended to be equal and universally applicable. The conditions are reflective of a recognition order foremost anchored in the notions of self-confidence and self-respect. Still, there are cases of actual practice that deviate from these norms.

Conclusion

In the above, we have sought to demonstrate that to clarify the nature of the EU's social constituency, the notion of recognition is useful, albeit it needs to be supplemented with a framework of analysis that helps to clarify who are the claimants and what are the claims. As our partial mapping showed, the process of clarifying the EU's social constituency was made difficult by important methodological and ethical problems. But even if we had the relevant data, it is still a daunting task to clarify the EU's social constituency because of the very complex nature of the EU itself.

We have suggested that the EU might make up a new recognition order. This EU-based emerging post-national European recognition order draws foremost on self-confidence and self-respect and promises to elicit a greater degree of reflexivity than is found in the nation-state. It also challenges the national self-esteem-based mode of recognition that has so long been taken for granted, in particular in interstate relations.

But this new recognition order still also has its roots in the international system of states, so that states play an unusually significant role in the struggle for recognition within the EU. States are critical in the forging of the EU, as well as in the channelling of demands. But within the EU far more than within the international realm, state-carried demands for recognition (with variable degrees of social imprint) have to vie for space with social movements and individual rights promoters. Through Europeanization, the state-carried national self-esteem-based mode has had to enter the fray of a highly complex and multifaceted European recognition struggle. Rather than entrenching and solidifying national collective identities, the institutional structure associated with the EU increasingly *challenges* national auto-recognition, i.e., the taken-for-grantedness of the national point of view.

Honneth appears to be hinting at this significant state role when he says that there might be a need for a fourth recognition principle, which incorporates collective actors. But what we see in Europe is not so much the emergence of a new collective mode of recognition, but rather how the established and very often taken-for-granted notion of – national – self-esteem-based collective modes of recognition are challenged and are compelled to come up with justifications.

This new recognition order is both frail and is facing serious challenges. The EU has committed itself to the standards of democracy and equal citizenship, partly in response to social criticism. At the same time, some of the member states have consistently sought to curtail the EU through placing constraints on it, so as to bar it from delivering on these commitments. Other states have pushed for the EU to take on commitments. Imposed constraints can themselves generate a dynamic in which social actors experience denial of recognition, precisely because of the EU's commitment to – but curtailed ability to comply with – the most central recognition principles. The EU's own search for institutional – and constitutional – recognition is thus intimately tied up with the social constituency's conception of the EU. This is a potentially vicious circle. The EU responds to social criticism for inadequate democratic legitimacy, but is barred from or held back by governments concerned with their own identity and interests. How vicious this circle turns out to be depends on the social 'take' or embrace of the expectations that the EU propounds, and for us to know this a comprehensive mapping along the lines suggested above is needed.

The story and the framework listed above could perhaps best be conceived within the setting of the EU's own struggle for institutional recognition and the entire reconfiguring of the European political landscape that emanates from this.

References

Ackers, L. 1999. *Shifting spaces: women, citizenship and migration within the European Union*. Bristol: Policy Press.

Alesina, A., Devleeschauwer, A., Easterly, W., Kurlat, S. and Wacziarg, R. 2003. 'Fractionalization', *Journal of Economic Growth* 8: 155–94.

Alston, P. (ed.) 1999. *The EU and human rights*. Oxford: Oxford University Press.

Aminzade, R. R. et al. 2001. *Silence and voice in the study of contentious politics*. New York: Cambridge University Press.

Austrian Government. 2000. Report by the Republic of Austria pursuant to Article 25 paragraph 1 of the Framework Convention for the Protection of National Minorities, ACFC/SR(2000)003, 30 June 2000.

Benhabib, S. 2002. *The claims of culture: equality and diversity in the global era*. Princeton: Princeton University Press.

CFR-CDF. 2004. *Report on the Situation of Fundamental Rights in the European Union in 2003*, EU Network of independent experts on fundamental rights (CFR-CDF), January 2004. Available at http://cridho.cpdr.ucl.ac.be/en/eu_experts_network/report_details.php?year=2003

Chahrokh, H., Klug, W. and Bilger, V. (principal authors) 2004. *Migrants, minorities and legislation: Documenting legal measures and remedies against discrimination in 15 Member States of the European Union*. Report submitted by the International Centre for Migration Policy Development (ICMPD), on behalf of the EUMC, 2004. Available at http://www.fra.europa.eu/fraWebsite/material/pub/comparativestudy/CS-Legislation-en.pdf

Charter of Fundamental Rights. 2000. *Charter of Fundamental Rights of the European Union*. Official Journal of the European Communities 2000/C 346/01–22.

Cypriot Government. 1999. Report submitted by Cyprus pursuant to Article 25, paragraph 1 of the Framework Convention for the Protection of National Minorities, ACFC/SR(1999)002 rev, 1 March 1999.

Czech Government. 2004. Second report submitted by the Czech Republic pursuant to Article 25, paragraph 1 of the Framework Convention for the Protection of National Minorities, ACFC/SR/II(2004)007, 2 July 2004.

Danish Government. 2004. Second Report submitted by Denmark pursuant to Article 25, paragraph 1 of the Framework Convention for the Protection of National Minorities, ACFC/SR/II(2004)004, May 2004.

Delanty, G. 1995. *Inventing Europe: idea, identity, reality*. London: Macmillan.

Eriksen, E. O. and Fossum, J. E. 2002. 'Democracy through strong publics in the EU?' *Journal of Common Market Studies* 40(3): 401–23.

Eriksen, E. O., Fossum, J. E. and Menéndez, A. J. (eds) 2003. *The chartering of Europe: The Charter of Fundamental Rights and its constitutional implications*. Baden-Baden: Nomos.

EUMC. 2003/2004. *Racism and xenophobia in the EU member states: trends, developments and good practice*. EUMC – Annual Report 2003/2004. Available at http://www.fra.europa.eu/fraWebsite/attachments/ar0304p2en.pdf

European Commission. 1996. *Euromosaic: The production and reproduction of the minority language groups in the European Union*. Office for Official Publications of the European Communities.

European Convention. 2003. *Draft Treaty establishing a Constitution for Europe*. CONV 850/03, Brussels, 18 July 2003.

European Council. 1993. *Presidency conclusions*. SN/180/93, Copenhagen, 21–23 June 1993.

Fearon, J. D. 2003. 'Ethnic and cultural diversity by country', *Journal of Economic Growth* 8: 195–222.

Finnish Government. 2004. Report submitted by Finland pursuant to Article 25, Paragraph 1 of the Framework Convention for the Protection of National Minorities, ACFC/SR/II(2004) 012 E, 10 December 2004.

Fraser, N. 1997. *Justice interruptus: critical reflections on the 'postsocialist condition'*. London: Routledge.

Fraser, N. 2003. 'Social justice in the age of identity politics: redistribution, recognition and participation', in: N. Fraser and A. Honneth (eds) *Redistribution or recognition?* London: Verso, 7–110.

Fraser, N. and Honneth, A. 2003. *Redistribution or recognition? A political-philosophical exchange*. London: Verso.

Gächter, A. 2003. *COMPSTAT: Comparative aspects*. Vienna: Center for Social Innovation. January 2003. Available at: http://www.compstat.org/Start/subnav_q2_wblau_dsd_folder/Comparative_aspects.pdf

German Government. 2005. Second Report submitted by Germany pursuant to Article 25, Paragraph 1 of the Framework Convention for the Protection of National Minorities, ACFC/SRII(2005)002, 13 April 2005.

Greenwood, J. 2003. *Interest representation in the European Union*. Basingstoke: Palgrave Macmillan.

Greenwood, J. and Aspinwall, M. 1998. *Collective action in the European Union*. London: Routledge.

Gutmann, A. 2003. *Identity in democracy*. Princeton: Princeton University Press.

Habermas, J. 1994. 'Struggles for recognition in the democratic constitutional state', in: C. Taylor and A. Gutmann (eds) *Multiculturalism*. Princeton: Princeton University Press, 107–49.

Habermas, J. 1996. *Between facts and norms: contributions to a discourse theory of law and democracy*. Cambridge, MA: MIT Press.

Habermas, J. 2000. *The postnational constellation*. Cambridge, MA: MIT Press.

Hobson, B. (ed.) 2003. *Recognition struggles and social movements*. Cambridge: Cambridge University Press.

Honneth, A. 1995a. *The struggle for recognition: the moral grammar of social conflicts* [trans. J. Anderson]. Cambridge: Polity Press.

Honneth, A. 1995b. *The fragmented world of the social: essays in social and political philosophy*. Albany, NY: State University of New York Press.

Honneth, A. 2003. 'Redistribution as recognition: a response to Nancy Fraser', in: N. Fraser and A. Honneth (eds) *Redistribution or recognition?* London: Verso, 110–98.

Hoskyns, C. 1996. *Integrating gender: women, law and politics in the European Union*. London: Verso.

Imig, D. and Tarrow, S. (eds) 2001. *Contentious Europeans: protest and politics in an emerging polity*. Lanham: Rowman and Littlefield.

Inglehart, R. 1977. *The silent revolution: changing values and political styles among Western publics*. Princeton: Princeton University Press.

Inglehart, R. 1990. *Culture shift in advanced industrial societies*. Princeton: Princeton University Press.

Italian Government. 1999. Report submitted by Italy pursuant to Article 25, Paragraph 1 of the Framework Convention for the Protection of National Minorities, ACFC/SR(1999)007, 3 May 1999.

Italian Government. 2004. Second Report submitted by Italy pursuant to Article 25, Paragraph 1 of the Framework Convention for the Protection of National Minorities, ACFC/SR/II(2004)006, 14 May 2004.

Kent, M. 2000. 'The Baltics: demographic challenges and independence', Population Reference Bureau. Available at: http://www.prb.org/Articles/2000/TheBalticsDemographicChallengesandIndependence.aspx

Kværk, G. O. 2003. Legitimering gjennom rettigheter? En studie av arbeidet med EUs Charter om grunnleggende rettigheter, og sivilsamfunnets bidrag til dette, ARENA Report No. 6/2003.

Kværk, G. O. 2007. Organised civil society in the EU constitution-making process, in: J. E. Fossum, P. Schlesinger and G. O. Kværk (eds) *Public sphere and civil society? Transformations of the European Union*. ARENA Report No. 2/07. Oslo: ARENA, 141–223.

Kymlicka, W. 1995. *Multicultural citizenship: a liberal theory of minority rights*. Oxford: Clarendon Press.

Kymlicka, W. 1998. *Finding our way*. Oxford: Oxford University Press.

Kymlicka, W. and Norman, W. (eds) 2000. *Citizenship in diverse societies*. Oxford: Oxford University Press.

Latvian Government. 2006. Report submitted by Latvia pursuant to Article 25, Paragraph 1 of the Framework Convention for the Protection of National Minorities, ACFC/SR(2006)001, 11 October 2006.

Lipgens, W. 1982. *History of European integration*. Oxford: Oxford University Press.

Lithuanian Government. 2001. Report submitted by Lithuania pursuant to Article 25, Paragraph 1 of the Framework Convention for the Protection of National Minorities, ACFC/SR(2001)007, 31 October 2001.

McAdam, D., Tarrow, S., and C. Tilly, C. 2001. *Dynamics of contention*. Cambridge: Cambridge University Press.

Menéndez, A. J. 2003. 'Rights to solidarity: balancing solidarity and economic freedoms', in: E. O. Eriksen, J. E. Fossum and J. E. Menéndez (eds) *The chartering of Europe*. Baden-Baden: Nomos, 179–98.

Milton, S. 1997. 'Registering civilians and aliens in the Second World War', *Jewish History* 11(2): 79–87.

Moravcsik, A. 2004. 'Is there a "democratic deficit" in world politics? A framework for analysis', *Government and Opposition* 39(2): 336–63.

OECD. 2006. *International migration outlook*. Paris: OECD.

Offe, C. 1987. 'Challenging the boundaries of institutional politics: social movements since the 1960s', in: C. S. Maier (ed.) *Changing boundaries of the political: essays on the evolving balance between the state and society, public and private in Europe*. Cambridge: Cambridge University Press, 63–105.

Polish Government. 2002. Report submitted by Poland pursuant to Article 25, Paragraph 1 of the Framework Convention for the Protection of National Minorities, ACFC/SR(2002)002, 10 July 2002.

Shaw, J. 2000. 'Importing gender: the challenge of feminism and the analysis of the EU legal order', *Journal of European Public Policy* 7(3): 406–31.

Sjursen, H. 2002. 'Why expand? The question of legitimacy and justification in the EU's enlargement policy', *Journal of Common Market Studies* 40(3): 491–513.

Slovenian Government. 2004. Second report submitted by Slovenia pursuant to Article 25, Paragraph 1 of the Framework Convention for the Protection of National Minorities, ACFC/SR/II(2004)008, 6 July 2004.

Soysal, Y. N. 1994. *Limits of citizenship: migrants and postnational membership in Europe*. Chicago: University of Chicago Press.

Spanish Government. 2006. Second Report submitted by Spain pursuant to Article 25, Paragraph 1 of the Framework Convention for the Protection of National Minorities, ACFC/SR/II(2006)002, 10 April 2006.

Swedish Government. 2001. Report submitted by Sweden pursuant to Article 25, Paragraph 1 of the Framework Convention for the Protection of National Minorities, ACFC/SR(2001)003, 8 June 2001.

Taylor, C. 1985. *Human agency and language*. Cambridge: Cambridge University Press.

Taylor, C. 1986. *Philosophy and the human sciences*. Cambridge: Cambridge University Press.

Taylor, C. 1989. *Sources of the self: the making of the modern identity*. Cambridge, MA: Harvard University Press.

Taylor, C. 1993. *Reconciling the solitudes: essays on Canadian federalism and nationalism*. Montreal and Kingston: McGill-Queen's University Press.

Taylor, C. 1994. 'The politics of recognition', in: C. Taylor and A. Gutmann (eds) *Multiculturalism*. Princeton: Princeton University Press.

Tilly, C. 1978. *From mobilization to revolution*. New York: Random House.

Trenz, H.-J. 2004. 'Language minorities in Europe: dying species or forerunners of a transnational civil society?' Paper presented at the ECPR Second Pan-European Conference on EU Politics *Implications of a Wider Europe: Politics, Institutions and Diversity*, Bologna, Italy, 24–26 June 2004.

Tully, J. 1995. *Strange multiplicity: constitutionalism in an age of diversity*. Cambridge: Cambridge University Press.

Weiler, J. H. H. 2001. 'Federalism without constitutionalism: Europe's Sonderweg', in: K. Nicolaïdis and R. Howse (eds) *The federal vision*. Oxford: Oxford University Press, 54–70.

Weiler, J. H. H. 2002. 'A constitution for Europe: some hard choices?' *Journal of Common Market Studies* 40(4): 563–80.

Williams, F. 2003. 'Contesting "race" and gender in the European Union: a multilayered recognition struggle for voice and visibility', in: B. Hobson (ed.) *Recognition struggles and social movements*. Cambridge: Cambridge University Press, 121–44.

Young, I. M. 1990. *Justice and the politics of difference*. Princeton: Princeton University Press.

8 Caesarean citizenship and its anti-civic potential in the European Union

Ireneusz Pawel Karolewski

Introduction

The issue of European citizenship has been subject to a heated debate in legal and social sciences from the beginning of the 1990s. The mainstream debate dealt above all with the potential of the European citizenship. While some scholars focused on the limitations of European citizenship in comparison with national citizenship, criticizing the underdeveloped character of European citizenship (Lyons 1996; Weiler 1996), others highlighted the constructive potential of it (Wiener 1998; Shaw 1998). However, one issue seems to be particularly marginalized in the debate on European citizenship. Although a wealth of research exists on the issue of European citizenship as a source of new transnational and supranational rights (Bellamy *et al.* 2006; Bauböck 2007; Delanty 2007), certain anti-civic features of the EU are explored to a lesser degree in the context of European citizenship. In order to approach the anti-civic potential of the EU, this chapter introduces the concept of Caesarean citizenship and argues that the anti-civic features of the European citizenship are counterproductive concerning the development of civic resources in the EU.

The concept of anti-civic potential of citizenship draws on the literature highlighting the exclusionary nature of citizenship as an instrument of social closure. In this vein, Rogers Brubaker argues that even democratic citizenship is a device of social closure and exclusion, as it necessarily discriminates between citizens and non-citizens and excludes the non-citizens from the polity (Brubaker 1994, 1999). This boundary-making mechanism of modern citizenship appears to be necessary, as citizenship integrates individuals within a community and excludes those outside of it. As Peter Wagner argues, modern states apply two main techniques of rule to politically integrate modern societies: liberty and discipline (Wagner 1994). While liberty is associated with democratic citizenship as a source of civil, political and social rights, the disciplining function of citizenship reflects the governance aspect of citizenship, as global population is governed by dividing it into subpopulations consisting of territorially closed, politically independent and even competing states (Hindess 1998; Joppke 2005). In this sense, citizenship is an instrument of social closure, whose architect and guarantor is the modern state and increasingly 'quasi-states' such as the European Union. However, these exclusionary mechanisms can be used in an excessive manner that promotes anti-civic potential of citizenship. While more traditional concepts of citizenship aim either for common good or highlight the individual's rights, Caesarean citizenship is associated with a mode of governance based on exclusion, which is presented as a remedy against the so-called 'society of risk' (cf. Beck 2002). Caesarean citizenship is based on the notion of collective self-preservation of citizens who unquestioningly support the state authority for the sake of their protection against (actual, potential and imaginary) enemies and threats. It finds its reflection in exclusionary policies of the state vis-à-vis the dangerous 'others' and establishment of institutions dealing with exclusion and surveillance. Didier Bigo coined in this context the term 'banopticon', which refers to a system of institutions and technologies used for discrimination between those with access and those to be monitored for possible detention and removal (Bigo 2002).

Even though these exclusionary practices, institutions and policies have occurred mainly in the post-9/11 nation-state, the EU has also increasingly dealt with immigration as a danger to European societies and created institutions dealing with exclusion of immigrants. After 2001 there has been a surge in the legislative output of the EU concerning internal security issues, in particular concerning immigration policies. Jörg Monar (2008: 109) points out that 'for the Justice and Home Affairs Council the year 2007 brought a record: the 164 texts adopted were not only an increase of nearly 40 per cent compared to 2006, but also the highest number of texts ever adopted during a single year.' Moreover, new programmes on internal security and immigration have been enacted and implemented, including the Hague and Stockholm programmes. As a result, the EU has continued to establish new institutions dealing with immigration, e.g. Frontex, as well as invested heavily in surveillance technologies designed to fend off immigration.

Against this background, immigration has become progressively defined and presented in the EU as a threat to the community's survival in its current economic, social and cultural form, thus strengthening exclusionary aspects of Caesarean citizenship. Even with its dedication to cosmopolitism and civility, the EU has established and applied exclusionary practices in the field of immigration policies, which are likely to espouse anti-civic effects. This chapter begins by discussing the concept of Caesarean citizenship. I will briefly discuss the theoretical roots of the concept and highlight its contemporary relevance. Additionally, I will explore the Caesarean citizenship in the context of immigration policies and point to its anti-civic potential. Here, I will contextualize Caesarean citizenship in the EU by reverting to the concepts of 'othering' and the banopticon. Afterwards, I will explore the concept of the European 'corporate security state', which is the institutional counterpart of Caesarean citizenship in the EU. Next, I will examine the immigration policies of the EU through the prism of the Caesarean citizenship and explore the institutions of the European 'corporate security state' in the field of immigration.

Caesarean citizenship

The roots of the Caesarean citizenship concept can be found in the writings of Thomas Hobbes and, in its modern version, in the works of Carl Schmitt (Hobbes 1996 [1651]; Schmitt 1996 [1932]). Within this tradition being a citizen means to think in categories of friend and enemy. Therefore, the Caesarean citizen is supposed to delineate politics as a perpetual struggle against enemies, be it internal (Hobbes) or external ones (Schmitt). Citizenship is thus about survival of the community, which can be only guaranteed by the effectiveness of political decisions in the face of danger and threat. Consequently, the citizens do not realize any political ideal of communitarian life nor do they act upon their individual rights. Rather, they authorize the 'Caesar', a political leader with sufficient power to guarantee the survival of the citizens in a hostile environment.

Hobbes stresses that a strong ruler is the only solution to political chaos that would otherwise tear society apart and claim the lives of its citizens (Frost 2004; Maritain 1950). With the conclusion of the Hobbesian 'contract of rule', citizens willingly surrender their political rights and pledge their obedience to the Leviathan (Hobbes 1990 [1682], 1991 [1642], 1996 [1651]). Consequently, the ruler is free to make laws according to his will, as long as he can guarantee the survival and security of his citizens. As a result, the Caesarean model of citizenship does not highlight the rights or communitarian obligations of citizens as much as the effectiveness of the state and the compliance of the citizens who submit to the authority in the face of potential danger. The decisional effectiveness of the ruler reflects the supply side of the Caesarean citizenship, while the citizens' willing compliance is linked to its demand side. The citizens demand state activity and effectiveness in dealing with potential dangers, enemies and threats.

Carl Schmitt argues in the same vein, as the very essence of politics is the ability of citizens to think of the 'others' in terms of 'enemies', which forges political bonds among citizens within the community at hand (Schmitt 1996 [1932]); cf. Rasch 2000; Sartori 1989). Consequently, the demand side of Caesarean citizenship stresses the eager compliance of the citizens, their subjecthood and their fear-induced support for the leader. On this basis, bonds of collective identity, loyalty, solidarity and even sacrificial readiness among citizens can develop. In contrast, the supply side of Caesarean citizenship relates to the ability of political elites to guarantee citizens' survival and safety. Caesarean citizenship becomes manifest when the demand and the supply side of the Caesarean citizenship meet in equilibrium. This occurs when the leader possesses the decisional authority, while the role of citizens is reduced to the confirmation of his decisions and compliance. In this way, 'politics of exception' or 'decisionist politics' are highlighted, as survival of the citizens is at stake and no decisional weakness of the state can be accepted. As Carl Schmitt puts it in the conclusion to *Legality and Legitimacy*, '[t]he people can only respond yes or no. They cannot advise, deliberate, or discuss. They cannot set norms, but can only sanction norms by consenting to draft sets of norms laid before them. Above all, they also cannot pose a question, but can only answer with yes or no to a question placed before them [. . .]' (Schmitt 2004 [1932]: 89).

The contemporary relevance

In the modern post-9/11 version, the Caesarean citizenship relates mainly to internal security policies as the major concern of the state. Concerning the demand side of the Caesarean citizenship, security policies become essential, as there is a shift from rights-endowed citizens towards neurotic citizens (Isin 2004; Lyon 1992). A neurotic citizen defines politics in terms of its permanent insecurity, which can only be dealt with by the state. That is why citizens' preference for liberty and freedom becomes surpassed by their fears of survival in view of risk and danger. However, state actions are not only a response to citizens' demands. Citizens become fear-induced by state actions and mass media reporting that often highlight catastrophic imagery and the worst-case scenarios (Sunstein 2005). Paradoxically, state actions in the field of internal security can strengthen citizens' neurotic reactions, rather than satisfy their need for more security. As a result, the activity of the citizen focuses more strongly on reporting potentially dangerous situations and spying on his compatriots, rather than on elections, public space and ensuring the accountability of the government.

In contrast, the supply side of Caesarean citizenship reflects the decisional effectiveness of the state and its surveillance activities. The ability to decide effectively in order to secure the survival of citizens is the Hobbesian criterion for state legitimacy. In Schmitt's writings, the president can rule using decrees, since through direct legitimacy of the president they acquire a normative superiority. While the inefficiency and perhaps even a tyranny of the parliamentary majority poses a danger for the rule of the demos, the Caesarean president in the ancient Roman manner redeems and rescues the decayed and corrupted republic. Consequently, the Caesarean citizenship is executive-accentuated at the expense of the parliaments. In the modern version, the mistrust in the effectiveness of parliaments strengthens the demand side of Caesarean citizenship, whereas on the supply side the executive branches develop escape strategies from parliamentary and judicial control. The surveillance activity of the state is directed both at the citizens ('surveillance society') and non-citizens (citizens versus suspects) (Lyon 2009; Scherrer *et al.* 2010). The surveillance activities of the state highlight the immanence of danger, insecurity and threat and thus mobilize the fear-induced citizenship (Debrix and Barder 2009). Therefore, the polity is characterized by 'data-flows, mutating surveillance agencies and the targeting and sorting of everyone' (Lyon 2010: 1).

While Hobbes and Schmitt are primarily concerned with the decline of the political order, they both underestimate the power of the state to apply Caesarean citizenship in an instrumental way. The state can stimulate the demand side of Caesarean citizenship by, for instance, inducing the citizens to believe in their ongoing insecurity, thus delivering grounds for the perpetual actions of the state. It can result in the so-called politics of insecurity targeted at maintaining or producing feeling of insecurity (Huysmans 2005, 2006). The state authorities can enhance the threat perception by highlighting existing threat images and/or by constructing institutions dealing with existing threats, whereby citizens cannot easily estimate for themselves whether these institutions are necessary. *On the one hand*, information on risk and threat is often ambivalent, since the so-called security experts offering their 'knowledge' in mass media are seldom reliable due to the secrecy concerning internal security policy (Behnke 2000). This ambivalence is particularly easy to manipulate in Western insurance-oriented societies with a high demand for regulation of risk (Aradau and van Munster 2007). *On the other hand*, the mere availability of risk and threat information in mass media enhances the salience of security matters in the citizenry. This can contribute to collective feelings of threat and danger, promoting diffuse perception of insecurity. As the citizens' perception of insecurity increases, the demand for state activity in the field of internal security policy is also likely to rise.

Caesarean citizenship, immigration and the anti-civic potential

In addition to the generation of the diffuse feeling of insecurity, governments tend to give the enemy a face and a name. By identifying the enemy, rather than only pointing to general threats, the state can enhance the identification of citizens with their own collectivity. This double identification (of the enemy and with its own collectivity) is a powerful identity technology associated with Caesarean citizenship. In this context, immigrants can be used as a negative point of reference for Caesarean citizenship and its politics of identity (Walters 2002; Roes 2004). By identifying immigrants-cum-suspects, the state shows that its surveillance activities are justified and it also highlights its decisional capacity. Jef Huysmans argues:

> Bureaucratic, corporate, academic and political actors most of the time represent migration policy as a reaction to an increasing migration pressure. Migration is thus approached like any other economic, social, or psychological challenge: a problem that presents itself in front of the policy-makers and that demands effective action. However, this approach hides the fact that questions relating to migration are posed in the context of a crisis of political identity in Europe today. In this process immigrants and refugees are not only a challenge to which one reacts but they also become anchoring points for political (self-) identification . . .
>
> Huysmans 2000a: 150

In this sense, immigration policy of the EU has (self-)identity-generating effects, as it highlights the difference between the citizen and the suspect and thus becomes part of the Caesarean citizenship. Therefore, the Caesarean identity technology inherent in immigration policy uses the very identifying process to strengthen collective responses and compliance of the citizens (cf. Muller 2004). In this sense, combating immigration as a diffuse threat goes hand in hand with attempts to identify immigrants as a specific point of reference for Caesarean citizenship. Therefore, Caesarean citizenship becomes associated with demarcation and a juxtaposition of the in-group in relation to the 'other', whereas the 'other' frequently acquires a more durable image. The 'othering' as a device for collective-identity-building tells 'us' who 'we' are by relating 'us' to 'them' (Billig 1995: 78). Generation of collective identity therefore responds to the needs of societies to create and recreate its own 'others'. In this sense, the construction of 'others' reacts to the symbolic or affective needs of the community members (Triandafyllidou 1998). Particularly in times of crises, the significant 'other' becomes activated in the collective identity of individuals, since the binary construction of 'us' versus 'them' helps in overcoming the crises by using 'blaming' and 'scapegoating' strategies vis-à-vis the 'others'. The 'others' unite the community by highlighting that the community is different and unique (Billig 1995: 80). For instance, the 'other' can be constructed as inferior, which boosts the feeling of supremacy and grandeur of a given collectivity and might lead to stigmatization of 'others'. If the 'other' is constructed as threatening through an enemy-accentuating political rhetoric, it may produce xenophobia and even violence against the 'others'. Therefore, politics of insecurity focusing on the 'others' can lead to anti-civic reactions of citizens against non-citizens.

In this context, immigrants are frequently 'constructed' as the 'others' that are depicted as a threat to the community's survival in its current social and cultural form. Didier Bigo uses in this context the term 'banopticon', which discriminates between those with access and those to be monitored for possible detention and removal. This banopticon supersedes the nation-state, as national governments of the EU strengthen their collaboration in exclusion of immigrants as suspected 'others'. In particular, the European Union uses banopticon technologies, as it governs effectively its external borders by applying exclusionary practices and carries out surveillance of the population within its borders (Amiraux 2010).

> The Ban-opticon is then characterized by the exceptionalism of power (rules of emergency and their tendency to become permanent), by the way it excludes certain groups in the name of their future potential behaviour (profiling) and by the way it normalizes the non-excluded through its production of normative imperatives, the most important of which is free movement (the so-called four freedoms of circulation of the EU: concerning goods, capital, information, services and persons).
>
> Bigo 2010: 35

The member states of the EU collaborate in the setting-up of institutions, funds and surveillance instruments which separate the neurotic European citizens from the dangers of the outside world, embodied by the 'others'. By constructing and implementing practices of exclusion, banopticon reassures the neurotic citizens and deters the 'others'. In this perspective, the EU external border controls assume the function of 'sorting machines' (Mau 2011), which monitor, screen and remove the suspected non-citizens, while allowing 'qualified bodies' to enter its territory. The border controls are supported by a number of monitoring institutions, data banks, screening devices and surveillance mechanisms including Frontex, Europol, the Schengen Information System and Eurodac. Simultaneously, these banopticon institutions and technologies strengthen the confidence of the EU citizens that they remain among themselves and separated from the dangers of the outside world. As the border controls are shifted from the member states to the external borders of the EU, the Europeanization of the Caesarean citizenship ensues. However, the banopticon operates far from the spotlight of the public opinion and evades increasingly the democratic control of parliaments. Moreover, the banopticon tends to expand its operations beyond the realm of the necessary (Bigo 2010). The policing and surveillance that takes place to classify and determine the 'others' can be applied to the rest of the population, as the use of technologies of biometrics and shared databases is easily enlarged and expanded. The banopticon is associated with the Caesarean citizenship, as the EU increasingly applies the politics of insecurity, which on the one hand maintains and promotes the fear of the neurotic citizens directed at the 'others'. On the other hand, the EU furthers state activity in the realm of surveillance, control and restrictions. By so doing, the EU shifts its focus on citizenship from political participation and democracy towards the field of internal security, which bases its legitimacy in the bureaucratic power of surveillance, control, separation and expulsion. The main objective of citizenship becomes its preservation against external threats, rather than political self-determination. It goes hand in hand with a construction of collective identity based on fear and insecurity of the neurotic citizen, who in order to preserve his collectively threatened lifestyle agrees to live in an increasingly disciplinary society.

These workings of the Caesarean citizenship in the EU are potentially anti-civic and contrast the more positive notion of European citizenship based on new transnational mobility rights. Caesarean citizenship highlights security concerns at the expense of individual liberty and civil and political rights (cf. Sunstein 2005: 204). Moreover, it sanctions the executive-dominated politics of exceptions to the detriment of parliamentary control. In the EU context, it deepens the existing democratic deficit of the EU through the expansion of executive powers, the executive escape from democratic accountability and overall secrecy surrounding security issues, which exacerbates the transparency deficits of the EU. Caesarean citizenship highlights the growing relevance of security politics on the one hand and the increasing demand for protection from the neurotic citizen on the other, measured, for instance, by new institution-building and legislative output in the field of security policies.

Certainly, there has been a duality of the security discourse in the EU, regarding especially immigration, where the EU asylum and immigration policies espouse two conflicting policy objectives – the objective of internal security and the objective of humanitarianism. While the security objective stresses the necessity to restrict immigration across EU borders, and to fend off irregular immigration, the humanitarian objective incorporates the human rights principles of freedom of movement and refugee protection. However, despite this duality, asylum and immigration policies have become dominated by the imperative to secure the borders against unwanted immigration (cf. Lavenex 2001).

The European 'corporate security state'

While the rights-based citizenship is associated with democratic and accountable state, the Caesarean citizenship finds its institutional counterpart in the institutional development of a 'corporate security state'. In the case of the EU the 'corporate security state' is not necessarily monolithic but rather reflects the multiple and differentiated form of the EU governance. The European 'corporate security state' consists equally of supranational security institutions such as Frontex or Europol and national police with military status, secret service, border guards and customs. They search inside and outside of the EU borders for threats from 'outside', which are mainly associated with immigrants, citizens of foreign origins or residents of disadvantaged suburbs (Bigo 2000).

The threat assessment related to immigrants becomes one of the main justifications for new supranational security institutions and more cooperation between the national security agencies. In this context, we can identify four characteristics of the developing European 'corporate security state': (1) the progressing Europeanization of Justice and Home Affairs; (2) the fusion of intergovernmental and supranational elements in the EU; (3) the 'executive escape' from the democratic accountability in the EU; and (4) the European banopticon.

First, there has been advancing Europeanization of security issues, including immigration policies (Favell 1998; Lavenex 2001; Lavenex and Uçarer 2004). At the institutional level, this refers both to the activities within the former first (community level) and the former third pillar of the EU (intergovernmental level) (Stetter 2008), which after the Lisbon Treaty constitute the Area of Freedom, Security and Justice (AFSJ) including both citizenship and immigration issues. At the level of the legislative output of the EU, there is a growing regulation of internal security issues, in particular concerning immigration policies. Jörg Monar (2008: 109) points out that in 2007 the EU legislated the highest number of legal texts in this field ever adopted during a single year. In 2010, the total annual output of the JHA Council dropped from 121 adopted texts in 2009 to 114 texts, but it is likely to merely indicate a slow start of the Stockholm Programme, which follows the Hague Programme

(Monar 2011: 145). In other words, the EU is expected to espouse a high legislative dynamic in the AFSJ in the years to come.

Second, even though there has been an increasing communitization of the EU with the Lisbon Treaty, the EU still remains composed of both supranational and intergovernmental elements. However, it means that also the intergovernmental elements are a part of the EU and its intergovernmental activities cannot be reduced to actions of the individual member states (cf. Uçarer 2001). Even prior to the Lisbon Treaty, the EU legislation concerning internal security (including the immigration issues) has occurred equally in both pillars. A case in point is the second generation Schengen Information System (SIS II) that has been legislated both in the first pillar (European Parliament and Council 2007) and the third pillar (Council 2006b). Furthermore, the research on the administrative dynamics of the EU suggests that there is also a growing fusion of administrative structures of the member states in the realm of internal security. This administrative fusion is characterized by routinized interactions among civil servants from different levels of the nation-states, based on technocratic expertise and consensus-orientation (Wessels 1998, 2000). In the case of internal security policies, the multi-level bureaucratic fusion underpins an evolution of the EU towards a 'corporate security state'. In the process, the bureaucracies of the member states dealing with internal security open up towards integration with bureaucracies of other member states.

Third, there has been a tendency of 'executive escape' from the democratic accountability in the EU member states through 'Europeanization' (Wagner 2006, 2010). The 'Europeanization' of some policy fields such as immigration control or counter-terrorism policies can be regarded as a strategy to increase the autonomy of member states' ministries from political, normative and institutional constraints of the national policymaking. Since the democratic constraints on the executive action in the EU due to the feeble position of the European Parliament are considerably weaker than in the member states, advancing coordination and institution-building among the national ministries in the EU can be interpreted as an attempt to escape the democratic constraints of their member states (cf. Lavenex 2004, 2006). The main actors are justice and interior ministry officials who attempt to expand their autonomy vis-à-vis their governments by mobilizing against security threats arising from asylum-seekers, foreign criminals and terrorists. In this way, officials can diffuse responsibility for policy ideas, disguise their own interests and also lend normative acceptance to more restrictive measures in the EU immigration policies (Maurer and Parkes 2007). Against this background, the European corporate security state is not merely a product of supranational European elites, but also of national officials striving for more Europeanization. This results, however, in a considerably reduced democratic accountability of the evolving European corporate security state.

Fourth, the EU increasingly attempts to come to terms with the discrimination between friend and enemy, the latter being mainly the irregular immigrants.

As a result, the EU applies technologies of the banopticon, based on data-gathering, surveillance and deterrence. The EU security apparatus deployed against the threats from outside ranges from common regulations concerning passports to potentially offensive weapon systems. For instance, the European Union has required of its member states (and non-members such as Iceland, Norway, Switzerland and Turkey) to implement biometrics in passports no later than 2012. Biometric features in passports and travel documents are used to verify the authenticity of the document and the identity of the holder, in order to sort out the irregular immigrants or immigrants-cum-terrorists. In addition, already in 2005 Italy purchased several Predator drones to patrol the borders of the Libyan Desert to fend off irregular immigrants to the EU. The unmanned aerial vehicles (UAV) not only carry the latest surveillance equipment but are also used by the US military to kill terrorists in different parts of the world. Moreover, the southern and eastern borders of the EU have become progressively more guarded, which mobilizes threat images in the European societies. 'On the new eastern borders of the EU, more than one billion Euros has been invested into Schengen data terminals, X-ray scanners, surveillance vehicles, electronic watchtowers with thermal cameras and underground detection cables with motion sensors' (Gammeltoft-Hansen 2006: 1). This and other measures reflect 'politics of insecurity' or 'politics of exception' involving an increased exploitation of threat images concerning immigration. As the 'politics of exception' highlights permanent danger and risk situations, it legitimizes the application of surveillance technologies and data-gathering about both citizens and non-citizens.

Caesarean citizenship and the immigration policies in the EU

In the context of the EU's Caesarean citizenship, immigration has been increasingly presented as a danger to public order, cultural identity and labour market stability. As a result, the banopticon has become enacted in the EU, with the purpose of discrimination between those with access and those to be monitored for possible detention and removal. Therefore, the EU has been establishing new institutions, funds and deploying surveillance and deterrence technologies that are to separate the neurotic citizen from the dangers of the outside world. In this context, Ruben Zaiotti (2007) suggests that the EU suffers from a 'gated community syndrome', which results from the 'Schengen culture of internal security', whose key tenet is the focus on security as the central feature of the political process (Melossi 2005). This focus entails the priority of security over other policy domains, fixation of the EU authorities and national states to protect Europe from internal and external threats and suspicion towards third countries' citizens (cf. Commission 2007b).

However, these institutional developments convey images of societal danger from a criminal and invading enemy. For instance, the term 'illegal migration', used in the EU's legal texts, promotes a rhetorical criminalization of immigrants, in particular asylum-seekers and refugees, and highlights the criminal threats stemming from them (Commission 2006a, 2006b). This criminalization ranges from threats to the labour market ('combating illegal unemployment') to 'fight against organized criminality' (Commission 2006c; Council 2007). It establishes a security discourse in the field of immigration, in which immigrants become increasingly associated with threat images (Verschueren 2007; Vermeulen 2007). Moreover, the EU immigration policy is brought together with the threat of terrorism, which stresses the existential threats of immigration (Council 2004a; Brouwer 2003; Adamson 2006). The imagery of an immigrant-cum-terrorist is even better suited for politics of insecurity, since being under threat from terrorism generates a higher degree of fear and worry in neurotic citizens than for instance the image of criminal immigrants.

Different types of immigrants reflect a broad range of threat images involved in the EU immigration policy, rather than an immigration policy, where both attraction and rejection strategies vis-à-vis the immigrants are applied in a balanced manner. As a result, the EU has defined the immigration issue mainly in terms of threat, rather than labour market requirements (Beutin *et al.* 2007). Some types of immigrants serve better the insecurity politics than others, where asylum-seekers and refugees are the types with the highest potential for threat image construction. However, by inducing the perception of 'the immigration problem' in terms of security, a collective image of immigrants as a threat is established which annihilates the perception of difference between different types of immigrants, thus paving the way for a defensive security politics in the EU. The fear-inducing policies of the EU are constructed both by the supranational political elites of the EU and the EU member states – often in a symbiotic manner, which reflects the multi-level character of the EU. For instance, according to a Commission proposal, the EU members have to collect personal data on air passengers coming into and leaving EU airspace. The information is to be collected in analysis units that make a 'risk assessment' of the traveller, which could lead to the questioning or even refusal of entry (Commission 2007a; European Parliament 2007; Pérez Asinari and Poullet 2004). The implementation of these policies is carried out by the member states but they are legislated in the EU and are implemented in its name.

Furthermore, the EU reacts oftentimes to national fears and specific national immigration preferences. For instance, despite the goal of the 'Blue Card proposal' to increase the EU's share in the global competition for skilled third-country workers, the Commission was aware of the member states' preferences to keep their control over the national labour markets and therefore it watered down its initially ambitious plans for an EU-wide admission procedure and left it under the control of the 27 national immigration systems (Monar 2008). Whoever the initiators of the restrictive EU policies are, they generate or strengthen threat images associated with immigration, which are not necessarily driven by a rational assessment of the current situation. Presenting immigration as a security issue (to public order, cultural identity and labour market stability) becomes a part of a discourse of insecurity. As a consequence, countering irregular immigration can result in a feeling of insecurity rather than establishing security.

The practices of Caesarean citizenship in the field of immigration policy consist, for instance, of categorization of friends and enemies as well as policies of exclusion. This realm of exclusion applies, for instance, the biometric technologies for identifying and authenticating threats. This identification entails the allocation of civil rights to refugees considered legitimate and rejection of civil rights to illegitimate refugees (Geddes 2001: 36; Geddes 2005). Caesarean citizenship is therefore mirrored in identification of the collective enemy, in terms of his authentication: biometrics, databanks and electronic surveillance are used to verify and to discriminate between the qualified others and the unqualified authentic others who are in turn subject to detention and deportation (Muller 2004; Walters 2002). As mentioned earlier, the insecurity politics of immigration produces a collective image of immigrants as a threat without differentiating between different types of immigrants. This is additionally reinforced by practices of externalization of border control. For instance, the EU obliges carrier firms such as airlines to return any illegal immigrant to their country of origin (Moreno Lax 2008; Guiraudon and Lahav 2000). These carrier firms are made accountable and punished with financial sanctions where immigrants are unable to present legal documents during EU border controls. Apart from undermining the basic principles of refugee protection, the EU shifts the traditional state practice of checking travel documents and returning irregular immigrants to private firms. However, this shift is likely to put legitimate refugees and irregular immigrants into one category of threatening immigrants who are to be prevented from entering EU territory, as the carrier firms are likely to avoid immigrants in general, as a strategy of reducing potential costs of sanctions and returning the immigrants (Svantesson 2006: 71).

On the one hand, the ever more restrictive immigration policies of the EU respond to the fears and insecurities of the citizenry. On the other hand, by showing decisiveness and by externalizing immigration problems, the EU highlights the seriousness of the problem and contributes to the dispersion of fear and 'affective epidemics' of insecurity (Faist 2002). The 'corporate security state' of the EU deals with the issues of immigration by using modes of European inter-state cooperation and often in isolation from judicial and parliamentary scrutiny. By stressing the link between asylum and internal security, the actors of the 'corporate security state' have been able to shift Justice and Home Affairs (now part of the AFSJ) from the margins to the core of the European Union (Maurer and Parkes 2006). Therefore, the European executives act in the field of immigration regulation as a part of the 'corporate security state' with the goal of deterring and deflecting asylum-seekers, thus enhancing the image of fortress 'Europe' and at the same time promoting the image of an effective and secure Europe.

However, the imagery of criminal and terrorist immigrants strengthens the fears of the neurotic citizens, which can promote a vicious circle of xenophobia. It is likely to polarize the European societies along the lines of citizens and suspects. In an extreme form it can foster prejudice against non-citizens, particularly if citizenship rests on ascriptive and ethnic traits of group membership. In his seminal work on 'cognitive prejudice', Henri Tajfel (1969) indicated that the 'blood-and-guts model' of citizenship could lead to dehumanization of out-groups and as a consequence to aggression against them. In polarized European societies of citizens and suspects, civic resources of trust and solidarity are turned into a general suspicion, panic and hysteria.

The European 'corporate security state' in the field of immigration policy

Let us turn now to the mechanisms and institutions of the 'European corporate security state' within its politics of insecurity in the area of immigration control. In recent years the EU has created a number of agreements and regulations that treat immigration as a security problem. One of the first steps towards a more restrictive EU immigration policy was the Council directive 2001/40/EC on mutual recognition of the expulsion of third country nationals. The directive, issued in 2001, stipulated that an expulsion decision made by any EU member state could be implemented in any other EU country. A more comprehensive framework for immigration policy in the EU was established by the Hague Programme in 2004. Its main goal was to implement an area of freedom, security and justice in the EU by 2010 by realizing common immigration and asylum policies agreed upon in Tampere in 1999. The Hague Programme focused mainly on the security aspects of the EU immigration policy, even though it was accompanied by some human rights rhetoric of the EU decision-makers (Vitorino 2004; Frattini 2005). In 2010 the Hague Programme was replaced by the Stockholm Programme (with the subtitle: An open and secure Europe serving and protecting the citizens), which makes fighting illegal migration a priority for the EU and formulates the goal of a common European asylum policy. In addition, the Stockholm Programme envisages more cooperation between security agencies and further mobilization of technological tools such as the European Criminal Records Information System (ECRIS).

Together with the goal of establishment of a common immigration and border policy, the EU began to create specialized agencies to implement and monitor the policy. The first institutional step was the Europol Convention, which was based on the Maastricht Treaty. It regulated the setting up of a European police office (Europol), which began its work in 1999 (Council 2006a). Europol focuses on combating cross-border crimes, expected to be situated in so-called illegal immigration networks. One of the many objectives of Europol is to prevent and combat illegal immigrant smuggling. Even though it was established in 1994 to a limited extent as an agency fighting the drug trade, its activities extended considerably. Currently, Europol assists the member states with intelligence analysis of transnational crime, facilitates the exchange of information and participates in multinational investigations. In this sense, Europol is a part of a surveillance and investigation system of the EU aimed at the irregular immigrants defined as a threat to the EU. Even though Europol officers still lack executive powers such as wire-tapping or house searches, the EU member states have agreed to grant Europol 'operational powers'. Europol now has considerable influence on multinational investigations, in particular due to its access to intelligence and personal data. Since Europol has access to around 150,000 personal data files, it raises serious concerns of parliamentary and judicial control of its activities (Europaeisches Parlament 2007). One of the many concerns relating to the executive and uncontrolled nature of Europol is the immunity of Europol officers, even if their activities infringe individual rights such as the right to privacy (Peissl 2003). Moreover, neither national courts nor the European Court of Justice have jurisdiction over Europol, as a result of the immunity granted to Europol staff and the inviolability of Europol's archives, which again leads us to imagery of a European Leviathan.

A further agency central to the EU immigration and asylum policy is the European Agency for the Management of Operational Cooperation at the External Borders (Frontex). The issue of so-called integrated border management (IBM) has been defined by the EU since 2001 as crucial. The agency was inaugurated in 2005 and was designed to assist the member states in their control of the EU borders. Even though border controls are the responsibility of the member states, Frontex's main tasks include coordination of external border cooperation between the member states, training of national border guards, risk analyses and monitoring of the research on control and surveillance of external borders. Moreover, Frontex supports the EU member states in organizing joint return operations of irregular immigrants. It works together with other EU bodies, most importantly Europol, but also with the Commission directorate-general Joint Research Centre. In addition to Frontex's activities, the Commission proposed in 2006 to establish rapid border interventions teams, which would assist in despatching staff with technical and operational know-how regarding border control and surveillance in crisis situations. Although Frontex was established as more than just a coordinating body, it has further expanded its powers and scope of activity in 2011 (Monar 2011). The agency's budget is also steadily increasing: from €6.3 million in 2005, it rose to nearly €42 million in 2007 and had topped €87 million by 2010. Frontex draws its main legitimacy from its dealing with an 'urgent and exceptional [migratory] pressure at the borders of a Member State' (European Parliament and Council 2007), which highlights the enactment of the 'politics of exception'.

However, the agency has been recurrently criticized for assisting in joint return operations (often involving violence against irregular immigrants), which can be regarded as a manifestation of its repressive powers, earning it the label of an 'expulsion agency'. The joint expulsion operations have repeatedly provoked demonstrations and protests by human rights activists. For instance, in May 2011 there were demonstrations at Brussels Airport and at the entrance of the closed detention centre against collective expulsion by

Frontex.[1] This time about 60 people protested against the collective expulsion of 61 Nigerians and Congolese from detention centres in Belgium, the United Kingdom, Germany, France, Switzerland, Poland, Sweden and Norway. On 23 May 2011 there was a protest and street party in front of the headquarters of Frontex in Warsaw. These demonstrations and protests reflect the more general critique of Frontex, which in its annual reports measures its success by focusing on statistical results referring to detection, apprehension and 'refusal of entry of illegal immigrants' at the main borders of the EU (Frontex 2006: 12). The 2007 Frontex report states that 130,000 third-country nationals were refused entry to the EU, while in the 2008 report the figure is 140,000 (Frontex 2007, 2008). Frontex reports do not make any reference to humanitarian aspects of its activities, related to protection of migrants, for instance, under Article 33 of the 1951 Geneva Convention. Simultaneously, Frontex is 'only too willing to comment on the growing number of "bogus asylum seekers" allegedly trying to cross the EU's borders, without referring to any method enabling it to distinguish between "bogus" and "genuine" asylum seekers' (Keller *et al.* 2011). Moreover, it can be argued that Frontex lacks proper democratic control, which causes concerns for the legitimization and accountability of its operations. This being generally problematic with regard to the overtly executive character of the EU immigration policy, it holds particularly true for the Frontex activities. The European Parliament is significantly isolated from Frontex information regarding, for example, the follow-up of its activities. It applies especially with regards to risk assessments, which are not delivered to the European Parliament (Jorry 2007). Against this background, the activities of Frontex reflect the executive and security-oriented character of the European 'corporate security state'.

Apart from institutions and funds, the EU deals with unwanted immigration and asylum on the basis of specialized data-gathering and data-processing systems which are crucial for the EU's surveillance operations. As argued above, by identifying the 'enemy', the identification of citizens with their own collectivity can be enhanced. This double identification (of the enemy and with its own collectivity) represents a powerful identity technology associated with Caesarean citizenship. The main EU information system is the Schengen Information System (SIS), which maintains and distributes data related to border security and law enforcement. The SIS stores data on physical characteristics of individuals, whereas in its follow-up version – SIS II – it will register biometric data (House of Lords 2007; McGinley and Parkes 2007). The Thessaloniki European Council from June 2003 called for a coherent approach on biometric identifiers (iris scans, facial recognition and fingerprints) to find EU-wide solutions for documents for third-country nationals, EU citizens' passports and information systems (Lodge 2004: 265; Council 2006b). Therefore, in addition to deterrence and expulsion strategies,

---

1 http://frontexplode.eu/2011/06/01/actions-against-frontex; http://zspwawa.blogspot.com/2011/05/protest-and-street-party-in-front-of.html, accessed on 1 January 2012.

the EU is digitalizing its borders and expanding the control over identity of individuals. Even though the EU's surveillance devices are mostly employed against immigrants from outside the EU (or Europe in the larger sense, since Norway and Iceland also use the SIS), EU citizens also become objects of observation and information-gathering, which clearly poses problems for civil rights (cf. Lodge 2005).

Furthermore, the Commission has proposed a Visa Information System (VIS), which is supposed to allow member states to exchange data on visas issued or denied in any of the EU states and thus to supplement the SIS II (Council 2004). The VIS is a further technological device for identifying irregular immigrants and thus it is believed to 'contribute to the prevention of threats to internal security' (Commission 2006d). The VIS represents the latest effort by the EU to establish control over 'the others'. This information system registers all visa applications and the fingerprints of individuals required to have a visa for the EU. It also includes data of the person or company that issued an invitation and is hence responsible for the cost of living of the visa applicant during their stay in the EU. Whereas SIS and SIS II target specifically cross-border criminal activity, the VIS is an instrument of less differentiating surveillance and control of immigrants, EU residents and EU citizens. The goal of the VIS is to identify those immigrants who legally entered the EU, but then illegally extended their stay. When the VIS is completed, the EU will be able to control the immigrant population in its territory, in addition to its territorial borders (Lahav 2004). The VIS system makes two types of identity search possible: verification and identification. Verification of identity consists of a check, carried out by the Biometric Matching System, comparing the fingerprints scanned during a border control with those in the biometric record attached to the visa (its duration is about 2 seconds). In contrast, identification consists of comparing the fingerprints taken during a border control with the contents of the entire database (its duration is about 10 minutes).

With the VIS still under construction, the EU possesses yet another information system that has already been operational since 2003. The Eurodac was set up to support the Dublin Regulation, which is to determine which member state is responsible for a given asylum application (Council 2000; Monar 2004; Huysmans 2000b). The system stores and processes fingerprints from asylum-seekers and captured irregular immigrants crossing the EU external border. In this sense, the Eurodac is an essential part of the supranational biometric control regime, functioning as an automated fingerprint identification system (Aus 2003, 2006). The Eurodac database was designed to curtail the possibilities for so-called 'asylum shopping' of individuals applying for asylum in more than one EU country. Therefore, the Eurodac allows a community-wide comparison of fingerprints of asylum applicants and hence the determination of which member state is responsible for the asylum procedure (Levi and Wall 2004; Liberatore 2007). Since a variety of instruments for controlling identity of immigrants exists, the EU attempts to enhance interoperability between the SIS II, VIS and Eurodac. The interoperability is also believed to be reached through linking the SIS II to the Europol information system. This should result in an EU surveillance network, with which the 'protective Union' hopes to fulfil its functions as a European Leviathan (cf. Kostakopolou 2000).

Conclusion

The EU immigration policies are strongly associated with politics of Caesarean citizenship. It uses images and scenarios of threat from 'bogus asylum-seekers' who are presented by EU agencies as a danger to the social integration and cohesion of the European societies. Biometric technologies, detention facilities and new methods of surveillance are increasingly employed to establish exclusionary and restrictive practices of the Caesarean citizenship in the EU. The respondent of these practices is the neurotic citizen who defines citizenship in terms of permanent insecurity. His preference for liberty and freedom becomes surpassed by his fears of survival in a risk society. Therefore, the insecure societies in Europe rely increasingly more on executive power of dividing politics of border and population controls as well as on the dispersion of networks of surveillance. The insecure society and neurotic citizens become an essential part of the modern Caesarean citizenship in the EU. However, the creeping creation of a European Leviathan in the form of a corporate security state does not solve the security problems of the Union citizens outright, as is the case in the Hobbesian state. Instead, it upholds or even strengthens collective feelings of insecurity and thus it is likely to promote a 'culture of fear' that makes citizens overreact to risks, rather than resolve problems of security.

Against this backdrop, Caesarean citizenship is closely associated with politics of insecurity and the demarcation between the citizen and the suspect, which can entail anti-civic effects. As the EU espouses a growing activity in the realm of surveillance, control and restrictions, it shifts its focus on citizenship from political participation and democracy towards the field of internal security, which bases its legitimacy in the bureaucratic power of surveillance, control, separation and expulsion. Therefore, the main objective of citizenship becomes its preservation against external threats, rather than political self-determination. These workings of the Caesarean citizenship in the EU are potentially anti-civic and contrast the more positive notion of European citizenship based on new transnational rights, as the Caesarean citizenship highlights security concerns at the expense of individual liberty and civil and political rights. The imagery of criminal and terrorist immigrants strengthens the fears of the neurotic citizens, which can promote a vicious circle of xenophobia. It is likely to contribute to further polarization in the European societies along the lines of citizens and suspects. In an extreme form it can foster prejudice against non-citizens, which can lead to dehumanization of out-groups and, as a consequence, to aggression against them. In a polarized society of citizens and suspects, civic resources of trust and solidarity are turned into a general suspicion, panic and hysteria.

Furthermore, the development of Caesarean citizenship is likely to exacerbate the existing democratic deficit of the EU through the expansion of executive powers, escape from democratic accountability and overall secrecy surrounding security issues. Therefore, it plunges the EU deeper into the democratic dilemma. Moreover, increasing trends of Caesarean citizenship contradict the vision of the EU as a community of values, in particular representing and promoting human rights. As, for instance, the EU refugee policies are criticized for undermining the civil rights of immigrants, the tension between the EU as the 'security producer' and the EU as 'the humanitarian' is likely to grow.

References

Adamson, F. B. 2006. Crossing borders: international migration and national security. *International Security* 31: 165–99.

Amiraux, V. 2010. 'Suspicion publique et gouvernance de l'intime: contrôle et surveillance des populations musulmanes dans l'Union Européenne', in: A. Scherrer, E.-P. Guitet and D. Bigo (eds) *Mobilité(s) sous surveillance: Perspectives croisées UE-Canada*. Outrement: Athena Editions, 73–87.

Aradau, C. and van Munster R. 2007. 'Governing terrorism through risk: taking precautions, (un)knowing the future', *European Journal of International Relations* 13: 89–115.

Aus, J. P. 2003. *Supranational governance in an 'area of freedom, security and justice': Eurodac and the politics of biometric control*. Paper presented at ARENA, University of Oslo, 18 November 2003.

Aus, J. P. 2006. 'Eurodac: a solution looking for a problem?' *European Integration Online Papers* 10 (6) http://eiop.or.at/eiop/texte/2006-006a.htm.

Bauböck, R. 2007. 'Why European citizenship? Normative approaches to supranational union', *Theoretical Inquiries in Law* 8: 439–74.

Beck, U. 2002. 'The terrorist threat: world risk society revisited', *Theory, Culture & Society* 19: 39–55.

Behnke, A. 2000. 'The message or the messenger? Reflections on the role of security experts and the securitization of political issues', *Cooperation and Conflict* 35: 89–105.

Bellamy, R. et al. 2006. *Making European citizens: civic inclusion in a transnational context*. London: Palgrave.

Beutin, R. et al. 2007. 'Reassessing the link between public perception and migration policy', *European Journal of Migration and Law* 9: 389–418.

Bigo, D. 2000. 'When two become one: internal and external securitisations in Europe', in M. Kelstrup and M. C. Williams (eds) *International relations theory and the politics of European integration, power, security and community*. London: Routledge, 171–204.

Bigo, D. 2002. 'Security and immigration: toward a governmentality of unease', *Alternatives* 27: 63–92.

Bigo, D. 2010. 'Globalized (in)security: the field and the banopticon', in: D. Bigo and A. Tsoukala (eds) *Terror, insecurity and liberty*. New York: Routledge, 11–48.

Billig, M. 1995. *Banal nationalism*. London: Sage.
Brouwer, E. 2003. 'Immigration, asylum and terrorism: a changing dynamic of legal and practical developments in the EU in response to the terrorist attacks of 11.09', *European Journal of Migration and Law* 4: 399–424.
Brubaker, R. 1994. *Citizenship and nationhood in France and Germany*. Cambridge, MA: Harvard University Press.
Brubaker, R. 1999. 'The Manichean myth: rethinking the distinction between civic and ethnic nationalism', in: H. Kriesi *et al.* (eds) *Nation and national identity: the European experience in perspective*. Zürich: Rüegger, 55–71.
Commission. 2006a. *Communication from the Commission on policy priorities in the fight against illegal immigration of third country nationals*, COM(2006) 402 Final, 19.07.2006.
Commission. 2006b. *Towards a comprehensive European migration policy*, COM(2006) 735 Final.
Commission. 2006c. *Communication from the Commission on policy priorities in the fight against illegal immigration of third country nationals*, COM(2006) 402 Final, 19.07.2006.
Commission. 2006d. COM(2006)332, p. 19.
Commission. 2007a. *Proposal for a Council Framework Decision on the use of Passenger Name Record (PNR) for law enforcement purposes*, 6.11.2007, COM (2007) 654.
Commission. 2007b. *Green Paper on Bio-Preparedness*, 11.7.2007, COM(2007) 399.
Council. 2000. *Council Regulation*, No 2725/2000.
Council. 2004. *EU Plan of Action on Combating Terrorism*, 10010/3/04, REV 3, 11.06.2004.
Council. 2006a. *Council Decision establishing EUROPOL*, SEC(2006) 1682.
Council. 2006b. *Council Conclusions on the SIS II, the SUS 1+ and the enlargement of the Schengen area*, 2768th Justice and Home Affairs Council meeting, Brussels, 4–5 December 2006, CONCL 3, 14292/04.
Council. 2007. *Decision establishing for the period 2007–2013 the Specific Programme 'Prevention of and Fight against Crime*, 2007/125/JHA, 12.02.2007.
Debrix, F. and Barder, A. D. 2009. 'Nothing to fear but fear: governmentality and the biopolitical production of terror', *International Political Sociology* 3: 398–413.
Delanty, G. 2007. 'European citizenship: a critical assessment', *Citizenship Studies* 11: 63–72.
Europäisches Parlament. 2007. *Arbeitsdokument zur Errichtung des Europäischen Polizeiamts* (EUROPOL), Ausschuss für bürgerliche Freiheiten, Justiz und innere Angelegenheiten, 19.2.2007, DT\652813DE.doc.
European Parliament. 2007. *Fighting terrorism can never be an excuse to violate human rights*. Press release, 12.12.2007.
European Parliament and the Council. 2007. *Regulation establishing a mechanism for the creation of Rapid Border Intervention Teams*, (EC) No. 863/200.7
Faist, Th. 2002. 'Extension du domaine de la lutte: international migration and security before and after September 11, 2001', *International Migration Review* 36: 7–14.
Favell, A. 1998. 'The Europeanisation of immigration politics', *European Integration Online Papers* 2, http://eiop.or.at/eiop/texte/1998-010a.htm.
Frattini, F. 2005. *The Hague Programme: a partnership for the European renewal in the field of freedom, security and justice*. Brussels: Centre for European Policy Studies, 14 July 2005, Speech/05/441.

Frontex. 2006. Rapport général de Frontex pour l'année 2006, http://www.frontex.europa.eu/annual_report, accessed on 1 January 2012.
Frontex. 2007. Rapport général de Frontex pour l'année 2007, http://www.frontex.europa.eu/annual_report, accessed on 1 January 2012.
Frontex. 2008. Rapport général de Frontex pour l'année 2008, http://www.frontex.europa.eu/annual_report, accessed on 1 January 2012.
Frost, S. 2004. 'Hobbes out of bounds', *Political Theory* 32: 257–73.
Gammeltoft-Hansen, T. 2006. *Filtering out the risky migrant migration control, risk theory and the EU*. AMID Working Paper Series 52/2006, Danish Institute of International Studies.
Geddes, A. 2001. 'International migration and state sovereignty in an integrating Europe', *International Migration* 39: 21–42.
Geddes, A. 2005. 'Europe's border relationships and international migration relations', *Journal of Common Market Studies* 43: 787–806.
Guiraudon, V. and Lahav, G. 2000. 'A reappraisal of the state sovereignty debate: the case of migration control', *Comparative Political Studies* 33: 163–95.
Hindess, B. 1998. 'Divide and rule: the international character of modern citizenship', *European Journal of Social Theory* 1: 57–70.
Hobbes, Th. 1990 [1682]. *Behemoth or the long parliament*. Edited by F. Tönnies, with an introduction by S. Holmes. Chicago: University of Chicago Press.
Hobbes, Th. 1991 [1642]. *The citizen (De Cive)*. Edited by B. Gert. Indianapolis: Hackett Publishing Company.
Hobbes, Th. 1996 [1651]. *Leviathan, or the matter, form and power of a commonwealth, ecclesiastical and civil*. Edited with an introduction by J. C. A. Gashin. Oxford: Oxford University Press.
House of Lords. 2007. *Schengen Information System II*. 9th Report of Session 2006–07. Report with Evidence. London: House of Lords.
Huysmans, J. 2000a. 'Contested community: migration and the question of the political in the EU', in: M. Kelstrup and M. C. Williams (eds) *International relations theory and the politics of European integration, power, security and community*. London: Routledge, 149–70.
Huysmans, J. 2000b. 'The European Union and the securitization of migration', *Journal of Common Market Studies* 38: 751–77.
Huysmans, J. 2005. *The politics of insecurity: security, migration and asylum in the EU*. London: Routledge.
Huysmans, J. 2006. 'International politics of insecurity: normativity, inwardness and the exception', *Security Dialogue* 37: 11–29.
Isin, E. F. 2004. 'The neurotic citizen', *Citizenship Studies* 8: 217–35.
Joppke, C. 2005. 'Exclusion in the liberal state: the case of immigration and citizenship policy', *European Journal of Social Theory* 8: 43–61.
Jorry, H. 2007. *Construction of a European institutional model for managing operational cooperation at the EU's external borders: is the FRONTEX Agency a decisive step forward?* Challenge Project: Liberty and Security, Research Paper 6.
Keller, S., Lunacek, U., Lochbihler, B. and Flautre, H. 2011. *Frontex Agency: which guarantees for human rights?* A study conducted by Migreurop on the European External Borders Agency in view of the revision of its mandate. European Parliament.
Kostakopolou, T. 2000. 'The protective union: change and continuity in migration law and policy in post-Amsterdam Europe', *Journal of Common Market Studies* 38: 497–518.

Lahav, G. 2004. *Immigration and politics in the new Europe: reinventing borders.* Cambridge: Cambridge University Press.
Lavenex, S. 2001. 'The Europeanization of refugee policies: normative challenges and institutional legacies', *Journal of Common Market Studies* 39: 851–74.
Lavenex, S. 2004. 'EU external governance in wider Europe', *Journal of European Public Policy* 11: 680–700.
Lavenex, S. 2006. 'Shifting up and out: the foreign policy of immigration control', *West European Politics* 29: 329–50.
Lavanex, S. and Uçarer, E. M. 2004. 'The external dimension of Europeanization: the case of immigration policies', *Cooperation and Conflict* 39: 417–43.
Levi, M. and Wall, D. S. 2004. 'Technologies, security and privacy in the post-9/11 European information society', *Journal of Law and Society* 31: 194–220.
Liberatore, A. 2007. 'Balancing security and democracy, and the role of expertise: biometric politics in the European Union', *European Journal on Criminal Policy and Research* 13: 109–37.
Lodge, J. 2004. 'EU homeland security: citizens or suspects?' *Journal of European Integration* 26: 253–79.
Lodge, J. 2005. 'eJustice, security and biometrics: the EU's proximity paradox', *European Journal of Crime, Criminal Law and Criminal Justice* 13: 533–64.
Lyon, D. 1992. 'The new surveillance: electronic technologies and the maximum security society', *Crime, Law and Social Change* 18: 159–75.
Lyon, D. 2009. *Identifying citizens: ID cards as surveillance.* Oxford: Polity Press.
Lyon, D. 2010. 'Liquid surveillance: the contribution of Zygmunt Bauman to surveillance studies', *International Political Sociology* 4: 325–38.
Lyons, C. 1996. 'Citizenship in the constitution of the European Union: rhetoric or reality?' in: R. Bellamy (ed.) *Constitutionalism, democracy and sovereignty: American and European perspectives.* Aldershot: Avebury, 96–110.
Maritain, J. 1950. 'The concept of sovereignty', *American Political Science Review* 44: 343–57.
Mau, S. 2011. 'Grenzen als Sortiermaschinen', in: H. Kleger (ed.) *Umstrittene Bürgerschaft: Grenzen, Identitäten und Konflikte.* Potsdam: Universitätsverlag, 72–81.
Maurer, A. and Parkes, R. 2006. *Asylum policy and democracy in the European Union from Amsterdam towards the Hague Programme.* Working Paper FG 1, SWP, Berlin, esp. pp. 3–4.
Maurer, A. and Parkes, R. 2007. 'The prospects for policy change in EU asylum: venue and image at the European level', *European Journal of Migration and Law* 9: 173–205.
McGinley, M. and Parkes, R. 2007. *Data protection in the EU's internal security cooperation: fundamental rights vs. effective cooperation?* SWP Research Paper 5, Berlin.
Melossi, D. 2005. 'Security, social control, democracy and migration within the constitution of the EU', *European Law Journal* 11: 5–21.
Monar, J. 2004. 'Justice and home affairs', *Journal of Common Market Studies* 42(Annual Review): 117–33.
Monar, J. 2008. 'Justice and home affairs', *Journal of Common Market Studies* 46(Annual Review): 109–26.
Monar, J. 2011. 'Justice and home affairs', *Journal of Common Market Studies* 49(Annual Review): 145–64.
Moreno Lax, V. 2008. 'Must EU borders have doors for refugees? On the compatibility of Schengen visas and carrier sanctions with EU member states' obligations to

provide international protection to refugees', *European Journal of Migration and Law* 10(3): 315–64.

Muller, B. J. 2004. '(Dis)Qualified bodies: securitization, citizenship and identity management', *Citizenship Studies* 8: 279–94.

Peissl, W. 2003. 'Surveillance and security: a dodgy relationship', *Journal of Contingencies and Crisis Management* 11: 19–24.

Pérez Asinari, M. V. and Poullet, Y. 2004. 'Public security versus data privacy: airline passengers' data, adoption of an adequacy decision by the European Commission', *Computer Law & Security Report* 20: 370–76.

Rasch, W. 2000. 'Conflict as a vocation: Carl Schmitt and the possibility of politics', *Theory, Culture and Society* 17: 1–32.

Roes, P. 2004. 'Securitization and minority rights: conditions of desecuritization', *Security Dialogue* 35: 279–94.

Sartori, G. 1989. 'The essence of the political in Carl Schmitt', *Journal of Theoretical Politics* 1: 63–75.

Scherrer, A., Guitet, E-P. and Bigo, D. 2010. *Mobilité(s) sous surveillance: perspectives croisées UE-Canada*. Outrement: Athena Editions.

Schmitt, C. 1996 [1932]. *The concept of the political*. Translated and with an introduction by G. Schwab. Chicago: University of Chicago Press.

Schmitt, C. 2004 [1932]. *Legality and legitimacy*, Translated and edited by Jeffrey Seitzer, with an introduction by John P. McCormick. Durham: Duke University Press.

Shaw, J. 1998. 'The interpretation of European Union citizenship', *Modern Law Review* 61: 293–317.

Stetter, S. 2008. 'Regulating migration: authority delegation in justice and home affairs', *Journal of European Public Policy* 7: 80–103.

Sunstein, C. R. 2005. *Laws of fear: beyond the precautionary principle*, Cambridge: Cambridge University Press.

Svantesson, M. 2006. 'The EU and illegal immigration: an ascending (in)secure community?' in: A. Boin, M. Ekenbergen and M. Rhinard (eds) *Protecting the European Union: policies, sectors and institutional solutions*. University of Leiden: National Defence College, 61–78.

Tajfel, H. 1969. 'Cognitive aspects of prejudice', *Journal of Biosocial Sciences* 1: 173–91.

Triandafyllidou, A. 1998. 'National identity and the Other', *Ethnic and Racial Studies* 21: 593–612.

Uçarer, E. M. 2001. 'From sidelines to center stage: sidekick no more? The European Commission in justice and home affairs', *European Integration Online Papers* 5, http://eiop.or.at/eiop/texte/2001-005a.htm.

Vermeulen, G. 2007. 'Mutual instrumentalization of criminal and migration law from an EU perspective', *European Journal of Migration and Law* 9: 347–61.

Verschueren, H. 2007. 'European (internal) migration law as an instrument for defining the boundaries of national solidarity systems', *European Journal of Migration and Law* 9: 307–46.

Vitorino, A. 2004. *The future of the European Union agenda on asylum, migration and borders*. Speech to the Conference of the European Policy Center and King Baudouin Foundation, Brussels, 4 October 2004.

Wagner, P. A. 1994. *Sociology of modernity: liberty and discipline*. London: Routledge.

Wagner, W. 2006. 'Guarding the guards: the European Convention and the communization of police-co-operation', *Journal of European Public Policy* 13: 1230–46.

Wagner, W. 2010. *Die demokratische Kontrolle internationalisierter Sicherheitspolitik: Demokratiedefizite bei Militäreinsätzen und in der europäischen Politik innerer Sicherheit*. Baden-Baden: Nomos.

Walters, W. 2002. 'Deportation, expulsion, and the international police of aliens', *Citizenship Studies* 6: 265–92.

Weiler, J. H. H. 1996. *Legitimacy and democracy of Union governance: the 1996 intergovernmental agenda and beyond*. Oslo: ARENA, Working Paper 22.

Wessels, W. 1998. 'Comitology: fusion in action: politico-administrative trends in the EU system', *Journal of European Public Policy* 5: 209–34.

Wessels, W. 2000. *Die Öffnung des Staates*. Opladen: Leske+Budrich.

Wiener, A. 1998. *European citizenship practice: building institutions of a non-state*. Boulder: Westview.

Zaiotti, R. 2007. 'Of friends and fences: Europe's neighbourhood policy and the gated community syndrome', *Journal of European Integration.* 29: 143–62.

Part III
Conceptual and theoretical considerations

9 From crisis to constitution?
Europe's path from culture to politics

Enno Rudolph

The crisis as a new beginning

Regardless of the calculated optimism of the influential EU governments, and in contrast to a significant majority, many Europeans believe that the euro has not taken a beating recently but that it has emerged victorious. For them the refusal of the United Kingdom to enter into a new fiscal union is not the loss of an indispensable member but the longed-for relieving of an insufferable burden. Britain has never really wanted to be a part of Europe, as is well known, and panicked at the imposition of replacing sterling with the euro as it did to the threatened relativization of its international political importance. David Cameron embodied the British psyche and fears as he vehemently rebelled against every additional scrutiny measure by the EU watchdogs over the City of London as if fighting off a new Armada.

Relief therefore on both sides of the Channel – albeit unbalanced. That on the continental side is greater, even if buried under an upsurge of indignation at the British sense of entitlement. Once Sweden, Hungary and the Czech Republic – for fear of their own courage to act like the British – have quickly included themselves, the EU can record a partial victory on the road to a realistic policy of concentrating on a truly workable membership: the road to a shift from the overstretched policy of the virtually indiscriminate 'widening' to one of selective 'deepening'. As Nice threatened to founder, the former French president Jacques Chirac and the former German chancellor Gerhard Schröder, in the heat of the moment but with conviction, called for a 'two-speed Europe'. Had they operated strategically back then and, above all, actually done what they said they would, the EU would potentially have been spared many troubles. He who doesn't listen must sense: now, under substantially increased pressure, takes place what could then have voluntarily been done, and now results in different selections than would perhaps have been the case then.

It is not the EU that has run into debt, but Italy, proclaimed the new prime minister of Italy, Mario Monti, recently. In doing so, he formulated a selection principle whose definition, and above all whose application, is no longer taboo: those countries that run into debt – de facto at the expense of the EU – damage the borders as well as the economic and political tolerance of the community of states so sorely that they threaten their very existence. What is politely expressed in EU resolutions – in which such sinners are threatened with punishment – reads in plain English: those that damage the borders will find themselves outside the community. Whilst the Italian government works feverishly to ensure it doesn't become a victim of the specifically formulated criteria, but internally already hindered as a result, the future of the EU hangs on achieving a new 'core Europe' (Habermas 2004; Garton Ash 1993; Böckenförde 1997). This cannot mean – not least because of the British withdrawal – either the old EEC or a size oriented towards cultural similarities. Cultural similarities then prove themselves to be indispensable requirements and resources when trying to sustainably stabilize a politically predefined union through identity-building (Cerutti and Rudolph 2010).

If one compares with political realism the recently developed fiscal union with the currently functioning EU, the latter has 26 members (minus X) at the moment, not 27. Of these, a not insignificant number are candidates for withdrawal according to the 'Monti criteria' – even if these withdrawals are not as voluntary as in the case of the United Kingdom, where the government could no doubt imagine the support of the majority of the population. It would in some cases – such as in Greece's – be a withdrawal that would meet temporary resistance from the affected government but not from the affected national population. Quite the contrary.

Only with such a brave and consistent shakeout following this concept will Europe have any prospect of coming out of this crisis strengthened. The new 'core Europe' only has a chance when as 'punishment' more concrete measures are announced than achieved so far: expulsion with immediate effect – without consideration of seniority (Italy), former strength (Spain), eastern integration (Hungary) or extenuating circumstances due to structural arrears (Greece). Countries such as France, Austria, the Netherlands, Germany and Finland must form the core and should – in some cases at the second attempt – quickly and energetically work towards providing this core with a constitution in order to secure it in the long term.

Constitution

In such a constellation the question of the likelihood of a European constitution again arises. It could be expected that this likelihood would have been improved for three reasons:

1 The countries in favour of a constitution would have learned from their mistakes.
2 A smaller and more stable entity can be more easily 'constituted'.
3 A core EU *with* constitution is politically weightier than one that is too large and diffuse *without*, and it acts as an incentive for candidate members to fulfil the terms of admission on a long-term basis.

Not coincidentally in this situation, Jürgen Habermas (2011) has produced a new monograph on the subject of the constitution of Europe. The study joins a debate that was under way long before the failure of the referenda in France and the Netherlands and in which both Habermas (2001) and primary political players, such as the former German chancellor Helmut Schmidt (2000), linked the question of the necessity and ability of the EU to have a constitution with the question of the democratibility of this confederation construct. While Schmidt positioned as starkly as he did directly the demand to make a guaranteed democratic suitability an absolute criterion for membership in the EU, Habermas warned of a situation in which a divide develops between governmental decisions on the one hand and democratic legitimation on the other, as was often the case between Brussels and the EU citizens affected by their decisions. Over the years the divide was too large, leading both to a desire for a constitution in a 'non-demos' situation as well as to taking the risk of adopting the constitution from the top–down and relying on a resulting evolution of a European populace.

Habermas highlights two reasons to hold on to Europe as a constitution project, 'all the more' at the current time:

- First, the current necessity for crisis management results in an 'economistic narrowing of perspectives'(Habermas 2011: 40) that needs to be corrected.
- Second, he notes that – generally as the upshot of a long evolution of rights and specifically as the result of European integration so far – a process of 'transnationalization of the popular sovereignty' has started to which it can be linked.

'When one considers the development of the European Union from these points of view, the path to a politically functional and democratically legitimate (core-) Europe is in no way blocked' (Habermas 2011: 47). Habermas therefore also advocates a 'core-Europe', one whose contours however are not as sharply defined as attempted in this chapter. It could constitute the following conditions, after prior selection through the use of the Monti criteria in which the countries able to partake in fiscal union start a new constitution coordination process:

- It must take place *synchronously* in the respective countries.
- It must present a *simplified*, i.e. readable, draft constitution for discussion.
- It must clearly state in the preamble *who belongs* (or can belong) *to the EU and why* and *what the long-term goal* of the EU is (for example whether it sees itself as a staging post on the road to a global union with a world constitution).

This process is, however, to be complemented by the launch of an extensive and of course international cultural-political information campaign which provides with appropriate particulars and materials clarification on which semantic convergence exists between the label 'European' as historical identifying feature of this union and the historic variable 'Europe': can the semantic convergence be explained by the conformities of geographical contingency alone, or also by such a 'cultural' form? On the understanding that cultural legitimization is rendered helpful, if not even essential, to work against that 'economistic narrowing of perspectives', it is forbidden to apply cultural-genealogical arguments – even to demonstrate which differences between cultural identity and political identity are acceptable in the interests of a successful EU constitution.

Excursus: culture as a source of political solidarity

While nations, communities or ethnic groups – earlier in Europe often represented by culture-defining protagonists such as epicists, poets or chroniclers – give their society a history, they often at the same time procure the status of a tendentially exclusive entity: in this way they institute identity. Still today we label – based on the German philosopher of the Enlightenment Johann Gottfried Herder – such an integrated entity as 'culture'. (Herder famously believed that this was primarily organized through the distinct language of the concerned ethnic group or nation, whose specific formation is in turn due to the eminent linguistic innovators of the respective linguistic community: Homer for the Greeks, Shakespeare for the English, etc.) However, the following points must be considered:

- The elements and building blocks from which such cultures organize themselves – namely religion, art, science, etc. – are themselves culture.
- These elements have assumed specific forms in the history of a particular culture, such as Anglicanism in England or Calvinism in parts of Switzerland. They nevertheless appear 'eccentric' – in other words, spanning different ethnic groups. As a result, a formed societal unit – if not so nationalistically determined – can never be exclusively defined through specific cultural profiles – neither linguistic nor scientific nor religious. *Culture is always a syncretism of cultures; culture is tendentially eccentric.*

On this understanding it would be more legitimate to speak from the outset of a European culture than of an English, Italian or German one. Culture is the name for the dynamic and contingent process of interconnectedness and differentiation, identity maintenance and insemination – an ensemble of contradictory tendencies which run through the concerned societies with the aid of some authentic and some appropriated adoptions. Even the idiosyncratic *complementarity of authenticity and adoption* appears to distinguish the history of Europe in a specific manner and to differentiate from other large historical formations such as China, the USA or the Arab world.

The French philosopher, Arabist and Europe researcher Remi Brague characterized this European idiosyncrasy in a pointed way. Europe, according to

Brague, is a continent of 'upstarts'. As a result, Europe is questionable, an 'illegitimate' adoption in which 'the supposed descendants of venerable ancestors (such as Greece, Rome) have been monopolised' (Brague 1993: 29). Byzantium by contrast, this historical empire, is a much more legitimate heir to the Old World – or, better said, the old worlds – and Brague provocatively adds that the Islamic world, including Turkey, stands alongside in equal ranking. This comparatively striking sparseness of Europe is, however, overcome. 'Europe's cultural poverty was also its opportunity', believes Brague: the European 'strivers' compensate for their poverty – which can be explained by the short lifetime of Europe, which ultimately has only existed since the Carolingians – through industriousness. Industriousness is a virtue that is distinguished through a series of fortunate side effects, of which two should be highlighted:

- First there is a specific *inquisitiveness for others* which can be explained by the equally elaborate as presumptuous adoption mentioned above. Those that adopt do not have their own relatives and integrate the other in an equally ownership-adopting as engaging way. The term 'cultural imperialism' has for a long time figured as a description of this competence. The historical narrative has provided the term 'Renaissance' with a view to the epoch before the dawn of the modern era, as we are used to reserving a specific historical form for the activation of the cultural memories of European elites. Renaissances clearly differentiate themselves, as Brague correctly identified, from restorations ('revivals') in that they do not, as for example in the case of the Reformation, rely on the 'pure', the 'undamaged sources' to secure their own tradition, but that they with inquisitive openness 'reach for the outside' so that they open up for what does not *eo ipso* belong to them. Renaissance is a name for the 'adoption' of forefathers and not for the rebirth of one's past in the strictest sense.
- This form of 'adoption' additionally leads to a sustainably effective training of the *virtue of inclusive tolerance*, and this is the second side effect of industriousness. Brague underlines that the type of cultural inquisitiveness under consideration here is much older than the voyages of discovery at the end of the fifteenth century and is thus to be evaluated as pre-imperialistic. A theoretical habitus of the competent and successful adoption of others therefore belongs to the cultural foundations of Europe and to the structured renaissances. A prototype of methodically organised cultural integration, which begins much earlier than any other 'process of theoretical inquisitiveness', occurred according to popular opinion as the modern era was looming and with the effect of the methodologically secured scientification which has driven our world views until today.

The dependence on external past – or, more specifically, on the successful adoption of external pasts – relativizes the personal standpoint historically and culturally. Past and external are not kept at a distance, nor personal interests monomaniacally adapted, but highly valued *per se*. Remi Brague formulates pointedly: 'Only in Europe is culture understood as history, and in turn history as culture' – only Europe has a cultural history. Europe's culture is its history, Europe's history is its culture: a historical process of adoption and inclusion, motivated through qualified inquisitiveness that would only later become an imperial attitude.

Culture as a policy instrument?

According to this analysis, Europe would be defined – from a cultural-genealogical perspective – as a historical project, in other words a more productive and more efficient historical process of cultural enrichment through the inquisitive and increasingly competent dealings with external histories. To be European therefore means nothing more than partaking in this process. This can be illustrated by the three examples of secularization, science and law.

Secularization

If the thesis that the history of Europe is a history of strategic adoption is correct, and if it is furthermore true that the Italian Renaissance is a prime example of successful adoption – making the other renaissances comparable with each other – then it is an idiosyncratic process of exciting and conflict-laden inclusions through which the history described as 'European' runs like a golden thread. It conspicuously connects the equally constructive as unorthodox adoption of the antiquity, namely the Roman and Greek on behalf of the humanists, in the 300 years between Petrarca and Giordano Bruno with the equally tendentially inclusive idea of the *universality* of humanity in the period of enlightened rationalism during the seventeenth and eighteenth centuries. In particular, however, with regard to the religion-critical initiatives of both periods from Bruno to Kant, it should be understood that it was by no means the Christian religion and its dogmatic fundaments that acted as the integrating power of these developments or as a bridge between them; instead, religion formed at most the increasingly faint backdrop from which these processes of emancipation of culture were lifted from their religious implementations. Seen in this way, Europe is the embodiment of a cross-national series of increasingly radical secularization movements, beginning with the humanists in the Italian Renaissance, continuing with the partially critically constructive and partially destructive classical enlightenment almost more or less simultaneously in different European countries, through to the partially agnostic and partially aesthetic 'demystification' of the world in the contemporary late modern age.

Science

Causally connected with these secularization movements is the development process of science. One sometimes finds the opinion that the leading role of science in particular is to be seen as a specifically European phenomenon, the success of mathematical physics a European achievement. On top of this comes the evidence that the birth of mathematics – including methodical natural science – occurred in a subsequently Europeanized Greece together with that of philosophy. Casting doubt on the humanistic state of mathematics would hardly question that of philosophy. In other words, for centuries the same is to be retained from natural sciences as from mathematical physics: they were – not least via the path of the previously described cultural adoption – equally effectively involved in the autonomization of the individual disciplines compared with religious or metaphysical ideologizations as science was. Secularization and science in overlap have culturally profiled Europe.

Law

The Berlin historian Heinrich August Winkler, an engaged European among the German-speaking humanities scholars of today, has repeatedly and in most cases not unpolemically asserted his arguments against the entry of Turkey into the European Union (Winkler 2005). Among his central theses is the argument that Turkey lacks the defining achievements of European societies, such as the separation of religion and politics or the specific legal traditions from Roman law through to the idea of international law in the spirit of Immanuel Kant and its impact. In order to substantiate these theses, it would be sensible and indeed necessary to demonstrate the specific meaning of the juridification of normative beliefs for the integration of societies (Habermas 2011: 44). As the memory of Roman law and its undisputedly paradigmatic meaning for European legal traditions are under suspicion of the adoption discussed above, it would be imperative to provide evidence of a specific European authorship and trusteeship for the integration function of the law – law understood as a form of continuation and stability of indispensable norms of the social coexistence. This particular function of the law, continuing and making pre-valid norms enforceable, is clear in two very different examples of law formation as known from the European history of legal theories: first, the social contract theory (for example in the sense of Hobbes or Rousseau), and second, the example of Kant's law of reason. The differences between these two types have been sufficiently discussed. The contract ensures law through consensus; it juridifies a convention. The law of reason in contrast explains in law what all people should want by virtue of the ability to reason their own common sense: their freedom mutually guaranteed.

Both legal forms, however, make the interests, norms as well as peace (Hobbes), equality (Rousseau) or freedom (Kant) 'sacrosanct' (like human dignity later in which these three partial norms are correspondingly concentrated) – and this through the function of law. In other words – apart from the undeniable marked difference that the authority of law is embodied by Hobbes through its absolute sovereignty, by Rousseau through the equally absolute peoples and by Kant through the autonomous rationality – the commonality of the belief in the indispensability of law as a form of continuation and suability remains a compulsorily acknowledged norm for all.

There is an indication that this evolved cultural sensibility for the indispensable function of law can be categorized as a specifically European achievement. One must, however, add that speakers who refer like Winkler to the legal tradition in order to distinguish between Europe and non-Europe are compelled to make plausible that it is an idiosyncrasy of the law in the previously defined sense to be genuinely and integrated European, that Europe is therefore defined as having created this law and turned it into a symbol of its culture.

Conclusion

An applied recapitulation of the European cultural history – especially when this can be considered a unique European characteristic, as asserted by Remi Brague – is essential not only under the premise that the future is generally dependent on the provenance, but also that Europeans need an answer to the question of what constitutes its core – over and above a contingent coalition of individual states capable of fiscal union. It is not only the historically effective motors of secularization and science as cultural integration promoters, but also the collective appreciation of legal continuation of once-achieved unifications that could prove to be indispensable for a new attempt – perhaps at the last minute – at a constitution for the European core.

References

Böckenförde, E. W. 1997. *Welchen Weg geht Europa?* München: Siemens Stiftung.
Brague, R. 1993. *Europa, eine exzentrische Identität.* Frankfurt: Campus.
Cerutti, F. and Rudolph, E. 2010. *Brauchen die Europäer eine Identität? Politische und kulturelle Aspekte.* Zürich: Orell Füssli.
Garton Ash, T. 1993. *In Europe's name: Germany and the divided continent.* London: Random House.
Habermas, J. 2001. *Braucht Europa eine Verfassung?*, in: J. Habermas (ed.) *Zeit der Übergänge.* Frankfurt: Suhrkamp, 104–29.
Habermas, J. 2004. *Gegenmacht Kerneuropa? Nachfragen*, in: J. Habermas (ed.) *Der gespaltene Westen.* Frankfurt: Suhrkamp.
Habermas, J. 2011. *Zur Verfassung Europas: Ein Essay.* Berlin: Suhrkamp.
Schmidt, H. 2000. *Die Selbstbehauptung Europas. Perspektiven für das 21. Jahrhundert.* Stuttgart: Deutsche Verlags-Anstalt.
Winkler, H. A. 2005. *Was hält Europa zusammen?* Stuttgart: Robert Bosch Stiftung.

10 Analysing European identity – the need for civic resources

Viktoria Kaina

Introduction

In May 2007, the leaders of 27 European nations met in Berlin to celebrate the fiftieth anniversary of the signature of the Treaties of Rome. On this occasion, they signed the Berlin declaration, which highlights the unequalled success of unifying a continent that used to be torn by hostility and hate, war and national jealousy: 'European unification has made peace and prosperity possible. It has brought about a sense of community and overcome differences.'[1] Less than two years later, in February 2009, leading politicians of many European governments warned about a new wave of protectionism in Europe (Frankfurter Allgemeine Zeitung, 2 November 2009). Facing a severe economic crisis of global extent, the governments of some EU member states are tempted to protect the well-being of their own country at the expense of other EU members, even at the risk of damaging the inner unity of the European Union. Instead of closing ranks, in order to help the European community out of the economic crunch, some EU governments only seek to save their country's interests by arguing and acting foremost from a national rather than a supranational point of view. Although the 2009 spring summit of the European Council could mitigate the conflict between the EU members, the subsequent crisis of the common European currency keeps the heads of the EU member states in suspense and comes with the risk of intensifying EU citizens' cognitive and emotional detachment from the European Union. In addition, the EU's 'paradox of success' makes it much harder to legitimize European decision-making and more likely to deepen the gap between national and European elites on the one hand and the European publics on the other (see the introduction to this volume).

Research on European integration is therefore facing the pressing question of what holds the European 'family' together in times of scarcity, conflict, danger and threat. Looking for answers to this question, a multitude of publications stresses the need for group cohesion in the European Union. The gradual emergence of a European collective identity which is entrenched in

---

1 For the complete Berlin Declaration see (www.eu2007/de/de/About_the_EU/Constitutional_Treaty/ BerlinerErklaerung.html – date of access: 2.5.2009).

the EU citizens' consciousness of sharing a coming fate is said to be a means of overcoming centrifugal tendencies due to the increased heterogeneity of today's European Union of 27 member states and nearly 500 million people. An increasing number of scholars accordingly believe in the need of a 'European identity' to weather the challenges ahead and prevent the EU from breaking apart, especially in heavy times (Kaina and Karolewski 2009).

Whereas the Berlin declaration takes a European sense of community already for granted, previous research on 'European identity' provides inconsistent evidence, contradictory conclusions and controversial diagnoses (ibid.). This disillusioning situation is mainly caused by lasting theoretical and methodological challenges in analysing collective identities in general and European identity in particular. Against this background, this chapter comprises two main parts. The first part in section 2 of this chapter offers a proposal for conceptualizing European identity research in order to ease observable scholarly schisms. In doing so, I will focus on two theoretical issues: first, the two-level nature of collective identities and, second, the need to distinguish between 'belonging to' and 'belonging together'. Taking up the insights of section 2, the second part of this chapter presents some ideas about measuring European identity. Focusing on the individual level in analysing collective identities, I will show in section 3 that European identity research may benefit from taking recourse to concepts that describe various civic resources such as interest, loyalty, trust and solidarity. The concluding section summarizes the main arguments.

Conceptualizing European identity research[2]

Despite a multitude of publications on 'European identity', research in this area still suffers from great conceptual problems (Kaina 2009; Kaina and Karolewski 2009). Regarding the content of the term 'identity', ambiguity is not only a typical trait of this notion but also its greatest impairment when it comes to its usefulness of an analytical category. Ten years ago, Rogers Brubaker and Frederick Cooper (2000) even recommended giving up the identity concept since it is far too extensile to be of use for systematic inquiry. Other scholars agree that there is not only a lack of a theoretically substantial notion of both 'identity' and 'collective identity' but also a problem of applying approved methods of measuring (Fuchs 2011; Abdelal et al. 2009b: 17ff; Herrmann and Brewer 2004: 4; Huntington 2004: 41; Mayer and Palmowski 2004: 578). However, most students do not concur with the appeal of banishing the identity concept from the social sciences because identity is too important for social life. They acknowledge that, in the long run, both individuals and human groups cannot live without identity. Having an identity, so the argument goes, is a 'psychological imperative' as well as a 'sociological

---

2 For a previous version of this section see Karolewski and Kaina (2011).

constant' (Greenfeld 1999: 38). Against this background, I unfold my proposal of conceptualizing European identity research by focusing on two issues: first, the two-level nature of collective identities and, second, the need to distinguish between 'belonging to' and 'belonging together'.

The two-level problem in analysing European identity

In his recent book, Thomas Risse (2010: 19) almost casually notes that studying collective identity needs a clear distinction between the *subjects* and *objects* of identification. Put differently, inquiry on collective identity has to make clear *who* identifies with *whom* or *what* – and *why* or *for which reason*, I would like to add. Risse's helpful proposal benefits from being straightforward and simple (in the good sense). Its capacity to avoid confusion in research on European collective identity is nonetheless constricted. This limitation is mainly caused by the two-level nature of collective identities. Accordingly, *collective* identities relate to *two* subjects at different analytical levels, namely *individual(s)* and/or a *group of people*. Therefore, Risse's analytical distinction may easily lose its clarity since a group of people may be both subject and object of identification. Thus, in the case of research on collective identities, the distinction between subjects and objects of and reasons for identification should be supplemented by distinguishing an *individual level* and a group or *collective level* (Table 10.1) (see also Duchesne 2008: 402, 403; Duchesne and Frognier 2008: 144, 145; Kaina 2009: 41).

This perspective offers two important advantages. First, a framework based on the aforementioned analytical distinctions and displayed in Table 10.1 may serve structuring the research agenda as well as systematizing different perspectives and several approaches in previous research on European collective identity. It might furthermore urge students of European collective identity to disclose their notion of 'collective identity', justify their research focus and clarify their research puzzles. Second, this framework is compatible with different perspectives in previous research on European collective identity by avoiding a scholarly schism between the collective and individual level of analysing (European) collective identity. I will explain this argument in greater detail.

I agree with Fuchs (2011: 35) that a great part of confusion in the research on European collective identity can be traced back to a misunderstanding.

Table 10.1 An analytical framework for research on European collective identity

		Levels of collective identity	
		Collective or group level	Individual level
Components of collective identity	Subject Object Reason		

However, I do not believe that this misunderstanding predominantly exists between scholars with a *normative* approach, on the one hand, and researchers with an *empirical* approach, on the other. While the latter deal with the question of whether, to what extent and for what reasons the EU citizens do *identify* with the European Union as a group of people and their European fellow citizens, the latter seek to find answers to the question of what the *content* or *substance* of a European collective identity could be. In doing so, most researchers dealing with the substance of a European identity in fact tend to offer mere normative arguments by deducing it from philosophical ideas, normative principles or legal documents (e.g., Delanty 1995; Habermas 2003; Habermas and Derrida 2003; Magnette 2007; Leiße 2009: 111–17; Meyer 2009; Přibáň 2009). However, there are also studies which are based on an empirical perspective using, for instance, discourse analyses or surveys among elites and non-elites in order to empirically explore the content of a European identity (e.g., Díez Medrano 2003, 2009; Bruter 2004a; Antonsisch 2008; Cerutti and Lucarelli 2008; Jenkins 2008; Schildberg 2010; Risse 2010). I accordingly feel the scholarly schism runs between the collective and individual level of analysing (European) collective identity rather than between normative and empirical perspectives.

Researchers coming from a socio-psychological or sociological tradition consider collective identity equivalent to the 'emotional sub-dimension' of *social identity* which, in turn, is part of the individual's self-concept (Esser 2001: 342, 345; Fuchs 2011: 36; Grundy and Jamieson 2007; Rutland *et al.* 2008). Those scholars consistently analyse collective identities at an individual analytical level since the *subject* of collective identity is a person who is related to a group of people in a certain way. Here, the aforementioned misunderstanding is being caused by a biased focus on individuals who are seen as the subjects of collective identities. However, as I have argued above, not only individuals but also a group of people can be studied as the subject of a collective identity – and several scholars do so (e.g., Delanty 1995; Habermas 2003; Habermas and Derrida 2003; Huntington 2004; Eder 2009).

We may explore this thought by referring to the two main ideas of identity which are prominent in studies on collective identities: first, identity as something a person or a group *is*; second, identity as something individuals or collectives *have* (Kaina and Karolewski 2006: 12).[3] The first idea is tantamount to a statement of 'who I am' or 'who we are'. Accordingly, it basically relates to a *definition* in terms of describing a self-image or self-concept, a *meaning* of 'me' and 'us', respectively. Identity as 'being' therefore helps to *classify*

---

3 In addition, some scholars consider identity as a resource persons or a group of people use, as something individuals or a collectivity *do* (see, e.g., Triandafyllidou and Wodak 2003: 215; Kaina and Karolewski 2006: 12). This idea of identity can be found in (socio-)linguistic approaches of identity research which is linked to an ethnomethodological/conversation analytic perspective (Triandafyllidou and Wodak 2003: 215). I believe this is an important and promising approach for studying *given* identities. As for European identity, however, the existence of a supranational collective identity is still a matter of dispute.

things, persons or groups of people (Triandafyllidou and Wodak 2003: 206). The second idea intrinsically refers to a *justification*. Since 'having an identity' relates to 'associating oneself with something or someone else' (ibid.), identity as 'having' always implies more or less unexpressed reasons for a subject's identification with somewhat.

The distinction of identity as 'being' and 'having' is strictly different from Kantner's (2006: 507f.) proposal to distinguish between 'numerical identification (or categorization)' and 'qualitative identity'. According to Kantner (2006: 508), 'numerical identification' means that all objects of the material, social and subjective world can be identified in space and time by a *neutral observer*. My proposition takes this already for granted and relates both ideas of identity as 'being' and 'having' to *self-reflections* of people or a group of people.

Due to the two-level nature of collective identities, it certainly makes sense to study both ideas of identity as 'being' and 'having' at an individual as well as collective level (see Figure 10.1). We just have to be precise about what we talk about and what we are interested in whenever we speak of the emergence of a 'European identity'. *On the one hand*, we may study the individuals' self-concept related to a group in that we ask, for instance, how far the Europeans consider themselves as Europeans, which pertains to 'who I am' (see cell *A*) (e.g., Westle 2003a; McLaren 2006; Bruter 2005; Green 2007; Grundy and Jamieson 2007; Scheuer and Schmitt 2007, 2009; Duchesne and Frognier

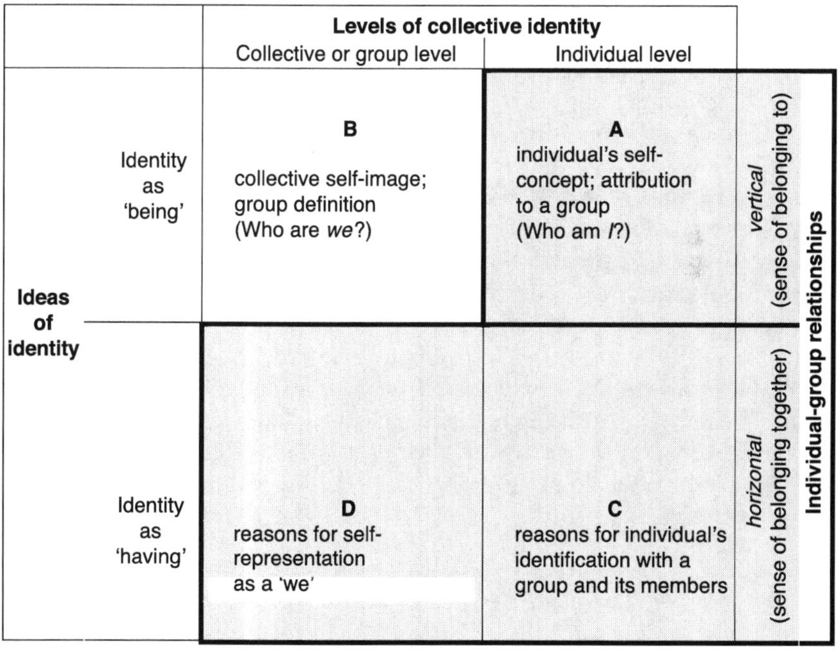

		Levels of collective identity	
		Collective or group level	Individual level
Ideas of identity	Identity as 'being'	**B** collective self-image; group definition (Who are *we*?)	**A** individual's self-concept; attribution to a group (Who am *I*?)
	Identity as 'having'	**D** reasons for self-representation as a 'we'	**C** reasons for individual's identification with a group and its members

vertical (sense of belonging to)
horizontal (sense of belonging together)
Individual-group relationships

Figure 10.1 Configuring research foci in studying European collective identity

2008; Caporaso and Kim 2009; Fligstein 2009; Kaina 2009; Thomassen and Bäck 2009; Risse 2010). But we also may deal with group definition and the image of the European collective self in that we ask, for instance, which contents give a meaning to 'who we Europeans are' (see cell *B*) (e.g., Delanty and Rumford 2005; Checkel and Katzenstein 2009; Kaelble 2009). In this context, we can study the degree of contestation of a European identity as well since *meaning* 'is the product of social activity, established inter-subjectively and may always be a matter of agreement or disagreement' (Triandafyllidou and Wodak 2003: 206; Abdelal *et al.* 2009a: 9).

On the other hand, we may empirically scrutinize for which reasons the EU citizens do identify with the collectivity of EU citizens (see cell *C*) (e.g., Bruter 2005; Green 2007; Grundy and Jamieson 2007; Kaina 2009, 2010). Furthermore, we may try to find out, first, what the reasons are 'we as Europeans' can be considered a collectivity or a 'we' (e.g., Caporaso and Kim 2009; Schönberger 2009; Thomassen and Bäck 2009); and second, how this collective sense of 'we-ness' is to be constructed (see cell *D*) (e.g., Cerutti and Lucarelli 2008; Kraus 2008; Eder 2009; Karolewski 2009). In other words, the *individual level* of collective identity describes a person's attribution to a collectivity or a group (*definition*) that is regarded as significant and precious for the individual's self (*justification*). In contrast, the *group level* of collective identity refers to the self-image of a group (*definition*) and the reasons for seeing 'us' as a collectivity and a 'we' (*justification*).

As to the group level, justification is primarily necessary to *act* inwardly and outwardly as a collectivity; group definition is mainly used to *present* the group both internally and externally as a community. This way, the group gives their members certain reasons to identify with it and enables others from outside the group to recognize it as a collective. That is, collective identities are both internally and externally defined (Schlesinger 2000: 1875; Herrmann and Brewer 2004: 6) and need the presence of a 'significant other' (of many: Tajfel 1982: 104; Wendt 1994: 389; Eisenstadt and Giesen 1995: 47; Delanty 2000: 115; Schlesinger 2000: 1873; Rumelili 2004: 32; Lepsius 2006: 114).

I believe the structure of Figure 10.1 is suitable to comprise not only different approaches of political scientists but also various positions from other disciplines in research on European collective identity, such as diverse perspectives of sociologists, socio-psychologists, historians and philosophers. In the following section, I will present some considerations on measuring European identity by focusing both on identity as 'having' and the individual analytical level of collective identity. Before I turn to this part of the chapter, however, I will offer some arguments on the second issue of analysing European collective identity.

Why we need to distinguish between 'belonging to' and 'belonging together'

Aside from the two-level nature of collective identities, Bettina Westle (2003b) argued some time ago that collective identities are based on two distinct kinds of individual-group relationships (see also Magnette 2007: 66). *First*, a person's self-attribution to a collective in terms of someone's *sense of belonging to* a group does admittedly need the group's acknowledgement (Meyer 2004: 22). Therefore, collective identity is based on a *vertical* relationship between individual and group (Westle 2003b: 120) resulting from the individual's experience of belonging by collective recognition. I relate this vertical type of individual-group relationships to the individual analytical level of collective identity (see Figure 10.1).

Second, the process of collective identity formation additionally depends on two crucial preconditions. It presupposes not only the common will of *belonging together* (Kocka 1995: 29), but also the group members' mutual acceptance as associates of one and the same collective (Gellner 1983: 7) and, in this special sense, the mutual acknowledgement as *equals* (Eisenstadt and Giesen 1995: 74). Consequently, collective identity is also based on *horizontal* relationships between the group members (Westle 2003b: 129) in terms of a *sense of belonging together*. In contrast to the vertical kind of individual-group relationships, I apply horizontal relations between group members both at the collective and the individual level of collective identity (see Figure 10.1). This is justified again by the two-level nature of collective identity since a *sense of belonging together* can not only be seen as a feature of a collectivity but also as a part of an individual's psychology.

These two different modes of individual-group relationships not only serve an analytical purpose but also pose a methodological challenge. In European identity research, the materialization of a European collective identity is said to be equivalent to a gradual emergence of a *sense of community* among EU citizens. The methodological challenge at hand refers to the question of whether people's *sense of belonging to* a group – in terms of a *vertical* relationship between an individual and a group – is really a fair indicator to measure their sense of *community* and *sense of belonging together*, respectively – in terms of *horizontal* relations between group members.

In fact, most empirical studies on a mass European identity start from the theoretical premise that an individual's collective identity can be considered as a feeling of belonging to a group. This theoretical commitment is caused by the fact that political science literature at the individual level of European collective identity is strongly influenced by socio-psychological or sociological concepts which are interested in the individuals' relationship with their social environment. In this tradition, collective identity describes one's identification with a group one feels attached to. Consequently, students of this branch of research on collective identity in general and European collective identity in particular mainly consider any kind of collective identity as *feelings of belonging to* social groups (e.g., Díez Medrano and Gutiérrez 2001: 754; Westle 2003a: 455; Croucher 2004: 40; Bruter 2005: 1). A lot of research on European collective identity therefore provides empirical analyses on how Europeans' feelings of attachment to the European Union have been developed over time.

The conceptualization of collective identity in terms of an emotional component of an individual's self-concept has both pros and cons. The most important benefit is seen in the possibility to study collective identities at the micro level of societies – i.e. the level of individuals (Westle 2003a: 455; Bruter 2005: 8). This advantage, however, is weakened by three conceptual shortcomings: first, putting the focus on individuals; second, the overemphasis of feelings; third, equalizing a sense of 'belonging to' and a sense of 'belonging together'.

I discussed the first conceptual issue in the previous sub-section. As for the second problem, the overemphasis of the affective component of attitudes entails a conceptual truncation. Along with other scholars, I assume that feelings of belonging to a group cannot emerge before the individual is aware of his/her group membership and – more important – before the group has become relevant for the person's self-concept. Social psychologists therefore argue that collective identity is built up on the psychological existence of the community (Castano 2004). More than 30 years ago, Henri Tajfel (1974, 1982) defined a person's knowledge of belonging to a group as one component of group identification (Tajfel 1982: 70, 102). According to his work, collective identities of individuals contain at least three attitudinal elements: cognitive, affective and evaluative orientations. With regard to cognitive orientations, social categorization and attribution serve as benchmarks which display commonalities between 'me' and 'others' and designate dissimilarities between 'me' and 'other others'.

Some sociologists who support a social constructionist view on collective identity challenge this outlook which leads us to the issue of equating 'belonging to' with 'belonging together'. These scholars (Jamieson 2002; Fuss and Grosser 2006) highlight the distinction between processes of categorizing self and others versus processes of coming to feel a sense of common identity or belonging together with others (Fuss and Grosser 2006: 213). 'Being categorized', so their argument goes, 'does not automatically mean to take on this label as an aspect of self-identity or to see oneself as *sharing something with others* so categorized. If and only if the category has profound consequences in terms of changed patterns of social interactions (does) the assignment to a certain category become (. . .) relevant for self-identity' (Fuss and Grosser 2006: 213f. – emphasis added; likewise: Kantner 2006: 507). This argument allows for two important insights: first, cognitive perceptions in terms of categorization and attribution are obviously not sufficient in order to conceptualize collective identity. This general detection, however, does not preclude that cognitive orientations are a necessary element of the collective identity concept at the individual level. Second, the argument nonetheless highlights that we should make an analytical distinction between individuals' sense of 'belonging to' and their sense of 'belonging together' since individuals' attribution to a group is different from their belief in *sharing* something *with* other group members (see also Figure 10.1).

There is also some empirical evidence corroborating this line of thought since people obviously may have a *sense of belonging to* a group without having *a sense of belonging together* with other group members. In their study on European collective identity among young adults, Daniel Fuss and Marita Grosser (2006: 228) found that some young people considered their sense of belonging to Europe as a consequence of their national citizenship status and origin: being a German is accordingly tantamount to belonging to the EU and, consequently, being a European, since Germany is a member state of the European Union. Hence, Fuss and Grosser (2006: 229, 236) call this kind of European collective identity 'status identity' since it is only a technical and unemotional statement of 'belonging to' without having any idea of 'belonging together'.

Against this background, another crucial question arises: how do cognitive perceptions of belonging mutate into emotional bonds? In other words, what turns people of a group, who are members of the same social category, into a *community*? This is a very important question because community membership has a 'higher' quality than the merely belonging to a social category does. The specific value of communities results from feelings of mutual commitment between the group members (Citrin and Sides 2004: 165; likewise: Eder 2009: 430; Risse 2010: 22). Due to these feelings of commitment, the awareness of 'belonging to' becomes tantamount to the awareness of 'belonging together' which, in turn, provides the background for one's willingness to show solidarity as well as readiness to make a personal sacrifice for the well-being of the collective and fellow group members.

Taking the research literature into account, there are several answers to the aforementioned question. Some scholars stress that (horizontal) *feelings of togetherness* develop inasmuch as people believe that the group is a *significant* collective whose state affects the fate of its members and which is valuable enough to give the group a specific worth (Estel 1997: 79). This argument is based on the plausible supposition that individuals only aspire to such memberships which give some kind of gratification in order to strengthen the individuals' self-esteem (see also Abdelal *et al.* 2009a: 4). Collectives or groups become valuable, for instance, if their insiders share 'precious' commonalities that make a difference to outsiders (Estel 1997: 79f.). In addition, psychologists argued that a sense of community depends on group members' 'sense of mattering' and that a positive sense of togetherness benefits from the group members' feeling that their association to the group is rewarding in that their needs will be met through group membership (McMillan and Chavis 1986: 9, 12).

Other researchers regard human interrelationships and social interactions as the fundamental driving force for an emerging *sense of belonging together* in that they convert cognitive perceptions into affective bonds (of many: Eisenstadt and Giesen 1995: 74; Delanty 1999: 269; Schlesinger 2000: 1874; Jamieson 2002; Mayer and Palmowski 2004: 577; Fuss and Grosser 2006: 212, 215). The group members' relationships and social interactions transform assumed or real commonalities into emotionally justified commitments. Taking recourse to these emotive certitudes, the collective self can experience continuity and develop the collective belief in a common fate (Smith 1992: 58). But this process depends on two essential conditions: people's mutual acknowledgement as group members (Gellner 1983: 7; Magnette 2007) as well as the modelling and stereotyping of common characteristics that make a difference to others (Hettlage 1999: 246). Based on certain 'codes of distinction' (Eisenstadt and Giesen 1995: 74), strategies of delimitation are used in order to define a border between inside and outside, in-group and out-group, 'us' and 'them'. Thus, delimitation and the group's recognition of individual membership are different sides of the same coin. It is accordingly likely that vertical relationships between individual and group generally precede the emergence of a horizontal sense of belonging together and are a necessary piece of a sense of community. However, when something predates another thing or is a part of this, both things cannot be equal and should be analytically distinguished.

The concept of 'belonging to' raises another theoretical problem in empirical, individual-centred research on European collective identity. That issue is basically caused by scholars' uncertainty about what the object of people's sense of 'belonging to' is: Europe, the European Union or the collective of Europeans? I agree with Sonia Lucarelli (2008: 23) that the very idea of collective identities refers to (a group of) *people*. Even when we speak about the 'identity' of interest groups, social movements, political parties, business companies or international organizations, we actually mean a group of people. Accordingly, my conceptualization of collective identity also differs from the proposition by Klaus Eder (2009: 427, 443), who defines collective identities as narrative constructions which are the objects of identification. My argument is that the object of collective identity is always a group of people, while there can be a variety of reasons for identification, such as a common story (e.g., Tilly 2003; Eder 2009), a set of values and principles (e.g., Cerutti 2008) or similar experiences (e.g., McMillan and Chavis 1986; Kielmansegg 1996).

Summing up my arguments, I will base the following considerations on three theoretical premises. *First*, I apply the notion of 'collective identity' to (a group of) people. *Second*, collective identity can be studied at two different analytical levels by differentiating an individual level and a collective or group level. *Third*, I change the notion of collective identity at the *individual level* of research in that I speak of one's *identification with a group and its members* rather than of *feelings of belonging*. The identification term includes several parts of individuals' orientation towards groups and underlines that identities are process-like and context-dependent (e.g., Wendt 1994: 386; Neumann 2001: 144; Triandafyllidou and Wodak 2003: 206, 208; Rumelili 2004: 32f.; Duchesne and Frognier 2008: 163; Lucarelli 2008: 26; Eder 2009: 442). Furthermore, the identification term avoids the common confusion of 'belonging to' with 'belonging together'. Since 'belonging to' and 'belonging together' conveys a different mode of individual-group relationship, we should not confound it with one another anymore. As a result, a sense of *community* among EU citizens should be operationalized by Europeans' (horizontal) sense of 'belonging together' rather than their (vertical) sense of 'belonging to'.

Measuring European identity and the need for civic resources[4]

Studies on collective identity in general and European identity in particular vary in how collective identity is treated as a *variable*. Thus, collective identity can be empirically analysed both as an *independent* and a *dependent* variable (Abdelal *et al.* 2009a: 3; Kaina 2006, 2009; Kaina and Karolewski 2009). Research concentrating on European identity as a *dependent variable* can be arranged in order of two batteries of questions (Kaina and Karolewski 2009). The first group is interested in the possible content of a European identity. Referring to Figure 10.1, these studies deal with 'identity as being' at the analytical group level of collective identity in that they seek to define a European collective self-image and search for answers to the questions of 'who we Europeans are'. The second group of scholars dealing with European identity as a dependent variable is interested in the prospects of a self-sustaining development of a European sense of togetherness among EU citizens as well as the obstacles to a shared sense of community at the European level. Exploring (collective) identity as a dependent variable at the individual level is furthermore focused on the issue if something 'is causing a person to adopt a particular identity' (Abdelal *et al.* 2009a: 3).

In contrast, studying identity as an *independent variable* is concerned with its impact on something else, such as a collectivity's capability of group integration and collective action or the group members' readiness to accept binding decisions they are affected by. Looking at the possibilities of studying European identity as an independent variable, there are already several studies focusing on the individual analytical level of collective identity (e.g., Citrin and Sides 2004; Mau 2005; Weßels 2007; Kaina 2009). These approaches are interested in the effects of a European identity, for instance, on citizen support of the integration process and the European Union. As for individuals, research on identity as an independent variable furthermore asks if 'identity is causing a person to do a particular thing' (Abdelal *et al.* 2009a: 3).

In the following, I will focus on three aspects. First, I treat collective identity as an *independent variable*. Second, I concentrate on the *individual level* in analysing European identity. Third, I apply my ideas about measuring European identity to EU citizens' *sense of belonging together* and their sense of community, respectively. In doing so, I will show that it can be fruitful for research on European identity to refer to analytical concepts that describe certain civic resources such as interest, loyalty, solidarity and trust. Furthermore, my proposal refers to surveys as one promising method in empirically analysing a shared sense of belonging together among EU citizens.[5]

---

4 This section is partly based on Kaina and Karolewski (2009).
5 Some researchers criticize the dominance of surveys in studying European identity and argue for more qualitative methods (e.g., Cerutti 2008: 9f). Referring to my proposal in systematizing different angles of European identity research (Figure 10.1), I argue for a mix of qualitative and quantitative methods which rather complement than preclude each other (see also Abdelal *et al.* 2009a). Apart from this, the appropriate method always depends on our research puzzle and what we are interested in.

Based on the supposition that a collective identity refers to affective attitudes of people, standardized questionnaires frequently contain questions which emphasize feelings of attachment in order to operationalize a common sense of community among EU citizens. Apart from my theoretical critique I presented above, answers to such general questions do not reveal much information about the degree or the sturdiness of a sense of belonging together among Europeans. The strength of any we-identity in terms of group members' sense of community has to be proven in case of conflicts, danger and threat.

On the whole, the current development in quantitative empirical research on a common sense of belonging together among EU citizens is still unsatisfying due to a shortage of standardized, longitudinal, reliable and valid data as well as suitable methods of measurement (e.g., Risse 2002, 2004: 253; Bruter 2004b: 187; Sinnott 2005; Kaina 2009). One cause of this situation can be found in the limitations of broad surveys on a vast multitude of issues. The design of questionnaires normally results in a trade-off between efficiency regarding time, money and the number of questions on the one hand, and the researcher's quest for profundity and complexity on the other. As a consequence of compromises detrimental to the latter goal, wide-ranging surveys often neglect the abstract nature of concepts in social research. Theoretical constructs such as 'collective identity', 'sense of community' or 'sense of belonging together' are abstractions of social reality and cannot be observed in a direct way. Thus, such concepts not only need a definition but also require reference to noticeable variables by defining appropriate indicators (see also Figure 10.2).

As for the definition, I use people's 'sense of belonging together' synonymously with their 'sense of community'. I am aware that this is a simplification which needs more elaboration in further research. Defining 'sense of community', I refer to a proposal by psychologists. Accordingly,

> sense of community is a feeling that members have of belonging, a feeling that members matter to one another and to the group, and a shared faith that members' needs will be met through their commitment to be together.
> McMillan 1976; quoted in McMillan and Chavis 1986: 9

Drawing on my theoretical premises, I modify this definition in two aspects. On the one hand, I do not confine someone's 'sense of community' to emotions. On the other hand, I conceptualize someone's 'sense of belonging together with others' as an orientation defined 'as anything people have in mind with respect to a specific object' (Niedermayer and Westle 1995: 44). The 'specific object' in our context is the European political community. Furthermore, my suggestion is mainly based on three points of view.

First, based on literature on national collective identities, I suggest that the quantitative empirical inquiry of citizens' orientations regarding the development and extent of a shared sense of community among Europeans can also provide knowledge about the *intensity* of those sentiments and the levels of identification with the European community in terms of EU citizens' sense of belonging

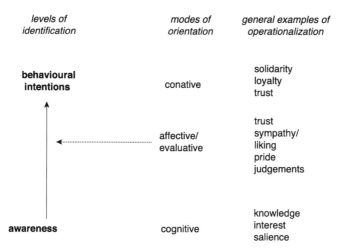

Figure 10.2 Systematizing EU citizens' orientations regarding a shared sense of belonging together

Source: Kaina (2009: 53); Kaina and Karolewski (2009).

together (Westle 1999: 37, 102f.; Huntington 2004: 49). If one agrees that 'the development of orientations begins with [. . .] awareness [. . .] and ends with behavioural intentions [. . .]' (Niedermayer and Westle 1995: 44), the phenomenon of any collective identity cannot be limited to affection, sympathy, pride or other affective modes of orientation. Rather, feelings express an advanced stage of identity and are probably not a sufficient condition, but in many situations a necessary condition for behavioural consequences.

Second, I accordingly assume that different *modes* of citizen orientations are relevant to the study of a shared sense of community among Europeans (see Figure 10.2). Therefore, cognitive orientations – such as knowledge, interest and salience – should be the basic attitudes (see also Estel 1997: 79; Fuss and Grosser 2006). That is, we have to form a picture of 'us' as well as to recognize that the specific 'we' is actually a significant category of self-identification, *before* we can develop any we-*feelings*. However, it is doubtful that cognitive orientations are automatically transformed into behavioural intentions (although Tajfel 1982 argues otherwise). As a rule, cognitions need some permanence to evolve habits that produce familiarity which, in turn, encourages social action. Moreover, before cognitive orientations become relevant for individual behaviour, they are generally influenced by the affective as well as the evaluative orientations of the individuals. Hence, I suppose that both behavioural intentions and concrete observable behaviour are the highest levels of identification. This proposition is based on the argument that evaluations and feelings have to prove themselves in certain situations of conflict, disagreement and danger – in other words, every time the readiness to pay a price on behalf of the community is needed. Since the proposed framework is focused on orientations, real individual behaviour is left outside this proposition.

Third, the examples of operationalization shown in Figure 10.2 are also theoretical constructs and require indicators as well. In this regard, further empirical inquiry into a shared sense of community among Europeans may profit from research on the so-called 'inner unity' of East and West Germans in the unified Germany. Just two examples may illustrate the argument. Are people ready to give up some of their cake by making personal sacrifices? The 'willingness of individuals to give up things they value for the sake of the collectivity and the acceptance of re-distributive policies' (Zürn 2000: 199) is the decisive question of acting in solidarity with others. Accordingly, people's intention to show solidarity throughout Europe could be measured, for example, by their willingness to accept a tax increase in order to financially support their poorer neighbours. Mutual sympathy could be measured by certain statements – standardized or open questioned – which reproduce distinctive images and reciprocal stereotypes. At the same time, findings of such kind may produce knowledge about the criteria of inclusion and exclusion. These results will also give some information about the reasons for coming closer together as well as the causes of the maintenance of barriers.

The proposal shown in Figure 10.2 brings about an important insight for measuring European identity in terms of a shared sense of European community. Dealing with Europeans' sense of belonging together as a variable, we should treat it as a construct of several components or elements (see also McMillan and Chavis 1986: 9) comparable, for instance, to the construct of the Authoritarian Personality (Adorno *et al.* 1950). From this follows two consequences for designing such a variable. First, we have to think about what these elements could be. One possibility to specify those elements might be to refer to the modes of individuals' orientations – i.e., *cognitions* (1), *feelings and evaluations* (2), and *behavioural intentions* (3). The second consequence deals with the challenge to theoretically justify those elements and relate them to suitable operationalization procedures. In doing so, it may be rewarding to take recourse to civic resources such as:

- citizens' interest in and knowledge about the community's matters
- citizens' mutual trust
- citizens' loyalty regarding the community, its leaders and civic obligations resulting from being a member of the community in question, and
- citizens' readiness to show mutual solidarity on behalf of the group and fellow group members.

Empirical studies on EU citizens' shared sense of belonging together may benefit from taking account of civic resources for at least two reasons. On the one hand, civic resources may serve as indicators for operationalizing the complex 'sense of community' construct by distinguishing different intensity levels of we-identification among EU citizens. On the other hand, taking recourse to civic resources in measuring Europeans' shared sense of community stresses the character of a European identity as a *political* identity.

These benefits, however, are accompanied by three challenges. *First*, civic resources and other examples of operationalization shown in Figure 10.2 are also constructs in need of gaugeable indicators.

Second, we have to think about how we can relate those resources such as trust, loyalty and citizens' readiness to show mutual solidarity to large groups – i.e. 'imagined communities' (Anderson 1991) where most group members interact as strangers. Psychological research on sense of community may be inspiring for future research on EU citizens' shared sense of belonging together. However, psychologists are foremost interested in *local* or small communities such as neighbourhoods and townships where social relationships are less anonymous and contingent than in large-scale communities with thousands or millions of group members. Thus, we should consider how psychological research on sense of community may enrich our research on a shared sense of belonging together among Europeans.

Third, we must clarify what kind of community we have in mind when it comes to the European Union. Referring to a distinction by Gusfield (1975), there are 'two major uses of the term community' (McMillan and Chavis 1986: 8). As McMillan and Chavis (1986: 8) have summarized, the first usage relates to a *territorial* and geographical idea of community such as neighbourhoods, cities and states; the second use refers to a *relational* notion regarding the 'quality of character of human relationships without reference to location' (Gusfield 1975: xvi) and developed around interest and skills such as professional or spiritual communities. As a first hypothesis, I assume we need both uses of community in studying a European sense of community. The territorial notion of community is needed inasmuch as the European Union has been established as a supranational authority, a Weberian *Herrschaftsverband*, at the European level (Karolewski and Kaina 2011). Thereby, territorial borders mark the geographical scope of political rule and define who is not only subject to certain obligations but also entitled to exclusive rights since s/he is recognized as belonging to the political community. The relational notion of (European) community becomes relevant when EU citizens develop a shared sense of community on the basis of common values, beliefs and interests that bind people together without and beyond territorially defined membership. Against this background, it might be promising to analyse as well whether and, if so, how both kinds of European communities are related. However, these considerations need both more theoretical elaboration and empirical clarification in future research.

Conclusion

As before in its history, the European Union has again reached a critical juncture. However, in contrast to previous setbacks and temporary crises, today's European Union is facing the partly unforeseeable repercussions of a 'too much too soon'-policy by national and European elites.[6] The EU's changing nature as a 'polity in between' and its 'paradox of success' (see the introduction to this volume) comes with the risk of overstretching the EU's capability of holding the union together. An increasing number of scholars accordingly believe in the need of a 'European identity' to weather the challenges ahead and prevent the EU from breaking apart, especially in heavy times (summarizing: Kaina and Karolewski 2009; see also Karolewski and Kaina 2011). Although there has been a surge of publications on 'European identity', our knowledge about collective-identity-building at the supranational level is still quite limited. This disillusioning situation is mainly caused by lasting theoretical and methodological challenges in analysing collective identities in general and European identity in particular.

Against this background, this chapter was aimed at offering some considerations on analysing European identity. In the first part (section 2), I offered a proposal for systematizing European identity research in order to ease observable scholarly schisms. In doing so, I outlined three theoretical premises for future research on European identity. *First*, the notion of 'collective identity' applies to (a group of) people. *Second*, collective identity can be studied at two distinct analytical levels by differentiating an individual level and a collective or group level. *Third*, the notion of collective identity at the *individual level* of research was changed by speaking of one's *identification with a group and its members* rather than of *feelings of belonging*. The identification term includes several parts of individuals' orientation towards groups, underlines that identities are process-like and context-dependent and avoids the common confusion of 'belonging to' with 'belonging together'. Since 'belonging to' and 'belonging together' conveys a different mode of individual-group relationship, we should not confound it with one another anymore. Consequently, a sense of *community* among EU citizens should be operationalized by Europeans' (horizontal) sense of 'belonging together' rather than their (vertical) sense of 'belonging to'.

Based on these conceptual props, I offered some ideas of measuring a shared sense of belonging together among EU citizens. In this context, I have argued that it can be fruitful to refer to civic resources such as trust or someone's readiness to show solidarity in order to operationalize a (European) sense of community. This promising approach nonetheless provokes new challenges for research on a European sense of community. For instance, we must reconsider the term community regarding a *community of strangers* and think about whether and, if so, how a territorial idea of (European) community is related to a relational notion of (European) community. Thus, European identity research promises to keep being a stimulating research area for a European Union in trouble.

---

6 The 'too much too soon'-diagnosis regarding the European integration process is borrowed from Richard Eichenberg and Russell Dalton (2007).

References

Abdelal, R., Herrera, Y. M., Johnston, A. I. and McDermott, R. 2009a. 'Introduction', in: R. Abdelal, Y. M. Herrera, A. I. Johnston and R. McDermott (eds) *Measuring identity. a guide for social sciences*. Cambridge: Cambridge University Press, 1–13.

Abdelal, R., Herrera, Y. M., Johnston, A. I. and McDermott, R. 2009b. 'Identity as a Variable', in: R. Abdelal, Y. M. Herrera, A. I. Johnston and R. McDermott (eds) *Measuring identity. a guide for social sciences*. Cambridge: Cambridge University Press, 17–32.

Adorno, T. W., Frenkel-Brunswick, E., Levinson, D. J. and Sanford, R. N. 1950. *The authoritarian personality*. New York: Harper and Row.

Anderson, B. 1991. *Imagined communities: reflections on the origin and spread of nationalism*. London and New York: Verso.

Antonsich, M. 2008. 'European attachment and meanings of Europe. A qualitative study in the EU-15', *Political Geography* 27(6): 691–710.

Brubaker, R. and Cooper, F. 2000. 'Beyond identity', *Theory and Society* 29(1): 1–47.

Bruter, M. 2004a. 'On what citizens mean by feeling 'European': perceptions of news, symbols and borderless-ness', *Journal of Ethnic and Migration Studies* 30(1): 21–39.

Bruter, M. 2004b. 'Civic and cultural components of a European identity: a pilot model of measurement of citizens' levels of European identity', in: R. K. Herrmann, T. Risse and M. B. Brewer (eds) *Transnational identities: becoming European in the EU*. Lanham, MD: Rowman & Littlefield, 186–213.

Bruter, M. 2005. *Citizens of Europe? The emergence of a mass European identity*. Houndmills: Palgrave Macmillan.

Caporaso, J. A. K. and Kim, M. 2009. 'The dual nature of European identity: subjective awareness and coherence', *Journal of European Public Policy* 16(1): 19–42.

Castano, E. 2004. 'European identity: a social-psychological perspective', in: R. K. Herrmann, T. Risse and M. B. Brewer (eds) *Transnational identities: becoming European in the EU*. Lanham, MD: Rowman & Littlefield, 40–58.

Cerutti, F. 2008. 'Why political identity and legitimacy matter in the European Union', in: F. Cerutti, and S. Lucarelli (eds) *The search for a European identity: values, policies and legitimacy of the European Union*. London: Routledge, 3–22.

Cerutti, F. and Lucarelli, S. (eds) 2008. *The search for a European identity: values, policies and legitimacy of the European Union*. London: Routledge.

Checkel, J. T. and Katzenstein, P. J. 2009. 'The politicization of European identities', in: J. T. Checkel and P. J. Katzenstein (eds) *European identity*. Cambridge: Cambridge University Press, 1–25.

Citrin, J. and Sides, J. 2004. 'More than nationals: how identity choice matters in the new Europe', in: R. K. Herrmann, T. Risse and M. B. Brewer (eds) *Transnational identities: becoming European in the EU*. Lanham, MD: Rowman & Littlefield, 161–85.

Croucher, S. L. 2004. *Globalization and belonging: the politics of identity in a changing world*. Lanham, MD: Rowman & Littlefield.

Delanty, G. 1995. *Inventing Europe: idea, identity, reality*. Houndmills: Palgrave Macmillan.

Delanty, G. 1999. 'Die Transformation nationaler Identität und die kulturelle Ambivalenz europäischer Identität. Demokratische Identifikation in einem postnationalen Europa', in: R. Viehoff and R. T. Segers (eds) *Kultur. Identität. Europa. Über die Schwierigkeiten und Möglichkeiten einer Konstruktion*. Frankfurt: Suhrkamp Verlag, 267–88.

Delanty, G, 2000. *Citizenship in a global age: society, culture, politics*. Buckingham: Open University Press.
Delanty, G. and Rumford, C. 2005. *Rethinking Europe: social theory and the implications of Europeanization*. London: Routledge.
Díez Medrano, J. 2003. *Framing Europe: attitudes to European integration in Germany, Spain, and the United Kingdom*. Princeton: Princeton University Press.
Díez Medrano, J. 2009. 'The public sphere and the European Union's political identity', in: T. C. Jeffrey and P. J. Katzenstein (eds) *European identity*. Cambridge: Cambridge University Press, 81–107.
Díez Medrano, J. and Gutiérrez, P. 2001. 'Nested identities: national and European identity in Spain', *Ethnic and Racial Studies* 24(5): 753–78.
Duchesne, S. 2008. 'Waiting for a European identity... reflections on the process of identification with Europe', *Perspectives on European Politics and Society* 9(4): 397–410.
Duchesne, S. and Frognier, A. 2008. 'National and European identifications: a dual relationship', *Comparative European Politics* 6(2): 143–68.
Eder, K. 2009. 'A theory of collective identity: making sense of the debate on a "European identity"', *European Journal of Social Theory* 12(4): 427–47.
Eichenberg, R. C. and Dalton, R. J. 2007. 'Post-Maastricht blues: the transformation of citizen support for European integration, 1973–2004', *Acta Politica* 42(2–3): 128–52.
Eisenstadt, S. N. and Giesen, B. 1995. 'The construction of collective identity', *European Journal of Sociology* 26(1): 72–102.
Esser, H. 2001. *Soziologie. Spezielle Grundlagen. Band 6: Sinn und Kultur*. Frankfurt and New York: Campus.
Estel, B. 1997. 'Moderne Nationsverständnisse: Nation als Gemeinschaft', in: R. Hettlage, P. Deger and S. Wagner (eds) *Kollektive Identität in Krisen. Ethnizität in Religion, Nation, Europa*. Opladen: Westdeutscher Verlag, 73–85.
Fligstein, N. 2009. 'Who are the Europeans and how does this matter for politics?', in: T. C. Jeffrey and P. J. Katzenstein (eds) *European identity*. Cambridge: Cambridge University Press, 132–66.
Fuchs, D. 2011. 'Cultural diversity, European identity and legitimacy of the EU: a theoretical framework', in: D. Fuchs and H. Klingemann (eds) *Cultural diversity, European identity and the legitimacy of the EU*. Cheltenham: Edward Elgar, 27–57.
Fuss, D. and Grosser, M. A. 2006. 'What makes young Europeans feel European? Results from a cross-cultural research project', in: I. P. Karolewski and V. Kaina (eds) *European identity: theoretical perspectives and empirical insights*. Münster: LIT Verlag, 209–41.
Gellner, E. 1983. *Nations and nationalism*. Oxford: Basil Blackwell.
Green, D. M. 2007. *The Europeans: political identity in an emerging polity*. Boulder and London: Lynn Riennier.
Greenfeld, L. 1999. 'Is nation unavoidable? Is nation unavoidable today?', in: H. Kriesi, K. Armingeon, H. Siegrist, and A. Wimmer (eds) *Nation and national identity: the European experience in perspective*. Zürich: Rüegger, 37–54.
Grundy, S. and Jamieson, L. 2007. 'European identities: from absent-minded citizens to passionate Europeans', *Sociology* 41(4): 663–80.
Gusfield, J. R. 1975. *The community: a critical response*. New York: Harper Colophon.
Habermas, J. 2003. 'Towards a cosmopolitan Europe', *Journal of Democracy* 14(4): 86–100.

Habermas, J. and Derrida, J. 2003. 'February 15, or what binds Europeans together: a plea for a common foreign policy, beginning in the core of Europe', *Constellations* 10(3): 291–7.
Herrmann, R. and Brewer, M. B. 2004. 'Identities and institutions: becoming European in the EU', in: R. K. Herrmann, T. Risse, and M. B. Brewer (eds) *Transnational identities: becoming European in the EU*. Lanham, MD: Rowman & Littlefield, 1–22.
Hettlage, R. 1999. 'European identity – between inclusion and exclusion', in: H. Kriesi, K. Armingeon, H. Siegrist and A. Wimmer (eds) *Nation and national identity: the European experience in perspective*. Zürich: Rüegger, 243–62.
Huntington, S. P. 2004. *Who are we? Die Krise der amerikanischen Identität*. Hamburg and Vienna: Europaverlag.
Jamieson, L. 2002. 'Theorising identity, nationality and citizenship: implications for European citizenship identity', *Sociológia* 34(6): 506–32.
Jenkins, R. 2008. 'The ambiguity of Europe: "identity crisis" or "situation normal?"', *European Societies* 10(2): 153–76.
Kaelble, H. 2009. 'Identification with Europe and politicization of the EU since the 1980s', in: J. T. Checkel and P. J. Katzenstein (eds) *European identity*. Cambridge: Cambridge University Press, 193–212.
Kaina, V. 2006. 'European identity, legitimacy, and trust: conceptual considerations and perspectives on empirical research', in: I. P. Karolewski and V. Kaina (eds) *European identity: theoretical perspectives and empirical insights*. Münster: LIT Verlag, 113–46.
Kaina, V. 2009. *Wir in Europa. Kollektive Identität und Demokratie in der Europäischen Union*. Wiesbaden: VS Verlag für Sozialwissenschaften.
Kaina, V. 2010. '"Wir" und "die Anderen" – Europäische Identitätsbildung als Konstruktion von Gemeinsamkeit und Differenz', *Zeitschrift für Politik* 57(4): 413–33 ('We' and 'the Others' – European identity building as a construction of commonality and difference).
Kaina, V. and Karolewski, I. P. 2006. 'European identity – why another book on this topic?', in: I. P. Karolewski and V. Kaina (eds) *European identity: theoretical perspectives and empirical insights*. Münster: LIT Verlag, 11–19.
Kaina, V. and Karolewski, I. P. 2009. 'EU governance and European identity', *Living Reviews in European Governance* 4(2) [online article].
Kantner, C. 2006. 'Collective identity as shared ethical self-understanding: the case of the emerging European identity', *European Journal of Social Theory* 9(4): 501–23.
Karolewski, I. P. 2009. *Citizenship and collective identity in Europe*. London: Routledge.
Karolewski, I. P. and Kaina, V. 2011. 'Does the European Union need a collective identity?', tabled paper for the 6th ECPR General Conference, Reykjavik, 25–27 August 2011.
Kielmansegg, P. G. 1996. 'Integration und Demokratie', in: M. Jachtenfuchs and B. Kohler-Koch (eds) *Europäische Integration*. Opladen: Leske + Budrich, 47–71.
Kocka, J. 1995. 'Die Ambivalenz des Nationalstaats', in: M. Delgado and M. Lutz-Bachmann (eds) *Herausforderung Europa. Wege zu einer europäischen Identität*. München: Beck, 28–50.
Kraus, P. A. 2008. *A union of diversity: language, identity and polity-building in Europe*. Cambridge: Cambridge University Press.
Leiße, O. 2009. *Europa zwischen Nationalstaat und Integration*. Wiesbaden: VS Verlag für Sozialwissenschaften.

Lepsius, M. R. 2006. 'Identitätsstiftung durch eine europäische Verfassung?', in: R. Hettlage and H. Müller (eds) *Die europäische Gesellschaft*, Konstanz: Universitätsverlag Konstanz, 109–27.

Lucarelli, S. 2008. 'European political identity, foreign policy and the Others' image', in: F. Cerutti and S. Lucarelli (eds) *The search for a European identity: values, policies and legitimacy of the European Union*. London: Routledge: 23–42.

Magnette, P. 2007. 'How can one be European? Reflections on the pillars of European civic identity', *European Law Journal* 13(5): 664–79.

Mau, S. 2005. 'Democratic demand for a social Europe? Preferences of the European citizenry', *International Journal of Social Welfare* 14(2): 76–85.

Mayer, F. C. and Palmowski, J. 2004. 'European identities and the EU – the ties that bind the peoples of Europe', *Journal of Common Market Studies* 42(3): 573–98.

McLaren, L. M. 2006. *Identity, interests and attitudes to European integration*. Houndmills: Palgrave Macmillan.

McMillan, D. 1976. 'Sense of community: an attempt at definition', unpublished manuscript. George Peabody College for Teachers, Nashville, TN.

McMillan, D. W. and Chavis, D. M. 1986. 'Sense of community: a definition and theory', *Journal of Community Psychology* 14(1): 6–23.

Meyer, T. 2004. *Die Identität Europas. Der EU eine Seele?* Frankfurt: Suhrkamp Verlag.

Meyer, T. 2009. 'Europäische Identität', in: T. Meyer and J. Eisenberg (eds) *Europäische Identität als Projekt. Innen- und Außensichten*. Wiesbaden: VS Verlag für Sozialwissenschaften, 15–30.

Neumann, I. B. 2001. 'European identity, EU expansion, and the integration/exclusion nexus', in: L. Cederman (ed.) *Constructing Europe's identity: the external dimension*. Boulder and London: Lynne Rienner, 141–64.

Niedermayer, O. and Westle, B. 1995. 'A typology of orientations', in: O. Niedermayer and R. Sinnott (eds) *Public opinion and internationalized governance: beliefs in government Vol. 2*. Oxford and New York: Oxford University Press, 33–50.

Přibáň, J. 2009. 'The juridification of European identity, its limitations and the search of EU democratic politics', *Constellation* 16(1): 44–58.

Risse, T. 2002. 'Nationalism and collective identities: Europe versus the nation-state?', in: P. Heywood, E. Jones and M. Rhodes (eds) *Developments in West European politics 2*. Houndmills: Palgrave Macmillan, 77–93.

Risse, T. 2004. 'European institutions and identity change: what have we learned?', in: R. K. Herrmann, T. Risse and M. B. Brewer (eds) *Transnational identities: becoming European in the EU*. Lanham, MD: Rowman & Littlefield, 247–71.

Risse, T. 2010. *A community of Europeans? Transnational identities and public spheres*. Ithaca and London: Cornell University Press.

Rumelili, B. 2004. 'Constructing identity and relating to difference: understanding the EU's mode of differentiation', *Review of International Studies* 30(1): 27–47.

Rutland, A., Cinnirella, M. and Simpson, R. 2008. 'Stability and variability in national and European self-identification', *European Psychologist* 13(4): 267–76.

Scheuer, A. and Schmitt, H. 2007. 'Zur Dynamik der europäischen Identität', *WeltTrends* 15(54): 53–68.

Scheuer, A. and Schmitt, H. 2009. 'Dynamics in European political identity', *Journal of European Integration* 31(5): 551–68.

Schildberg, C. 2010. *Politische Identität und Soziales Europa. Parteikonzeptionen und Bürgereinstellungen in Deutschland, Großbritannien und Polen*. Wiesbaden: VS Verlag für Sozialwissenschaften.

Schlesinger, P. 2000. '"Europeanness" – a new cultural battlefield?', in: J. Hutchinson and A. D. Smith (eds) *Nationalism: critical concepts in political science*. London and New York: Routledge, 1866–82.
Schönberger, C. 2009. 'Stiftet die Unionsbürgerschaft europäische Identität?', in: P. Müller-Graff (ed.) *Der Zusammenhalt Europas – In Vielfalt geeint*. Baden-Baden: Nomos, 55–71.
Sinnott, R. 2005. 'An evaluation of the measurement of national, subnational and supranational identity in crossnational surveys', *International Journal of Public Opinion Research* 18(2): 211–23.
Smith, A. D. 1992. 'National identity and the idea of European unity', *International Affairs* 68(1): 55–76.
Tajfel, H. 1974. 'Social identity and intergroup behavior', *Social Science Information* 13(2): 65–93.
Tajfel, H. 1982. *Gruppenkonflikt und Vorurteil. Entstehung und Funktion sozialer Stereotypen*. Bern: Huber.
Thomassen, J. and Bäck, H. 2009. 'European citizenship and identity after enlargement', in: J. Thomassen (ed.) *The legitimacy of the European Union after enlargement*. Oxford: Oxford University Press, 184–207.
Tilly, C. 2003. 'Political identities in changing polities', *Social Research* 70(2): 605–20.
Triandafyllidou, A. and Wodak, R. 2003. 'Conceptual and methodological questions in the study of collective identities: an introduction', *Journal of Language & Politics* 2(2): 205–23.
Wendt, A. 1994. 'Collective identity formation and the international state', *American Political Science Review* 88(2): 384–96.
Weßels, B. 2007. 'Discontent and European identity: three types of Euroscepticism', *Acta Politica* 42(2–3): 287–306.
Westle, B. 1999. *Kollektive Identität im vereinten Deutschland. Nation und Demokratie in der Wahrnehmung der Deutschen*. Opladen: Leske & Budrich.
Westle, B. 2003a. 'Europäische Identifikation im Spannungsfeld regionaler und nationaler Identitäten. Theoretische Überlegungen und empirische Befunde', *Politische Vierteljahresschrift* 44(4): 453–82.
Westle, B. 2003b. 'Universalismus oder Abgrenzung als Komponente der Identifikation mit der Europäischen Union?', in: F. Brettschneider, J. van Deth and E. Roller (eds) *Europäische Integration in der öffentlichen Meinung*. Opladen: Leske + Budrich, 115–52.
Zürn, M. 2000. 'Democratic governance beyond the nation-state: the EU and other international institutions', *European Journal of International Relations* 6(2): 183–221.

Index

amalgamation support 66
anti-civic 5
Area of Freedom, Security and Justice (AFSJ) 203–4
Authoritarian Personality 242
autonomy rationale 133, 137, 138, 141

back regions 126
bad political system 47, 53
Bang, H. 126
banopticon 197, 201, 202
Belgium 178
beneficial single market 46
Benhabib, S. 188
Bigo, D. 197, 201
bottom–up participation 125, 131
Brague, R. 224–5
Brubaker, R. 196, 230
Bücker, N. 6
Bulgaria 105, 113, 160

Caesarean citizenship 8, 198–203; anti-civic potential in the European Union 196–213; contemporary relevance 199–200; EU immigration policies 205–8; European corporate security state 203–5; European corporate security state in the field of immigration policies 208–12; immigration and anti-civic potential 200–3; politics of insecurity 200; security policies 199
Cammaerts, B. 140
catness 155–7
catnet 155, 157
Central and Eastern Europe (CEE): civic resources for democracy 105–23
Charter of Fundamental Rights of the European Union 185
Chavis, D. M. 240, 243

civic identity 61
civic resources: European democracy in Central and Eastern Europe (CEE) 105–23; European identity analysis 229–44; European identity measurement 239–43; European policy evolution 128–30; European Union governance 126–8; interactive policymaking 130–2; mobilizing through e-participation in the European public sphere 125–42; multilingualism 132–3; multilingualism consultation 133–9; social capital 106–9; and their relevance for EU studies 4–6
claims and claimants 154–9; access 187–8; categories 159; combined *catnet* strength of the nation-state **157**; handling 186–9
'closed' networks 21, 109, 110, 112, 115, 119
Coleman, J. 83, 108
Coleman, S. 140
collective identity 5, 9, 15, 16, 17n 2, 231–4, 234–8, 239–41, 244; affective attitudes 240; citizens' orientations 240–1; correlations with support for the authorities and the regime of European Union **29**; *dependent variable* 239; distribution **25**; *independent variable* 239; operationalization and structure indicators of 18–24
collective thinking 110, 111, 120
community problem 82
congruence dilemma 82
Cooper, F. 230
core Europe 222, 223
corporate security state 203–5; characteristics 203–5; European immigration policies 208–12;

'Europeanization' 203, 204; 'executive escape' 204
Council of Europe Framework Convention for the Protection of National Minorities 162–3
crisis: 'core Europe' 222; European constitution 221–8, 222–4; 'Monti criteria' 222; new beginning 221–2
cultural identity 61
culture 221–8; law 227–8; policy instrument 226–8; poverty 225; religion 226; science 226–7; source of political solidarity 224–6
culture governance 126
Czech Republic 164–5, 173

Dahl, R. 82
Dalakiouridou, E. 129
Danish Personal Data Protection Act 161
Data Protection Directive 161
Debate Europe 129–30
decoupling 125–42
Delhey, J. 6–7
democracy 82; European Union civic resources in Central and Eastern Europe (CEE) 105–23
democratic deficit 127
Denmark 168
diffuse support 39, 39n 5, 71
disastrous single market 55
discourse 42n 10
division of labour 125

e-participation: civic resources mobilization in the European public sphere 125–42; European policy evolution 128–30; European Union governance 126–8; interactive policymaking 130–2; multilingualism 132–3; multilingualism consultation 133–9
Easton, D. 6, 38
Easton's concept of political support 16–17
Eder, K. 238
Eldholm, M. 8
Entman, R. 42
Estonia 113
ethnic identity 163
ethnic minorities 163–8; 25 EU member states **166–7**; categories 164
Eurobarometer 53, 83, 97; surveys 41n 9
Eurodac 211
EUROPA 127, 129, 138

Europe 20n 5; trust in co-Europeans and support for European unification 51–76
European Bureau for Lesser-Used Languages (EBLUL) 180
European citizenship 196
European constitution 222–4; coordination process 223–4; crisis 221–2, 221–8; holding reason 223
European Criminal Records Information System (ECRIS) 208
European Election Study (EES) 65
European identity 15, 50, 53, 61, 67; analytical framework for research **231**; 'codes of distinction 238; collective 231–2, 234; conceptualization 236; configuring research foci **233**; distinction 233; identification 231; individual-group relationships 235; 'inner unity' 242; justification 233, 234; measurement 239–43; need for civic resources 229–44; numerical identification 233; operationalization 242; qualitative 233; research conceptualization 230–8; *sense of belonging* 234–8, 244; sense of community 243; social 232; 'status identity' 237; systematizing EU citizens' orientations **241**; two-level problem 231–4; variables 239
European Monitoring Centre on Racism and Xenophobia (EUMC) 161–2
European police (Europol) 202, 203, 208–9
European policy: e-Participation Preparatory Action plans 130; participation evolution 128–30; Plan D 129–30; Tell Barroso 130; White Paper on European Governance 129
European public sphere: civic resources mobilization through e-participation in the 125–42; governance participation 126–8; policy evolution 128–30
European Union (EU): caesarean citizenship and immigration policies 205–8; Caesarean citizenship anti-civic potential 196–213; challenges for a polity in between 1–3; citizens' image of and support for 37–56; citizens perception 51–5; civic resources and their relevance for EU studies 4–6; civic resources for democracy 105–23; corporate security state 203–5; corporate security state in the field of immigration policies 208–12; correlation between

Index

indicators of identification and of trust **28**; Europe's blues and Europe's future 1–9; examining political support in European integration studies 38–42; framing in Eastern Germany and Poland 43–5; identification and trust as resources of support for 15–34; identity and the need for civic resources 229–44; indicators of identity **19–20**; new recognition order 180–6; preliminary application and evaluation 151–4; representative samples of voting population in 16 Western and Eastern European countries (2007) **19**; social constituency conception 184–6; social constituency conceptualization 146–92; social constituency tentative mapping 159–80; transnational frames 45–7
Euroscepticism phenomenon 2, 86

Fearon, J. D. 160
Finland 169, 178
Fossum, J. E. 8
Framework Convention for the Protection of National Minorities 165
framing 6, 42; citizens perception of EU 51–5; country's main benefits from EU membership **54**; country's main disadvantages from EU membership **55**; Eastern German EU 47–8; EU frames in Eastern Germany and Poland **44**; European in Eastern Germany and Poland 43–5; Polish EU 48–51; ranking of the most important frames in Eastern German sample **47**; ranking of the most important frames in the Polish sample **48**; research design and methods 42–3; transnational frames 45–7; typology of EU frames **52**
Fraser, N 149, 153
Frontex 202, 203, 209–10
Fuss, D. 237

general social trust 21, 63
Germany 174, 184
global player 48
Gotze, J. 140
governance: democratic legitimacy 127, 128; European Union participation 126–8; properties of a multi-tiered European public sphere **128**; public sphere 127–8
Grosser, M. 237
Gypsy linguistic minority 162

Habermas, J. 8, 223
Habermasian postnational constellation 8
Herder, J. G. 224
Hix, S. 2
Hobbes, T. 198, 200
Hobson, B. 154
Honneth, A. 147–8, 149, 150, 151–3, 188
Huysmans, J. 200

identification 6; appendix 32–4; collective identification distribution **25**; correlation between indicators of identification and trust of national and European identification **23**; distributions 24–7; distributions of identity and trust 24–7; factorial structure of indicators of identification and trust **23**; multiple regression: support of identification and horizontal trust **30**; multiple regressions for subgroups **31**; relationship between trust and 27–8; resource of support for the European Union 15–34; theoretical considerations 15–18; and trust as resources of European unification 28–31
identity 6–7, 61
identity approach 59
immigrant minorities 168–70; 25 EU member states **171–2**; citizenship 168–9; naturalization 169
immigration: Caesarean citizenship and anti-civic potential 200–3; EU policies 205–8; 'sorting machines' 202
immigration policies 205–8; 'Blue Card' 206; European corporate security state 208–12; refugees 207
inherent necessity 48
input-oriented legitimacy 82, 92
institutional confidence and citizens' support for supranational decision-making 80–99
institutional trust 7
integrated border management (IBM) 209
Interactive Policy-Making (IPM) 130–2; tool 7
international community 45, 51
international trust 65
interpersonal trust 110, 111, 120
Italy 178

Jackman, R. 111

Kaina, V. 7, 9
Kant, I. 227
Kantner, C. 233

Index 253

Karolewski, I. P. 8
Kozeluh, U. 142

language minorities 178–80; 25 EU member states **181–3**; 'mother tongue' 178
Latvia 170
legitimacy 17n 2, 39
Letki, N. 110
Lisbon Treaty 203–4
Lithuania 170
Loveless, M. 7
Lucarelli, S. 238
Luhmann, N. 83

Maastricht Treaty (1992) 80
Maastricht Treaty (1993) 1
mapping: EU social constituency 159–80
market economy 122
McMillan, D. W. 240, 243
membership variable 41n 9
Miller, R. A. 111
Mishler, W. 111
mistrust 16n 1
modernization 48–9
Monar, J. 197
Monti criteria 222, 223
Muller, E. N. 111
multilingualism 132–3; consultation 133–9; online discussion forum 133–9
mutual trust 16n 1

national auto-recognition 153
national discrimination 46, 55
national identity 61, 67
Netherlands 169
netness 155–7

online discussion forum 133–9; phase 1 135–6; phase 2 136–8; phase 3 138–9
output-oriented legitimacy 82, 92

people's Europe 45, 53
permissive consensus 2
Poland 113
policies 40
policy competence **90**; preferred level and citizens' trust in European institutions **93**; preferred level and EU's democraticness citizen assessment **92**; preferred level for cross-border problems **95**; preferred level for welfare and identity issues **96**
political attitudes 107

political authorities 38
political community 38
political culture 107
political group membership 115, 120, 121
political regime 38
political support: citizens perception of EU 51–5; Easton's model **39**; European integration 38–42; model of people's EU attitudes 41
political system 38n 4
politics 221–8; culture as source of solidarity 221–8
polity in between 1
positive socialization 109
Post-Maastricht blues 2
problem-solving rationale 125–42
professional group membership 115, 121
protection and power 49–50
psychological insecurity 109, 112, 113, 115, 117, 119, 120, 121
Putnam, R. D. 107–8

re-legitimizing rationale 125–42
recognition 5; denial 158, 188; enlargement 189–90; expectations 154; framework 147–8, 149–51, 152, 155, 157–8, 159; gap 188, 190; order 148, 153–4, 191; politics 147, 154
recognition framework 147–8, 149–51, 152, 155, 157–8, 159; denial 151; failure 150; legal 150; modern 149–50
recognition order 8, 148, 153, 180–6, 191; expectations 183; principles 149–51; self-confidence 149–50; self-esteem 151; self-respect 150–1
recognition politics 147, 153–4
religious minorities 170, 173–7; 25 EU member states **175–7**; informed estimates 173; Jewish 173–4; Judaism 173; self-identification 173; self-reporting 173
Risse, T. 231
Romania 105, 160
Rose, R. 111
Rudolph, E. 8

Scharpf, F. W. 82
Schengen Information System (SIS) 210, 211–12
Schmidt, H. 223
Schmitt, C. 198, 199, 200
schools of democracy 106, 110, 112, 115, 119

self-confidence 149–50
self-esteem 151
self-respect 150–1
Seligson, M. A. 111
sense of belonging 234–8, 244
sense of community approaches 60–3; cultural threat 62–3; national and European identity 60–2
Slovakia 113
Smith, E. 129
Smith, S. 7
social capital (SC) 15; civic resources 106–9; collective thinking 111; collective thinking and support for the European Union (EU) **114**; democratic culture 107–8; explanations 107; interpersonal trust 111; literature 109–10; methodology 111–13; results 113–19; social networks 108–9; support for the European Union in CEE **117–18**; trust and collective thinking **113**; trust and support for the European Union (EU) **114**; VGA 'closed' networks, and psychological insecurity **116**; voluntary group activity (VGA) 108
social constituency 8; claims and claimants 154–9; enlargement 189–90; EU conception 184–6; European Union conceptualization 146–92; handling claims 186–9; new recognition order 180–6; preliminary European application and evaluation 151–4; recognition framework 149–51; tentative mapping 159–80
social group membership 112, 121
social identification theory (SIT) 15
social trust database 65–6; dependent variables 66; independent variables 66–7; testing against data 65–7
social trust 16
society of risk 197
socioeconomic status 121–2
solidarity 5, 7
specific support 39, 59
successful transformation 50
support: citizens' image of and support for European Union 37–56; Easton's model of political support **39**; examining political support in European integration 38–42; institutional confidence for supranational decision-making 80–99; people's EU attitude model **41**; research design and methods 42–3

supranational decision-making appendix 99; empirical results 84–98; institutional confidence and citizens' support 80–99; net trust in the Council of the European Union **85**, **86**; net trust in the European Central Bank **85**; net trust in the European Commission **85**; net trust in the European Parliament **84**; preferred level of policy competence and citizens' trust in European institutions **93**; preferred level of policy competence and EU's democraticness citizen assessment **92**; preferred level of policy competence for cross-border problems **95**; preferred level of policy competence for welfare and identity issues **96**; preferred policy authority at the national and European level **89**; preferred policy competence **90**; theoretical considerations 81–3; trust in EU institutions **88**; trust in European and national institutions **87**
system-oriented participation 126

Tajfel, H. 236
tentative mapping: categories 160; data availability 161–3; ethnic minorities 163–8; immigrant minorities 168–70; lack of data and implications 180; language minorities 178–80; recognition data 160; religious minorities 170, 173–7
threat to national identity/sovereignty 55
threats of enlargement 48, 55
Tilly, C. 148, 155
top-down participation 125, 131
transnational frames 45–7
transnational trust 7, 63–5; trust in co-Europeans and support for European unification 51–76
trust 5, 6, 7, 39n 6, 83, 98; appendix 32–4, 75–6; co-Europeans and support for European unification 51–76; correlation between indicators of identification and trust of national and European identification **23**; correlations between the different indicators of trust in people **24**; determinants of support for European integration - trust + identity model **71**; determinants of support for European integration - trust model **70**; distributions 24–7; distributions of identity and trust 24–7; factorial structure of indicators of identification

and trust **23**; and identification as resources of European unification 28–31; impact on support for European integration **72**; multiple regression: support of identification and horizontal trust **30**; multiple regressions for subgroups **31**; relationships between identification and 27–8; resource of support for the European Union 15–34; results: trust in co-Europeans and taste for European integration 68–74; salience for support - geographical differences **74**; sense of community approaches 60–3; support for European integration by level of trust **69**; testing social trust approach against data 65–7; theoretical considerations 15–18; transnational trust 63–5; trust in people - distribution **25**
trust + identity model 68

unification 31n 11
Uslaner, E. 63
utilitarianism 106

Van Audenhove, L. 140
Visa Information System (VIS) 211–12
voluntary group activity (VGA): 108, 112; political group 112; professional group 112; social group 112

Wagner, P. 196
Weberian *Herrschaftsverband* 1
Weiler, J. H. H. 186
Westle, B. 6, 234–5
Winkler, H. A. 228
Winkler, R. 142
World War II 48
Wright, S. 134, 140, 141–2

Zaiotti, R. 205

Taylor & Francis
eBooks
FOR LIBRARIES

ORDER YOUR FREE 30 DAY INSTITUTIONAL TRIAL TODAY!

Over 23,000 eBook titles in the Humanities, Social Sciences, STM and Law from some of the world's leading imprints.

Choose from a range of subject packages or create your own!

Benefits for you
- Free MARC records
- COUNTER-compliant usage statistics
- Flexible purchase and pricing options

Benefits for your user
- Off-site, anytime access via Athens or referring URL
- Print or copy pages or chapters
- Full content search
- Bookmark, highlight and annotate text
- Access to thousands of pages of quality research at the click of a button

For more information, pricing enquiries or to order a free trial, contact your local online sales team.

UK and Rest of World: **online.sales@tandf.co.uk**
US, Canada and Latin America:
e-reference@taylorandfrancis.com

www.ebooksubscriptions.com

A flexible and dynamic resource for teaching, learning and research.